D1572557

Hall-Scott

The Untold Story of a
Great American Engine Maker

Other SAE titles of interest:

Chrysler Engines
1922–1998
By Willem L. Weertman
(Order No. R-365)

Pioneers, Engineers, and Scoundrels
The Dawn of the Automobile in America
By Beverly Rae Kimes
(Order No. R-358)

The Romance of Engines
By Takashi Suzuki
(Order No. R-188)

For more information or to order a book, contact SAE International at
400 Commonwealth Drive, Warrendale, PA 15096-0001;
phone (724) 776-4970; fax (724) 776-0790;
e-mail CustomerService@sae.org;
website http://store.sae.org.

Hall-Scott

The Untold Story of a
Great American Engine Maker

Francis H. Bradford

and

Ric A. Dias

Warrendale, Pa.

For permission and licensing requests, contact:

SAE Permissions
400 Commonwealth Drive
Warrendale, PA 15096-0001 USA
E-mail: permissions@sae.org
Tel: 724-772-4028
Fax: 724-772-3036

Library of Congress Cataloging-in-Publication Data

Bradford, Francis H.
    Hall-Scott : the untold story of a great American engine maker / Francis H. Bradford, and Ric A. Dias.
      p. cm.
    Includes bibliographical references and index.
    ISBN-13: 978-0-7680-1660-4
    1. Hall-Scott Motor Car Company. I. Dias, Ric A. II. Title.

TL215.H35B73 2007
    338.7'629046--dc22

                                 2006051118

SAE International
400 Commonwealth Drive
Warrendale, PA 15096-0001 USA
E-mail: CustomerService@sae.org
Tel: 877-606-7323 (inside USA and Canada)
        724-776-4970 (outside USA)
Fax: 724-776-0790

SAE International is committed to preserving ancient forests and natural resources. We elected to print *R-368 Hall Scott - The Untold Story Of A Great American Engine* on 30% post consumer recycled paper, processed chlorine free. As a result, for this printing, we have saved:

  6 Trees (40' tall and 6-8" diameter)
  2,672 Gallons of Wastewater
  1,074 Kilowatt Hours of Electricity
  295 Pounds of Solid Waste
  579 Pounds of Greenhouse Gases

SAE International made this paper choice because our printer, Thomson-Shore, Inc., is a member of Green Press Initiative, a nonprofit program dedicated to supporting authors, publishers, and suppliers in their efforts to reduce their use of fiber obtained from endangered forests.

For more information, visit www.greenpressinitiative.org

CONTENTS

ACKNOWLEDGMENTS

This project has demonstrated a historian's dependence on others as I had not thought possible. Because evidence of the history of Hall-Scott is widely scattered and the caches of materials in any one place are generally small, we have had to rely on many people. I have tried to address everyone who helped Francis (Brad) Bradford and me on this project, but I regret that someone no doubt will be unintentionally overlooked or not given the proper thanks that he or she deserves.

Many people yielded to our request to read the manuscript, or critical parts of it with which they have expertise, including Lorry Dunning, Jay Eitel, Stan Grayson, Robert Neal, John Perala, and Bill West. Our book is infinitely stronger because of their diligent efforts.

Some contributors have personal connections to the Hall-Scott story and have shared invaluable family possessions with us. Taylor Scott opened his personal collection and that of his family (Taylor's great-grandfather, Leland, was secretary at Hall-Scott and was Bert Scott's brother), in which he has invested a great amount of time and money in compiling. William Nelson was the last Hall-Scott president, and his grandson, who shares his name, provided us with excerpts of his grandfather's autobiography and access to company records and Hall-Scott ads. Deb Brill wrote a thorough book on her family's company and then assisted in locating relevant materials. Bruce Balough has family connections to the Hercules Engine Company, and he assisted this project by providing a company history and Canton-area resources. Joe Bradford, Brad's son, dug for data in the Berkeley area and served as contact person between his father and me.

Many people supplied Hall-Scott-related materials, such as photos or literature, or loaned or gave to us Hall-Scott artifacts. Some steered us to sources. These generous people include Jack Alexander, Rick Anderson, Mike Axford, Eli Bail, Tom Batchelor, Dave Blaisdell, Mike Britt, Robert Bronson, Glen Chaffin, Don Coucher, Dick DeLuna, Keith Denison, Stan DeVore, Lorry Dunning, Keith Ernst, Doug Gigstad, Josh Houghton, Robert Jantz, Ivan Jaques, Dave Keister, Myron Kiesling, Beverly Rae Kimes, Jody Kirsan, David Linley, Mike Lusher, John Montville, Robert Neal, Tony Pasqualone, Pierre Phliponeau, Vern Racek, Dave Read, Howard Reinke, John Reynolds, Tom Sharpsteen, Craig Smith, Dan

Taylor, Jim Wagnon, Bill West, and Rouhalde Wilfried. Wayne McDougall not only shared from his own collection but introduced me to other sources and made available to me photos from Cleo Burnette and Ronald Tate.

Several people conducted considerable and indispensable research that they supplied directly to us. These folks include Lorry Dunning (a historical consultant), David Linley, Robert Neal, John Perala, Tom Shafer, Ronald L. Warren, and Bill West. These individuals spent far too much time at the post office and in front of a photocopier, mailing to me and reproducing material that could have been found nowhere else. Our e-mail exchanges alone would fill a book. Tom Shafer also accommodated me in his home for an entire week for a research trip. That's real dedication to this project.

Several individuals with firsthand experience in operating Hall-Scotts completed interviews that were either taped or written. These generous people include Tom Batchelor, John Bodden, Dick Brown, Dick DeLuna, Jim Dixon, Jody Kirsan, Wayne McDougall, Pierre Phliponeau, Jim Ryan, Craig Smith, and Rouhalde Wilfried. They gave this book its "voice."

Folks associated with Glover Ruckstell have begun to illuminate this well-connected and influential but still under-appreciated character, through their own work and by their help with this project. Glen Chaffin, who sells Ruckstell axles, began the ball rolling for us with his helpful Web site and his essay on "Roxy." Sara Bartley, photo curator at the Howard W. Cannon Aviation Museum, and Dennis McBride, curator of the Boulder City Museum, steered me to relevant people. Sandra Ruckstuhl offered advice from the family history she has assembled. Ronald L. Warren is one of the few authors who have written on Ruckstell, and he was very helpful in acquiring data and background. Giacinta Koontz found essential documents at the San Diego Aerospace Museum and steered me to Gene Tissot, the son of Glover's mechanic, who provided the photos of Ruckstell used in this book. Gene is the only person I have met who has actually spoken with Roxy. These two generous people also reviewed our writing on Ruckstell.

Securing material on Hercules was surprisingly difficult, especially given that the company was in business until rather recently and produced so many engines—exponentially more than Hall-Scott, in fact. Former Hercules Engine Company personnel and related folks did much to aid our project. Jack Dienes and Robert Klotz of Hercules Components directed me to sources. Bruce Balough contributed historical materials from his family collection. Jack Fidler, Jack Scheetz, and Jim Sullen submitted to repeated queries from me and generously gave of their time and opinions, plus a brochure or two. Janet Metzger at the Wm. McKinley Presidential Library & Museum in Canton, Ohio, and Barbara Powers of the Ohio Historic Preservation Office provided much-appreciated photos and other hard-to-find data on the company. They were quick, efficient, and friendly.

Northern State University (NSU) made it possible for me to contribute my part in this project. NSU library staff, especially Jackie Hansen and Carolyn Blanchard, cheerfully and promptly filled the innumerable requests I made for technical help or to locate books, newspaper microfilms, journal article reprints, and other arcane and obscure bits. Plus, they isolated essential items that, without their particular skills and tenacious efforts, would never have been found. NSU covered the costs associated with photocopying, printing, electronic scanning, postage, telephone calls, and research trips, and gave me a one-semester sabbatical from teaching. Tara Coulthard, Ann Eisenbiesz, Karen Elliot, Chance Glasford, Linda Gray, Brian Harding, Jeanie Hoffman, Tania Stulc, Jim Rappe, Mandy Reid, Bobbi Jo Rissmann, John Romeo, Russell Vincent, and College of Arts and Sciences deans Jay Ruud, Dan Tallman, and David Grettler all played a much-appreciated part in this project. Note that Chance Glasford and Mandy Reid scanned more than 500 Hall-Scott images to aid this project.

The personnel at several libraries opened their resources for our use. Special thanks are deserved by the highly skilled staff at the Transportation Library and the Bancroft Library of the University of California, Berkeley; the Department of Special Collections of the University of California, Davis; the Oakland (California) Public Library; Mary Nelson at the Wichita State University Department of Special Collections; Flint (Michigan) Public Library; Alan Renga at the San Diego Aerospace Museum; Kyle Wyatt and Ellen Halteman at the California State Railroad Museum; Judith Kirsch at the Benson Ford Research Center at The Henry Ford; Ken Cardwell of the Berkeley Historical Society; Paul Snyder of the Stumptown Historical Society; and Kimberly Bowden at the Haggin Museum.

Assisting Brad with his 1989 history of Hall-Scott, which is the first full-length treatment of the company, were John E. "Speed" Glidewell, Alma Searing, John Tucker, John Webb, and Claire Wikander, all former Hall-Scott employees like Brad, Jay Eitel, Tom Sharpsteen, Richard Strad, Bill West (whose name has appeared at several points in this section and could not have been a stronger supporter), Philip D. Edmund of the Smithsonian Institution, and Roy T. Budmiger of Oslo, Norway.

Brad was among the last Hall-Scott employees left in Berkeley in 1958 when the company closed the plant, and he helped with the shutdown. He saved hundreds of photos, letters, brochures, plans, and other items from being sent to the landfill. This material served as the basis for his unpublished 1989 Hall-Scott history work, which was the starting point for this book. His tenacious commitment to the company, its story, and its people is amazing. Therefore, it is with particular sadness that I report that Brad passed away in November 2005, as this manuscript was being prepared for submission. He gave years to the company and then years more to chronicling its history. Needless to say, Brad was quite pleased when SAE International offered us a contract to publish this book.

Most of the illustrations and written materials used in this project came from our personal collections. In the illustration captions and endnotes, if no credit is given, then the material came from the holdings of Bradford or Dias.

Brad dedicated his 1989 Hall-Scott manuscript to his wife Helen "for her patience." Considering how much time, attention, and money went into the entirety of this project—from Brad's manuscript that was finished in 1989 to the present book—I cannot imagine a more appropriate dedication. Thus, I continue his acknowledgment in this book. It appears that Brad and I have been similarly blessed with terrific spouses. Both Helen Bradford and Kim Stanley-Dias supported their husbands, inexplicably perhaps, as we lavished inordinate amounts of time, money, and affection not on either of them but on a history project—and on an old engine maker, no less. I could not have asked for a more generous and steadfast supporter as I worked on the Hall-Scott story early in the morning, late in the evening, over weekends, and on holidays. I took trips and side trips, fielded phone calls at dinner, and had my focus diverted for years. A bright red 2150-pound Hall-Scott truck engine resides discretely in our backyard, while several shelves in our house overflow with Hall-Scott memorabilia. Kim, similar to Helen with Brad, only encouraged me. That's love. Therefore, this book is sincerely dedicated to Helen Bradford and Kim Stanley-Dias.

Ric Dias
January 2006

INTRODUCTION

Whatever happened to Hall-Scott?

Hall-Scott engines have been remembered for having great power, long lives, and even good looks. Enthusiasts of classic airplanes, trains, boats, trucks, buses, fire equipment, and engines often recall the company and its products with great admiration—even fondness. Forty years after the last new Hall-Scott left a factory, people still sing the praises of these engines. For decades, the motoring press heaped favorable reviews on Hall-Scott for its products. Although Hall-Scott produced tens of thousands of engines of acknowledged high quality and performance, the company nevertheless closed its doors after a 48-year run. Another company kept the Hall-Scott name alive on new engines for another decade and then discontinued the line. This provokes an obvious question: Why did a company that designed and built such capable and respected products fail in the marketplace?

Hall-Scott has a fascinating history. While its primary endeavor was building gasoline-powered internal combustion engines, Hall-Scott did not hesitate to branch into making other promising products. For example, in its early years in the 1910s, the company manufactured motorized railroad cars of various sizes and configurations—for passengers, freight, or maintenance—with many powered by Hall-Scott engines and transmissions. In that same period, Hall-Scott also sold engines to the airplane market and briefly became a leading firm in the design and manufacture of aircraft propulsion. Lured by the awesome sales potential of a young and rapidly growing sector of the engine market, the company abandoned making aviation engines and motorized railcars in the 1920s to serve the booming truck and bus businesses. Also during the 1920s, Hall-Scott briefly built an innovative two-speed rear axle for the Ford Model T but did not remain in the axle business after this successful venture. During both world wars, Hall-Scott contributed significantly to the war effort. In World War I, the company built hundreds of aircraft engines for the American military and for a handful of Allied countries. In World War II, Hall-Scott built thousands of motors for naval vessels and tank transporters. And in the early Cold War, Hall-Scott attempted to embrace the rise of high technology by purchasing a few small electronics firms. A narrow and one-dimensional company Hall-Scott most definitely was not.

Hall-Scott personnel and fans have pointed proudly to a host of significant advances and firsts in engine design from the company. Although some of these claims can be contested by other firms or individuals, the list includes claims of being the first American engine maker to use a full-flow oil filter and the first American aircraft engine maker to use die-cast aluminum pistons. Hall-Scott was early among American engine makers to make widespread use of the overhead camshaft and "hemi" head. Hall-Scott also was an early user of aluminum in engine crankcases to minimize weight. The first airplane to make an international mail flight was Hall-Scott powered. Hall-Scott participated in significant ways to assist American military efforts in both world wars. Arguably, Hall-Scott's finest hour came in its role (through cofounder E.J. Hall) in the design of the much heralded Liberty motor of World War I. Patents held by Hall-Scott personnel number in the dozens.

The story of Hall-Scott, as small a company as it might have been, points to issues of national scope. The company was born in an era when American entrepreneurs could successfully enter auto, truck, and engine making. Gasoline and diesel engines, along with the automobile, were invented in the late nineteenth century, only a few years before Hall-Scott commenced production. At this time, the technology used in making engines was simple; thus, the skills and tools needed to be competitive were easily within the reach of a hard-working and skilled individual with minimal capital. Hall-Scott enjoyed a measure of success in the ensuing decades in its volatile and crowded industry, watching as most of its competitors disappeared. But by the post-World War II period, engine making (and associated fields) had become much more sophisticated and capital intensive. Entrepreneurs were not entering the engine and auto industries and achieving success as they had done around 1900. Although Hall-Scott had built tens of thousands of engines and other items, it did not have the needed capital, and perhaps the right management, to develop and diversify its product line to remain competitive. The contraction of the number of American engine, auto, and truck makers continues into the twenty-first century. Hall-Scott was only one of the thousands of casualties caught in this slow and merciless grind.

The most frequently cited reason for the demise of Hall-Scott was that it did not have a successful line of diesel engines. To wit, as the company's fortunes sank to new lows in the late 1950s, Hall-Scott leadership described the primary reason for losing its (already small) market share as competition from other engine makers, especially those that made diesel power units. A 1975 magazine article on an E.J. Hall-built car explained the demise of Hall-Scott as resulting from Hall-Scott not having a successful diesel as that type of motor came to dominate commercial engine uses. Indeed, other Hall-Scott insiders and interested observers have likewise noted that lacking a viable diesel engine program left Hall-Scott at a pronounced disadvantage.

Not having a successful line of diesel engines is an adequate, short explanation for the failure of Hall-Scott. Few other commercial engine makers have survived without having diesels, or very many, in their product offerings; Lycoming and Wisconsin are examples. On the other hand, simply because a company builds diesel engines has been no guarantee for success. This point is cogently driven home by the shared fate of three other San Francisco Bay Area engine makers: Atlas-Imperial, Enterprise, and Union. These firms produced large diesel marine engines, and all are long gone. This one factor—not having a successful diesel engine—is an essential piece of the puzzle to explain the death of Hall-Scott, but it fails to provide a complete answer.

Current literature does not offer a detailed history of the company, much less why it closed its doors. References to Hall-Scott can be found in many books but offer only a limited portion of the story. Excluding books that mention the company, which are great in number because Hall-Scott engines powered so many different kinds of vehicles for so many years, a diligent researcher can collect nuggets of Hall-Scott information from trade publications, company brochures, company annual reports, newspapers, business publications, and other hard-to-find esoteric sources in scattered places. However, large volumes of information on the company in any one place are fantastically difficult to find, and this has hampered efforts to write a complete and published Hall-Scott history. This is the first book on this much discussed and greatly admired company.

The present book grew from "A History of the Hall-Scott Motor Car Company," an unpublished manuscript written by Francis H. (Brad) Bradford in 1989. Bradford worked as an engineer at Hall-Scott for 18 years, and he helped oversee the plant shutdown in 1958. Recognizing the great worth contained in the materials that he was ordered to throw away, he squirreled away boxes of letters, photos, brochures, and drawings. Most of the Hall-Scott records nonetheless were lost. The company leadership had little regard for saving company materials for posterity. With his "insider" Hall-Scott connections, Brad enjoyed access to materials that were not available to others. Uniquely armed with these resources, Brad created the first detailed account of Hall-Scott. Copies of the manuscript can be found at several repositories around Berkeley, where

Hall-Scott maintained its main factory and Brad lived. For Brad, this effort was a labor of love. He spent more than a decade making his own manuscript, and three years contributing to this present collaborative book project.

This book builds on the primary documents isolated by Brad and supplements them with period newspapers, trade journals, business publications, more recent books, and other sources. The troublesome scarcity of materials on Hall-Scott has not been solved, but a determined attempt has been made to find what materials do exist. Perhaps a future researcher can tell more of this story by finding materials that have yet to be uncovered. This study aims to place the Hall-Scott Motor Car Company in its rightful position as an American engine maker of importance and as a barometer of the changing face of engine making in the twentieth century.

CHAPTER ONE

HALL-SCOTT'S FOUNDERS AND FORMATIVE YEARS

The founders of Hall-Scott, Elbert J. Hall and Bert C. Scott, possessed some complementary talents that strengthened their enterprise and allowed it to buck the automotive industry trend of companies having a brief life span. Hall brought with him impressive mechanical talents, while Scott provided management experience, funding, and connections to local businesses. What's more, Hall and Scott picked an advantageous time in which to launch their venture. By the time Hall-Scott made the last engine in its own factory some 50 years later, however, the American engine industry had undergone a slow and fundamental change, and openness to entrepreneurial newcomers was no longer the case. In its first ten years of operation, though, Hall-Scott took advantage of opportunities as they came along, often responded to the market effectively, carved out a niche in which it could compete, and pushed along its industry.

Hall, Scott, and Their New Company

Elbert John Hall, sometimes called "Al" by friends, was born in San Jose, California, in 1882. [1-1] From an early age, Hall demonstrated an uncanny ability to understand, improve, and build machines, most notably gasoline-powered internal combustion engines. Thinking about engines and things mechanical seemed to dominate his thoughts. A 1918 article on Hall appearing in his hometown newspaper wrote that as a boy, "throughout his brief school career, his engine pictures and models were his playmates; the other children were distant grandstand spectators and the teacher, a necessary nuisance." [1-2] Hall was a decent but not great student and, according to this article, seemed largely bored with the subject matter presented. Hall "listened intently to his teacher, when it was urgently necessary, and at all other times drew pictures of engines both large and small, with the assistance of a squeaky slate-pencil and a curling tongue, much to the admiration of the rest of the small-fry." Hall's inauspicious academic career ended in the seventh grade. Evidence could not be found that he ever attained a diploma or credential of any kind, although he may have taken some sporadic courses, such as night classes, when he was older. Hall's mechanical abilities were inborn, augmented by experience.

The subjects of many of Hall's drawings, gasoline engines, were still in their infancy at the time, having been invented only a few years earlier in Europe. Otto of Germany had patented his four-cycle engine in 1876, the first practical example of the basic combustion process ultimately used in most gasoline engines. Gasoline engine technology quickly made its way across the Atlantic Ocean to the United States, and applications using this versatile power plant mushroomed in number. The new technology came to California shortly before Hall began his mechanical tinkering. New as they were, engines captured his imagination and helped lead to his first job. That same 1918 newspaper article stated that shortly after quitting school, Hall left home and boarded with a local baker. [1-3] Young Hall assumed his sick brother's position, driven to take the job for several reasons, in part because of "that tempting looking motor in Keyes' candy place next door." Hall drew and designed motors when not baking, preparing himself for the next phase of his engineering training, when he would start working on engines.

As a 17-year-old boy, Hall obtained a position with a farmer, fixing engines that pumped water for irrigation. [1-4] His duties of tinkering with pumping engines and other devices in the Santa Clara Valley did not last long. I.L. Burton, the San Francisco company that had sold Hall's employer the problem-prone Atlas engine that had won young Elbert his job, requested his skills at its operation. Burton reportedly said to Hall's employer, "Send that boy to me, he's just the sort I want." [1-5] So in 1901, Hall began a stint at the I.L. Burton Machine Works. Burton sold engines for a variety of uses, and while there, Hall designed gasoline engines for his employer. Around this same period, Hall also designed a small industrial motor of some acclaim, the "Doak," which was marketed by the well-known West Coast-based company Henshaw, Bulkley and Co. [1-6] In 1902, even though not yet 20 years of age, Hall acquired a half-interest in I.L. Burton. Hall continued working with engines, inside and outside the walls of Burton, including repowering cars with improved engines to better climb San Francisco's legendary hills and to race. From these humble beginnings, E.J. Hall's impressive engineering career had begun. Henry Ford, Jesse Vincent,

Clessie Cummins, and many others who became famous in the automotive field in the early twentieth century did so without the benefit of having college engineering degrees. This career path is virtually unheard of in engine building a hundred years later.

Hall formally entered the automobile business when he joined the newly formed Heine-Velox Company of San Francisco. Gustav Heine had immigrated to the United States in the 1870s. After succeeding as a piano maker, he tentatively inched into the car business in 1904, assembling all of three cars by 1906. [1-7] Heine historian Tikker wrote that Hall served as "works driver, repairman, chauffer, salesman and general partner," and several newspaper accounts credited Hall with helping in the design of the Heine-Velox car. [1-8] It is unclear, however, if Hall had any engineering input in the creation of the Heine-Velox motor. Heine-Velox had two engines, both with in-line four-cylinder designs. Their cylinders were cast in pairs of two and had overhead valves, producing either 30–35 or 40–45 hp. [1-9] The Heine-Velox car was impressive, being

In his business operations, as in this Heine-Velox car, the headstrong Gustav Heine was in the driver's seat, and Elbert Hall was in the passenger's seat.

both fast and quick, boasting of many clever features, and having a body that came in several styles. The ever-confident Heine actually posted a $5,000 wager that his car could beat any other auto of similar displacement. [1-10]

But whatever chance Heine-Velox had of achieving success, which was nil, ended in April 1906 when a massive earthquake and ensuing fire ravaged San Francisco, including the Heine-Velox shop. Realistically, Heine-Velox was not going to become a major auto maker, and total production can be counted on the fingers of one hand. Heine continued to dabble with auto making after the earthquake and fire, but he did so without the aid of Elbert Hall. By this point, Hall had clearly caught the car "bug" that had bitten so many other like-minded entrepreneurs in America.

While working for various employers in the early twentieth century, Hall "wrenched" on race cars and did some racing himself. Six months after the earthquake, Al Hall made the pages of the *San Francisco Chronicle* as part of a team that tried, and failed, to set a new record driving from San Francisco to Los Angeles by car. [1-11] In November, that same team finished the trek and established a new record of 18 hours 13 minutes—in a 40-hp Columbia. His brother Harold shared Elbert's interest in racing and engine design, and they circulated in racing circles for years to come.

After Hall left Heine-Velox, sources disagree on exactly what he did next, where, and when. Several sources tell of his hard work in rebuilding San Francisco after the earthquake and fire, which clearly occupied many people's time. As life returned to normal in the Bay Area, Hall might have briefly assumed leadership of a technical school, Cogswell College, a fact all the more interesting given how little formal education he had. In 1907, Hall, along with Bert Saunders, began work as a dealer for the San Jose-based manufacturer of the Sunset. Sunsets enjoyed success in the Bay Area, both as road cars and as race cars, selling hundreds of vehicles early in the century. The *San Francisco Chronicle* in April 1907 reported that Hall and Saunders had "taken the local agency of the Sunset car, announce that they have established their offices with the Middleton Motor Car Company... At the same time they have resumed their duties with that firm as demonstrators." [1-12] And in 1907, Elbert Hall was listed in the San Jose City and Santa Clara County Directory as "supt." of the Occidental Motor Car Company, which had the same address as the Victory Motor Car Company, maker of the Sunset. [1-13] The exact timing and relationship here is unclear. However, some evidence suggests that while working with Sunset, in whatever capacity, Hall might have begun building his own car—the Comet.

Hall's name is clearly linked to the Comet, and all indications are that he designed the entire vehicle. It appears that the first couple of examples were built in San Jose, and then production moved to San Francisco, with one record dating the move having been accomplished by December 1908. [1-14] Little is known about the Comet today because the firm produced so few motor cars, a small fraction of the hundreds of Sunsets produced. During the brief and sharp national business panic of 1907, Comet production ceased in San Jose. But it did not extinguish Hall's irrepressible desire to build engines, nor did it bury the Comet name.

Hall regrouped his efforts and moved the operation to San Francisco. He opened Hall's Auto Repair in San Francisco, where he worked on cars of all makes and assembled a small number of second-generation Comet cars. Hall's Auto Repair was associated with a car dealership, owned first by C.S. Middleton and later by Walter C. Morris, which sold Autocars and Columbias. [1-15] This was not a dedicated automobile production operation, but it is clear that Hall was dedicated to producing the Comet.

The outstanding characteristic of the Comet was not its chassis nor its body, but rather its power plant. The Comet's overhead valve, 201-cubic-inch, four-cylinder, four-inch bore and stroke engine was relatively small and high-revving by the standards of the day, estimated at producing only 18–25 hp. But that was more than adequate to propel the 102-inch wheelbase

Hall's V-8-powered Comet.

auto. [1-16] Hall preferred the overhead valve arrangement in his engines, and that made his designs stand apart. Most auto engines of the time—and for several decades afterward, for that matter—arranged the valves alongside the cylinders, coinciding their reciprocal movement with that of the pistons. That more conventional "side valve" arrangement carried some advantages, but facilitating free breathing of the engine was not among them. The overhead valve configuration employed by Hall was more complicated and costly to build, but it also allowed the engine to develop more power and to reach higher revolutions. Hall was not wedded to the four-cylinder layout, though. A few later Comets came with additional cylinders, at least one with an in-line six and, most surprisingly, a small number with a V-8. [1-17] Although all Comet cars were considered lively performers, the eight-cylinder-powered Comet must have most closely lived up to its suggestive, celestial name.

Hall's V-8 was a particularly sophisticated engine for its day, with two banks of four cylinders, arranged in a "V" pattern. The arrangement made for a compact, weight-efficient, and rigid design. Today, "V" engines are common, but they were quite rare at that time. No company had yet mass-produced an automotive V-8. All were produced in very limited quantities, similar to Hall's, and few companies even tried. In fact, a V-8 was not mass-produced for automobiles until Cadillac undertook the challenge for the 1915 model

Close-up of the Comet V-8. Note the exposed valvetrain, individually cast cylinders, and long head bolts.

year, so Hall's design was truly noteworthy. In Hall's engine, the banks of cylinders laid at a 90-degree angle to each other, with each individual cylinder bolted to the crankcase. The engine displaced 402.1 cubic inches and produced 60–80 hp. [1-18] Even with the awesome performance the engine must have been able to achieve, production of the eight-cylinder Comet was quite low. Leland Scott, Bert Scott's brother, remembered that Hall built a single eight-cylinder car for his family. However, the family never called it a Comet but rather the "Special Car." [1-19] The Scott family kept a picture of this auto, with the name "Special Car" written on it, on display. Photographs of the V-8 powered car, which could have received continued customizing after being first assembled, show a small, attractive, two-door runabout, with racy lines, a curved windshield, and a jaunty top.

During its brief production life, the Comet, with any of these engines, quickly made an enviable name for itself at West Coast speed events. The remarkable performance of the Comet, even with the four-cylinder engine, deserves special attention. In 1908, an automobile race was held at an oval track in Santa Rosa, California, where a Comet, probably powered by the four-cylinder engine, literally blew away the competition. [1-20] Frank Free, not one of the Hall boys, piloted the little Comet that day. One publication reported, "Seven of the ten motor races were captured by a little California-made car, the Comet." The Comet not only outperformed the other cars but "merely played with them... it would allow the other cars to pass it, and in the next [lap] it would shoot by them in front of the grandstand." In fact, the Comet so dominated the events it entered that race organizers finally barred it from further competition. Beyond dominating the racing that day, the Comet broke a speed record, being the first car on the West Coast to break a mile a minute for two successive miles on an oval track. [1-21] While E.J. Hall was building a reputation for himself as a race driver, more important was that he was building a name as being "a clever motor designer." Publications treated the Comet car as a newcomer, making its "coming out party" dramatic, indeed. The Comet race car in that 1908 Santa Rosa race could run circles around its competitors, in part because Hall's motors—four, six, and eight cylinders—had the same basic valve layout found in many cars operating in the early twenty-first century. On the other hand, most of the cars choking on the Comet's dust had engine valvetrains more akin to what are found on less sophisticated lawnmowers today.

The performance of the Comet was not limited to a special version, "souped up" for that Santa Rosa race. Hall claimed that all Comets could reach 45 mph from a standstill, driving up three blocks of San Francisco's very steep Powell Street, even while having to traverse the cable car tracks and the uneven cobblestone street surface. One source, Hall-Scott engineer John E. "Speed" Glidewell, writing in 1956, claimed that the car "could climb a 32 per cent grade in high gear from a standing start." [1-22] In spite of the undeniable performance and handsome lines of the car (one write-up said its "long, narrow body, low hung, gives the Comet a racy appearance, which is most attractive"), Hall assembled very few examples. [1-23] The company attempted to lure buyers with ads that stated, "A guarantee of 75 miles an hour goes with every $1,500 Comet sold." [1-24] Perhaps Hall took a cue from his former employer Heine using this sales tactic. But it was a crowded market. By 1908, when Hall's Comet car shined so spectacularly in that Santa Rosa race, some 515 companies had already entered the auto industry. It was also the year Ford introduced its revolutionary Model T. Hall's achievement in engine building made him a name to watch in the fledgling industry, even as his Comet car immediately went the way of most of its competitors and slipped into permanent obscurity. Most estimates place total Comet production at six to eight cars.

In 1909, Hall began a new association with colleague Bruce Kennedy, opening the short-lived Hall-Kennedy Engineering Works. [1-25] While Hall worked with Kennedy, sporadic production of the second-generation Comet continued, as did production of the successful engines that had powered earlier Comet automobiles. Now these engines were actually being fitted into airplanes, too, which made perfect sense, given the superior performance characteristics of the engines.

In fact, it was in the 1908–1909 period when Hall designed and built his V-8. Most noteworthy of the applications for the advanced engine was an experimental aircraft called a "helicopter," which was designed and built by Peter English. [1-26] The craft had two propellers that were highly variable in their orientation, with the intent to be able to power the futuristic-looking craft straight upward, forward, backward, and so forth. Optimistic plans for testing were announced in local newspapers in 1908 and 1909, but the ambitious airship met a disappointing ending. A 1909 airplane guide reported that it was "Tried in its shed July, 1909, it broke loose and damaged itself badly." [1-27] This was a fairly high-profile experiment, even though it failed, and it gave the young engine designer some "buzz" in aviation circles. In an era when most gasoline engines still had low revolutions per minute and were heavy and painfully unreliable, Hall produced engines that were head and shoulders above the competition in reliability, output, and power-to-weight ratio. Their light weight and high performance made them natural for airplane propulsion. Unfortunately, records of how many of these engines Hall (or Hall and Kennedy) produced have not survived.

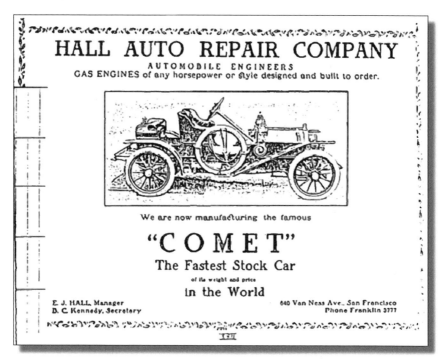

A Comet newspaper ad, judging from the Hall-Kennedy name, from 1908–1909. (Courtesy of Bill West.)

Also during 1908–1909, Hall developed an important relationship with Bert Scott. Bert Carlisle Scott was a contemporary and a fellow northern Californian, being born in 1881 to George and Cannie (Carlisle) Scott in Oakland. [1-28] George had moved west from New York during the California Gold Rush to make his fortune, and he became a business leader of considerable influence. He rose from being a bookkeeper to a railroad company president, along with holding leadership positions in lumber companies, banks, and other concerns. George sent his boys to (Leland) Stanford University. In fact, he named one of his sons Leland Stanford Scott, so impressed was he with the founder of that school. Bert received his education at area schools, culminating with his graduation from Stanford, majoring in political science. He took positions in his father's companies, as did other Scott family members. Between genetics and training, Bert Scott was destined to become a business leader somewhere.

Working for his high-powered father, Bert acquired some measure of material success, allowing him the luxury of purchasing a new car. In 1908, Scott purchased an Autocar automobile from C.S. Middleton and took it to Hall for a mechanical inspection at his San Francisco garage. [1-29] While Hall was looking over Scott's new Autocar, he took his customer for a drive in his own creation, which Scott described as being "a Comet Car, four cylinder engine, valve in head, 4" bore 4" stroke, that he had designed and built," and that "he and Frank Free raced...week ends, winning most of the events." Almost 40 years later, Scott remembered that ride, writing that Hall "took me out in the car for a trial spin and I recall going up Powell Street from a standing start at Sutter Street, and exceeding 40 M.P.H. when we reached the top of the grade at California Street." Scott reported being "very much intrigued with [the] performance of the car," so he placed an order with Hall to build a similar car for him. Greatly enamored with the spunky machine, Scott convinced two friends to buy models as well. After taking delivery in December 1908, Scott first drove the auto in the manner it was originally intended, as a passenger car, but later stripped it down and raced it, with Harold Hall at the wheel. The beginnings of a business relationship had been laid down.

Scott immediately recognized Hall's amazing mechanical aptitude. Although he appreciated these as related to auto racing, Scott also wanted to apply his skills in a very different realm. Bert's father George was a partner in the Scott & Van Arsdale Company, which owned the small Yreka Railway in northern California. Bert had gained practical and valuable business experience working as a secretary for Scott & Van Arsdale, and he had a familiarity with the firm's rolling stock. While the rail company operated steam locomotives that hauled a number of standard rail cars, it also ran a small gasoline-powered unit that carried a few passengers and some freight. Such gasoline-powered rail vehicles, called "motor cars," were a common sight on tracks across America through the early twentieth century.

The particular car operated by the Yreka Railway was a McKeen, a fairly popular vehicle, and had a power plant made by Fairbanks-Morse, a respected manufacturer of heavy-duty engines. Underwhelmed by the tepid pulling power of the vehicle, Scott likewise found the motor cars used by other firms little better. While motor cars filled a niche in rail, their engines developed limited torque and their automobile-like transmissions and clutches delivered little power to the wheels, all of which prevented them from hauling heavy loads. [1-30] Years later, Scott wrote, "Hall & I made the round trip on the car [that operated between Sacramento and Roseville] to look it over and check performance." [1-31] He observed that the McKeen "could pull a light weight passenger trailer, but could not handle standard freight cars." Finding such performance unsatisfactory, Scott continued, "It was my idea that a motor car could be built with passenger and baggage compartments, to handle three or four standard freight cars, and that a car of that type could be used on the Yreka Railroad to supplant the steam locomotives, and effect a very considerable saving in operating expense." On this trip, the two young men agreed that together they could build such a superior vehicle.

Hall and Scott's first product, finished in 1909. (Courtesy of Taylor Scott.)

The initial motor car project between Hall and Scott was a joint enterprise. For the new vehicle, Hall created an entirely original engine. Rather than fitting the car with one or more of his existing lightweight, high-speed engines, in his San Francisco shop Hall designed and built a new four-cylinder in-line unit with large displacement that operated at low speeds. No model name or number was affixed to this (and later similar) early rail engines; instead, references to them identify them only by their bore and stroke measurements. Hence, this rail power plant was referred to as the "8 × 10 engine" because each cylinder had an 8-inch bore and a 10-inch stroke. In the 1910s, Hall-Scott ultimately built versions of the 8 × 10 engine in four-, six-, and eight-cylinder configurations, corresponding roughly to 2010, 3014, and 4019 cubic inches, respectively. In Hall and Scott's motor cars, starting with this first unit, power flowed from the engine through an automotive-type clutch, which was coupled to a four-speed transmission that passed power to the propeller shaft, which finally delivered power to the wheel "trucks." This setup made it similar to the McKeen. Of particular interest in this vehicle was a Hall-designed mechanism that allowed the driver to select those four gears whether going forward or backward by simply throwing a lever. This one feature alone would be of great usefulness to the car operator because trains riding on rails, unlike automobiles driving on roads, have fewer opportunities to turn around. Hall's design would allow the motor car to go forward or backward easily and with equal speed and pulling power. Functional and clever, this feature would also appear on future rail cars designed by Hall.

Another picture of Hall and Scott's 1909 motor car. The first few cars had wooden bodies. (Courtesy of Taylor Scott.)

For his part, which was the "business end" of the arrangement, Bert Scott signed with a local coach builder, Holman and Company of San Francisco, to fabricate the frame of the car and the wooden body. Risk to Hall and Scott was minimized by the Yreka Railroad agreeing to purchase the completed car after its construction and successful testing. Scott's family and business connections paid dividends here. With a guaranteed buyer in hand, construction of the motor car moved forward. Holman and Company assembled the car in its San Francisco facility, and Hall designed and built the drivetrain for the car—engine, propeller shaft, clutch, and transmission—in his shop. After three months, the various pieces were put together, the car was tested and found successful, and the new owners took possession. According to Scott, the little car "was very satisfactory, supplanting steam locomotive operation, and the

The engine compartment of Hall and Scott's first car.
(Courtesy of Taylor Scott.)

saving offset [the] cost of the car within a few years," as he had predicted it would. [1-32]

Encouraged by this initial success, the two men decided to continue making rail engines and cars; thus, they formed the Hall-Scott Motor Car Company in 1910. [1-33] With financial assistance from George Scott, land and buildings were purchased at 5th Street and Snyder Avenue in West Berkeley, where virtually all Hall-Scott production took place over the next 48 years. [1-34] Snyder Avenue's name later changed to Heinz, as it remains today. The new street designation came from the condiment company of that name, which built a plant on Snyder and convinced the city of Berkeley to change the name of the street in its honor, over the unsuccessful objections of Hall-Scott. [1-35] The Hall-Scott physical plant grew in the years ahead, extending the site from 5th Street eastward to 7th, ultimately comprising almost 13 acres. For many decades, the mailing address of Hall-Scott was either 2750 or 2850 7th Street. For a few of its early years in business, Hall-Scott listed its general offices as being in San Francisco's Crocker Building. In fact, Bert spent much of his time running the

An early shot of the Hall-Scott West Berkeley plant and crew, with a rare reference to the Comet. Hall-Scott quickly ceased mentioning the Comet.

affairs of the company from there, but there is no evidence that engine production ever moved across the bay. [1-36] Dividing the responsibilities within the company appears to have been an obvious choice. Speed Glidewell wrote that at Hall-Scott, Hall "was the Engineer and B.C. Scott was the money manager, and I imagine it was a good thing that the latter was so." [1-37]

The west side Berkeley location of Hall-Scott afforded the new company several advantages. Around its factory were transportation services, a skilled labor pool, and a handful of industrial enterprises that could serve Hall-Scott. The most important single such business was Macaulay Foundry, which began operations in 1896. [1-38] Only two months after the 1906 earthquake, Macaulay erected a new shop in West Berkeley, pouring its first "heat" of iron on June 20, before the roof had even been finished. Beginning in 1910, Macaulay provided Hall-Scott with most of its iron and aluminum for blocks, crankcases, heads, manifolds, and other items. Being one of the premier foundries on the West Coast, Macaulay could fill the needs of Hall-Scott, big or small, simple or sophisticated. The long-wearing nature of Hall-Scott engines and their early use of aluminum, plus the ability of Hall-Scott to construct specialized machining equipment, were all made more possible by having a first-rate "hot metal shop" literally around the corner. If E.J. Hall could imagine something made of metal, Macaulay could pour and mold it. Hall-Scott never operated a foundry of any size.

After forming the company in 1910, Hall-Scott built a number of motorized rail vehicles over the next eleven years, sometimes in conjunction with other companies such as Holman. A Hall-Scott brochure, probably printed in 1920, described its product line spanning "varying types embodying a wide range of utility, power and construction," from "the large 50 to 70-foot passenger cars seating from 40 passengers upwards, down to small track or inspection cars and industrial locomotives." [1-39] These units included fully enclosed vehicles "in appearance designed to resemble either light type of regular railway car or

With the controls located next to the engine, operators of Hall-Scott motor cars were treated to an assault of noise, odor, and heat.

automobile motor bus," highway trucks converted to run on rails, or small open locomotives, built "for any gauge," with "speed ranges from 30 to 40 miles per hour, unless otherwise specified." Although a builder of proven engines, Hall-Scott did not exclusively use its own engines in its rail cars but offered engines from well-known competitors such as Buda, Continental, and Wisconsin. [1-40] Heavy-duty vehicle manufacturers often used different brands of engines, depending on customer demand and performance characteristics of the engines. Hall-Scott customers could specify gasoline, distillate, or kerosene as fuel for their cars. All but forgotten today, distillate is a cruder petroleum fuel than gasoline and, at the time, was quite a bit cheaper. It was not uncommon for commercial engines in the period to burn distillate, or to even start on gasoline but switch to distillate once under way, to reduce operating costs. And like its first unit built in 1910, "all Hall-Scott cars operate in either direction with the same speed, this being a feature of the Hall-Scott patented transmission. The value of this feature is, of course, apparent, and the necessity in many instances of turning the car at the end of a run is obviated." [1-41]

It is unknown how many rail cars of different types were produced by Hall-Scott, but records show that the company made a total of 23 motor cars. [1-42] The number might not have been huge, and almost all were built for companies in the American West, with one notable exception. Hall-Scott built its last two motor cars for the Kowloon-Canton Railway in China in 1921. "Speed" Glidewell wrote that one of the motor cars sold to this Chinese railway returned to the Berkeley factory in the early 1950s for an engine overhaul, a record Glidewell described as being "not too bad for service life." [1-43] Long life of that Chinese car aside, Hall-Scott's tiny production pointed to the fact that Hall-Scott never became a major player in rail, even in its immediate area.

The most interesting motor car constructed by Hall-Scott might have been a special fighting model created for the U.S. War Department around World War I. [1-44] Weighing approximately 100 tons, the 62-foot-long boxcar-like machine had steel plating 3/4 inches thick on its sides and 1/2 inch on its roof, which would give its operators some protection against attack. Leland Scott, Bert's brother and secretary of the company, called it a "monster, really to[o] big and heavy, and not practical," a description that seems entirely fitting. [1-45] To mitigate the effects of cold, heat, vibration, and noise, a felt liner resided between the inner and outer walls. Offensively, the car sported an array of guns—from machine guns fitted in each corner to numerous gun ports found around it. An auxiliary gasoline engine powered internal electric lights, an exterior 1000-watt searchlight, and an air compressor that was used to start the main engine and to operate the air brakes. Hall-Scott provided the chief

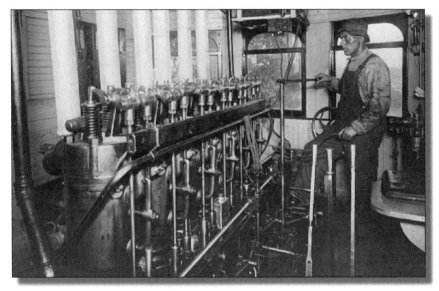

The engine compartment of the fifth Hall-Scott motor car, built for Nevada Copper Belt and delivered in 1911, with a six-cylinder, 150-hp Hall-Scott engine. (Courtesy of the California State Railroad Museum Library.)

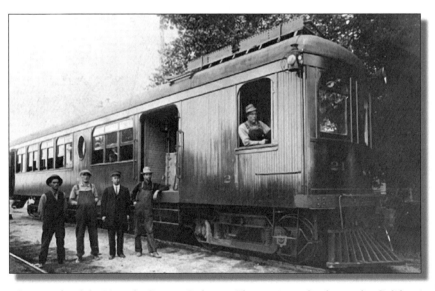

The outside of the Nevada Copper Belt car. The car is on display at the California State Railroad Museum, with its Hall-Scott engine still intact. (Courtesy of the California State Railroad Museum Library.)

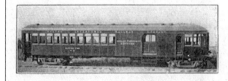

*A 1914 ad showing the second and seventh Hall-Scott motor cars. As can be gleaned
from the dates given, motor car sales got off to a rather modest start.*

*These three Hall-Scott motor cars—the eleventh, twelfth, and thirteenth—were
all 60 feet long and had steel bodies and six-cylinder 150-hp engines. They were
delivered to the Salt Lake and Utah Railroad in 1914.*

18

power unit of the unique car, bolting together two in-line four-cylinder engines to make a "straight 8," the two individual engine crankshafts connected to form a functional single engine. With a bore and stroke of 10 inches by 12 inches, the engine probably was the only one like it ever produced by Hall-Scott. The eight-cylinder behemoth displaced approximately 7536 cubic inches and developed 300 hp. Coupled to a three-speed transmission (with three gears available in either forward or backward mode, in typical Hall-Scott fashion), the fighting vehicle could attain a top speed of 60 mph and pull several loaded freight cars. Considering that Hall had squeezed 100 hp from a lightweight V-8 aircraft engine of only 785 cubic inches, this rail engine was a different kind of motor than he had made for airplanes and autos, one instead valued for its high torque for pulling power and low engine speed to promote long life and fuel economy. Paring weight in trains from components such as engines is not nearly the critical function it is in aviation, with the trains' wheels planted on rails, so Hall did not try to maximize its power-to-weight ratio. Such an enormous engine would have consumed heroic amounts of fuel, so Hall-Scott mitigated its high operating costs slightly by having the engine start on highly volatile gasoline and then switch to run on lower-cost distillate once under way. The U.S. government purchased the single Hall-Scott armored rail car, and this vehicle can be viewed as an experiment that showcased imaginative and productive capabilities of Hall-Scott and its range of ability, but not one that led to any derivative rail machines.

The Hall-Scott war motor car. Unfortunately, its fate is unknown.

The engine for the Hall-Scott war car. It appears that Hall-Scott made only one of these power plants.

According to Bert Scott, "the manufacture of rail motor cars...was the reason for Hall-Scott Motor Car Company," hence the name chosen for the enterprise, but it was another year after completing the first unit that the company received another order. [1-46] In spite of lacking motor car orders, the young company nonetheless had plenty of engines to sell in 1910—those engines Hall had already designed and built for automobiles and aircraft before joining forces with Scott. Entering the auto business had little appeal to Hall and Scott in 1910 (although Hall reentered the auto business in 1930). Concerning the possibility of becoming an automobile maker, Leland Scott recalled that Hall and Scott "knew the only way one could produce them and come out financially, would be on a production—assembly line—and they had plenty to keep them busy, without getting into this phase." [1-47] The founders had already seen the writing on the wall when it came to auto making in the 1910s—capital and technology intensive, mass production was the only way a company could reasonably hope to succeed. But no evidence was found to suggest that either Hall or Scott had some special attraction to serving the rail industry either. Customers did not exactly knock down the doors of Hall-Scott for more motor cars, but making rail cars of different types was a natural transition, given the successful motor car built for George Scott. There was some local demand for rail vehicles by timber and rail companies; it was a small market the company could exploit. Trying to find patterns or reasons for why Hall-Scott built a particular product, however, from the 1910s onward is often difficult to discern and usually does not seem to betray a single program or theme. In fact, years later, a parent company of Hall-Scott accused the two men of not giving sufficient thought when launching a new product or product line.

Autos brought Hall and Scott together, and rail provided the first paying customer, but aviation kept the doors open at Hall-Scott Motor Car Company through the 1910s. Hall-Scott aircraft products quickly earned the company an international reputation as an engine builder. For its first five years of operation, Hall-Scott Motor Car Company fielded four aircraft engines, with the smallest power rating being the four-cylinder A-1 ("A" for aircraft). [1-48] Advertised as a 32-hp engine, the A-1 could develop 40 hp when altered to run at the slightly higher engine speed of 1500 rpm. The A-1 had its cylinders laid out in-line, with each having a 4-inch bore and a 5-inch stroke, displacing a total of 251.3 cubic inches (compared to the 4-inch bore and stroke, 201-cubic-inch Comet engine). It had a cast iron head with pressed-on steel water jackets (perhaps copper at first) for containing coolant, as opposed to having passages in the iron through which coolant flowed. The head, however, had passages inside for coolant flow. Three main bearings supported its hand-forged crankshaft. The A-1 weighed 165 pounds, making it suitable for small, light aircraft. In addition to that first engine, in the early 1910s the company offered three closely related V-8s: the A-2 (4-inch bore and stroke, 402 cubic inches, 60 hp at 1400 rpm, 260 lb), the A-3 (4-inch bore and 5-inch stroke, 502.6 cubic inches, 80 hp at 1400 rpm, 290 lb), and the A-4 (5-inch bore and stroke, 785.4 cubic inches, 100 hp at 1200 rpm, 535 lb). These four engines featured the same construction (all the V-8s shared a 90-degree angle between the banks of cylinders), differing chiefly only in their number of cylinders, displacement, and the capacities and capabilities arising from those size differences.

Many other talented people such as Hall were building or tinkering with aviation engines in America around this same time. Glenn Angle's *1921 Airplane Engine Encyclopedia* offers at least 25 examples of startup aviation engine makers in the United States that built at least one engine around 1910 and lasted only a few years. To avoid a similar fate, Hall-Scott needed to make successful motors and to conduct a winning promotional effort. To distinguish itself, Hall-Scott purchased large and sometimes full-page ads in prominent national aviation magazines to pitch its line of engines. Advertisements from as early as 1910 show the company aggressively aiming its products at aviators. One such ad from 1910 showed two aircraft motors, the A-1 and the A-2, describing their

A 1911 ad for the first Hall-Scott aviation engine, the A-1, claiming industry leadership.

The Hall-Scott A-4, the fourth aviation engine offered by the company.

Side view of the Hall-Scott A-4 engine.

The Last Flying Hall-Scott?

Although a handful of Hall-Scott aviation engines are on display in America and elsewhere, there is probably not more than a single Hall-Scott aviation engine that has seen any flying time in decades. The Old Rhinebeck Aerodrome in Rhinebeck, New York, probably has the last Hall-Scott engine powering an airplane, shown here. The engine is a 1911 Model A-3, serial number 50, rated at 80 hp. It powers a reproduction 1911 Curtiss Model D Pusher, built in the 1970s by Aerodrome founder Cole Palen. Palen made an accurate reproduction of a Curtiss, right down to its controls (turn wheel for rudder, push and pull wheel for elevator, lean in the swivel seat to bank the

aircraft). The engine was restored by Kurt Muller and Jim Stover, two impressive mechanics who also have the restoration of a Liberty V-12 under their belts. While the craft is still capable of flight, generally its time airborne today consists of short hops off the runway. But in 2003, Aerodrome personnel took the plane to an Australian air show, where the plucky craft circled the entire field. With the Hall-Scott V-8 roaring behind him, shown here is Old Rhinebeck Aerodrome pilot Dan Taylor flying the Curtiss Model D Pusher. (Photos courtesy of Old Rhinebeck Aerodrome.)

strong suits as "Simplicity—Lightness—Strength—Constant Power." [1-49] In a 1911 ad, the company told potential buyers, "Its absolute simplicity of design, accessibility to parts, ease of adjustment and light weight, particularly adapt it for use of beginners in aviation as well as professional work in lighter type machines." [1-50] The price of the A-1 was $1,500 for the complete engine, and $1,650 with radiator, copper gas tank, and connections. That certainly was a great amount of money for the time but was comparable to the price of engines made by other firms. [1-51] The eight-cylinder A-2 carried a price tag of $2,000. [1-52]

The basic engine design Hall used in these aviation motors, while their genesis may have been in automobiles, worked quite well in airplane applications. Hall favored the overhead valve arrangement in his engines for several reasons. In a 1929 publication for the Society of Automotive Engineers, of which Hall was a long-time member, he wrote that an "overhead-valve engine is not necessarily any more durable than is an L-head [which is also known as a side-valve or flat-head] engine, because engine life is largely a matter of good design and proper material," but rather in how the two types produce their power. [1-53] According to Hall, overhead valve engines develop more torque at higher revolutions per minute. "The L-head engine," continued Hall, "has good torque up to an engine speed of about 1000 r.p.m., but the torque decreases at higher speeds. On the contrary, the overhead-valve engine will carry a satisfactory torque up to an engine speed of 5000 rpm, or even 7000 to 8000 rpm if necessary..." Thus, he explained, this is why "the L-head has never made good in airplane work...because the speed at which the power is taken off is too high for the torque characteristics of the engine." As an aside, Hall noted, "Merely due to design, about 5 per cent better fuel economy can be obtained with the overhead valve type than with the L-head type." Not an aviator himself, Hall nonetheless understood what aviators wanted in an engine, and Hall-Scott gave it to them.

The victories tallied by these capable motors encouraged Hall-Scott to work winning into its ad campaign, which would appeal to racers, enthusiasts, and "barnstormers." By 1911 and 1912, Hall-Scott ads mentioned specific instances in which Hall-Scott-powered planes won racing victories, set records, and accomplished startling feats. For example, in the August 1912 edition of *Aeronautics*, a Hall-Scott ad referenced two recent air races where a high percentage of the planes used Hall-Scott power—"50% Total Entries Los Angeles" and "75% Oakland International Meet." [1-54] A 1911 ad for the A-2 listed a number of racers using Hall-Scott engines who "are having real professional success with them. Why not place your order now and save yourself a chance of disappointment with any other make." [1-55] A Hall-Scott V-8 engine propelled Bob Fowler's "daring and successful flight across the Panama Canal," according to a 1913 ad. [1-56] Hall-Scott might have been a young West Coast company, but its market ambitions stretched far beyond the borders of its home region. To obtain a Hall-Scott catalog, interested people had to write to a national aviator of some reputation, Captain Thomas S. Baldwin, located far from the Berkeley factory: Madison Square, New York, New York. [1-57] A Hall-Scott ad from 1913 claimed that its 100-hp V-8 engine was "the most powerful (for aviation purposes) on the American market today." [1-58] Hall-Scott could list among its customers "Sure Shot" Kearny, who was described by one 1912 ad "doing more flying than any other aviator in the country," and who used an A-2. [1-59] Hoping to lure additional barnstormers to fly with Hall-Scott engines, that same 1912 ad said Sure Shot Kearny "never disappoints, never fails to fill flying dates as contracted for." And the money could be lucrative. That ad referenced a two-man team who made $4,000 for three days of flying.

Before World War I, Hall-Scott was perhaps the best-known maker of aircraft engines in the United States behind Curtiss. [1-60] Companies and individuals today recognized as pioneers and leaders were quick to adopt Hall-Scott aviation engines. Boeing, the world's largest aerospace company for many years, powered its first airplane, the B&W Model 1 of 1916, plus its next several planes, with Hall-Scott engines. [1-61] One writer reviewing the early California aviation scene opined, "Soon a Hall-Scott motor was the ambition of every early experimenter" because its engines "were unusually powerful in relation to weight and what was more important they were reliable." [1-62] Within only three years, Hall-Scott had shot from being a small startup engine maker to a prominent firm powering winning race planes and aviation record setters.

California was a great place to build aircraft engines in the 1910s, and aviation was a natural market for Hall-Scott to exploit. In 1911, one national aviation publication wrote, "California is an earnest rival of New York state in the number of aviators and flying fields." [1-63]. Barnstormers and other flyers were common at California county fairs and other outdoor events. Some aviators who would become quite famous for their aircraft, flying, and flying schools and for using Hall-Scott engines, such as Glenn L. Martin, were already making national names for themselves as Hall-Scott was getting off the ground. With E.J. Hall's success at powering aircraft before teaming with B.C. Scott, plus the growing demand for high-performance aviation engines in California, developing and selling Hall's engines as Hall-Scotts was a smart move.

Glenn Martin is shown here in 1911 with a Hall-Scott V-8-powered plane in southern California. A car salesman in 1909, Martin became a daredevil "birdman" and then rose to lead the influential Martin Company. (Courtesy of Taylor Scott.)

Hall-Scott V-8 engines received a great amount of attention, and not only from aviators. Cadillac Automobile Company introduced its first V-8 for its 1915 models after studying the powerful performance of the Hall-designed V-8. Engineers at Cadillac took one of Hall's eight-cylinder motors, tested it, and tore it apart to study it. [1-64] As it turned out, though, the final Cadillac design was quite different from Hall's design. In terms of similarities, both motors had eight cylinders with the banks 90 degrees to each other. [1-65] The Cadillac V-8 displaced 314 cubic inches and, rather than using built-up design as in Hall's design, had two banks cast of four cylinders. Furthermore, the Caddy did not use pressed-on water jackets as employed by Hall, but rather used a more sophisticated water jacket cast into the block. The Cadillac V-8 had only three main bearings for its crankshaft, whereas Hall's (at least for the Hall-Scott A-3, for which this detail is certain) had five. Although Hall's V-8 had overhead valves, the Cadillac V-8 sported side valves. Cadillac used side valves until adopting overhead valves in its V-8 in 1949. Nonetheless, despite these differences, the story of the large General Motors showing interest in

The V-8 "Special Car" owned by Leland Scott, Bert's younger brother. (Courtesy of Taylor Scott.)

tiny Hall-Scott naturally became widely repeated by those who worked at Hall-Scott. The Scott family kept the story alive for decades, handing it down across generations. In the late 1970s, shortly before his death, Leland Scott told of how E.J. Hall advised General Motors research chief Charles F. Kettering, "Why not get something really new and different like an eight cylinder engine." [1-66] Kettering responded with "Who in the world has an eight

It is possible that the Special Car was the Hall V-8-powered auto that Cadillac engineers purchased to study when designing their own V-8. (Courtesy of Taylor Scott.)

cylinder?" Hall told him, "Well, Lee Scott out in California has one I designed for him." Kettering then supposedly called Scott, asked how much it would cost to buy the car and, when told $5,000, said, "Fine. Put it on a freight, and send it in all haste to me." This would not be the last time a major auto maker took an interest in the ideas of E.J. Hall.

One thoughtful (and practical) feature in Hall's engines was his practice of sharing a large number of important parts. For example, all three Hall-Scott aviation V-8s sprung from the same basic design—a shared crankcase with two banks of cylinders attached to it at a 90-degree angle to each other. The three V-8s could swap cylinders, pistons, connecting rods, and valvetrains, depending on the model. With their many similarities, perhaps they could better be described as being a "family" of engines, as opposed to different and discrete ones. This practice allowed Hall-Scott to market several different engines, ones to meet a variety of customer demands, but not have entirely different designing, machining, and parts support for each one. A high degree of parts interchangeability would drive down the designing, machining, manufacturing, and stocking costs for Hall-Scott. This was especially important for a small young firm lacking great amounts of capital. Hall-Scott began using interchangeable parts for multiple engines in 1910 and continued the practice—indeed, relied on it—throughout its years as an engine maker.

It is not surprising that these first Hall-Scott products might appear somewhat strange to people who are more accustomed to looking at gasoline engines produced a century later. In large part, the dated appearance of the Hall-Scott A-1, A-2, A-3, and A-4 engines comes from the many exposed parts not visible on more modern motors. In Hall-Scott aircraft power plants, the cylinders were bolted to the crankcase (a common construction given several names, including the "built-up" or "separate cylinder" design), with long cylinder bolts circling the circumference of the cylinders in clear view. More surprising to a modern eye was the exposed valvetrain on these engines. Pushrods, rocker arms, and valve springs all were visible and plainly vulnerable to the harsh environment of moisture, dirt, and other hazards. This exposure did not foster long life for these parts or effectively dissipate the heat and friction that came from their constant, rapid oscillating and reciprocating action. The compromised ability of parts to deal with these challenges restricted the high-speed operation of the engine. These important parts naturally required lubrication, and being exposed meant that lubrication was done by hand. Engine operators only two decades later did not even give thought to the valvetrains of their engines. By then, the valve gear of virtually all engines were fully enclosed and pressure lubricated.

This less-than-ideal situation was precisely what E.J. Hall needed to pique his engineering prowess, and only a few years later, he rectified this situation.

For 1915, Hall-Scott introduced a new engine, the A-5, which represented an early turning point for the young company. [1-67] The A-5 was the first Hall-Scott in-line six-cylinder aircraft engine, which is somewhat noteworthy. But that is not what made it significant. Far from having exhausted his potential of engineering ideas, Hall designed the A-5 to be more sophisticated than anything he had yet created. He substantially improved the manner by which fuel and exhaust entered and exited the cylinders in the A-5 by dropping the overhead valve (pushrod) arrangement hitherto used on all Hall-Scotts, with valves actuated by an overhead camshaft (often referred to as an "overhead cam" design). By situating the camshaft directly above the valves, Hall could dispense with pushrods, thereby simplifying valve action. With fewer moving parts making for more efficient valve function, an overhead cam engine can "breathe" better, allowing for quicker throttle response and potentially higher maximum engine speed. Higher engine speed (revolutions per minute) generally allows

Hall-Scott workers standing around an A-5, with some of the more significant features of the engine visible here.

an engine to produce more horsepower, and an engine that can run at a wider range of speeds allows machines greater flexibility of operation. Having the entire valvetrain placed together, above the cylinders, also expedites repair because the head, with the valvetrain, can be removed all at once as a unit. An overhead cam design is more expensive to build, however, than the more common overhead valve or side valve designs. Its greater expense has been a prime reason why overhead cam design has seen limited usage for the last 100 years. It has long dominated race cars and expensive European passenger cars but did not make its way into broad use, including in heavy-duty engines, until the late twentieth century. Starting with the A-5 in 1915, overhead cam design became an E.J. Hall "trademark" on the engines he designed and on all engines sold by Hall-Scott thereafter, making it most unusual for a heavy-duty engine maker.

In addition to a new valve arrangement, Hall gave the A-5 a feature that became standard for his future engines—a combustion chamber having a dome shape at the top. Hall-Scott literature sometimes referred to this as being domed, and other times called it "semi-spherical." More recently outside of Hall-Scott literature, such a shape came to be called a hemispherical or "hemi" head. Hall canted the valves of the A-5 over a few degrees from the vertical axis of the cylinder to allow them to pass gas and exhaust more smoothly and to improve mixing in the combustion chamber. Hall and many other engineers looking to boost performance since the 1910s have recognized that a hemispherical shape promotes the passage of air and fuel in the cylinder, improves combustion with the cylinder, and therefore enhances performance. Today, the connotation many people have with a hemi head is one of high performance, and Hall certainly had this in mind when he included it in the A-5.

The Hall-Scott A-5 displaced 824.7 cubic inches, with each cylinder having a 5-inch bore and a 7-inch stroke. These measurements became common cylinder dimensions for future Hall-Scott engines. Weighing 525 pounds and producing 125 hp, the A-5 boasted a respectably low 4.2 pounds per horsepower, making it a competitive aviation engine. Another version of the A-5 followed shortly thereafter, the A-5a, which had a slightly larger bore measurement of 5.25 inches, thus increasing its displacement to 909.2 cubic inches and bumping its power output up to 150–165 hp (depending on the maximum engine speed model chosen). The A-5 (and its variants, the A-5a, A-7, and A-7a) did not take full advantage of this higher engine speed opportunity afforded by having an overhead camshaft, and these new motors had maximum speeds that were roughly the same as earlier Hall-Scott aircraft motors, about 1200–1500 rpm.

Beyond the valvetrain, head, and combustion chamber improvements, Hall enhanced engine cooling in the A-5, too. Hall designed the coolant in the A-5 to flow through passages cast into the iron head and cylinder walls. Foundry men at Macaulay were able to successfully cast Hall's boldest ideas into alloy iron (or more tricky aluminum), aiding the evolution of Hall-Scott engines. [1-68] Previously on Hall's aircraft engines, a pressed-on steel sleeve containing coolant surrounded the cylinders and abutted the head. While the integral casting design was heavier than that of the sleeve, the cast method far more reliably contained the coolant, and it dissipated engine heat more effectively. Even with the added mass from the thicker iron walls, at 575–600 pounds the A-5 was still lightweight for how much power it developed. Its power-to-weight ratio measured an impressive 3.75–4.2 lb/hp, depending on the model. This was a potent selling point to aviators.

It is not surprising that sales of the high-tech A-5 and A-5a quickly took off, with buyers from various states and countries. Uncle Sam discovered the strengths of the A-5 the hard way—after buying other motors of inferior ability. During the American military's "Punitive Expedition" of 1916–1917 into Mexico, in a vain attempt to hunt down the wanted bandito Pancho Villa, B.D. Foulois, captain in the U.S. Signal Corps, First Aero Squadron, reported to Washington, "In view of the fact that the present aeroplane equipment of the First Aero Squadron is not capable of meeting the present military conditions, it is urgently requested that the following number of aeroplanes, motors, and spare parts be purchased," including two Martin and two Curtiss aircraft, each

A Hall-Scott envelope from 1916.

1917 Hall-Scott Racer

Although Hall-Scott never marketed an automobile, its engines have appeared under the hoods of a handful of autos. These cars have not been regular production models, but rather special, hand-built machines. Without a doubt, the most widely seen and appreciated example of a Hall-Scott-powered car is the fabulous World War I-era replica racer owned by Californian Dick DeLuna. In the 1990s, DeLuna learned from individuals familiar with Hall that E.J. had wanted to build a racer around 1916 or 1917 using one of his company's aviation engines mated to a Reo three-speed transmission and frame. Hall had hoped to enter the car in the 1917 Vanderbilt Cup Race, but he never got around to building it. Upon hearing the story, the proposition of building such a car intrigued DeLuna, who then assembled the talent needed. DeLuna picked Tom Batchelor of Nevada to complete the power-train and Dennis Webb of California to hand-fabricate the body. Batchelor rebuilt a well-preserved A-7a (one of the 1,000 built by Nordyke & Marmon) and secured the Reo parts. But Batchelor faced a host of problems peculiar

to the aviation nature of the engine. Because it was designed to power early aircraft, the A-7a had no flywheel or starter, it used counterclockwise rotation, and its magneto ignition made an awkward match

to an auto electrical system. The low turning speed and great torque of the engine presented their own challenges. How would the engine be geared to attain racing speed? Not possessing an existing differential that would work in such a vehicle, Batchelor fashioned gears with an unusual 2:1 final drive ratio. Webb created a body of highly polished aluminum, secured by thousands of rivets, that is reflective of racers of the period. The project took more than five years to complete, and the stunning results speak for themselves. DeLuna's Racer has run the San Diego Speed Festival, Monterey Historic at Laguna Seca, and Good Wood Festival of Speed, and it was shown at Pebble Beach in the Race Car Class. As far as driving the one-of-a-kind machine, DeLuna says that "it does feel big" and with so much torque on tap in a chassis using World War I-era technology, "you have to respect it tremendously." Having 110 hp, 428 ft. lb. of torque, and tall gearing, the 2800-lb car can reach a speed of 100 mph. With its (mechanical) service brakes on only the rear wheels, however, high speeds would be a nerve-wracking proposition for most modern drivers. Whether moving or stationary, though, DeLuna's 1917 Hall-Scott Racer is a thrilling automobile. (Photos and information courtesy of Dick DeLuna and Tom Batchelor.)

fitted with "Hall-Scott 125 hp 6 cyl. motors." [1-69] Hall-Scott also sold A-5 or A-5a engines to foreign governments to power military aircraft, frequently trainers. Detailed export data are unavailable, but one record shows that Russia purchased 300 engines. [1-70] Countries, especially in Europe, braced for war in the 1910s, and Hall-Scott benefited, as did many other American businesses, as money flowed to fund the buildup.

Hall-Scott was not finished creating permutations of the basic A-5 when it offered the slightly larger-displacement A-5a. Following the practice Hall-Scott used with many of the new engines that it introduced, the Hall-Scott six-cylinder A-5 soon had a four-cylinder partner, the A-7, which also had a slightly larger version (again having a 0.25-inch bore increase), the A-7a. The four-cylinder A-7 had the same 5 × 7-inch cylinder measurements seen in the A-5; however, with

The front of the Hall-Scott A-7a. (Courtesy of Taylor Scott.)

only 549.8 cubic inches of displacement, the smaller engine developed 90–100 hp at 1400 rpm and weighed 410 lb. The A-7a displaced 606.1 cubic inches and developed 100–110 hp at 1400 rpm. The A-7a also might have been the first Hall-Scott model to come with a Miller carburetor option, but this is not entirely clear. Such an option points to Hall's friendship with West Coast racing figure Harry Miller, as well as Hall's continued commitment to delivering high performance in his machines. The A-7 was a serious motor and therefore found its way into a number of aircraft, including the Boeing Model C trainer, 50 of which were ordered by the U.S. Navy. In an unusual example of bad press for Hall-Scott, one Boeing historian in the 1960s called the A-7a "unreliable." [1-71] It is unclear if this was a widespread opinion in the 1910s and 1920s. In air power, being an unreliable engine carries even more serious possible consequences than when powering a truck or tractor.

The A-5 and A-5a had many mechanical similarities to the A-7 and A-7a, but the

new four-cylinder engines had a critical difference "under the skin" that set
them apart from their earlier counter-
parts—aluminum pistons. Hall-Scott
was possibly the first American aviation engine maker to use lightweight
aluminum as opposed to iron for its
pistons. [1-72] Around this time, other
engineers were beginning to use aluminum alloy for pistons in cars, including
Harry Miller, who had already attained
legendary stature among racers. Technically, the A-7 pistons were the "first
to incorporate the thick section aluminum piston principle, which was patented jointly by Hall and the Aluminum
Company of America." [1-73] With the
obvious benefits derived from lowering
the weight of internal moving parts,
other engine makers quickly followed
suit. Aluminum pistons later became
common in automotive, truck, marine,
and industrial engines, and Hall-Scott
helped push along this advance, as
it did with other features, making its
contribution to the improvement and
growing sophistication of the internal
combustion engine.

*The rear of the Hall-Scott A-7a. Note
the long bolts securing the cylinder.
(Courtesy of Taylor Scott.)*

In the spring of 1917, Hall-Scott finished preliminary testing of the A-8
airplane engine. The A-8 was the most powerful Hall-Scott airplane engine
built to date and its first V-12. Just how much power was generated by the
engine is of some dispute, but even the low figures reported were impressive.
Hall-Scott claimed in an advertisement that the A-8 produced 300 hp, which
probably is accurate. However, an article from 1918 in *Motor Age* and an entry
in the *1921 Airplane Engine Encyclopedia* reported that the A-8 produced
450–500 hp, which probably is optimistic [1-74] With so much power on
tap, the A-8 would be able to propel much larger aircraft and to higher speeds
than had any previous Hall-Scott engines. In fact, so powerful was the A-8

that tests in July 1918 had to be halted when Hall-Scott engineers determined that the A-8 was too much for the test stand being used. Hall-Scott erected another engine stand with a capacity of 600 hp, which would handle the A-8 and still retain a comfortable margin of safety. The twelve cylinders of the A-8 each had a 5-inch bore and a 7-inch stroke, and the engine displaced 1649.3 cubic inches. Following a well-established Hall-Scott practice, the A-8 shared cylinder dimensions and engine parts with other Hall-Scott models. But the twelve-cylinder was not simply two six-cylinder A-5 engines bolted together. Instead, the A-8 engine reverted to Hall-Scott's earlier use of pressed steel jackets around the cylinders for cooling. No rationale could be found in available records to explain why this "de-evolution" occurred, but such a feature would pare quite a bit of weight off the big engine. Sources put the weight of the A-8 at approximately 1000 lb. [1-75] By adding the A-8 to its engine lineup, Hall-Scott was positioning itself to move into powering larger commercial and military aircraft. Building and testing of the largest and most powerful Hall-Scott aircraft engine came at a good time for the company as the United States entered World War I in 1917.

The Hall-Scott V-12 aviation engine, the A-8.

From 1910 to 1917, Hall-Scott grew substantially in the range and quantity of products it made, the number of workers it employed, and the earnings it reported. Late in 1910, the company launched its aviation engine line. Hall-Scott's first year was successful by any reasonable standard, with the company posting a modest net earnings figure of $7,061.66 for the year (actually ten months, ending December 31, 1910). [1-76] In November 1911, *Aeronautics* wrote, "The Hall-Scott Company find business brisk, and are extremely busy at their factory. Their pay roll [*sic*] shows that they are now employing nearly forty men, and they have been running overtime for the past few months, and it looks as if they would continue to do so for the next few months to come." [1-77] Hall-Scott also was selling propellers—first a $50 spruce model and then one of mahogany for $75—by late 1911. Important new engine models followed. Hall-Scott production numbers from the period are sketchy, but net earnings are available; thus, it is known that the company usually made money from 1910 to 1917. For the period February 1910 to December 31, 1916, Hall-Scott reported a cumulative $447,312.79 in net earnings. [1-78] Although 86% of the earnings for that period came from 1916 alone, note that Hall-Scott

For its first few years of operation, Hall-Scott marketed engines and even propellers. Shown here being assembled are an auto engine, several aviation engines, and a propeller. (Courtesy of Taylor Scott.)

lost money in only one of those years, 1914, with a net loss of $14,716.91. Overall, Hall-Scott ran a profitable operation before World War I. The high net earnings that Hall-Scott reported in 1916 gave managers a taste of how lucrative the Great War would be.

World War I and Hall-Scott

Through the summer of 1914, Europe lurched into fighting a wider and wider war. Austria's declaration of war on Serbia on July 27 initiated a domino effect of similar actions across the continent. While the conflict began in Europe, within a couple of years the war sucked in countries from around the globe. The United States remained officially neutral for almost three years, in fact, conducting business with both sides. *Commercial Car Journal* found a silver lining to this dark cloud of war, saying in August 1914, "While the war is in progress, all industries in the European countries are practically at a stand-still." [1-79] It forecast a very long war, inasmuch as European nations had been preparing to fight for so long. This meant that "The general war which is now raging throughout Europe must, in a very short time, produce great prosperity in the United States."

The growing involvement of America in World War I had a profound effect on American industrial production, as it siphoned raw materials, finished goods, and labor for the war effort, especially beginning in the spring of 1917. Hall-Scott was not immune to this impact. In the early 1910s, Hall-Scott ordered less than 20 tons of metal from Macaulay Foundry every year, but that figure jumped to 100 tons in 1916, a date that brought volume production of the A-5 and its variants, and more than doubled again in 1917 when America changed its role in the war. [1-80] The war also halted the market introduction of the Hall-Scott high-performance A-8. A full-page ad in *Aviation* dated November 1917 showed a drawing of a Hall-Scott V-12 and reported that the "exhaustive tests [of the A-8 were] completed May 1st, 1917" but did not offer its price or even if it was available for purchase. [1-81] It was rather curious for a company to advertise an engine that still was not ready for sale, or an engine having its introduction postponed by the war. An article from *Motor Age* dated October 1918, five months later, stated, "This engine is just undergoing its final testing at the California plant of the company." This statement suggests that development of the A-8 had been either ongoing or on hold since the spring of 1917 but, either way, still was not available at that later date. [1-82] The war prevented the introduction of the A-8 engine and brought other huge changes to the Berkeley-based engine company.

On April 6, 1917, Congress granted President Woodrow Wilson his request for a declaration of war to be brought against Germany. This action threw the United States headlong into the European conflict, supporting the "Allies." America's entry would make a critical difference in the outcome of the war, in part because the United States could out-produce all of the enemy "Central Powers" countries combined. The Great War had quickly descended into a horrifying stalemate after it began in 1914, at least on the Western Front; therefore, Allied leaders hoped that the infusion of fresh American "doughboys," along with the promise of limitless materiel from the American industrial juggernaut, would break the deadlock and turn the tide of war.

As seen across American industry, auto, engine, boat, and truck makers availed their services to the government with the advent of war. By that time, the plants of American auto and related industries were already producing copious amounts of industrial goods for the Allies, including a few engines for British and French planes. F.E. Moskovics, an auto executive with Nordyke & Marmon, wrote an article in 1919, titled "What the Motor Car Industry Did in the War," saying, "The Society of Automotive Engineers...opened offices in Washington [D.C.] immediately after war was declared. The society was very largely instrumental in furnishing the various departments with the technical men needed." [1-83] The National Automobile Chamber of Commerce, which represented management, similarly availed itself and opened an office in the capital. In fact, a member of this body chaired the Automobile Committee of the newly formed War Industries Board of the U.S. government. Because of its much greater size than the aviation industry, the auto industry could supply munitions, machinery, and an array of vehicles for the American war effort, including aircraft and aircraft engines. Moskovics was not overstating his case when he asserted that the automobile industry played a "modest contributing factor" in the outcome of the war.

Producing aircraft became a top priority to American war planners. General John "Blackjack" Pershing urged American leaders to rush three things to the American Expeditionary Force in Europe: airplanes, tanks, and gas. [1-84] The American aircraft industry did not have nearly the productive capacity to fill such a great demand, let alone in the massive quantities suggested by Pershing. Thus, the auto industry and related fields such as trucks and engines had to interdict in the American wartime aircraft design and production program. Total American aircraft production from 1903 through April 14, 1917 amounted to a paltry 666 units. In June 1917, the War Department announced a program to produce 22,625 planes, so the auto industry was a natural source

Testing aviation engines at Hall-Scott, circa 1917.

for the massive and coordinated production needed. [1-85] The government opened an assortment of agencies to oversee aircraft and aircraft-engine making, including the Aircraft Production Board.

The American automotive engineering community plugged itself into the Allied air war effort immediately. Given the sad condition of Allied aircraft design and production to date, it was none too late. The airplane made its appearance as a war machine in World War I, and Germany of the Central Powers had taken the best advantage of this new technology. By 1917, the Allied governments were producing sixty different aircraft engines, while the Germans made only five engines and in sheer number out-produced all of the Allies. [1-86] The Germans also built perhaps the finest aircraft motor at the time, the Austro-Daimler, designed by Ferdinand Porsche. [1-87] American policy makers wanted to consolidate Allied engine production under U.S. government regulation to maximize design, production, and distribution resources. Lieutenant H.H. Emmons, chief of the U.S. government Engine Production Department, said that two men—Howard Coffin, chairman of the Aircraft Production Board, and Edward A. Deeds, an engineer, industrialist, and member of the Aircraft Production Board—determined that "three courses were available to them: 1 - To send a commission of experts abroad to study the engines used by the Allies. 2 - To encourage the production in this country of such suitable foreign engines as had already been put in production in the United States. 3 - To develop a suitable engine from the talent and facilities available in this country in automobile and allied industries. Action was taken along each of these three lines." [1-88] According to Emmons, an American commission reviewed the possible engines currently available that could be used to successfully power the Allied air campaign and determined that of all the foreign makers, the two best engines came from Rolls-Royce (Great Britain) and Lorraine-Dietrich (France). But these two engines, good as they were, did not lend themselves to American mass production, with its widespread use of interchangeable parts and machine assembly tended by operators, rather than skilled craftsmen working by hand. The Wright-Martin Aircraft Corporation had begun the initial stages of producing a model from the French luxury car maker Hispano-Suiza, but at 150 hp, the commission deemed it too small. Likewise, domestic aviation makers had little to offer. Emmons mentioned only a small number of domestic engine makers having the needed aviation experience to be taken seriously, one of them being the Hall-Scott Motor Car Company. Emmons said of Hall-Scott that it "had for several years been manufacturing aviation equipment for use by foreign governments" and that "E.J. Hall, of that company, had traveled in Europe at about the beginning of the war and had inspected the engines made both by the Allies and by the Germans." However, he did not mention any Hall-Scott engines specifically, even the stillborn A-8. After its review of the marketplace, the Aircraft Production Board could not find an engine anywhere that was currently in production and available to American plane makers that satisfied its demands. Therefore, a new engine would have to be designed and built, in great numbers and quickly.

Deeds continued to assemble the team needed to design suitable engines for the war effort. In May 1917, he and other members of the Aircraft Production Board received a visit from distinguished engineer Jesse G. Vincent of the Packard Motor Car Company, one of the premier American automobile producers. Although best known for its prestigious automobiles, Packard also produced trucks and marine engines. More recently, Vincent had been designing aviation engines, finishing a 250-hp V-12 in early 1917. [1-89] However, until that point in time, Vincent had never actually designed a marketed aircraft engine. Vincent shared with Deeds some ideas of what the new Allied aircraft engine should look like, such as having a high power-to-weight ratio,

E.J. Hall as an officer in the U.S. Air Service during World War I. (Courtesy of Wichita State University Libraries, Department of Special Collections.)

maximum performance, minimum fuel and oil consumption, and standardized engine parts. The Board recognized in Vincent the kind of engineer it needed to lead the project to a successful outcome, but he could not complete the design work alone. E.J. Hall was an obvious choice to work with Vincent, and Deeds suggested that Hall be added to the team. [1-90] Hall and Vincent met on the morning of May 29. Hall did not need to be summoned to appear in Washington in May; he had been in town since March, meeting with government men concerning his company's engines. [1-91]

The selection of Hall to consult in Washington for the war effort was not an unusual decision. Hall had worked in a small company, but he had been in the engine business at that point for about 10 years. Because these were the early days of engine making in America, that was a substantial period. Considering his humble beginnings, however, Hall's rise in prominence in engineering circles was meteoric. According to Moskovics, Hall "actually had more aerial motor experience than any other American engineer," while Vincent had "more experience on details of the Mercedes-type air motors," widely considered a leading aviation engine, more than anyone in the country. [1-92] Interestingly, these two respected and successful engineers shared a lack of advanced formal schooling, but nonetheless both possessed superior technical abilities. According to a Hall-Scott brochure, both men were "highly skilled engineers, capable, energetic, veritable geniuses of the gas engine." [1-93]

The two engineers had never met before this wartime encounter, knowing each other only by reputation. But the newness of their association did not seem to hinder their productivity. Their task was to design a standardized line of military aircraft engines with the highest levels of performance and reliability that could take full advantage of the sophisticated American industrial might. This meant the engines needed to be able to be mass-produced using interchangeable parts. The engines also had to avoid the use of too many untried features.

In a story that has taken on the qualities of legend, on May 29, 1917, Hall, Vincent, and a few associates were locked in a suite of the New Willard Hotel in Washington, DC. [1-94] Deeds gave them the needed relevant materials on current Allied air power. Moskovics, who attended the first two days of meetings, reported that "all their preliminary calculations and sketches were completed in five days" after being "locked up" together. [1-95] At midnight on June 4, Hall and Vincent met with members of the Aircraft Production Board and other military leaders to show them their drawings. [1-96] The Board approved the plans and ordered that the first prototype engines, of eight and twelve cylinders, be produced immediately for testing. Four- and six-cylinder engines were scheduled for production later.

Hall and Vincent left for Detroit and the Packard factory on June 7 to supervise the building of the first "Liberties." Hall obtained Hall-Scott crankshaft dies from the A-7a and A-5a to facilitate the project. [1-97] In all, skilled men from more than two dozen auto companies contributed in this marathon effort to make the initial motors. About a month after the drawing started, an eight-cylinder Liberty motor sat ready for testing, an amazingly rapid turnaround time in engine design, which can often take years to proceed from conception to the first working example. [1-98] During the next few months, Hall spent time in engine and airplane manufacturing sites in several states, and then in a few Allied European countries, to oversee production and testing.

In spite of E.J. Hall's critical input in the creation of the Liberty motor, and the close similarity between existing Hall-Scott aviation engines and the Liberty, Hall-Scott did not win a contract to build Liberty motors. Simply put, Hall-Scott was too small to contribute meaningfully in the production phrase of the Liberty program. The government wanted to take full advantage of the awesome American industrial output, and that meant not only using interchangeable parts, with which Hall-Scott was well versed, but also mass production, which Hall-Scott simply could not muster. Hall-Scott had produced hundreds of engines since 1910 but had nowhere near the enormous production capacity needed to efficiently and quickly churn out Liberties in the volume required. Therefore, larger companies that produced automobiles built Liberties. This practice ensured maximum production, even if it created engines that, according to one aviation historian, "varied considerably from maker to maker. A good Liberty was extremely reliable, a bad one pitiful." [1-99]

Although the first example of the Liberty motor was the eight-cylinder version, the twelve-cylinder was produced in the largest numbers, owing to its greater power and smoothness. Ultimately, builders manufactured only two of the four-cylinder models, 52 of the six-cylinder, 15 of the eight-cylinder, and 20,478 of the twelve-cylinder. [1-100] So many were produced, in fact, that surplussed Liberties powered airplanes, boats, and even a handful of automobiles well after the war. In spite of their thirst for fuel (which was not out of line, given their power), their pressing need for periodic maintenance, and their uneven reliability record, Liberty motors saw widespread postwar usage and in 1938 resumed production in England for powering Cruiser and Cavalier tanks. The Liberty motor was an engine that almost refused to die.

The long-term success of the Liberty is closely related to its high degree of technical sophistication that allowed it to produce so much power from a relatively light package. This is a highly desired trait in aviation engines. The degree to which aviation technology had sped forward in the first two decades of the twentieth century can be inferred from the constantly shrinking power-to-weight ratios in aircraft engines. For their history-making 1903 flight in North Carolina, the Wright brothers used a 12-hp engine that weighed 152 lb, producing 12.7 lb/hp. In 1910, Hall-Scott sold its A-1 engine, which developed 32 hp and weighed 165 lb, producing 5.2 lb/hp. In 1918, the Liberty 12-A developed 421 hp and weighed 844 lb, which comes to only 2 lb/hp, about one-sixth of the figure of the 1903 Wright engine.

It would be difficult, if not impossible, to create out of thin air in only one month an engine of the sophistication required by the government. Obviously, the final product would reflect features and aspects familiar to and favored by both of the men who designed it. In a joint statement, signed by both Hall and Vincent, the two men reported to the Aircraft Production Board in a May 31, 1917, letter with their initial recommendations, "In laying down this motor, we have without reserve selected the best possible practice from both Europe and America. Practically all features of this motor have been absolutely proved out in America by experimental work and manufacturing experience in the Hall-Scott and Packard plants, and we are, therefore, willing to unhesitatingly stake our reputations on this design providing we are allowed to see that our design and specifications are absolutely followed." [1-101] This statement seems to be borne out in an inspection of the Liberty motor.

While the Liberty engine was no clone of the aircraft engines designed by E.J. Hall for his firm in the 1910s, the new Liberties bore a striking resemblance to engines made by Hall-Scott, especially the most recent A-8. [1-102] These similarities began with the relationship among the Liberty models. The Liberty motor is perhaps more accurately termed a "family" of related engines of four, six, eight, and twelve cylinders with interchangeable pistons, rods, valvetrains, and other parts. Interchangeability of parts had been a Hall-Scott hallmark of its engines since 1910, for both its aircraft and rail engines. The Liberty Motor was not cast "en-bloc" of iron, but rather was "built up" with individual steel cylinders bolted to the upper crankcase, another Hall-Scott feature on every one of its aviation motors built since 1910. The coolant in the Liberty flowed through steel jackets affixed to the cylinders, as seen in many Hall-Scott motors, including the A-8. All Liberties had the same cylinder dimensions of 5 × 7 inches, measurements corresponding to many Hall-Scotts, including the A-8. A camshaft situated on top of the cylinders of the Liberty (overhead camshaft) opened and closed the valves, something seen on all Hall-Scott models introduced since 1915. The Liberty had heavy-duty aluminum pistons, a feature found on Hall-Scotts beginning with the introduction of the A-7. The first Liberty shared identical "bevel gear, piston rings...crankshaft dies" with the Hall-Scott V-12 engine, along with a "seven-bearing crankshaft" and "direct drive" as opposed to geared drive of the propeller. Finally, the V-12 Liberty and the V-12 Hall-Scott A-8 produced roughly the same horsepower. To be accurate, these were not features exclusive to Hall-Scott. They were shared with Hall-Scott engines and Liberties. They did not necessarily become part of the Liberty motor because of Hall's input.

The Liberty engines and the latest Hall-Scott aviation engines, especially the V-12 A-8, were not mirror images of each other. The Liberty V-12 engine had a

The V-12 Liberty.

45-degree angle between the banks of cylinders, whereas the Hall-Scott V-12 had a 60-degree angle. Transverse sections and exterior pictures of the two V-12s show a close correspondence between designs but differences in the intake and exhaust manifolds, carburetion, and other external components. The Liberty also had a slightly larger bearing surface than the Hall-Scott A-8. Therefore, the Liberty motor was a close match to the Hall-Scott A-8 and, argued by some (especially those connected to Hall-Scott), a direct derivative.

War often acts as a catalyst for technological advance, and World War I certainly jump-started engine development. The Liberty engine ranks among the greatest of the technical achievements, certainly in engine design, that emerged from this particularly bloody war. The *San Francisco Examiner* bragged in a brief article, "A portion of the credit for the celebrated new 'Liberty Motor,' said to be the fastest and finest airplane motor in the world, is claimed by Berkeley, inasmuch as E.J. Hall of the Hall-Scott Motor Company of that city had a hand in designing it," although the source might be dismissed as being biased for its native son. [1-103] Similarly, automotive executive Moskovics said of the Liberty motor and the larger U.S. aviation program, "It is not too much to say that at the time the armistice was signed our aircraft program was the largest, our two-seated planes the best, our fighting motors the best, our equipment and detail the best and our arrangement for repair and maintenance the best—of any belligerent—and all this was done by Army executives trained in the motor car industry and the motor car manufacturers themselves." [1-104] In his 1920 book, *The Story of the Engine*, which was devoted to engine (broadly defined) development through the ages, author Wilbur Decker wrote in the preface that this power plant was a "crowning example in mechanical achievement." [1-105] Decker subtitled the book *From Lever to Liberty Motor* to underscore his admiration for the Liberty.

Clearly, Hall and his company derived much satisfaction from their contribution in developing the Liberty. Hall's involvement in the war began in 1917 with surveying the engines available and helping design the Liberty, and continued afterward. [1-106] He adapted the French Le Rhone engine to American methods of production, acted as a "troubleshooter" starting U.S. production of the British De Haviland airplane, traveled to France at the bequest of General Pershing, and became chief of the Air Services Technical Section. For his impressive work in support of the war effort, Hall received a promotion in rank from major to lieutenant colonel and a Distinguished Service Medal from the U.S. government. The government gave Hall an honorable discharge in December 1918. In terms of national and international impact and service, World War I might have been E.J. Hall and Hall-Scott's finest moment.

While Hall did considerable globetrotting during the war, back in Berkeley, instead of producing Liberty motors or their parts, Hall-Scott focused on selling smaller aircraft engines, mostly for training aircraft, and spare parts. Hall-Scott built 1,250 A-7a engines for use in trainers, and auto maker Nordyke & Marmon built 1,000 more under license. [1-107] Therefore, the A-7 (and the A-7a) was the largest-selling Hall-Scott engine to date, and by a huge margin. It was the biggest moneymaker as well. Not only did Hall-Scott realize massive profitability during the war years of 1917 and 1918 by selling engines, but Nordyke & Marmon paid Hall-Scott a handsome royalty of $300 for every A-7a it built. [1-108] For the war years of 1917 and 1918, the net earnings of Hall-Scott shot up to $1,737,759 and $2,638,307, respectively. These are impressive figures for almost any company, but especially so for a company the size of Hall-Scott. [1-109] Hall-Scott was small and flexible enough to take advantage of this sudden change in demand. A few years later, a report on Hall-Scott looked back to the war years and said, "At the conclusion of the War, the Hall-Scott Company was in a very strong financial position with greatly expanded manufacturing facilities and a wide reputation as gas motor manufacturers." [1-110] Clearly, both E.J. Hall and Hall-Scott did very well in World War I.

A small portion of the enormous sale of hundreds of engines and spare parts Hall-Scott made for Russia during the war. (Courtesy of Taylor Scott.)

In spite of Hall's pivotal role in designing this engine and other contributions to the war effort, his personal recognition in the Liberty engine project has remained relatively low key. The similarities between the finished Liberty motor and earlier Hall-Scott engines are clear, the use of Hall-Scott dies for parts in the first Liberties is documented, and the government recognition of Hall's work is a matter of public record. Jesse Vincent has received most of the notoriety, though. Not to diminish Vincent's impressive efforts, but Hall has been accorded more of an "also starring" marquee position to Vincent's "top billing." In Dickey's book on the Liberty motor, the overwhelming majority of the quotations from the two men are credited to Vincent. Dickey does not appear to have had a personal axe to grind when writing his book, nor did he attempt to minimize Hall's contributions. E.J. Hall did not exactly make it easy for historians to divine his part in this story because he left little of a written record. Dickey wrote that Vincent, on the other hand, was a "prolific and lucid writer," and a primary source that Dickey used was "filled with [Vincent's] correspondence... It is regrettable that so little evidence is left of [Hall's] role in the Liberty project." [1-111] Perhaps those closer to the project could more clearly see Hall's critical input into the success of the Liberty. Harold Hicks, a young man fresh out of engineering school, joined Hall on the Liberty program in December 1917 to "make it proper for production." [1-112] The way Hicks remembered it, "Actually, Hall did most of the work because he had considerable experience in aviation engine design, having really built up and tested more aviation engines than Vincent had ever seen. That is Colonel Vincent of Packard Motors. To everyone that really knew, the credit should be given more to Hall than to Vincent." Hicks' loyalty to Hall is commendable, but the task at hand facing these men was so large, and the contributions made by the primary figures were so impressive, that suggesting that Hall deserves some kind of apology or perhaps should now receive more credit than Vincent is not worthy of either man.

Such an argument has already has been waged, however. Ironically, right after World War I ended, another conflict broke out—this one a war of words—over who got credit for creating the Liberty. An early shot came in *Motor West* magazine, which printed a statement dated January 1919 from Hall-Scott that read, "The man who contributed most to the making of the Liberty engine has said the least." [1-113] The article was one of two run by the publication on who deserved more credit for developing the Liberty, a choice *Motor West* deferred on making outright. Perhaps costing him a more visible place in history, Hall appears to have found it easier to create new engines than self-congratulatory statements.

Packard moved quickly to put Vincent's, and Packard's, names into the public record and general memory as leading the Liberty program. For example, Packard released a statement titled the "Real Story of the Liberty Motor," which appeared, among other places, in that same January 1919 issue of *Motor West*. Placed into some context, the Versailles Treaty had not yet been wrapped up, but Packard and Hall-Scott were already "planting their flag" on their conquest. Setting the record straight, at least by its own reckoning, Packard argued, "It is popularly though[t] that the Liberty Motor was created in a few days, some months after we entered the war, and that it was a composite production of many manufacturing plants. Actually, this motor had been under development by the Packard Motor Car Co. nearly two years before its adoption in final form by our Government." [1-114] The piece did mention E.J. Hall, once, but it omitted Hall-Scott altogether. The Packard statement conveniently ignored the government documentation of Hall and Hall-Scott's pivotal participation. Packard also produced a booklet by the same name as the aforementioned article, "The Real Story of the Liberty Motor," that argued its leadership in the Liberty program and the similarities of the Liberty to existing, prewar Packards. Before the war, Packard did not market an aviation engine, much less a line of such engines, but in 1915 began a program to develop aviation models. Having plenty of talent to accomplish such a task, the company was successful, and the engines that were built looked and performed much like the Liberties. In "The Real Story," though, the Liberty project came off sounding largely as a solo effort. When introducing Hall, it described him, amazingly, as only "an engineer who had built some motors for the Russian government." [1-115] Packard's great size, scope, and visibility gave it the ability to mount the kind of media campaign needed to put Vincent's name in the public imagination.

Hall-Scott also undertook an outspoken effort to shape the record of its contribution to the successful and heralded Liberty. In a media bid that might seem like grandstanding, the company released a booklet called "Pertinent Facts About the Liberty Motor," probably in 1919 or 1920. Arguing that it had been provoked, Hall-Scott said, "Forced into the arena by the unreserved statements in many so-called 'True Stories of the Liberty Engine' published in this country, we reluctantly protest against such statements contained therein..." [1-116] The publication pointed out, in great detail and using more than 25 pages of text packed with letters, examples, government records, and photographs, E.J. Hall's personal investment in the project (without using quotes attributed to him) and the many similarities between the Liberty and existing Hall-Scott engines. Calling the two men "gentlemen—highly skilled engineers, capable, energetic, veritable geniuses of the gas engine," Hall-Scott was more reluctant to give any specific credit to Vincent's employer, which the pamphlet obliquely referred to as "an eastern automotive company." Packard came off as a "bad guy" in this story, but Vincent did not. It is not known how many of these pamphlets were published by Hall-Scott, but examples can be found across America. A small company such as Hall-Scott could not hope to compete with a firm the size of Packard in terms of getting the nation's attention, but Hall-Scott still made the effort.

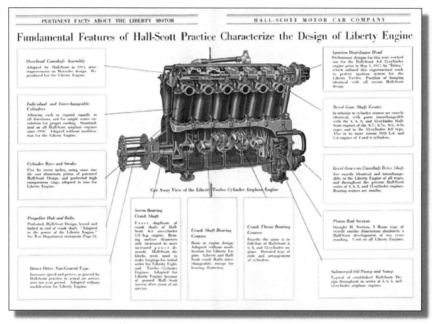

Although the type is difficult to read here, this is an example of the Hall-Scott argument in the public relations war with Packard over who was most responsible for designing the Liberty, taken from the "Pertinent Facts About the Liberty Motor" brochure. (Courtesy of Wichita State University Library, Department of Special Collections.)

In an even more provocative way of connecting itself to the Liberty, Hall-Scott referred to its Liberty motor connection in its ads for several years after the war. When introducing a new marine motor in the early 1920s, a Hall-Scott ad claimed that it embodied "the highest quality material and workmanship that made the Liberty Aircraft Engine unquestionably the present day premier

An overt Liberty connection can be seen on this Hall-Scott brochure cover, probably from 1919. Strongly worded text inside also linked Hall and Hall-Scott to the Liberty. (Courtesy of Robert Neal.)

aviation equipment." [1-117] Writing in the *Port of Oakland Compass* in 1933, Hall-Scott assistant sales manager C.G. Patch pointed out, "The history of the Liberty Engine is closely interwoven with that of Hall-Scott as it was designed by Col. E.J. Hall of the Hall-Scott Company and Col. Vincent of Packard. In the original layout many standard Hall-Scott parts were used and in its final form there was little deviation from the company's regular design." [1-118] Such overt references had largely faded in Hall-Scott ads by the advent of the 1930s. With the widespread recognition and universal admiration of the Liberty engine, at least through the 1920s, this was an advertising point that Hall-Scott management decided it could not squander. What benefit the company and Elbert Hall derived from this public back-patting is unclear.

Hall-Scott wove a more tangible connection between itself and the Liberty by basing some of its postwar engines on the famous (and contested) wartime aviation motor. As the fighting in Europe wound down slowly in the closing months of 1918, Hall-Scott announced a new aviation engine to its lineup, the L-6. Weighing only 502 lb, the L-6 still created 212.6 hp at 1666 rpm, making for an impressive 2.45 lb/hp. [1-119] In the L-6, Hall-Scott used higher-strength, lower-weight steel than more conventional and heavier iron for its cylinders. The use of steel led to many performance gains in the L-6, such as its ability to use a higher compression ratio and a higher operating temperature and to achieve a higher maximum engine speed. Engineers carefully removed all excess metal from the engine to ensure minimum weight. All of these differences contributed to the fact that the L-6 weighed about a hundred pounds less than the six-cylinder A-5 but developed more than an additional 40 hp. A four-cylinder version of the L-6, the L-4, followed shortly thereafter, which basically was an L-6 with two cylinders lopped off. [1-120] This smaller stable mate of the L-6 produced 125 hp at 1700 rpm. Both the L-4 and L-6 used the now familiar 5 × 7-inch bore and stroke internal cylinder dimensions, making their pistons and some other parts interchangeable. The magazine *Motor Age*, a publication that did not focus on aviation, was impressed enough to run an article on the introduction of the L-6, calling it "a considerable advance in design." Although the government (specifically, the U.S. Navy) was an early buyer for the L engines, the engines also became available for public consumption. The up-and-coming Boeing company used the L-4 in its BB-1 passenger plane and the L-6 in its B-1 mail-passenger flying boat and BB-L6 passenger plane. [1-121]

As was pointed out by *Motor Age* writers in their review of the L-6, the steel cylinders in the L-6 were "similar to the type perfected for the Liberty engine." Comparisons between the Liberty motor and new Hall-Scott models were natural, given their similarities in power and construction. In fact, Hall-Scott bought numerous Liberty parts from the government, which it had in abundance, to build its "new" engines. Although the Hall-Scott L engines were new, technically speaking, perhaps they could be more accurately described as being "pretty new," being closer to warmed-over Liberties, although they

HALL-SCOTT

Liberty Type Airplane
Engine Installations

for

Standard J-1
United States Government
Training Planes

*A brochure promoting the application of the Hall-Scott postwar
L-series engines in the government's standard training plane.
(Courtesy of the San Diego Aerospace Museum.)*

were not Liberties. And their "L" designation made it impossible not to associate them to the Liberty; it underscored, or even begged, a close relationship.
While that was an association worth exploiting, given the widespread and

L-4 Engine Test in Fuselage

Aᴌ details have been carefully worked out for ideal installations of Hall-Scott Types L-4 and L-6 engines in Standard J-1 Training Planes. Provision has been made for gasoline emergency gravity tank in upper wing, radiators of ample capacity, with shutters for altitude and cold climatic conditions, exhaust manifold carried back, away from pilot and passengers. (See photograph on front cover.) Extra drift wires, engine bed supports, change in stagger of plane so that the ship is perfectly balanced, extra strut from fuselage to landing gear with proper braces, extra oil reserve tank and larger gasoline tank for six hours continuous flying. In fact, everything has been done to make the equipment practically fool proof, and easily handled by the average airplane pupil so as to provide for ideal commercial use.

According to Mr. Pickup, of the Durant Aircraft Corporation, Oakland, Calif., this plane practically flies itself, cannot be stalled, and is the easiest and most pleasing equipment he has ever operated.

If more people about to start in the airplane game, or those that have been misled by the purchase of planes that are soon underpowered and give trouble, investigate the possibilities of the Standard J-1 plane with Hall-Scott equipment, it will further this industry in the United States rather than discourage it.

The person or company interested in private or commercial aviation possibilities should correspond with us for details upon these airplanes before investing in their equipment.

HALL-SCOTT MOTOR CAR CO., Inc.

Sales Department
BERKELEY, CALIFORNIA

That same brochure showing how the L-4 sits in the trainer's fuselage. Note the radiators alongside the engine. (Courtesy of the San Diego Aerospace Museum.)

The Hall-Scott
Type L-4, 125 H. P. Installation

For on short commercial or passenger carrying flights, the Type L-4, 125 H. P. installation shown above is admirably fitted. This gives a remarkable climb with two passengers, is economical on fuel and exceptionally dependable.

With the extra fuselage supports, engine bed braces, etc., as worked out by Hall-Scott engineers, vibration is diminished and smooth running qualities obtained.

Shown is the L-4 in the trainer, with body panels removed. (Courtesy of the San Diego Aerospace Museum.)

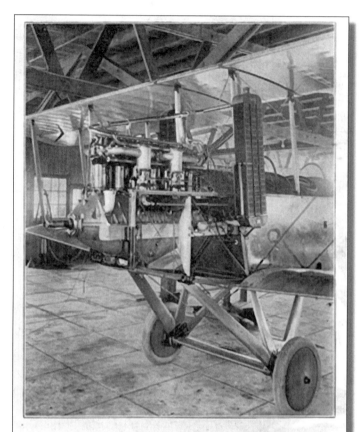

The Hall-Scott
Type L-6, 200 H. P. Installation

THE U. S. Government is offering for sale a quantity of training planes. This has presented a wonderful opportunity to obtain in conjunction with Hall-Scott Four and Six Cylinder Liberty Type engine installations the most up-to-date two passenger commercial or exhibition planes that the market affords, at a most reasonable cost.

Hall-Scott engineers, who during the war period obtained in Europe invaluable knowledge of the world's best in airplane design and construction, have pronounced the Standard J-1 U. S. Government training plane, equal to the best in European design and performance, when equipped with higher power, as provided by Hall-Scott Four and Six Cylinder Liberty Type engines.

The Hall-Scott L-6, 200 H. P. installation, shown above, is unsurpassed for long duration flights or climb with two passengers aboard.

Shown here is the larger and even more obtrusive L-6 in the trainer, with the body panels removed. (Courtesy of the San Diego Aerospace Museum.)

The history-making L-4-powered Boeing, shown with its airmail cargo, 1919. (Courtesy of Taylor Scott.)

positive opinion of the Liberty aviation engine, this decision might have been the opening salvo between Packard and Hall-Scott in their debate over the origins of the Liberty.

As with earlier Hall-Scott aviation engines, the L-4 and L-6 soon claimed their share of race victories and "firsts." The most interesting example might have occurred in 1919 when a Hall-Scott L-4-powered Boeing Model C made the first international airmail flight between Seattle, Washington, and Vancouver, BC, Canada. [1-122] Similar to the L-6, the four-cylinder L-4 was intended for civilian aircraft, which was a rapidly expanding market in the 1910s and one in which Hall-Scott had made amazing progress in powering during the span of only one decade.

By the end of the 1910s, Hall-Scott employees and managers could look back at ten years of success in the engine business. This was quite an amazing feat, considering the track record of most other engine and vehicle firms. Hall-Scott had not made a serious assault on the automobile, truck and bus, or marine engine businesses as it had so aggressively charged into aviation. It had produced rail cars, too. Clearly, the most important "niche" in the engine business for Hall-Scott during the 1910s was in aviation. World War I thoroughly occupied the energy of the company and its resident engineering "superstar," E.J. Hall, and had only reinforced the Hall-Scott commitment to air power to close the decade. Therefore, it would have been reasonable to speculate that when the war's cease-fire took effect at 11:00 a.m. on November 11, 1918, Hall-Scott might then have gone on to become a leading aviation engine producer. With less assurance perhaps, a similar prediction could have been made of Hall-Scott in rail. Hall-Scott had not given rail the attention in the 1910s that one might think, inasmuch as rail was so important to the formation of the company in the first place; however, it still targeted that sector of the market. Hall-Scott could have naturally and seamlessly turned its considerable talents to improving engines in rail and even to becoming a force to be reckoned with there, too. The next two decades until the outbreak of the next world war, however, brought a number of surprising twists in the Hall-Scott story.

References

1-1.   *National Cyclopaedia of American Biography, Vol. XLIII*, University Microfilms, Ann Arbor, MI, 1967, pp. 493–495. Much of Hall's early years described in this chapter are taken from this source unless indicated otherwise.

1-2.   *San Jose Mercury Herald*, April 14, 1918, p. 13.

1-3.   Ibid.

1-4.   Ibid.

1-5.   Ibid.

1-6.   *National Cyclopaedia of American Biography, Vol. XLIII*, University Microfilms, Ann Arbor, MI, 1967, pp. 493–495. It is unclear of when Hall might have designed the Doak, which was accomplished with, and named after, John Doak. Letter from J. Perala to R. Dias, July 31, 2004.

1-7.   Kevin Scott Tikker, "Gustav Heine and His Cars," *Automotive History Review*, No. 15, Fall 1982, pp. 10–11.

1-8.   Ibid., p. 11. *San Francisco Chronicle*, March 10, 1907, p. 4. Article courtesy of John Perala. See also *San Jose Mercury Herald*, April 14, 1918, p. 13.

1-9.   *The Automobile*, February 1, 1906, pp. 308–310. *San Francisco Chronicle*, October 8, 1905, p. 41. Both sources courtesy of John Perala.

1-10. *San Francisco Chronicle*, March 10, 1907, p. 4. Courtesy of John Perala.

1-11. *San Francisco Chronicle*, October 20, 1906, p. 8. *San Francisco Chronicle*, November 9, 1906, p. 9. Both sources courtesy of John Perala.

1-12. *San Francisco Chronicle*, April 17, 1907, p. 9. *The Oakland Tribune*, December 31, 1908, p. 13. For the Sunset-Victory link, see *San Jose Herald*, April 21, 1907, p. 46. All three sources courtesy of John Perala.

1-13. Letter from J. Perala to R. Dias, July 31, 2004.

1-14. Kevin Scott Tikker, "Gustav Heine and His Cars," *Automotive History Review*, No. 15, Fall 1982, p. 12. *Motor Age*, December 24, 1908, p. 15. *Motor Age* article courtesy of John Perala. Letter from J. Perala to R. Dias, July 31, 2004. Beverly Rae Kimes, *Standard Catalog of American Cars, 1805–1942*, third edition, Krause Publications, Iola, WI, 1996, p. 365.

1-15. Letter from J. Perala to R. Dias, July 31, 2004.

1-16. Letter from B. Scott to J. "Speed" Glidewell, May 8, 1956. Beverly Rae Kimes, *Standard Catalog of American Cars, 1805–1942*, third edition, Krause Publications, Iola, WI, 1996, p. 365. Letter from J. Perala to R. Dias, July 20, 2005.

1-17. Letter from J. Perala to R. Dias, July 31, 2004. The official entries for the 1909 race listed a #6, driver E.J. Hall, representing Hall-Kennedy Engineering, in a Comet with a 301.58-cubic-inch engine, suggesting a six-cylinder. *The Oakland Tribune*, October 22, 1909, p. 8. Article courtesy of John Perala. Many decades later, Leland Scott confirmed through his wife that one six-cylinder Comet was built. Letter from Bev Scott to M. Rosen, January 2, 1979. Letter courtesy of Taylor Scott.

1-18. *Cycle and Automobile Trade Journal*, November 1910, pp. 252–253, stated when reviewing the Hall-Scott A-2 aviation engine, "About a year and a half ago Mr. Hall built the 8-cylinder motor which this company is now marketing and which is similar in every respect, except for minor improvements." The higher power figure could have come at a higher, 1400 rpm versus 1200 rpm rating. Therefore, basic A-2 measurements and capacities will be assumed in the V-8 Comet.

1-19. Letter from Bev Scott to M. Rosen, December 26, 1978. Courtesy of Taylor Scott. The same photo is used in Beverly Rae Kimes, *Standard Catalog of American Cars, 1805–1942*, third edition, Krause Publications, Iola, WI, 1996, p. 365, and in Warren Miller, "Hall's Comet," *Antique Automobile*, March–April 1975, p. 23, and is described as a Comet.

1-20. *Motor Age*, September 3, 1908. Race officials treated the Comet as a racing special, as opposed to a production car, because so few were produced. Letter from J. Perala to R. Dias, July 20, 2005.

1-21. *Motor Age*, September 3, 1908. See also *The Oakland Tribune*, August 24, 1908, p. 8, and *The Oakland Tribune*, December 31, 1908, p. 13. Last two sources courtesy of John Perala.

1-22. J.E. "Speed" Glidewell, "A Brief History of Hall-Scott Motor Company," unpublished address, 1956, p. 1. Letter from J. Perala to R. Dias, July 20, 2005.

1-23. *The Oakland Tribune*, December 31, 1908, p. 13. Courtesy of John Perala.

1-24. Beverly Rae Kimes, *Standard Catalog of American Cars, 1805–1942*, third edition, Krause Publications, Iola, WI, 1996, p. 365.

1-25. *National Cyclopaedia of American Biography, Vol. XLIII*, University Microfilms, Ann Arbor, MI, 1967, p. 493. Although secondary sources often mention a Comet Company by name, sources from the time period suggest that such a company might never have existed.

1-26. Letter from J. Perala to R. Dias, July 31, 2004. *The Oakland Tribune*, September 30, 1908 p. 2. *San Jose Herald*, March 3, 1909, p. 1. Both articles courtesy of John Perala.

1-27. Fred Jane, ed., *All the World's Air-Ships*, Sampson, Low, Marston & Co, Ltd., London, UK, 1909, reprint, Johnson Reprint Corporation, New York, NY, 1968, p. 302.

1-28. Scott family histories, written by Rena Scott (no date) and Beverlee Scott, 1976. Courtesy of Taylor Scott.

1-29. Letter from B. Scott to J. "Speed" Glidewell, May 8, 1956.

1-30. Mike Shafer, *Vintage Diesel Locomotives*, Motorbooks International, Osceola, WI 1998, p. 11. Focused attention on motor cars can be found in Edmund Keilty, *Interurbans Without Wires: The Rail Motorcar in the United States*, Interurbans, Glendale, CA, 1979.

1-31. Letter from B. Scott to J. "Speed" Glidewell, May 8, 1956.

1-32. Ibid. The savings racked up by this Hall-Scott motor car are discussed in "Hall-Scott Motor Cars," *Railway Age Gazette*, June 19, 1914, p. 1525. Latter source courtesy of California State Railroad Museum Library.

1-33. There is controversy over whether Hall-Scott formed in 1909 or 1910. Bert Scott gave the date as 1910 in a 1956 letter to Speed Glidewell. Letter from B. Scott to J. "Speed" Glidewell, May 8, 1956. Kenneth Scott also cited 1910 in a company history, *Port of Oakland Compass*, March–April 1937, p. 3. The Oakland and Berkeley City Directory of 1911 contained a Hall-Scott Motor Car Company listing, but the 1910 directory did not, suggesting a 1910 appearance. Directory courtesy of the Berkeley Historical Society. "Report on Hall-Scott Motor Car Company, Berkeley, California," unpublished report, 1931, loose sheet. Report courtesy of Taylor Scott. This was a report written by the parent company of Hall-Scott, which tried to explain the weak financial performance of Hall-Scott and included a page with earnings and losses from 1910 to 1930. In fact, it reported that the 1910 year ending in December included only a ten-month period. But a Comet racing in late 1909 (with Harold Hall driving) was cited as representing the Hall-Scott Motor Car Company, *San Jose Herald*, November 29, 1909, p. 6. Article courtesy of John Perala. Other secondary sources sometimes offer a date of 1909.

1-34. Letter from L. Scott, Jr. to M. Rosen, August 25, 1978.

1-35. J.E. "Speed" Glidewell, "A Brief History of Hall-Scott Motor Company," unpublished address, 1956, p. 1.

1-36. Letter from Bev Scott to M. Rosen, January 25, 1979. Courtesy of Taylor Scott.

1-37. Letter from J. "Speed" Glidewell to G. Borgeson, July 5, 1984. Courtesy of San Diego Aerospace Museum.

1-38. Anthony Kirk, *Founded by the Bay; The History of Macaulay Foundry, 1896–1996*, Macaulay Foundry, Berkeley, CA, 1996, pp. 15–26.

1-39. Hall-Scott Railway Motor Cars, catalog #10, brochure, circa 1920.

1-40. Francis Bradford, "A History of the Hall-Scott Motor Car Company," unpublished manuscript, 1989, p. 6. Courtesy of Bancroft Library, University of California, Berkeley, BANC MSS 93/104c.

1-41. Hall-Scott Railway Motor Cars, catalog #10.

1-42. Edmund Keilty, *Interurbans Without Wires: The Rail Motorcar in the United States*, Interurbans, Glendale, CA, 1979, p. 47. A general description of the construction used in these cars, in the bodies and drivetrains, at least of those built through 1913, can be found in "Hall-Scott Motor Cars," *Railway Age Gazette*, June 19, 1914, p. 1525. Article courtesy of California State Railroad Museum Library.

1-43. J.E. "Speed" Glidewell, "A Brief History of Hall-Scott Motor Company," unpublished address, 1956, p. 1.

1-44. *Metal Trades*, February 1919, pp. 94–95. Edmund Keilty, *Interurbans Without Wires: The Rail Motorcar in the United States*, Interurbans, Glendale, CA, 1979, p. 47.

1-45. Letter from Bev Scott to M. Rosen, January 25, 1979. Courtesy of Taylor Scott.

1-46. Letter from B. Scott to J. "Speed" Glidewell, May 8, 1956.

1-47. Letter from Bev Scott to M. Rosen, January 25, 1979. Courtesy of Taylor Scott.

1-48. The descriptions for these Hall-Scott aviation models came from Glenn Angle, *Airplane Engine Encyclopedia*, Otterbein Press, Dayton, OH, 1921, pp. 229–238, unless otherwise stated.

1-49. *Aeronautics*, September 1910, no page number (n.p.)

1-50. *Aeronautics*, May 1911, n.p.

1-51. Ibid. The price of the four-cylinder Comet was roughly the same as the price of this engine.

1-52. *Cycle and Automobile Trade Journal*, November 1910, p. 253.

1-53. E.J. Hall, "Reducing Transportation Cost by Means of Engine Design," Society of Automotive Engineers, Northern California Section Paper, SAE Paper No. 290010, SAE International, 400 Commonwealth Dr., Warrendale, PA, 1929, pp. 69–70.

1-54. *Aeronautics*, August 1912, n.p.

1-55. *Aeronautics*, July 1911, n.p.

1-56. *Aeronautics*, May 1913, p. 200.

1-57. *Aeronautics*, August 1912, n.p.

1-58.   *Aeronautics*, June 1913, p. 240.

1-59.   *Aeronautics*, November 1912, n.p.

1-60.   Herschel Smith, *Aircraft Piston Engines*, Sunflower University Press, Manhattan, NY, 1986, p. 16. Smith rates the Hall-Scott as being of comparable quality with the better-known Curtiss.

1-61.   Peter Bowers, *Boeing Aircraft Since 1916*, Funk & Wagnalls, New York, NY, 1968, pp. 32–36.

1-62.   Kenneth Johnson, *Aerial California: An Account of Early Flight in Northern and Southern California, 1849 to World War I*, Dawson's Book Shop, Los Angeles, CA, 1961, p. 75.

1-63.   *Aeronautics*, October 1911, p. 143.

1-64.   John Heilig, *The Cadillac Century*, Chartwell Books, Edison, NJ, 1998, p. 16. *National Cyclopaedia of American Biography, Vol. XLIII*, University Microfilms, Ann Arbor, MI, 1967, p. 493.

1-65.   Glenn Angle, *Airplane Engine Encyclopedia*, Otterbein Press, Dayton, OH, 1921, pp. 229–238. James Lenzke, *Standard Catalog of Cadillac, 1903–2000*, Krause Publications, Iola, WI, 2000, pp. 14–15, 34–35. John Gunnell, *Standard Catalog of V-8 Engines*, Krause Publications, Iola, WI, 2003, pp. 35–36.

1-66.   Letter from Bev Scott to M. Rosen, December 26, 1978. Courtesy of Taylor Scott.

1-67.   Francis Bradford, "A History of the Hall-Scott Motor Car Company," unpublished manuscript, 1989, p. 12. Courtesy of Bancroft Library, University of California, Berkeley, BANC MSS 93/104c.1-68. Anthony Kirk, *Founded by the Bay; The History of Macaulay Foundry, 1896–1996*, Macaulay Foundry, Berkeley, CA, 1996, p. 26.

1-69.   Maurer Maurer, *The U.S. Air Service in World War I, Vol. II*, U.S. Government Printing Office, Washington, DC, 1978, p. 78.

1-70.   Francis Bradford, "A History of the Hall-Scott Motor Car Company," unpublished manuscript, 1989, p. 13. Courtesy of Bancroft Library, University of California, Berkeley, BANC MSS 93/104c. "Pertinent Facts About the Liberty Motor," pamphlet, Hall-Scott Motor Car Company, circa 1920, p. 3, F. Leroy Hill Collection, MS 95-03. Pamphlet courtesy of Wichita State University Library, Department of Special Collections.

1-71. Peter Bowers, *Boeing Aircraft Since 1916*, Funk & Wagnalls, New York, NY, 1968, pp. 38, 40.

1-72. Philip Dickey, *The Liberty Engine, 1918–1942*, Smithsonian Institution Press, Washington, DC, 1968, p. 25. *National Cyclopaedia of American Biography, Vol. XLIII*, University Microfilms, Ann Arbor, MI, 1967, p. 493.

1-73. *National Cyclopaedia of American Biography, Vol. XLIII*, University Microfilms, Ann Arbor, MI, 1967, p. 493.

1-74. *Motor Age*, October 10, 1918, pp. 38–39. Glenn Angle, *Airplane Engine Encyclopedia*, Otterbein Press, Dayton, OH, 1921, pp. 233–234. *Aviation*, November 15, 1917, p. 507.

1-75. *Motor Age*, October 10, 1918, pp. 38–39. Glenn Angle, *Airplane Engine Encyclopedia*, Otterbein Press, Dayton, OH, 1921, pp. 233–234. "Pertinent Facts About the Liberty Motor," pamphlet, Hall-Scott Motor Car Company, circa 1920, p. 7, F. Leroy Hill Collection, MS 95-03. Pamphlet courtesy of Wichita State University Library, Department of Special Collections.

1-76. "Report on Hall-Scott Motor Car Company, Berkeley, California," unpublished report, 1931. Courtesy of Taylor Scott. This report was written by the parent company of Hall-Scott, which tried to explain the weak financial performance of Hall-Scott and included a page with earnings and losses from 1910 to 1930.

1-77. *Aeronautics*, November 11, 1911, p. 180. Courtesy of Bill West.

1-78. "Report on Hall-Scott Motor Car Company, Berkeley, California," unpublished report, 1931, loose sheet. Courtesy of Taylor Scott.

1-79. *Commercial Car Journal*, August 15, 1914, p. 9.

1-80. Anthony Kirk, *Founded by the Bay; The History of Macaulay Foundry, 1896–1996*, Macaulay Foundry, Berkeley, CA, 1996, p. 29.

1-81. *Aviation*, November 15, 1917, p. 507.

1-82. *Motor Age*, October 10, 1918, p. 39.

1-83. *Motor Age*, January 30, 1919, p. 26.

1-84. Ibid.

1-85. Philip Dickey, *The Liberty Engine, 1918–1942*, Smithsonian Institution Press, Washington, DC, 1968, pp. 2–3.

1-86.   Ibid., p. 8.

1-87.   Herschel Smith, *Aircraft Piston Engines*, Sunflower University Press, Manhattan, NY, 1986, p. 29.

1-88.   *Motor Age*, December 5, 1918, p. 16.

1-89.   Herschel Smith, *Aircraft Piston Engines*, Sunflower University Press, Manhattan, NY, 1986, p. 48.

1-90.   Philip Dickey, *The Liberty Engine, 1918–1942*, Smithsonian Institution Press, Washington, DC, 1968, p. 14. *Motor Age*, January 30, 1919, p. 26. "Pertinent Facts About the Liberty Motor," pamphlet, Hall-Scott Motor Car Company, circa 1920, pp. 3, 17, F. Leroy Hill Collection, MS 95-03. Pamphlet courtesy of Wichita State University Library, Department of Special Collections.

1-91.   "Pertinent Facts About the Liberty Motor," pamphlet, Hall-Scott Motor Car Company, circa 1920, p. 17, F. Leroy Hill Collection, MS 95-03. Courtesy of Wichita State University Library, Department of Special Collections.

1-92.   *Motor Age*, January 30, 1919, p. 26.

1-93.   "Pertinent Facts About the Liberty Motor," pamphlet, Hall-Scott Motor Car Company, circa 1920, p. 3, F. Leroy Hill Collection, MS 95-03. Courtesy of Wichita State University Library, Department of Special Collections.

1-94.   Ibid., pp. 4, 17–18. *National Cyclopaedia of American Biography, Vol. XLIII*, University Microfilms, Ann Arbor, MI, 1967, pp. 493–494.

1-95.   *Motor Age*, January 30, 1919, p. 26.

1-96.   Ibid. "Pertinent Facts About the Liberty Motor," pamphlet, Hall-Scott Motor Car Company, circa 1920, p. 18, F. Leroy Hill Collection, MS 95-03. Pamphlet courtesy of Wichita State University Library, Department of Special Collections.

1-97.   Philip Dickey, *The Liberty Engine, 1918–1942*, Smithsonian Institution Press, Washington, DC, 1968, p. 16. "Pertinent Facts About the Liberty Motor," pamphlet, Hall-Scott Motor Car Company, circa 1920, pp. 11, 18, F. Leroy Hill Collection, MS 95-03. Pamphlet courtesy of Wichita State University Library, Department of Special Collections.

1-98.   Philip Dickey, *The Liberty Engine, 1918–1942*, Smithsonian Institution Press, Washington, DC, 1968, p. 17.

1-99. Herschel Smith, *Aircraft Piston Engines*, Sunflower University Press, Manhattan, KS, 1986, p. 50. Bill Gunston, *World Encyclopedia of Aero Engines*, fourth edition, Patrick Stephens Limited, Newbury Park, UK, 1998, p. 106.

1-100. Philip Dickey, *The Liberty Engine, 1918–1942*, Smithsonian Institution Press, Washington, DC, 1968, p. 66.

1-101. "Pertinent Facts About the Liberty Motor," pamphlet, Hall-Scott Motor Car Company, circa 1920, p. 23, F. Leroy Hill Collection, MS 95-03. Courtesy of Wichita State University Library, Department of Special Collections.

1-102. "Pertinent Facts About the Liberty Motor," pamphlet, Hall-Scott Motor Car Company, circa 1920, F. Leroy Hill Collection, MS 95-03. Courtesy of Wichita State University Library, Department of Special Collections. Glenn Angle, *Airplane Engine Encyclopedia*, Otterbein Press, Dayton, OH, 1921, pp. 229–238, 305–314.

1-103. *San Francisco Examiner*, September 15, 1917, p. 7.

1-104. *Motor Age*, January 30, 1919, p. 26.

1-105. Wilbur F. Decker, *The Story of the Engine; From Lever to Liberty Motor*, Charles Scribner's Sons, New York, NY, p. vi.

1-106. *National Cyclopaedia of American Biography, Vol. XLIII*, University Microfilms, Ann Arbor, MI, 1967, pp. 493–494. "Pertinent Facts About the Liberty Motor," pamphlet, Hall-Scott Motor Car Company, circa 1920, F. Leroy Hill Collection, MS 95-03. Pamphlet courtesy of Wichita State University Library, Department of Special Collections.

1-107. Francis Bradford, "A History of the Hall-Scott Motor Car Company," unpublished manuscript, 1989, p. 13. Courtesy of Bancroft Library, University of California, Berkeley, BANC MSS 93/104c.

1-108. "Report on Hall-Scott Motor Car Company, Berkeley, California," unpublished report, 1931, p. 5. Courtesy of Taylor Scott.

1-109. Ibid., loose sheet.

1-110. Ibid., p. 5.

1-111. Philip Dickey, *The Liberty Engine, 1918–1942*, Smithsonian Institution Press, Washington, DC, 1968, p. x.

1-112. "The Reminiscences of Mr. Harold Hicks," Vol. I, p. 4, Oral History Section, The Henry Ford, Dearborn, MI.

1-113. *Motor West*, January 15, 1919, p. 14.

1-114. Ibid., p. 24.

1-115. "The Real Story of the Liberty Motor," pamphlet, Packard Motor Car Company, circa 1920, p. 6. Courtesy of Robert Neal.

1-116. "Pertinent Facts About the Liberty Motor," pamphlet, Hall-Scott Motor Car Company, circa 1920, pp. 1, 3, F. Leroy Hill Collection, MS 95-03. Courtesy of Wichita State University Library, Department of Special Collections. An early connection made between a Hall-Scott engine and the Liberty can be seen in a press release from Hall-Scott that was published in *Automotive Industries* in November 1918, in which the A-8 was said to have pressed steel jacketed-type cylinders "similar to those which are used in the construction of the Liberty engine." *Automotive Industries*, November 14, 1918, p. 836. Latter source courtesy of California State Railroad Museum Library.

1-117. Stan Grayson, *Engines Afloat, From Early Days to D-Day, Vol. l: The Gasoline Era*, Devereux Books, Marblehead, MA, 1999, p. 81.

1-118. C.G. Patch, "The Story of Hall-Scott Engines," *Port of Oakland Compass*, September 1933, pp. 5–6.

1-119. *Motor Age*, October 10, 1918, p. 38.

1-120. Glenn Angle, *Airplane Engine Encyclopedia*, Otterbein Press, Dayton, OH, 1921, pp. 233–234.

1-121. Peter Bowers, *Boeing Aircraft Since 1916*, Funk & Wagnalls, New York, NY, 1968, pp. 32–41.

1-122. Ibid., p. 39.

CHAPTER TWO

HALL-SCOTT'S
ROARING EARLY '20S

The years between the two world wars, particularly during the 1920s, were some of the most interesting in the history of Hall-Scott. During its second decade in business, Hall-Scott introduced a handful of new engines, and, as during its first decade, many had industry-leading features and performance. This continuing evolution and expansion of the Hall-Scott product line took a surprising turn as management moved the company more aggressively into

A post-World War I photo of Elbert Hall.

A post-World War I photo of Bert Scott.

71

some new markets—tractor, truck, bus, industrial, and marine. The company continued to sell more than engines, too, although it retreated from serving rail (the market that had brought Hall and Scott together) and aviation (the market that had put Hall-Scott "on the map"). These years were also perhaps the most

An aerial view looking north of industrial West Berkeley, circa 1920. The Hall-Scott plant is just south and west of the prominent, five-story Peet Brothers (later Colgate-Palmolive) building in the center of the photo. (Courtesy of Berkeley Historical Society.)

As suggested by this photo, Berkeley in the 1920s was a bustling and diverse city, with the University of California to the east and the manufacturing sector, known as West Berkeley, to the west near the bay. (Courtesy of Berkeley Historical Society.)

pivotal for the company. Decisions made during this period set Hall-Scott on a course for the rest of its history and, for a brief while, made Hall-Scott an industry member of significance.

E.J. Hall and Hall-Scott's Postwar Diversions

E.J. Hall had built his reputation on designing and building engines, but Hall and his company nonetheless deviated from their primary mission on occasion. Hall and Hall-Scott even undertook work for other engine and vehicle makers after World War I. For example, Hall continued dabbling in race engines in the postwar era, in marine and auto mostly, often helping some big names on development projects—men such as Jimmy Murphy, Ralph de Palma, and Harry Miller. [2-1] Hall-Scott engineer "Speed" Glidewell remembered, "DePalma [sic] even had new engine blocks, heads, cranks etc. made there [at the Hall-Scott plant] and temporily [sic] left many in storage." [2-2] Hall had raced years before this time, and he maintained friends and business connections who raced. Hall's wife wrote, "Before 1910 all automobile racers in the Bay region were bringing their cars to his shop to be improved or repaired." [2-3] E.J. Hall liked to go fast and to build competitive race machines. Examples of individuals, especially on the West Coast, taking Hall-Scott aircraft engines and putting them in boats, race cars, or performance street cars into the 1920s were fairly common.

Years after helping launch Hall-Scott into the busy 1920s, it appeared that Hall still possessed a genuine love for tinkering with motors. Glidewell described Hall as a "very serious minded engineer, inventor and inovator [sic] and was 'at it' all hours of the day. In the early twenties...I was on night shift in the shop and it seemed that around ten p.m. to midnight you could expect him to come in and circulate around to see how everyone was doing." [2-4] By this point, Hall might have been a decorated veteran and respected engineer, but his approach to his work still had some of the innocent and playful attitude of a boy. Glidewell said, "When there was a new experimental engine on the dynamometer [Hall] would get fidgety and anxious to see it go. He'd sometimes get impatient and yank the throttle open—maybe she'd stick up—if so he'd have a bit of a sheepish grin on and tell the guys to fix 'er up and we'll try it again. He was not what you would call a tough task master but he knew what he wanted." Hall had plenty of energy, ideas, and desire to be a prolific engineer, as well as the open-mindedness to take advantage of whatever business opportunity might present itself.

An instance of one Hall-Scott foray out of engine making was its production of the Ruckstell axle. This two-speed axle was made specifically for the Ford Model T. The Model T, which Ford Motor Company built from 1908 to 1927, was so popular and pivotal that it is often said to have "put America on wheels." Henry Ford did not invent the automobile, nor did he build the first auto in America. But with the introduction of the Model T, Ford Motor Company brought the purchase of a new car within the reach of common Americans as no other automaker had done. Relatively reliable, tough, cheap, simple, and flexible in uses, about 15 million "Tin Lizzies" were sold by Ford by 1927, even though the basic design had changed little. By 1927, a new Model T cost only $290. Popular as it was, the Model T still suffered from some undeniable shortcomings, with limited top speed and low engine power being prime among them. These weaknesses were exacerbated by the car having only two forward gears, which did not allow the small engine to work in its peak horsepower range in many instances. Further reducing its effectiveness, while the transmission of the Model T was engaged in "low," the driver had to keep a pedal depressed. To answer drivers' need for speed, aftermarket devices to "soup up" the lethargic 20-hp Ford could readily be found in magazines and auto shops in the 1920s. One aftermarket cylinder head sold by Laurel Motors Corporation of Anderson, Indiana, sported twin overhead cams with four valves per cylinder, an advanced design that its promoters claimed would double the horsepower of the Model T. [2-5] Model T drivers also could select from a number of aftermarket transmissions and transmission alterations that promised to rectify some of the weaknesses of the Model T. Such devices included the $75 Crump auxiliary transmission and the $60 Woodward "2-in-1" transmission. [2-6] Clearly, a large market abounded for items that improved the performance of Ford's popular car and truck, needing only the right enterprising minds to tap into that market with the right products.

In the Ruckstell axle, Hall-Scott capitalized on the runaway success, and ample room for improvement, of the Model T. More accurately, the Ruckstell product was not an entire axle nor was it a differential, but *The Motor Truck* described it as "built up as a part of a new differential case and as such becomes a connecting link between the ring gear and the differential case." [2-7] Ruckstell buyers could purchase one of two kits: one for the Model T, or another for the Model TT. The Model TT was the heavy-duty truck version and had a different differential than the Model T. The kits were relatively easy to install; almost any garage could handle the job. With either kit, the Ruckstell provided two more forward gear ratios to the standard two, giving the vehicle added pulling power for heavy loads or hills. The Ruckstell also added another reverse ratio and accomplished its improvements with uncharacteristic smoothness and

Looking northwest at the Hall-Scott plant in the early 1920s, with its "saw tooth" roof evident. The Ruckstell sales office is the small white building to the right of Hall-Scott. (Courtesy of Taylor Scott.)

ease. Said *The Motor Truck*, "The Ruckstell axle gives for the first time in automotive history an absolutely fool proof shift." Advertisements hawked the price of a new Ruckstell axle, with installation, at $69.99, which seems cheap today. But back then, a used Model T could be purchased for that sum or less. However, the robust gain in the performance of the Model T with the addition of this small unit was so great that Ruckstell sales remained

This close-up of the same area better shows the proximity of the Hall-Scott plant and the Ruckstell sales office. They were located across the street from each other. (Courtesy of Taylor Scott.)

strong for years. "Speed" Glidewell, perhaps guilty of a bit of hyperbole, opined, "This 2-speed axle made an automobile out of the Model T." [2-8] Even

if Glidewell's opinion was a
bit over the top, the success of
the Ruckstell unit was undeniable. Yet another measure
of the worth of the Ruckstell
was that Henry Ford approved
selling the axle through Ford
dealerships in new cars, a rar-
ity at Ford. [2-9] According
to Mrs. E.J. Hall, "Due to its
excellent service and the great
confidence that Mr. Ford had
in my husband's talent, the
Ford Company then consented
to allow the Ford dealers to sell
it." [2-10]

*The Hall-Scott connection to the Ruckstell axle
can be gleaned from its name stamped into this
part of the component. (Courtesy of Joshua
Houghton.)*

The Hall-Scott connection
with this component began in World War I when Colonel Hall worked with
Captain Glover E. Ruckstell in the Air Service. Ruckstell, rather like Hall,
had a varied engineering and racing career. He invested more time in racing
than did Hall, and he drove competitively for an auto maker-sponsored team
of some stature, Mercer. After the war, Ruckstell went to work at Hall-Scott,
for a brief time having "charge of the aeroplane motor department," but that
assignment did not last long. [2-11] By 1921, Ruckstell, who like his friend
Hall had far-reaching skills and ambitions, had gathered financing and launched
the Ruckstell enterprise, a project done in coordination with Hall-Scott. The
San Francisco Bulletin described Ruckstell as a "former idol of the speed
fans," who was launching what might become "one of the greatest industrial
plants of the motor car industry on the Pacific Coast." Ruckstell secured the
rights to make the component and then used his employer, Hall-Scott, as the
sole place of manufacture. This would be an unusual, but profitable, turn for
Hall-Scott.

It appears that earlier forms of what came to be known as the Ruckstell axle,
the principal one known as the Perfecto axle, had trouble selling in sufficient
quantity. Other multi-speed axles were being made at the time, but none was
a runaway bestseller. "Former cowboy, now an automotive engineer," Charles
Starr appears to have been instrumental in creating the basic component Ruckstell brought to Hall-Scott, which then also received input from famed race
car builder Harry Miller and E.J. Hall. [2-12] "Speed" Glidewell, who had

just begun his long career at Hall-Scott as an engineer in 1920, wrote that in 1921, he "unpacked the first castings that came down from Bellingham, Washington where they had been made… However the design was found to be rather clumsy and expensive to build so Hall Scott [*sic*] redesigned it and produced it in quantity." [2-13] Ruckstell does not appear to have actually designed or engineered much on the axle itself, in spite of his name being attached to it. Instead, his contribution was bringing the axle to Hall-Scott. The Hall-Scott/Ruckstell arrangement turned around the fortunes of Perfecto and Hall-Scott.

The primary focus of Hall-Scott had been on engine making through the 1910s, but engine sales slumped badly after the war ended; thus, the Ruckstell deal came at a propitious time. Management set aside part of its

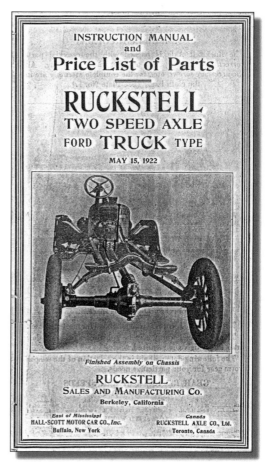

Brochure for the Ruckstell truck axle; note the Berkeley address.

factory, augmented with a $100,000 infusion of Ruckstell-owned machinery, to build the axles. [2-14] According to *The Oakland Tribune*, "The Ruckstell organization has offices adjoining the Hall-Scott factory and the officials of the axle company are in a position to supervise the manufacture of their unit." Thus, Hall-Scott and Ruckstell management remained physically separate. Hall-Scott left marketing to the Ruckstell Sales and Manufacturing Company, which maintained offices across America. Hall-Scott concentrated on manufacture. The Ruckstell assembly line in the Hall-Scott Berkeley plant produced large numbers of the axle, with estimates running as high as 600 to 800 per day at

Glover "Roxy" Ruckstell

Born in San Francisco in 1891, Glover Edwin Ruckstell was a slightly younger contemporary of fellow Californians Elbert Hall and Bert Scott. Like Hall, he lacked a high school or college diploma, although he did attend a couple of years of high school and took some classes at a business college. And like Hall and Scott, Ruckstell appreciated many kinds of machines and enjoyed going fast. "Roxy" raced cars across America in the early twentieth century, winning some contests and walking away from a couple of spectacular crashes. For several years, he drove for the team sponsored by auto maker Mercer. During World War I, Ruckstell and Hall worked together on the Liberty and De Haviland plane projects, with Ruckstell earning the rank of captain. Following the war, Ruckstell brought the axle, which came to bear his name, to his new employer, Hall-Scott. The Ruckstell/Hall-Scott relationship ended after a few years, but Ruckstell seems to have left on good terms. Resumes

he wrote years later included the names E.J. Hall, Leland Scott, and Frederick Whitaker from Hall-Scott (as well as Edsel Ford and C.F. Kettering!). After leaving the axle business, Ruckstell sunk his money into an up-and-coming industry—commercial aviation. After learning to fly, Glover (which he pronounced "gluver") helped form Grand Canyon Airlines in 1931, using Ford Tri Motor planes to ferry customers on sightseeing trips. He liked to fly Hollywood stars around the Grand Canyon, adding an element of glamour to the enterprise. Ruckstell was a man of some style, liking nice clothes and sporting a perfect dark tan year round. (This can be seen in the two photos on the left that include him: in the photo of the group standing beside an airplane, and in the upper left of the other photo where he is standing and wearing a pilot's uniform.) The airline was not much of a moneymaker, though, and after a few years, Ruckstell eased out of air travel and into boat and bus tours, hotels, and other tourist accommodations with the Grand Canyon–Boulder Dam Tours Company. Living and working near Lake Mead, he spent quite a bit of time on the water. His speedboat, an expensive and flashy Gar Wood (shown above, although Ruckstell is not in the photo), was Hall-Scott powered. A member of the Society of Automotive Engineers since 1917, he continued dabbling in engineering, too. Glover Ruckstell passed away in California in 1963. Some things connected to this fascinating man live on. People can still take air tours of the Grand Canyon, and new reproduction Ruckstell axles are still available today for Ford Model T's. (Photos courtesy of Gene Tissot.)

Instructions on how to shift a Ruckstell-equipped Ford transmission. (Courtesy of Tom Sharpsteen.)

its peak, and production running from 1921 to 1925. [2-15] In total, Hall-Scott probably assembled more than 200,000 Ruckstell axles.

There is some conflict among sources over who terminated the axle-making deal. Hall-Scott leadership maintained that by 1925, the end was in sight for the peak popularity of the axle. Because Hall-Scott had exploited the most lucrative part of the "bubble" of opportunity that existed with Ruckstell production, it terminated the arrangement. [2-16] This makes little sense, though, because Hall-Scott at that time was making great amounts of money from selling axles but was losing money from making engines. In 1925, Ruckstell signed a contract with Eaton Axle and Spring Company, which maintained that it was approached to purchase the axle operation, and it went on to produce about 400,000 units. [2-17] Ruckstell production began in Cleveland at the Eaton plant a year before Ford ceased production of the Model T.

With the advent of the Ruckstell axle, Hall-Scott reached volume production at its plant, a first for peacetime.

Ruckstell production had seen Hall-Scott through some lean times, making the company profitable when it otherwise would have lost a considerable amount of money. Turning out volume numbers of the Ruckstell axle covered up the otherwise dismal financial performance of Hall-Scott; axle making "yielded a very fine return," according to a 1931 company audit. In fact, Hall-Scott ended three years of losing money after the war and returned to profitability in 1923 precisely because of making the axles. [2-18] Even after axle production in Berkeley ended, carryover from Ruckstell operations made 1926 a profitable year for Hall-Scott, the last year it would report a profit until 1929. Production of this interesting automotive item, even if Hall-Scott did not develop the axle, demonstrates some of the wide technical range Hall-Scott possessed, and the company strategy of "batch" production, to carry it through tough financial times and stay in business.

E.J. Hall also participated in several engineering projects outside his own company with established vehicle firms and individuals. Both General Motors and Ford tapped the fertile mind of E.J. Hall in the early postwar period—such was his high visibility and respect in engineering circles. For General Motors, Hall designed a new engine and rear axle for the Buick in 1922. [2-19] But

Hall spent much more time with Ford than with General Motors. Henry Ford's son Edsel owned a pleasure boat with a Hall-Scott engine, so the Ford family respected Hall's work. But Hall also worked on some high-profile projects at Ford Motor Company. [2-20]

For Ford, Hall worked on both auto and rail projects. On the automobile side of the Ford shop, it appears that E.J. Hall designed and Hall-Scott built an experimental six-cylinder engine for the Model T. A former chief inspector at Hall-Scott during the 1920s, Oliver Searing, wrote a letter in 1969, stating, "Circa 1924 Henry Ford commissioned Col. Hall to design and build 6 cylinder engines for the Model T." [2-21] A few photos exist of the side-valve, 212-cubic-inch, six-cylinder power plant. It was a little unusual for Hall to have designed a side-valve engine, given the look of his engines since the mid-1910s; possibly Ford demanded that Hall go in that direction. Longer than the standard four-cylinder Ford engine, use of this Hall-Scott unit, referred to as the "Little Six," would have required modifying the Model T to accommodate it. This aspect alone could have doomed the engine from seeing regular production. "Speed" Glidewell wrote, "Ford finally decided to go to a V-8 engine which would not lengthen the car," to replace its long-standing use of four-cylinder engines. [2-22] Hall-Scott even built lines in its Berkeley

Hall's Little Six for the Ford Model T. (Courtesy of Taylor Scott.)

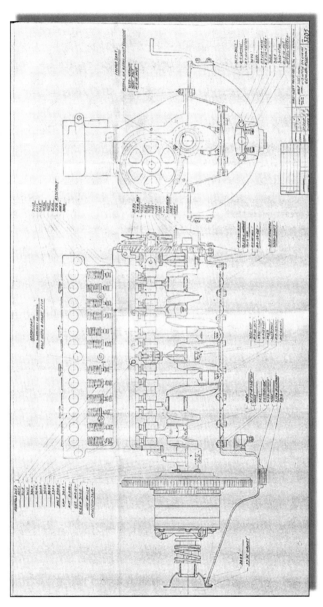

A blueprint for the Little Six, dated 1919.

plant to assemble the engine. But little written evidence can be found about the engine. Books on the Model T make no mention of a Hall-Scott-designed six, so this story continues to be wrapped in mystery.

Over and above his possible involvement in developing a new engine for the Model T, E.J. Hall contributed some fresh ideas to the Ford engineering program, namely, by designing gasoline-powered rail cars for Ford. [2-23] Harold Hicks, who had worked with Hall in the Army during the war, ironing out bugs in the Liberty, came to Ford in the spring of 1919 at Hall's bequest. Hicks described Hall as being "looked upon as an authority" who "really had a reputation in the entire world. The Liberty engine had been a great success." [2-24] Hall's work on the Liberty, plus Hall-Scott building motor cars, brought him to the attention of Ford for his own motorized rail car program. And Hall drove the engineering work on the rail project. According to Hicks, "neither Mr. Ford nor Edsel took much part in the design." It appears that Hall's lack of formal engineering education showed in the way he approached his work. Hicks said, "Of course, he was a very brilliant man, that is, he was shrewd. He was a good designer. He didn't actually get on the board and make a design himself because his draftsmanship was rather crude. He could control a design and tell what was wrong with it, and he worked with the men." But Hall's lack of formal engineering training did not faze Henry Ford, who "was never very impressed" that Hicks had graduated from the University of Michigan College of Engineering.

For Ford, Hall designed two related engines: a four-cylinder (with 5-inch by 7-inch bore and stroke measurements, the same as the A-5, the A-7, and the Liberty), laid on its side under the floor between the frame rails, about midway the length of the car; and an eight-cylinder, basically two of the fours connected together. [2-25] The four was rated at about 75 hp, and the eight around 150 hp. [2-26] Hall shuttled back and forth between Berkeley and Dearborn as needed, never staying long at either place. Testing in 1919 and 1920 of the Hall-engined cars revealed satisfactory performance and no glaring drivability problems. In fact, when a Ford supervisor boarded a car with the engine idling, he asked Hicks, " 'Say, where are the engines in this car?' He was standing on the engine while it was running. It was running that smoothly." [2-27] Although the cars ran well, their cost savings over electric drive were debatable, which doomed them for large-scale production. This horizontal, mid-ship, underfloor design might not have pushed Ford products in a new direction, but it planted a seed in E.J. Hall and had important consequences for the Hall-Scott company in the decades ahead.

Elbert Hall's passion for and success at auto racing led him to circulate with some of the leading figures in American racing, even years after he had abandoned competitive driving. Engine designer Harry Miller created some of the most technologically advanced, elegant, and winning engines of the early twentieth century, for names as prestigious as Duesenberg, and E.J. Hall continued to push the evolution of engine design through their association. According to auto historian Griffith Borgeson, Hall's ideas had "a subtle but vast influence on American racing engine design." [2-28] Hall's aircraft engines of the 1910s sported sophisticated and efficient valvetrains; therefore, Hall earned a reputation as a man with something to say about cylinder heads, combustion chamber shape, camshafts, and valves. Miller consulted with Hall on the tricky problem of designing the profile of camshaft lobes to extract maximum performance. [2-29] E.J. Hall's name has been mentioned in some books focused on early auto innovators, but sadly, his name and real contributions are recognized little outside those rather esoteric publications.

Outside of working for the two auto giants, Ford and General Motors, and a giant among racers, Harry Miller, Hall-Scott and E.J. Hall entered into an interesting and important agreement with International Harvester Company (IHC) in 1926. [2-30] A respected company that already produced its own heavy-duty engines, IHC contracted with Hall-Scott to build two sizes of four-cylinder engines for use in its trucks. A 1926 article in *Commercial Car Journal* reported that Hall-Scott would make engines for IHC at the rate of "about 50" per week, at an American Car and Foundry plant in Detroit, leaving the Berkeley plant "devoted to the manufacture of marine engines." [2-31] By this date, American Car and Foundry (ACF) had purchased Hall-Scott, a sale that will be addressed in Chapter 3. The announced division of engine-making duties never occurred, though, and the Hall-Scott Berkeley plant made the IHC engines. Because the yearly production numbers of Hall-Scott hovered in the 250-unit range, much to the disappointment of optimistic ACF executives, dividing up the Hall-Scott engine making was never needed. International did most of the initial engineering of the new models, with Hall-Scott applying only a little final "touching up"; thus, it did not take long for engines to begin emerging from the Berkeley plant. From 1927 through the early 1930s, the Hall-Scott 312-cubic-inch Model 151 and the 390-cubic-inch Model 152 powered an assortment of medium-sized IHC trucks in the range of 2-1/2 to 5 tons, such as the HS-54, W-4, HS-71, W-3, HS-104C, and HS-404C. [2-32] Bradford and Glidewell reported that these Hall-Scott-powered Internationals saw severe service in hauling earth at the construction of the Hoover Dam. [2-33] Contractual stipulations prevented Hall-Scott from selling these

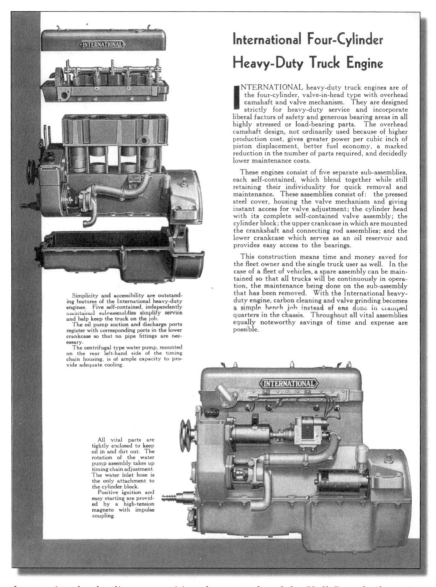

International Four-Cylinder Heavy-Duty Truck Engine

INTERNATIONAL heavy-duty truck engines are of the four-cylinder, valve-in-head type with overhead camshaft and valve mechanism. They are designed strictly for heavy-duty service and incorporate liberal factors of safety and generous bearing areas in all highly stressed or load-bearing parts. The overhead camshaft design, not ordinarily used because of higher production cost, gives greater power per cubic inch of piston displacement, better fuel economy, a marked reduction in the number of parts required, and decidedly lower maintenance costs.

These engines consist of five separate sub-assemblies, each self-contained, which blend together while still retaining their individuality for quick removal and maintenance. These assemblies consist of: the pressed steel cover, housing the valve mechanism and giving instant access for valve adjustment; the cylinder head with its complete self-contained valve assembly; the cylinder block; the upper crankcase in which are mounted the crankshaft and connecting rod assemblies; and the lower crankcase which serves as an oil reservoir and provides easy access to the bearings.

This construction means time and money saved for the fleet owner and the single truck user as well. In the case of a fleet of vehicles, a spare assembly can be maintained so that all trucks will be continuously in operation, the maintenance being done on the sub-assembly that has been removed. With the International heavy-duty engine, carbon cleaning and valve grinding becomes a simple bench job instead of one done in cramped quarters in the chassis. Throughout all vital assemblies equally noteworthy savings of time and expense are possible.

Simplicity and accessibility are outstanding features of the International heavy-duty engines. Five self-contained, independently maintained sub-assemblies simplify service and help keep the truck on the job.

The oil pump suction and discharge ports register with corresponding ports in the lower crankcase so that no pipe fittings are necessary.

The centrifugal type water pump, mounted on the rear left-hand side of the timing chain housing, is of ample capacity to provide adequate cooling.

All vital parts are tightly enclosed to keep oil in and dirt out. The rotation of the water pump assembly takes up timing chain adjustment. The water inlet hose is the only attachment to the cylinder block.

Positive ignition and easy starting are provided by a high-tension magneto with impulse coupling.

International sales literature, citing the strengths of the Hall-Scott-built engine. (Courtesy of Keith Ernst.)

models to any other truck makers as long as IHC bought them. Therefore, after terminating the IHC agreement, the Models 151 and 152 were rebadged as the Models 165 and 167 and powered trucks, buses, and industrial uses into the early post-World War II period. These engines also became the basis for the long-lived Hall-Scott marine "Fisher Jr." Around 1931, it appears Hall-Scott delivered the last of its Models 151 and 152 engines for IHC (although IHC continued to market them a short while longer), with the total production of the two models reaching around 6,000 units. [2-34]

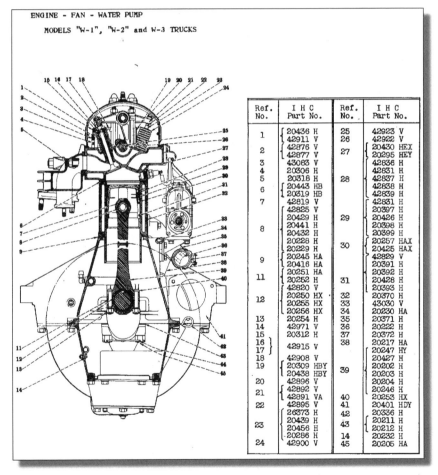

ENGINE - FAN - WATER PUMP

MODELS "W-1", "W-2" and W-3 TRUCKS

Ref. No.	IHC Part No.	Ref. No.	IHC Part No.
1	20436 H / 42911 V	25	42923 V
2	42876 V / 42877 V	26	42922 V
3	43083 V	27	20430 HEX / 20295 HEY
4	20306 H		42836 V
5	20318 H		42831 H
6	20443 HB / 20319 HB	28	42837 H
7	42819 V / 42825 V		42838 H
	20429 H		42839 H
	20441 H		42831 H
8	20432 H		20397 H
	20228 H	29	20426 H
	20229 H		20398 H
9	20245 HA / 20416 HA		20399 H
	20251 HA		20257 HAX
11	20252 H	30	20245 HAX
	42820 V		42829 V
	20250 HX		20391 H
12	20255 HX		20392 H
	20256 HX	31	20428 H
13	20254 H		20393 H
14	42971 V	32	20370 H
15	20312 H	33	43030 V
16 / 17	42915 V	34	20230 HA
18	42908 V	35	20371 H
19	20309 HBY / 20438 HBY	36	20222 H
20	42896 V	37	20372 H
21	42892 V / 42891 VA	38	20217 HA / 20247 HY
22	42895 V		20427 H
	26373 H		20202 H
23	20439 H	39	20203 H
	20456 H		20204 H
	20286 H		20246 H
24	42900 V	40	20253 HX
		41	20401 HDY
		42	20336 H
		43	20211 H / 20212 H
		14	20232 H
		45	20205 HA

Cylinder view of the Model 151/152 engine, made for International Harvester. Note the typical Hall-Scott features. (Courtesy of Keith Ernst.)

The proof of truck value is performance. The increasing popularity of Internationals among long-distance haulers is evidence of dependable and economical transportation.

This International hauls slack from nearby mines to the power plant of the Union Power Company, Ltd., Drumheller, Alta.

Heavy-duty Internationals are popular with coal dealers. These sturdy trucks with dependable power provide unusual pulling ability for hard going without sacrificing speed for good roads.

The Model W-2 tractor-truck with refrigerated semi-trailer is used by many dairies for hauling milk from the country.

Public utilities find the International Model W-2 with its complete equipment well adapted to line construction and maintenance work. Bodies, winches, derricks, and all types of equipment are provided for every line truck need.

Some types of International Harvester trucks powered by four-cylinder Hall-Scott engines. (Courtesy of Keith Ernst.)

The timing of this deal certainly worked out well for Hall-Scott, being in the depths of the Great Depression. Hall-Scott made only 44 "Harvesters" in 1927, amounting to merely 6% of its total engine production, but that percentage shot up to 64% in 1928 (with 1,235 Harvesters made), 82% in 1929 (with

Made in small numbers, the Models 151- and 152-based Fisher Jr. was marketed until World War II.

3,245 Harvesters made), and then 70% in 1930 (with 1,366 Harvesters made), before production fell off drastically. [2-35] ACF reported that this was a profitable arrangement for Hall-Scott. In fact, it was critical to the affairs of the company and mitigated the damage from the great amounts of money it had lost elsewhere from 1927 to 1930. [2-36] Companies sought the skill and resources of E.J. Hall and Hall-Scott, who had become respected engineering and engine-making "guns for hire" in the 1920s. After the ACF purchase in 1925, however, that happened less frequently.

Hall-Scott Abandons Some Products and Adopts Others

In the 1910s, E.J. Hall had established himself with his exciting engines as one of the most capable and promising air power engineers in America. Hall-Scott had the geographical location to take advantage of the air power market, with so many airplanes and airfields in California. Numerous racing victories by Hall-Scott-powered planes led Hall to being picked to participate in the high-profile Liberty program, where Hall (and by extension, Hall-Scott) made his most historically significant contributions. Given a military commission during World War I, a prestigious award for his wartime efforts, and plenty of favorable press for Hall and his company, you might think that would be

Model P-167
Industrial Power Unit

HALL-SCOTT MOTOR CAR COMPANY
DIVISION OF AMERICAN CAR AND FOUNDRY MOTORS CO.

Factory and General Offices
2850 Seventh Street, Berkeley, Calif.

Southwestern Factory Branches	Northwestern Factory Branches	Eastern Factory Branches
210 East Tenth Street LOS ANGELES, CALIFORNIA	907 Western Avenue SEATTLE, WASHINGTON	217 West Fifty-Seventh Street NEW YORK CITY
R. V. Morris & Co. 836 Columbia Street SAN DIEGO, CALIFORNIA	270 Sixteenth Street PORTLAND, OREGON	500 East Jefferson DETROIT, MICHIGAN

Another application of the "Harvester" engine was the Model 167 industrial engine, a brochure of which is shown here.

INDUSTRIAL a.c.f. *Hall-Scott* POWER UNITS

Model P-167 Four Cylinder Industrial Power Unit

THE Hall-Scott Model P-167 Four Cylinder Industrial Engine is applicable for use as motive power for concrete mixers, rock crushers, trench diggers, hoists, pumps, pressure blowers, power shovels, air compressors, electric generators, power saws, cranes, oil producing and many other types of industrial machinery.

It is of four-cylinder overhead valve type with $4\frac{3}{4}''$ bore and $5\frac{1}{2}''$ stroke and develops 60 brake horsepower at 1800 R.P.M., and is designed to take any standard power take-off, reduction gear or clutch unit.

The P-167 unit was designed for compactness, light weight and reasonable low cost. It is a completely housed unit with removable side doors, which makes it applicable to both indoor and outdoor use. These doors may be opened by sliding or removed by lifting them out when in close quarters. A heavy duty type radiator with heavy protecting grid is included in this unit. A control panel with complete set of instruments and engine controls is also provided.

The Model P-167 Industrial Engine is constructed of several complete units or assemblies which feature accessibility and simplicity of design. This type of

Magneto side of Hall-Scott Model P-167 power unit, with side door removed, showing magneto, generator and water pump; also showing starter and storage battery.

construction allows for the easy removal of cylinder head, cylinder block, etc., for repairs or maintenance.

Only the finest materials are used in the construction of this engine. All parts are of ample size to withstand hard usage and are all thoroughly tested and inspected before assembly into engines.

All of the usual Hall-Scott mechanical features are included in this engine, with the addition of an *improved carburetion and air temperature control system,* which adds greatly to the performance of this engine. A special Hall-Winslow oil filter is included, which keeps lubricating oil free from dirt and other foreign matter. *Generator, starter and storage battery are optional equipment and can be furnished at additional cost.*

The many *mechanical features incorporated in its design,* together with its *outstanding performance,* makes it a *very substantial and reliable power plant for industrial uses.*

For further information on these industrial units communicate with the nearest Hall-Scott Branch Office or write to the factory at Berkeley, California. Special information will be furnished upon request.

Carburetor side of Hall-Scott Model P-167 power unit, with side door removed, showing carburetion and exhaust systems and oil filter. Connections to operating panel are also shown.

RUGGED CONSTRUCTION ∞ LONG LIFE

A view of the Model 167 engine. Its external similarities to the Models 151 and 152 and the Fisher Jr. are evident.

encouragement enough for Hall to develop more aviation engines after the war ended. And many people predicted that the aircraft market would soar after the war ended, which must have encouraged Hall-Scott leadership to stay in air power and bring out the L engines. Paradoxically, though, this was not the case. Almost as quickly as Hall-Scott burst onto the aviation scene in the 1910s, the company retreated from there in the 1920s.

Hall-Scott did not follow up on the L-4 and L-6 with any new aviation engines. The L-4 and L-6 were good engines, and, being derived from the Liberty, they represented modern aircraft design and performance when they appeared. Because of their sparkling performance, Hall-Scott L engines even powered a few boats and race cars. But these engines marked the end of the line for the Hall-Scott aviation power program. When Hall-Scott pulled out of aircraft engine making entirely in the 1920s, it was still rather early in the market life of the L-4 and L-6. Rather than stay with the Liberty-based L engines or even move beyond them, Hall-Scott decided to turn its engineering focus elsewhere.

There are reasonable conjectures as to why Hall-Scott abandoned aviation in the 1920s, but conclusive company information has not been located. Francis Bradford argued that the company dropped the making of aviation engines to concentrate on "more lucrative" sectors of the engine market. [2-37] Supporting Bradford's contention was the market inundation of thousands of surplus Liberty engines after World War I. The government possessed almost 12,000 such engines at the close of the war, plus mountains of spare parts. [2-38] Only a few new airplanes could even use a V-12 Liberty, but some could, which exerted a downward pressure on aircraft engine prices and demand industry-wide. Wisely, Hall-Scott took advantage of this super-abundance of Liberty parts by purchasing large quantities of valves, cylinder barrels, water pumps, and other components at bargain prices and then using them in its own engines, both aviation and marine. [2-39] Hall-Scott could at least enjoy some benefit from the overabundance of Liberties and could bring out new engines without having to sink the needed research and development money into all-new models—a benefit for a small company.

It is clear that the aircraft industry headed into a brutal shakedown period around 1920. One historian wrote, "No industry ever fell so far so rapidly as did the young aircraft industry" after the end of World War I. "By the summer of 1919 some 90% of peak production capacity had been liquidated." In the years that followed, "Many firms were either liquidated or turned to other business pursuits." [2-40] Before the war, total American aircraft production first topped 100 in 1915, peaked at 14,020 in 1918, and then receded to a level of roughly 250 to 450 per year in the early 1920s. That was not enough production to support much of an industry or to provide a decent market for airplane engine makers. Few of the better-known aircraft companies in the 1910s made planes in the 1920s, or at least under the same name. Hall-Scott was such a well-known company, and as the aircraft market fell on hard times in the early 1920s—indeed, as the national economy sputtered—Hall-Scott lost money, an aggregate $566,594 for the years 1920 to 1923. [2-41] These losses were quite large by Hall-Scott standards, and they were the first back-to-back years of loss the company had endured. This was an especially dramatic turn of fortune, given that Hall-Scott had posted spectacular net earnings during the war years of 1917 and 1918, with more than $4.46 million. The postwar period saw Hall-Scott facing some serious profitability problems, so aircraft probably was abandoned because it did not pay, as suggested by Bradford. Several authors have noted that Hall-Scott might have been the leading American maker of water-cooled aircraft engines before World War I behind only Curtiss, but that prominent position still did not translate into long-term market presence. [2-42] Outside of profitability, the company that purchased Hall-Scott in 1925, ACF, likely wanted to concentrate Hall-Scott production for vehicles it made, and airplanes were not part of its product mix. Therefore, Hall-Scott quietly dropped its aircraft engine program in the early 1920s.

After World War I, Hall-Scott managers might have felt that the aircraft engine market was not where it should be in investing time and talent, but managers and engineers at Lycoming, Continental, Curtiss, and a few other companies did. In the 1920s, with a swamped market or not, and with or without E.J. Hall's leadership, aviation engine technology throttled forward. Planes became faster, and their bodies became sleeker. Big airplanes grew even bigger, and for small planes, a whole new market in private airplane ownership grew after the war, even if the numbers remained rather small. Aviation engines became more compact, reliable, and efficient, which facilitated a new market for small planes. And engines quickly moved away from the type that Hall-Scott had made. The most significant departure in engine design came with the growth of the air-cooled "radial" engine (in which the cylinders radiate outward from the crankshaft similar to spokes of a wheel) that had been popularized during the war. Later, the horizontally opposed air-cooled engine became popular. Such engines divide their cylinders into two horizontal banks, opposed to each other, "flat," and connected to a central crankshaft. The air-cooling feature frees the engine of weight and cost, while the horizontal layout makes it easier to fit into the pointed nose of small aircraft. Continental Motors historian William Wagner quoted an aviator from the time as saying that this new type of motor was "perhaps the single most important factor in the growth of our modern private aircraft industry." [2-43] Similarly, aviation historian Herschel Smith observed, "Every [aviation] piston engine in production today, outside of the Soviet bloc, is of the opposed type." Thus, after World War I, aviation engines veered in a direction quite different than Hall-Scott products had tracked. [2-44] Hall-Scott did not develop opposed types, nor were any of its engines ever air-cooled, nor did the company ever build a sleeve valve engine (which replaced the reciprocating "poppet" valves seen on most engines, with a holed sleeve that runs with the piston to transfer intake and exhaust), nor did the company adopt any of the other major technological developments of the period. The forward march of new technology in Hall-Scott aircraft power abruptly stopped with the introduction of the L engines—in other words, with Hall's part in the Liberty motor program.

Hall-Scott also turned its back on another market that it had served in its first decade—rail motor cars. Although it no longer made motor cars after 1921, Hall-Scott continued into the 1930s to make a few engines for rail units of varying sizes and uses. The few examples Hall-Scott produced of its motor car and 8 × 10 motor car engine established it as only a minor supplier of rail power anyway. Not only did Hall-Scott produce few such engines, but it waited a rather considerable time before improving on the 8 × 10 engine. Ten years might not seem like a long period, but major engine advancement came so quickly in the early twentieth century that "modern" engines could become obsolete within a few years. Hall-Scott did not neglect the aviation industry as it did rail before World War I, with a steady stream of ever-better aircraft engine models emerging from the Hall-Scott Berkeley plant through 1917.

E.J. Hall realized that his company needed to produce a substantially improved rail engine if it wished to remain competitive in that market. Thus, after World War I, Hall finally focused his attention there. In 1920 or 1921, he and three Hall-Scott draftsmen—Charlie Gray, George Mye, and August Schlesinger—began designing what would become the Model 350 to address this need. [2-45] This was no warmed-over existing engine; the Model 350 was an all-new, heavy-duty, medium-speed, six-cylinder gasoline engine that developed impressive power. A circa-1930 Hall-Scott engine horsepower chart lists the output of the Model 350 as 424 hp at 1200 rpm and 1965 ft. lb. of torque at 1000 rpm. [2-46] A full-sized locomotive installed two such units in its engine compartment, making for well over 800 hp and some 4000 ft. lb. of torque. While not able to out-muscle large steam locomotives that produced several thousand horse-power, a Model 350-powered locomotive could still pull a string of passenger or freight cars. Hall-Scott produced very "torquey" engines, which often had torque numbers being twice the horsepower figure. It is highly desirable for heavy-duty engines to have considerable "grunt" at low revolutions per minute, and Hall-Scott always gave its customers plenty of that.

The Model 350 was a large engine, displacing 2386 cubic inches with bore and stroke measurements of 7 inches by 9 inches, and was of more modern design than Hall's previous rail engines. [2-47] The Model 350 reflected some practices Hall-Scott employed in its aircraft engines, such as using domed or "semi-spherical" combustion chambers, dual ignition, an overhead camshaft (driven by a vertical shaft that came up through the engine and turned a bevel gear that rotated the camshaft), and two valves per cylinder. These features simultaneously improved performance and eased valvetrain adjustment or replacement. Beginning in the early 1920s when the firm began using "en-bloc" design, it used what it called "unit construction." In the Model 350, Hall designed the engine to have a two-part crankcase, a block (which had all six cylinders cast integrally—"en-bloc"), and a head (which contained the valvetrain), so that one

The great weight of the 350 series engines made them a better fit for stationary applications, as shown here, and for rail.

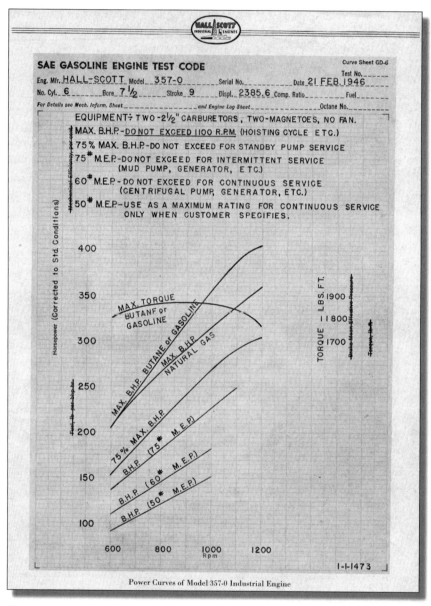

Power Curves of Model 357-0 Industrial Engine

The power curve of the 350 series. The industrial version came to be known as the Model 357, which is shown here.

"unit" could be replaced singularly, without replacing the others. This made rebuilding cheaper and easier, and extended the life of the engine. Hall and his engineering team gave the Model 350 a lower crankcase made of aluminum for lighter weight, and they fitted the engine with an electric starter. The new model also had a fully enclosed and pressure-lubricated valvetrain. Therefore, unlike the previous Hall-Scott rail engine, the Model 350 did not require regular hand lubrication while operating. Making engines less labor intensive to operate, and thus cheaper to run, was a critical consideration in designing rail engines after World War I and was a subtext driving the revolutionary developments then being made in powering locomotives. By the 1920s, development of the internal combustion engine made it vastly simpler to operate than the powerful and well-established, but dangerous and temperamental, steam engine. Steam engines required constant attention and adjustment by several skilled operators. In the 1920s, a locomotive with Hall-Scott Model 350 power could be a modern and cost-efficient unit for some rail lines.

The Model 350 that E.J. Hall and his associates designed differed in another fundamental way from the previous generation of Hall-Scott rail engines—it was designed with "gasoline-electric" operation in mind. In locomotive applications, the Model 350 was coupled to a direct-current generator that powered electric motors connected to the wheels of the locomotive. In this regard, the Model 350 kept up with an industry trend away from the gasoline-mechanical arrangement Hall-Scott had used with its first motor car in 1910 through its last such car sold to a Chinese railroad in 1921. That earlier system severely limited the pulling ability of the train. Through the 1910s, small locomotives made by other companies had also moved away from using the gasoline-mechanical arrangement, increasingly adopting a gasoline-electric drive. Gasoline-electric enjoyed growing acceptance over gasoline-mechanical because it simultaneously simplified operation, boosted operating efficiency, and dramatically increased maximum payload. Steam locomotives, especially large ones, were hard on tracks, with their great weight and powerful motions generated when transmitting power and braking. As gasoline-electric became more attractive over gasoline-mechanical, this newer technology became more competitive with steam, at least with smaller locomotives. General Electric produced its first working gasoline-electric motor car, nicknamed a "Doodlebug," in the early twentieth century. [2-48] The commercial success of the Doodlebug was mixed, but it pointed to the new direction for powering locomotives, small and large. One rail historian noted that by 1930, even "most of the remaining [gasoline-mechanical] McKeens had been rebuilt with electric transmission." [2-49]

Even as Hall-Scott gradually shed its participation in making entire rail cars, it still promoted the use of its engines in rail vehicles made by other companies. The Hall-Scott Model 350 did not achieve much success in the 1920s, with only 95 built between 1926 and 1929 (the only years numbers are available), but it was produced in much greater numbers than the old 8 × 10 engine. [2-50] Of those Model 350 engines, it is unclear how many went to locomotives, and Bradford wrote only that "many railroads" used the new engine. [2-51] The West Coast's Southern Pacific was among them, and, according to Bradford, its first Model 350-powered locomotives began service in February 1929. The maiden run of a Hall-Scott Model 350-powered Southern Pacific locomotive came on the Los Angeles to San Francisco route. These trains ran nearly the length of California, pulling freight and passengers from Los Angeles to Eureka. According to historian J.B. McCall addressing the "dieselization" of American rail, gasoline-electric locomotives such as these Hall-Scott-powered Southern Pacific units proved cost effective only in "short-haul service where schedules were slow and tonnage was light. In this service the railcars were generally a cheaper way to produce transportation than the steam-powered trains they replaced but, if either speed or heavy tonnage was required, the cost advantage over steam power vanished quickly." [2-52] Not nearly enough customers found the Model 350 an attractive power option for locomotives, though. By 1931, a report on Hall-Scott called its rail engine program a "liability" for the company, suggesting, "Its inventory should be liquidated as far as possible, and no money spent in expanding or modifying the product…" [2-53] The Hall-Scott Model 350 was its most viable entry in the gasoline-electric locomotive segment of the 1920s, although it hardly pointed the industry in a new direction.

Similar to many Hall-Scott engines, while initially built to serve the rail power need, the Model 350 soon became available to other customers. In its industrial form, it was known as the Model 357-0 and powered large pumps and generators. As a marine engine, Hall-Scott dubbed the Model 350 the "Voyager." Hall-Scott usually named its marine engines, rather than simply assigning a number designation to them. There is no evidence that this large engine ever powered trucks or buses. Its hefty 7000-pound weight obviously limited its mobile applications. From 1921 until 1937, the Model 350 was by far the largest and most powerful engine sold by Hall-Scott. Hall-Scott marketed this engine in various configurations into the early post-World War II period.

As rail companies began to choose diesel over gasoline to fuel their locomotives in the 1920s and 1930s, the economics of selling gasoline-burning engines to rail companies dimmed considerably. This trend did not provide the Hall-Scott Motor Car Company much incentive to pour additional resources into

General Electric
Gas-Electric Rail Car Equipment

Suitable for Use With the

HALL-SCOTT Special Rail Car Engine
Model 350

HALL-SCOTT ENGINE WITH GE GENERATOR

A 1920s Hall-Scott brochure promoting the Model 350 engine with a General Electric generator for rail use.

the Model 350, and there is no evidence that the Model 350 became the basis for other models of varying displacement or cylinder number. Likewise, Hall-Scott management did not feel inclined to invest money in developing other rail engines, for that matter. During this period, rail engine development was heading down a track that Hall-Scott engineers had no desire or perhaps sufficient resources to go—compression ignition.

Important development of the diesel engine after World War I was making the diesel amenable to more applications. Gasoline engines, which ignite fuel by a spark, witnessed constant improvement in the early twentieth century. But so did diesel engines, which ignite fuel by the heat from very high compression. Led by several companies, including Alco (American Locomotive Company), General Electric, and General Motors (through its purchase of the Winton Engine Company and Forming Electro-Motive Division [EMD] in 1930), gasoline-electric drive for large locomotives received a growing challenge from diesel-electric drive from the late 1910s. As a newer technology than gasoline, diesel lagged behind gasoline in market acceptance because of some peculiar and thorny impediments. [2-54] One barrier was the great weight inherent in diesel engines, in part a function of their construction to cope with the higher stresses of diesel combustion. Fuel delivery was another obstacle. Early examples relied on highly compressed air to deliver fuel to the cylinders, requiring bulky, heavy, and problem-prone compressors and high-pressure lines. Starting these ponderous engines with their high compression ratios was a great challenge, with early diesels sometimes being turned over using gasoline or other highly volatile fuel and then switching to cheaper fuel oil once running. Starting diesels in cold weather was a serious issue to operators, as it remains somewhat so decades later. The relatively low maximum engine speed and great weight of diesels made them less attractive in vehicles that needed to accelerate frequently, such as cars or trucks. Complete combustion of diesel fuel was problematic, with early diesels producing prodigious amounts of smelly and sooty exhaust. Although gasoline and kerosene had well-established refining and distribution networks by the 1910s, the fuel oil used in diesels was comparatively difficult to obtain. Technical support also was an issue, as was the high purchase price. We could conclude that it simply might have been easier to accept gasoline and forget about trying to make the problem-fraught diesel easier to live with.

But what kept engineers, businessmen, government figures, and others so focused on improving the diesel was its greatly alluring and superior operating efficiency over gasoline engines. Diesel engines can produce up to 25% higher fuel mileage over gasoline engines of comparable horsepower. They have no ignition systems to "tune up." Diesel fuel is a cruder petroleum product than gasoline and, given the tax structure of states in the early twentieth century, was cheaper by several cents or more per gallon. Compounding these savings is the greater ruggedness of diesel engine construction, which can make diesel engines long-lived. Although a diesel engine costs more to purchase than a gasoline engine of similar power, operating savings can recoup the higher upfront costs of a diesel unit in short order, especially if the engine is used heavily. All of these problems were not conquered, but they were greatly alleviated in the 1920s and 1930s, making diesel power more acceptable to customers needing these engines in rail, marine, stationary uses, tractors, trucks, and buses.

In the rail market, General Electric, with Ingersoll-Rand, led the way with the release of the first commercial diesel-electric locomotive in 1918. [2-55] Because Europe dominated diesel development at that point, early General Electric diesel "switcher" locomotives used an English-made engine. [2-56] Several makers followed this locomotive unit with their own diesel-electrics in the early 1920s, and improved models continued to appear. EMD's power-ful and efficient FT, released in 1939, silenced the remaining disbelievers. By the end of World War II, railroads had purchased well over 1,000 FT's. [2-57] As was frequently said about these new diesel locomotives, all you did was "turn 'em on and let 'em run," a phrase never made in reference to any steam locomotive. With shocking speed, diesel-electric overtook steam and quickly dominated American rail power.

Hall-Scott did not offer a diesel engine challenge to Alco, General Electric, or General Motors in this tidal change. Rather than compete and bring out its own large compression ignition engine, Hall-Scott simply left the motor car market in 1921 and faded from the locomotive market, leaving rail to the diesel build-ers. As seen in air power, competitors in rail raced ahead with new models. The Model 350 and other Hall-Scott engines powered a few locomotives and small rail cars in the years ahead, and the company continued to advertise its engines for rail service into the 1930s. However, in the 1920s, the Hall-Scott Motor Car Company remained a minor presence in rail power.

During this same time period, while turning its back on powering planes and making rail cars, Hall-Scott squarely refocused its talents on the booming trac-tor, truck, bus, and industrial engine market with zeal. The promise for growth in the truck and bus sector after World War I was bright. Said a writer from *Commercial Car Journal* in an article dated 1917, "Just as almost everyone in the early stages of this automobile age had made up his mind that some day he was going to buy an automobile, but concluded that he would wait until the machine was perfected...before substituting the motor truck for the horse-drawn truck. The late war has proved the absolute reliability and efficiency of the motor truck... This is going to make that line of business very good." [2-58] If Hall-Scott management thought it might be less risky to focus its resources on building engines for trucks and buses rather than for airplanes and trains, it was not a bad bet. In fact, a prime reason for the national downfall of the steam train in the postwar years was the proliferation of truck and bus service in that era. One rail historian wrote, "The rise of highway transportation cut the tap root of rail passenger traffic by the mid-1920s and was soon taking significant freight traffic from the rails as well." [2-59] In a sense, the Hall-Scott decision to build truck and bus engines strengthened that market and simultaneously undermined the competitiveness of the gasoline-electric locomotive. Following the old adage of "If you can't beat 'em, join 'em," the departure of Hall-Scott from rail and aviation into truck and bus in the 1920s was a logical and well-timed business decision—given its reluctance to commence diesel building, of course.

Heavy-duty truck engine manufacturing already was a crowded field, though. Established independent engine companies (and not vehicle companies that made their own engines) with some name recognition after World War I included Buda, Continental, Hercules, Herschell-Spillman, Hinkley, Le Roi, Lycoming, Waukesha, and Wisconsin. With several dozen truck makers on the market at any one time, even if most did not stay in business very long, the opportunity to get a company's engine into a truck as original equipment manufacturer (OEM) was enhanced. Hall-Scott designed and built engines to power both types of applications right after the war.

A West Coast vehicle maker, Holt Manufacturing Company, was instrumental in enticing Hall-Scott to develop engines for new applications—vehicles Hall-Scott had not yet addressed in its product line. In the 1920s, Hall-Scott moved into powering buses, trucks, and boats, actually by first making a brief but successful pit stop with tractors.

Holt, headquartered in Stockton, California, about 65 miles from the Hall-Scott plant in Berkeley, is better known today through the firm it helped create by means of a merger, the Caterpillar Tractor Company, now headquartered in Peoria, Illinois. Holt had become a leader in its field by pioneering the crawler tractor in the early twentieth century, producing models for the civilian market and having thousands of its tractors drafted for service overseas in the Great War. E.J. Hall supplied an engine of fresh design for a new Holt tractor model after World War I. The tractor, known as the T-35 and later as the 2 Ton, was a

The Holt T-35 tractor. (Courtesy of Tom Sharpsteen.)

smaller tractor than the one on which the company had built its reputation. In fact, the T-35 was the smallest in the Holt lineup at the time. The petite size of the T-35 was reflected in a price that kept it accessible to more operators. But it was still a capable machine, and, in one ad, Holt called the T-35 "*the* Supreme Small Tractor." [2-60] In 1921, the tractor debuted for sale, and it continued to be sold until 1928.

The Holt Manufacturing Company expected small tractors to become more popular after World War I for use in logging, agriculture, and construction; thus, it was hoped that the T-35 would fill a critical new market niche. Complicating the immediate future of Holt as a successful tractor company was a burden of its own making. When the war ended, the U.S. government possessed 9,000 tractors, about a third of them Holts. [2-61] That was far more than Uncle Sam needed, and because the tractors were ready for heavy-duty work in the civilian market, the government disposed of most of them at bargain prices. Being simultaneously squeezed by the flood of cheap full-sized tractors from the military, the sharp competition from the numerous small start-up companies making tractors, and the depressed agricultural sector after the war all underscored the propitious timing for Holt to introduce a small tractor with a highly efficient motor.

The exact association between Holt and Hall-Scott regarding this new tractor project was nebulous then and for years has remained unclear. In fact, some recent authors continue to cite Holt Manufacturing as the sole maker of the T-35 engine, designated first as the Model MS-35 and later as the Model M-35. One author stated unequivocally, "Holt, and later Caterpillar, made all components of the tractor, except for the Eisemann magneto and Kingston carburetor." [2-62] Because so many authors have overlooked the involvement of E.J. Hall and Hall-Scott in major projects and technological advances over the years, this oversight, while unfortunate, is by no means unusual.

During the period that Holt manufactured the T-35, there seemed to have been few common and widely read references that connected Hall-Scott to the little tractor. One example was *Western Machinery World*, which in its January 1922 issue told its readers that the engine "was designed by Pliny E. Holt, vice president in charge of engineering of the Holt Manufacturing Company, and Colonel E.G. [*sic*] Hall, one of the designers of the Liberty motor and a foremost automotive engineer." [2-63] The February issue of that publication also ran an article titled "Operations in the Production of 'Caterpillar' Motors" that focused on the manufacture of the T-35 engine. Four pages of text and photos (of which there were 15) went into detail about the construction and features of the engine but made no mention of Hall-Scott. The article only stated, "The manufacture of the transmission and other tractor parts at the Holt company's plant in Stockton has been described in detail in an earlier article," leaving the reader to assume that the story and photos of manufacture were based on operations at Holt's Stockton plant. [2-64]

But one source established a clear Hall-Scott connection to the little Holt tractor. Utilizing a number of period materials, author Lorry Dunning in his book *Ultimate American Farm Tractor Data Book* described the T-35 engine as a "Hallscott [*sic*] MS 35 vertical, valve-in-head." [2-65] More recently, looking through Holt company records, Dunning found conclusive proof that not only did E.J. Hall design the T-35 engine, but Hall-Scott Motor Car Company built hundreds of engines and spare parts for Holt. In a letter dated November 24, 1920, E.J. Hall wrote to Pliny Holt about "a proposed engine for use in caterpillar tractor." [2-66] Although only drawings were available at this stage, Hall presented Holt with "photographs of a blackboard drawing" and some descriptions, such as, "The size of this engine was 4-3/4" × 6" or 5" × 7"." Hall made no reference to any earlier communications between the two men or the two companies, so this can be assumed to be an early or even initial exchange concerning a tentative project. Holt must have approved of what he saw in Hall's letter, because Holt and Hall-Scott signed a deal on March 31, 1921. [2-67] This is interesting, but this date puts Hall-Scott participation in the T-35 project rather late in the development cycle of the tractor. With planning for the new T-35 beginning around 1918 and its market release in 1921, it is hard to imagine that Holt had not considered other power plants before receiving this letter from Hall. [2-68] Some evidence suggests that the motor took little time to design and build, though. In 1969, E.J. Hall's widow wrote, "The engine was designed, built and delivered tested [*sic*] in 28 days and was called the T-35." [2-69] If that is true, it makes this engine all the more interesting and impressive. Whatever the particulars were of the Hall-Scott and Holt relationship, production of the MS-35 engine began in the Hall-Scott plant that same year, with Mr. Holt's enthusiastic approval of the program. Pliny Holt remarked to a friend who wanted to tour the Hall-Scott facility, "I am sure that you will be interested in going through the plant there, as the way

The Holt T-35 tractor was popular, with more than 10,000 eventually built through 1928. (Courtesy of the University of California, Davis, Department of Special Collections. Found by Lorry Dunning.)

they have tooled up for building our motors is one of the cleverest things in the manufacturing line I have ever seen." [2-70]

After early discussions about what form the engine would take, the two companies agreed that Hall-Scott should build a four-cylinder unit with bore and stroke dimensions of 4" × 5-1/2" (which equaled 276.5 cubic inches), develop about 25 horsepower, and have a governed engine speed of 1000 rpm. [2-71] The basic dimensions and capacities of the T-35 engine seem in line with other tractor power plants of the day.

By January 1922, Hall-Scott had filled the initial order of 100 engines placed by Holt. [2-72] Those first 100 units were considered "experimental" while Holt and Hall-Scott worked together, usually smoothly, to get the engine to perform and appear as desired. [2-73] Given that Hall-Scott was untested in the tractor field, Pliny Holt plowed ahead cautiously in his collaboration with the Berkeley engine maker. The performance and appearance of the first MS-35s satisfied Holt management. Therefore, the initial purchase of 100 engines was followed by a second contract signed in December 1921, which specified 520 more, and then a third contract that was signed in October 1922 and ordered another 315. [2-74] Numerous running changes took place from the first lot through the third—from specifying that heat-treated stock be used for machining connecting rod bolts, to adopting radiator caps having more tension. After the third contract, the total engines delivered to Holt totaled 935, which terminated Hall-Scott participation in the 2 Ton project. Dunning cited 1,350 T-35 tractors being made in Stockton before production moved to Peoria, of which 935 received Hall-Scott MS-35 engines. After this time, the tractors received Waukesha-made M-35s, which basically were the same engine but with small improvements. [2-75] It is not known why this Holt and Hall-Scott relationship ended.

Holt Manufacturing might have been satisfied with the new Hall-Scott tractor engine, but a person would not know that from looking at the engine. Finding any clear evidence of the role of Hall-Scott in the development or production of this engine is impossible. The name "Holt" was prominently cast into both sides of the valve cover, with the name as conspicuously cut into both sides of the radiator frame. When Hall sent Holt his blueprint sketches in 1920, the "Hall-Scott" name was boldly cast into the block—not so on the production engine. No external evidence on the T-35 or MS-35 betrayed even the hint of a relationship with Hall-Scott. In fact, in a third contract signed between Holt and Hall-Scott in October 1922, point 13 stated, "No name plates, inscriptions or other designation or data shall be placed on said engines manufactured

A close-up of the Hall-Scott-built MS-35. (Courtesy of Lorry Dunning.)

hereunder, except those of Purchaser," which was Holt. [2-76] The contract continued, "Purchaser will supply its own standard name plates to Manufacturer for placing on said engines, and may also have the inscription or designation of the trade mark 'HOLT' or 'CATERPILLAR' placed on each of said engines." Holt, and later Caterpillar, made no attempt to credit Hall-Scott on the MS-35 engines or in any T-35 ads.

Although the Hall-Scott origins and early manufacture of the MS-35 are now documented, some elements of that engine bear the mark of E.J. Hall-inspired design more than others. Among the most notable Hall-Scott type of features in the MS-35 was its overhead camshaft. That feature was at home in a high-performance aircraft engine such as the A-5 but was most unusual in a tractor motor. The engine also had a domed combustion chamber—a hemi head. But other features of the MS-35 would make this an unusual motor to come from Hall-Scott. The single aspect that most made the MS-35 unlike any other Hall-Scott engine offered until that time was the use of "en-bloc" construction. Hall used the "built-up" method on all Hall-Scott engines through World War I.

En-bloc construction casts the cylinders together, as opposed to bolting each cylinder to the crankcase. This results in the engine having more rigidity. En-bloc construction was favored for automotive and heavy-duty engines by this time, so the MS-35 was in keeping with industry trends. Around 1920, Hall-Scott began making its engines en-bloc such as the Model 350; the MS-35 probably was that first model. So the MS-35 engine not only carried over some Hall designs, but also pushed forward the development of the engine-making skills of the company and its ability to fill the power needs of more consumers.

For the Hall-Scott Motor Car Company, this collaborative project with Holt marked a significant break from the past. By providing power for the T-35 tractor, Hall-Scott entered a new and potentially lucrative market. Hall-Scott might not become a major supplier of tractor engines in the future, and maybe it could have, but its brief involvement changed the development of Hall-Scott.

Hall's successful work with Holt led directly to Hall-Scott beginning a new relationship with Fageol Motors Company that had long-term and deep importance for the Berkeley engine maker. [2-77] Fageol Motors, led by brothers Frank and William Fageol and Louis Bill, manufactured trucks, buses, tractors, and a few cars in Oakland, California, and Kent, Ohio, from 1916 to 1939. [2-78] During its history, Fageol produced some unusual and forward-thinking vehicles, with distinctive performance and styling. One Fageol automobile produced right before America entered World War I used a Hall-Scott 125-hp, six-cylinder A-5 aviation engine, which would have made for a very fast car, and an expensive one, too. A bare A-5 engine sold for $4,700, a bare Fageol car chassis cost $9,500, and a "fully loaded" model cost a king's ransom for that time: more than $12,000. [2-79] Thus, it is no surprise that Fageol moved few units. But carrying a steep price did not deter Fageol from marketing a vehicle. In the 1920s, Fageol priced its trucks at $3,000 to $5,700, much higher than most of the competition but, according to one automotive historian, "typical of California-built vehicles which had to be capable of climbing long, steep grades." [2-80] Fageol is an early example of a truck maker that geared its products for the driving peculiarities of the American West, a practice still seen to some degree in the twenty-first century.

Vehicles of many types saw their business expand after World War I, but the passenger coach business grew from nothing to prominence almost overnight. Addressing this sudden growth, David Beecraft, president of the Society of Automotive Engineers, said in 1922, "The development of the motor bus for city or rural transportation is one of the major developments of the motor car industry today." [2-81] Not only did the production of these vehicles increase

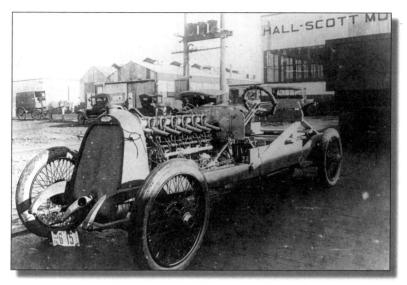

Demand for war production strained the production capacity of Hall-Scott, preventing it from supplying nearby Fageol with A-5s for its autos in 1917. Shown here is the potent Fageol in bare chassis with its Hall-Scott aviation engine.

Fageol ads teased potential buyers with a wide range of models, but the ads usually were drawings, not photos, because precious few Fageols were actually produced.

109

in number, but the innovation seen in them came quickly, too. Before World War I, the vehicles that carried numbers of people, either urban or interurban, were often elongated passenger cars. Others were little more than a box built atop a truck chassis. But these cobbled-together vehicles often were not up to the rigors of the job, especially concerning the peculiarities of moving people as opposed to freight. Residents of the American West increasingly began looking to buses to carry passengers across long distances and up and down the steep grades of the region, having a less dense rail network than the East among its far-flung cities. [2-82] It is little surprise that western states, particularly California, were national leaders in spurring increased bus (and diesel) usage. Both Hall-Scott and Fageol, given their California location, were uniquely situated to take full advantage of this up-and-coming segment of the heavy-duty vehicle market.

To meet this demand for a better way to carry people, Fageol introduced a totally new type of vehicle in 1921, the Safety Coach. The Safety Coach was among the first modern coaches or buses. In fact, the industry publication *Transit Journal* does not even list any "motor buses" as being produced before 1922, so the Safety Coach amounted to a gigantic step forward in carrying passengers over long distances. [2-83] The new Fageol bus had a heavy-duty chassis that nonetheless claimed an industry-leading low ground clearance of around 22 inches for a multi-passenger vehicle, a wide track (about 70 inches between the center of the front tires), and powerful braking (for that time). The ultra-low and wide Safety Coach carried 22 people, with a door for each row of seats to greatly facilitate entry and exit. Such a remarkable coach needed an exceptional engine to power it—one that could generate the great amount of torque needed to flatten steep, long hills. Fageol contacted Colonel Hall in neighboring Berkeley to fill the power needs for the new Safety Coach, even though Hall-Scott had not marketed an engine specifically for buses or trucks to that point. After all, Hall had designed engines for trains, planes, a light tractor model, and several automobiles—one of which was a Fageol, no less.

Managers from the bus maker could approach Hall-Scott because Fageol had been a Hall-Scott customer already and was a fellow East Bay manufacturer; therefore, Fageol management was familiar with Hall-Scott products and was aware of the impressive reputation of the company. Specifically, Fageol wanted to use a modified Hall-Scott/Holt tractor engine in its bus. Although similar to the Holt tractor engine, there were some differences. [2-84] The Fageol engine had a 1/4-inch greater cylinder bore, making it 4-1/4 inches, and it used aluminum rather than iron in its crankcase. Different sources reported a range of 55–62 hp at a governed 1800 rpm, 800 rpm greater than the MS-35. [2-85]

The cover of a Fageol Safety Coach brochure. (Courtesy of Tom Shafer.)

Hall-Scott renamed the engine the HSF-4. With the low gearing and heavy weight of these buses, the 60-odd horsepower in the engine could propel a Fageol Parlor Bus (a more luxurious version of the Safety Coach) to a top speed

The Fageol Safety Coach Chassis

THE Light Weight, Heavy Duty FAGEOL-HALL SCOTT MOTOR, Showing Clutch, Transmission, and Radiator Mounted.

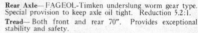

Frame—6 inch pressed steel channel weighing 8 lbs. per foot, hot riveted throughout. 9 cross members.

Wheelbase—Standard 218 inches. Can be furnished to suit body requirements.

Motor—Fageol - Hall - Scott. Four water cooled cylinders cast in block. Detachable overhead valve and cam shaft head with single cam for both intake and exhaust. Bore 4¼"x5½" stroke. Horse power, 28.9 S. A. E. rating, actual 62 H. P. at 1800 R. P. M. Three point suspension on Thermoid pads. Maximum motor speed 1800 R. P. M. controlled by enclosed governor.

Lubrication—Forced feed lubrication through hollow crank shaft to main and to connecting rod bearings and camshaft by gear pump.

Carburetor—Zenith.

Ignition—Delco ignition, starting and lighting.

Controls—Spark and throttle mounted on steering column, and accelerator pedal for foot. Gearshift lever and hand brake mounted in center.

Cooling System—Water circulation by centrifugal pump. Fan driven by internal silent chain through a friction clutch. Radiator mounted in unit with motor.

Clutch—Brown-Lipe heavy duty. Unit with motor.

Transmission—Brown-Lipe "selective". Four speeds forward and one reverse. Direct on third. Overgear of 25% on fourth. Possible speed on overgear at 1800 R. P. M., with 5.2:1 rear axle reduction, 49 M. P. H.

Front Axle—FAGEOL-Timken drop forged "I" beam axle of extra large cross section. Timken taper roller bearings throughout. Heavy steering knuckles.

Rear Axle—FAGEOL-Timken underslung worm gear type. Special provision to keep axle oil tight. Reduction 5.2:1.

Tread—Both front and rear 70". Provides exceptional stability and safety.

Brakes—Service an emergency brakes internal expanding on rear wheels. Size 21" diameter 4" wide, ¼" asbestos wire woven brake lining. 4 shoe Timken type.

Springs—Chrome Vanadium, half eliptic, flat. Front 11 leaves, 41"x2½", rear 10 leaves, 56"x3". Spring brackets are Meyers reservoir lubricating type. Gruss air springs in front.

Steering—Worm and nut non-reversible. Heavy type. 20" mahogany steering wheel.

Fuel Supply—29 gallon tank mounted at rear, fitted with three way valve, holding six gallons of reserve fuel. Stewart Vacuum System.

Battery—6 volt, mounted on running board.

Standard Equipment—Electric horn, tools, jack, extra tire carrier, full set lights, motometer.

The "U" shaped frame members are proportioned to be stronger than the frame channels themselves.

The powerful brakes, large enough for a 3½ ton truck, provide safety for the passengers.

The inside of the Fageol Safety Coach brochure shows the Hall-Scott engine, with the names of both companies clearly visible on the engine. (Courtesy of Tom Shafer.)

112

of 36 mph. Such speed apparently was considered adequate, for *The Motor Truck* writers made no mention of the Safety Coach's sloth. Even if the top speed of the Safety Coach did not make it a race car, perhaps the illusion of breathtaking speed could be conjured up from its engine having what *The Motor Truck* described as "Liberty aeroplane type overhead valves." [2-86] Hall's connection with designing the famous Liberty engine would follow him and his company for decades.

The new Hall-Scott HSF-4 power plant quickly won the admiration of drivers, owners, and members of the motor press. A caption for a

This photo shows the wide track of the Safety Coach. (Courtesy of Motor Bus Society.)

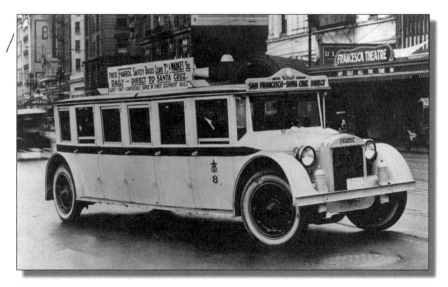

A Safety Coach on its way from San Francisco to Santa Cruz, circa 1922. (Courtesy of Motor Bus Society.)

photo of the engine in the January 1925 edition of *The Motor Truck* referred to the HSF-4 as the "Celebrated Hall-Scott Motor That Is Used by The Fageol Motor Truck Company." [2-87] So enamored were the editors of the magazine with the HSF-4 that they gave the engine an entire article in a later edition. The article spoke not only to the quality of the HSF-4, but also to the entire Hall-Scott line. The writer claimed, "Among the several power plants that the writer has seen, none is superior to the Hall-Scott, an engine designed by Col. E.J. Hall, one of the designers of the Liberty Aeroplane Engine, a former engineer of General Motors and the Ford Motor Company." [2-88] *The Motor Truck* writers were particularly impressed with Hall-Scott's use of high-quality steel and careful fabrication techniques, such as seen in the crankshaft. For each piece of steel used to make a crankshaft, called a "billet" in this crude stage, Hall-Scott personnel drilled and lab analyzed it to determine if it contained the correct carbon content. If it did, it was then heated, cooled, and reheated several times and very carefully, using "the finest type of instruments known for heat control and temperature readings," and then machined. Finally, the crankshaft was ready to install—having a "310 Brinell hardness, where it has a tensile strength of 140,000 pounds per square inch. At this hardness it is almost impossible to scratch the crank with a file." The engine had an overhead camshaft and a heavy-duty, extra-wide chain for operating accessories such as the generator that would last "about 10 times that obtainable in the average equipment." Even something as innocuous as the radiator fan drew praise. Compared to most automobile and truck fans that were lightweight and belt driven, the new fan blades of the Hall-Scott engine "...are shaped to move a great amount of air... The blades are unusually heavy, and are riveted securely in a heat treated chrome nickel steel spider...," turned by "heavy shafts that are accurately machined, heat treated and ground." The attention that Hall-Scott engineers devoted to designing and building the HSF-4 engine to cope with the rigors of bus service won the respect and even affection of these writers. Frank and William Fageol must have possessed some measure of confidence in this engine because they put their name on it—the name "Fageol–Hall-Scott" was embossed on the valve cover and block.

The HSF-4 powered the first Fageol 22-passenger buses, and a larger six-cylinder version of the engine followed, the HSF-6, for the Fageol 29-passenger Safety Coach. The Safety Coach instantly became a critical and commercial success. Sales of Safety Coaches took off quickly, with 260 sold in 1923 and 503 in 1924. [2-89] Fageol expanded its bus offerings to include models such as the luxurious 28-passenger Parlor Bus. Similar to the Safety Bus, these other vehicles also used Hall-Scott four- and six-cylinder engines. Because Fageol found a ready market for its Safety Coaches and other buses east of the Mississippi, it set up an eastern sales office and even an assembly plant in Kent, Ohio, which operated independently of the California branch. [2-90] The substantial number of Hall-Scott engines finding their way into Fageol products alone might have been enticement enough for Hall-Scott to focus on powering trucks and buses and to move away from powering aircraft and trains in the 1920s.

Always on the cutting edge of developments in the western truck and bus markets, Fageol found Hall-Scott engines well suited to its vehicles, and the company remained a buyer of Hall-Scott engines through the 1930s. But Fageol certainly did not use Hall-Scotts exclusively; in fact, Fageol used Waukesha engines heavily, too. Fageol management was always looking ahead at promising trends and new technology and therefore was an early user of aluminum frames and diesel engines in America. Fageol struggled, as most companies did, to remain in business through the Great Depression, only to be purchased in 1939 and renamed Peterbilt. Peterbilt used the old Oakland plant of Fageol until 1960 and offered Hall-Scott engines. [2-91] Hall-Scott continued to power trucks and buses in the decades ahead; in fact, these became the last engines made by the company.

Hall-Scott Tests the Water in the Marine Market

Similar to trucks and buses, marine applications became important to Hall-Scott after World War I. Ironically, the engine market for boats was even more crowded than the market for trucks and buses, so success in powering boats might have been more difficult. Whereas only a handful of truck and bus engine producers could be found in the 1920s and 1930s, the number of marine engine makers surpassed truck and bus makers by a factor of several fold. The April 1931 edition of *Motor Boating* magazine, which catered mostly to fans of race boats, yachts, and other large pleasure boats, listed the major American boat and marine engine makers for comparison. [2-92] The magazine included 37 "Leading Marine Engines" (gasoline), 15 "Leading Diesel Engines," and 9 "American Outboard Engines" makers. Some name duplication among these lists shrinks the total number, but only by a small bit. Six of the firms in the list of "Leading Marine Engine" makers also were found in the "Leading Diesel" category (Buda, Consolidated, Maybach, Murray & Tregurtha, Standard, and Winton). Only one outboard engine maker was repeated in the other two lists (Elto), which is not surprising inasmuch as outboards usually power smaller boats. Removing those six repeated gasoline and diesel engine firms and the one outboard supplier renders a total of 54 "leading" American marine engine makers in 1931. Even if it is acknowledged that some of the firms in this total were divisions, subsidiaries, or associated in some other way with another engine maker, 54 remains a large number—about five times larger than the number of "leading" American truck and bus engine makers in the same period. If Hall-Scott management was looking to point its compass into a less competitive sector of the engine market than aircraft and rail, marine might not have been the most promising choice.

The 1931 engine listing in *Motor Boating* reveals that the marine power market was inhabited by companies with a varied product diversity. Few of these engine makers enjoyed popular name recognition, known by people "on the street." That small number of engine companies would include companies such as fire-truck producer American-La France (which called its marine motors Alfco) and auto makers Chrysler and Packard. Some large boats used Liberty engines for years after World War I, and into the 1930s, these celebrated war motors possessed the kind of name recognition that is difficult to buy. They were converted to marine use and marketed by several firms. Many marine engine makers also lacked the name recognition of Chrysler or Packard, but they had histories as engine makers and sold engines for vehicles that did not float. Companies in this category included Buda, Cummins, Fairbanks-Morse, Lycoming, and Winton. Finally, a large number of firms focused exclusively or nearly so on marine power and were known and respected in marine circles, such as Atlas-Imperial (located for years in Oakland near Hall-Scott), Gray, Kermath, Scripps, and Van Blerck. Most companies that made boat motors served the marine market exclusively, such as this last group. A few makers in this group of solely marine suppliers fielded only a single model or a small number of models, such as Vimalert that had but one model in 1931 (a twelve-cylinder gasoline engine developing 400 hp, it was a "marinized" Liberty engine). However, many more built different engine models, such as Superior, which fielded 34 diesel engine models (two-, three-, four-, five-, six-, and eight-cylinder engines, covering a range of 35–840 hp). Marine power clearly was an eclectic market; therefore, achieving a firm beachhead in it after World War I would be a real challenge. Hall-Scott would not be unusual in simultaneously serving marine and other types of customers, nor would it be unusual in that it had only recently entered that market; new firms were continuously moving into and out of marine. Besides, a few Hall-Scott engines, intended by the factory to power airplanes, had already found new homes in the engine bays of a few select boats. These craft, such as the handful of cars sporting high-performance Hall-Scott aircraft engines, could be audacious performers. The existence of these few high-profile boats begged the question of whether Hall-Scott would take the next step and market marine engines. Still, Hall-Scott would have to introduce a dramatic product just to be noticed in these crowded waters.

Two closely related engines released right after the war propelled Hall-Scott to some success and visibility in marine circles: the LM-4 and the LM-6. Neither of these models began as a marine engine, though. Their designation betrayed their origin ("L" for Liberty engine) and their application ("M" for marine). As seen in the Hall-Scott postwar aircraft engine program, the company elected to exploit its close connection to the Liberty engine by dipping into the Liberty parts bin for its first marine motors. These Liberty parts often were similar to Hall-Scott parts anyway. The four-cylinder LM-4 produced 125 hp; the six-cylinder LM-6 (and LM-6a) produced 200 hp (at least at first). These numbers are similar to the numbers of the wartime motors on which they were based. [2-93] The LM engine came in several versions. The LM-6 and LM-6a used many interchangeable parts and produced equal power but differed in their cylinder construction. The LM-6 used cast iron for the cylinders, whereas the LM-6a used steel cylinders with a copper water-jacketed manifold. This difference in construction made for a difference in weight. Because these marine engines used water that was drawn from around the boat for cooling, operating the LM-6a in sea water made it subject to rapid degradation. Therefore, the steel-cylindered LM was suitable for operation only in freshwater. In fact, Hall-Scott recommended, "For general all-around use we strongly recommend the cast iron cylinder motor as being smoother, more durable and dependable." The iron LM-6 weighed 1290 pounds, and the steel LM-6a weighed 1165 pounds, about 135 pounds less. The LM-4 weighed 1070 pounds, not that much less than its six-cylinder sibling; however, the LM-4 created 75 less horsepower. The cylinder dimensions of the LM, with all models using a common 5-inch bore and a 7-inch stroke, might sound familiar—they were the same as those of the Liberty engine. A Hall-Scott brochure dated 1920 referred to some boats receiving their LMs, and winning races, in 1919, making for an introduction following quite soon after the end of World War I. The use of Liberty parts afforded Hall-Scott several advantages, one being speed at bringing new engine models to market.

The LM boasted of having many of the outstanding features of the Liberty, in addition to its respectable output. All LM engines carried over the use of an overhead camshaft, twin ignition, aluminum pistons, and hemispherical combustion chambers from the latest Hall-Scott aircraft engines, and the six-cylinder LM had a seven-main-bearing crankshaft. The six-cylinder models quickly benefited from some evolutionary improvements, such as acquiring an enclosed camshaft and the steel-cylindered LM-6a soon reporting a revised horsepower

117

The cover of an LM-6 brochure.

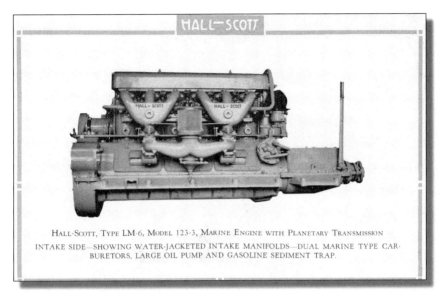

HALL-SCOTT, TYPE LM-6, MODEL 123-3, MARINE ENGINE WITH PLANETARY TRANSMISSION
INTAKE SIDE—SHOWING WATER-JACKETED INTAKE MANIFOLDS—DUAL MARINE TYPE CAR-
BURETORS, LARGE OIL PUMP AND GASOLINE SEDIMENT TRAP.

The intake side of the Hall-Scott Liberty-based LM-6.

figure of 250 hp at 1900 rpm. Another variant, the LM-6f, came with iron
cylinders, a planetary transmission, and a feature not seen on earlier Hall-Scott
engines or the production Liberty, a "semi-supercharger." [2-94] The charging
of air into the engine implied in the name came from a novel source—the airflow
created by the spinning flywheel of the engine. Superchargers are belt- or gear-
driven pumps that force extra air into the engine, sometimes increasing performance tremendously. The Hall-Scott "semi" version was decidedly tame. The
LM-6f pipework from the flywheel delivered air under light force to the intake
manifold for induction into the engine. The charging effect by this device was
mild and was not driven by belt or gear—hence, the semi-supercharger name.
E.J. Hall received a patent for this device. Although it probably did centrifuge
some of the dust out of the incoming air, it did not make for a reported increase
in engine performance, and it did not become a regular feature on Hall-Scott
engines in the years ahead, let alone those of other companies. Regardless,
the semi-supercharger was interesting, and during this time period, Hall-Scott
engines bristled with clever features. The LM also claimed a very early use
of a full-flow oil filter. Charles Winslow, a pioneering engineer known for his
work in lubrication, said, "The first oil filter that was ever built and applied
directly to an engine was designed and built by [myself] in Vallejo, California,
and applied to a Hall-Scott engine in Berkeley, California..." [2-95] Declaring

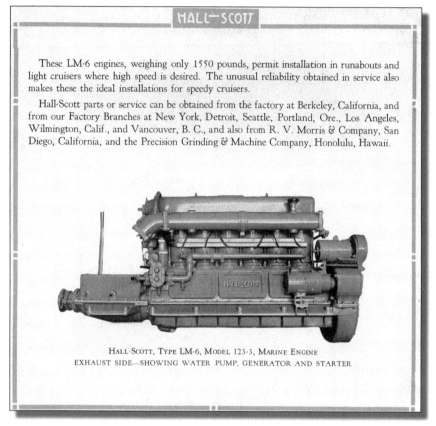

HALL-SCOTT

These LM-6 engines, weighing only 1550 pounds, permit installation in runabouts and light cruisers where high speed is desired. The unusual reliability obtained in service also makes these the ideal installations for speedy cruisers.

Hall-Scott parts or service can be obtained from the factory at Berkeley, California, and from our Factory Branches at New York, Detroit, Seattle, Portland, Ore., Los Angeles, Wilmington, Calif., and Vancouver, B. C., and also from R. V. Morris & Company, San Diego, California, and the Precision Grinding & Machine Company, Honolulu, Hawaii.

HALL-SCOTT, TYPE LM-6, MODEL 123-3, MARINE ENGINE
EXHAUST SIDE—SHOWING WATER PUMP, GENERATOR AND STARTER

The exhaust side of the Hall-Scott LM-6.

"firsts" is often a recipe for enticing pitched arguments among claimants, but Hall-Scott might have a legitimate position here.

The true test of the success of an engine is in real-world use, not on blueprints or on specifications charts, and the LM engine enjoyed immediate success in the water. Maritime historian Stan Grayson called Hall-Scott, now having the LM, an "important force in power boat racing." [2-96] Hall-Scott wasted no time in beginning to crow about the racing success racked up by boats using the new LM engines. The LM-6 made an immediate splash on the racing circuit with numerous victories. In 1919, W.R. Kemp's boat *N'Everthin'* won the Barthel Trophy Race and the Miller Chance Run, and it "broke all American records for displacement boats for 10 miles in American Power Boat Association races at

Detroit." [2-97] A Hall-Scott brochure bragged that the reliability of the engine negated the need for a mechanic to accompany the driver, but that "the outstanding feature of this equipment is the fact that it [the LM-6] is fully eight hundred pounds lighter than any present-day 200 H.P. stock marine engine." The boats *Miss Los Angeles* and *Adieu* won many races with Hall-Scott LM power, too, including the coveted Fisher Trophy in 1921 and 1922. [2-98]

As good as the LMs were, Hall-Scott needed to move away from bolting its separate cylinders to the crankcase, as it had done in aircraft engines. Casting an engine with its cylinders integral increases rigidity and compactness more than does the built-up method. Such an "en bloc" engine might weigh more, but it would make for a more stable, smooth, and compact power plant. Hall-Scott needed to take this major engineering step to maintain its competitive position in the marine market.

Responding to the need for an iron en-bloc marine engine, and having cruised off of scavenged World War I Liberty parts for five years, Hall-Scott released the HSR ("R" for reduction geared) and HSM ("M" for medium duty or direct drive) series of engines around 1925. [9-99] Based on the new four- and six-cylinder engines used to power Fageol buses, Hall-Scott pulled off some engineering "double dipping" again with this new marine engine series. Churning out 60–70 hp in four-cylinder form (4-1/4 × 5-1/2-inch bore and stroke, 312 cubic inches) and 90–100 hp as a six-cylinder (4-1/4 × 5-1/2-inch bore and stroke, 468 cubic inches), these new marine engines were not as powerful as the ones they replaced. It is no surprise that, given their non-aviation origins, the new engines were quite a bit heavier than the L engines. The reduction-geared four-cylinder HSR was 1750 pounds, and the six-cylinder was 2200 pounds; the direct-geared engines were a couple hundred pounds lighter. Worth noting is that some HSM series engines came equipped with the semi-supercharger seen on the earlier LM engines. The light "blower" did not seem to alter performance statistics. In fact, the HSM appears to have been the last Hall-Scott engine series to use this novel item. As expected, the HSM and HSR sported some typical Hall-Scott features, such as an overhead camshaft, hemi head, full-flow oil filtration, and the use of aluminum to save weight. In a Hall-Scott brochure, the company made sure to establish a tie to past glories, saying, "The type HSM engines and also the well known LM equipments have the advantage over other makes in that they are designed, built and tested in the largest and best equipped marine engine plant in the United States and under the direct supervision of Colonel E.J. Hall." [2-100] References to the Liberty Motor were absent; perhaps readers were assumed to make that connection from Hall's military rank. But the HSR and HSM missed the popular 250-hp target that the

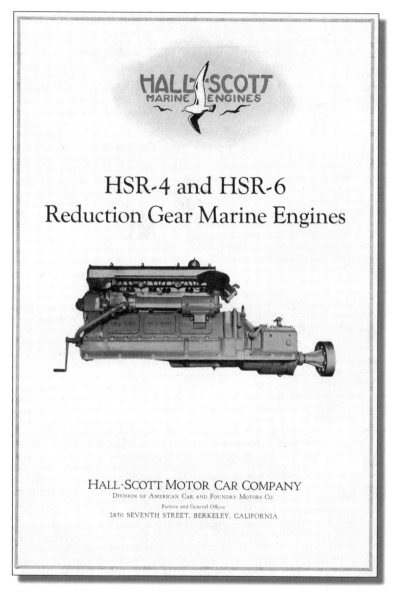

Cover of an HSR brochure. Note the crank attached to the engine.

LM hit. Hall-Scott needed another six-cylinder, en-bloc, iron alloy engine with upwards of 250 or more horsepower if the company was going to be a serious contender in the racing/yachting/work boat marine engine market.

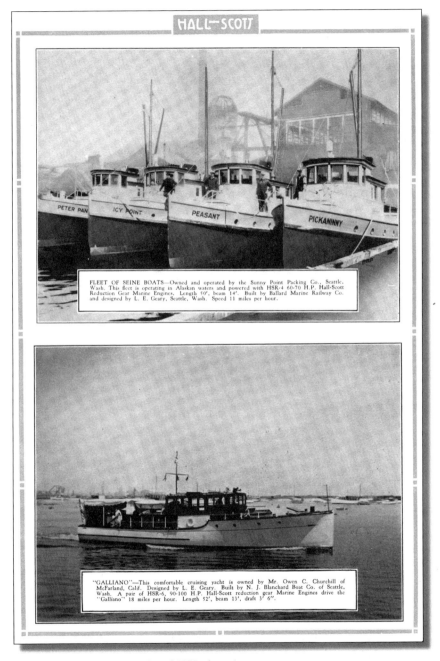

Applications of the HSR-4 and HSR-6 engines.

HALL-SCOTT, TYPE HSR-4, 60-70 HORSE POWER, FOUR-CYLINDER MARINE ENGINE
MANIFOLD SIDE, SHOWING CARBURETOR AND SPECIAL OIL FILTER

H.S.R.-4 SPECIFICATION

4-Cylinder; Bore, 4¼ in., Stroke, 5½ in., Piston displacement, 312.09 cu. in.
60-70 Brake Horse Power at either 600 or 900 R. P. M. of propeller shaft.
Fuel consumption, .6 lbs. per brake horse power hour.
Weight, 1750 lbs. complete. Shipping weight, approximately 2500 lbs.

Type HSR-4 engine is of the same general design and construction as the Type HSR-6, the only difference being in the number of cylinders and rated horse power. The same equipment and accessories are furnished. The high quality workmanship characteristic of all Hall-Scott engines, and the same high grade materials have been used throughout.

HALL-SCOTT, TYPE HSR-4, 60-70 HORSE POWER MARINE ENGINE
WATER PUMP SIDE, SHOWING SPECIAL LARGE GENERATOR

The intake (top) and exhaust (bottom) sides of the Hall-Scott HSR-4.

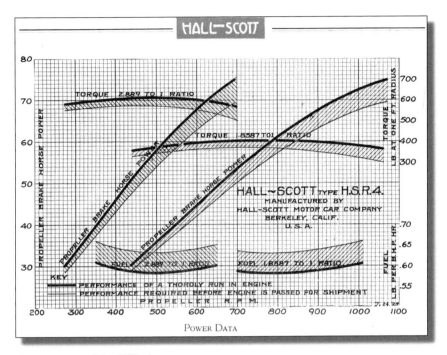

Power curve of the HSR-4.

After World War I, by moving into making engines for tractors, buses, trucks, and boats, Hall-Scott positioned itself to serve a more diversified and potentially more lucrative market. The Hall-Scott enterprise had enjoyed an exciting first 15 years of operation, rising from being a small-scale engine and rail-car maker to becoming a broad engine maker of some international presence. The early 1920s brought continued success to Hall-Scott, which reflected the overall economic good times in the nation. The Hall-Scott story mirrored another business trend of the decade: horizontal integration. In the mid-1920s, Hall-Scott ceased being an independent company and began a new phase in its history.

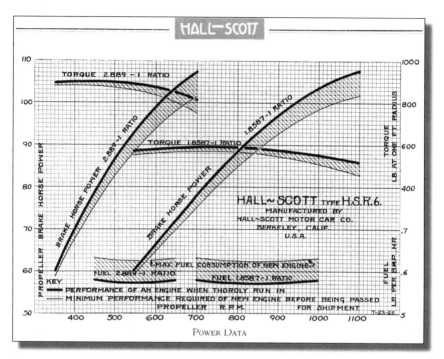

Power curve of the HSR-6.

References

2-1.   Francis Bradford, "A History of the Hall-Scott Motor Car Company," unpublished manuscript, 1989, p. 20. Courtesy of Bancroft Library, University of California, Berkeley, BANC MSS 93/104c.

2-2.   Letter from J. Glidewell to G. Borgeson, July 5, 1984. Courtesy of San Diego Aerospace Museum.

2-3.   Letter from Mrs. E. Hall to T. Sharpsteen, June 15, 1969. Courtesy of Tom Sharpsteen.

2-4.   Letter from J. Glidewell to G. Borgeson, July 5, 1984. Courtesy of San Diego Aerospace Museum.

2-5.   *The Motor Truck*, February 1926, p. 63.

2-6.   *Commercial Car Journal*, August 15, 1917, p. 38. *Commercial Car Journal*, October 15, 1917, p. 35.

2-7.   *The Motor Truck*, January 1925, p. 44.

2-8.   J.E. "Speed" Glidewell, "A Brief History of Hall-Scott Motor Company," unpublished address, 1956, p. 2.

2-9.   *Motor West*, April 15, 1926, p. 26.

2-10. Letter from Mrs. E. Hall to T. Sharpsteen, June 15, 1969. Courtesy of Tom Sharpsteen.

2-11. *San Francisco Bulletin*, July 2, 1921, p. 3. Courtesy of John Perala. See also *The Oakland Tribune Annual Book*, 1922, p. 92.

2-12. *Motor West*, April 15, 1926, p. 26. Letter from J. Glidewell to G. Borgeson, July 5, 1984. Letter courtesy of San Diego Aerospace Museum.

2-13. Letter from J. Glidewell to G. Borgeson, July 5, 1984. Courtesy of San Diego Aerospace Museum.

2-14. *The Oakland Tribune Annual Book*, 1922, p. 92.

2-15. Glidewell estimated production peaked at 750 units daily. J.E. "Speed" Glidewell, "A Brief History of Hall-Scott Motor Company," unpublished address, 1956, p. 2. In 1922, *The Oakland Tribune* estimated production had reached 100 per day and said the factory hoped for 500 daily soon. *The Oakland Tribune Annual Book*, 1922, p. 92. Oliver Searling, chief inspector at Hall-Scott in the 1920s, put the production number at 600–800 per day. Letter from O. Searling to T. Sharpsteen, July 11, 1969. Searling letter courtesy of Tom Sharpsteen.

2-16. "Report on Hall-Scott Motor Car Company, Berkeley, California," 1931, p. 6, unpublished report. Courtesy of Taylor Scott.

2-17. *The New York Times*, September 2, 1925, p. 36. "Report on Hall-Scott Motor Car Company, Berkeley, California," 1931, p. 6, unpublished report. Report courtesy of Taylor Scott. Ruckstell production numbers provided in a letter from G. Chaffin to R. Dias, October 31, 2005. *The History of Eaton Corporation 1911–1985*, The Eaton Corporation [Cleveland, OH], 1985, p. 15.

2-18. "Report on Hall-Scott Motor Car Company, Berkeley, California," 1931, p. 6, also loose sheet, unpublished report. Courtesy of Taylor Scott.

2-19. *National Cyclopaedia of American Biography, Vol. XLIII*, University Microfilms, Ann Arbor, MI, 1967, p. 494.

2-20.   Letter from J. Kirsch (researcher at The Henry Ford) to R. Dias, March 24, 2004.

2-21.   Letter from O. Searing to T. Sharpsteen, July 11, 1969. Courtesy of Tom Sharpsteen.

2-22.   Letter from J. Glidewell to G. Borgeson, July 5, 1984. Courtesy of San Diego Aerospace Museum. Oliver Searling, plant inspector during this period, also mentioned the engine and operations set up in Berkeley to make them. Letter from O. Searling to T. Sharpsteen, July 11, 1969. Searling letter courtesy of Tom Sharpsteen.

2-23.   *National Cyclopaedia of American Biography, Vol. XLIII*, University Microfilms, Ann Arbor, MI, 1967, p. 494. Edmund Keilty, *Interurbans Without Wires; The Rail Motorcar in America*, Interurbans, Glendale, CA, 1979, p. 182.

2-24.   "The Reminiscences of Mr. Harold Hicks," p. 12, Vol. 1, Oral History Section, The Henry Ford, Dearborn, MI.

2-25   Ibid., pp. 8–11.

2-26.   Ibid., p. 10. Hicks said the four-cylinder engine produced 75 hp; Keilty reported that only one car was made and was propelled by two 80-hp engines. Edmund Keilty, *Interurbans Without Wires; The Rail Motorcar in America*, Interurbans, Glendale, CA, 1979, p. 182.

2-27.   "The Reminiscences of Mr. Harold Hicks," p. 20, Vol. 1, Oral History Section, The Henry Ford, Dearborn, MI.

2-28.   Griffith Borgeson, *The Golden Age of the American Racing Car*, second edition, SAE International, Warrendale, PA, 1998, p. 107.

2-29.   Mark Dees, *The Miller Dynasty; A Technical History of the Work of Harry A. Miller, His Associates, and His Successors*, second edition, Hippodrome Publishing, Moorpark, CA, 1994, pp. 76, 79.

2-30.   Francis Bradford, "A History of the Hall-Scott Motor Car Company," unpublished manuscript, 1989, p. 38. Courtesy of Bancroft Library, University of California, Berkeley, BANC MSS 93/104c. *Commercial Car Journal*, December 20, 1926, p. 46.

2-31.   *Commercial Car Journal*, December 20, 1926, p. 46.

2-32.   *Commercial Car Journal*, July 1930, pp. 90, 94, 96.

2-33.   Francis Bradford, "A History of the Hall-Scott Motor Car Company," unpublished manuscript, 1989, p. 38. Courtesy of Bancroft Library, University of California, Berkeley, BANC MSS 93/104c. J.E. "Speed" Glidewell, "A Brief History of Hall-Scott Motor Company," unpublished address, 1956, p. 2.

2-34.   "Report on Hall-Scott Motor Car Company, Berkeley, California," 1931, p. AA-9, unpublished report. Courtesy of Taylor Scott. William Nelson, Hall-Scott binder, financial section, p. 13. Courtesy of William Nelson. Nelson kept many handwritten or typed company records in a binder. Letter from K. Ernst to R. Dias, April 17, 2005.

2-35.   "Report on Hall-Scott Motor Car Company, Berkeley, California," 1931, pp. AA-5–AA-8, unpublished report. Courtesy of Taylor Scott. William Nelson, Hall-Scott binder, financial section, p. 13. Courtesy of William Nelson. Nelson kept many handwritten or typed company records in a binder.

2-36.   "Report on Hall-Scott Motor Car Company, Berkeley, California," 1931, pp. 29, CC-8, CC-9, unpublished report. Courtesy of Taylor Scott.

2-37.   Francis Bradford, "A History of the Hall-Scott Motor Car Company," unpublished manuscript, 1989, p. 18. Courtesy of Bancroft Library, University of California, Berkeley, BANC MSS 93/104c.

2-38.   Philip Dickey, *The Liberty Engine, 1918–1942*, The Smithsonian Institution Press, Washington, DC, 1968, p. 74.

2-39.   Francis Bradford, "A History of the Hall-Scott Motor Car Company," unpublished manuscript, 1989, pp. 17–18. Courtesy of Bancroft Library, University of California, Berkeley, BANC MSS 93/104c.

2-40.   Donald Pattillo, *Pushing the Envelope; The American Aircraft Industry*, The University of Michigan Press, Ann Arbor, MI, 1998, p. 39.

2-41.   "Report on Hall-Scott Motor Car Company, Berkeley, California," 1931, loose sheet, unpublished report. Courtesy of Taylor Scott.

2-42.   Bill Gunston, *World Encyclopedia of Aero Engines*, Patrick Stephens Limited, Newbury Park, UK, 1998, p. 85. Herschel Smith, *Aircraft Piston Engines, From the Manly Balzer to the Continental Tiara*, Sunflower University Press, Manhattan, KS, 1986, p. 16.

2-43.   William Wagner, *Continental! Its Motors and Its People*, Aero Publishers, Fallbrook, CA, 1983, p. 57.

2-44. Herschel Smith, *Aircraft Piston Engines, From the Manly Balzer to the Continental Tiara*, Sunflower University Press, Manhattan, KS, 1986, p. 191.

2-45. Francis Bradford, "A History of the Hall-Scott Motor Car Company," unpublished manuscript, 1989, p. 9. Courtesy of Bancroft Library, University of California, Berkeley, BANC MSS 93/104c. Bradford speculated that much of the design work was done in Detroit because Brill was expected to be a major user of the engine, but Brill never became an exclusive, or even heavy, user of Hall-Scott power. Edmund Keilty, *Interurbans Without Wires; The Rail Motorcar in America*, Interurbans, Glendale, CA, 1979, pp. 85–101.

2-46. Horse Power Chart—Hall-Scott Engines, n.d.

2-47. Francis Bradford, "A History of the Hall-Scott Motor Car Company," unpublished manuscript, 1989, p. 9. Courtesy of Bancroft Library, University of California, Berkeley, BANC MSS 93/104c. The Model 350 was unusual from other Hall-Scott engines, in that it had a two-piece head, with each piece covering three of the cylinders.

2-48. Mike Schafer, *Vintage Diesel Locomotives*, Motorbooks International, Osceola, WI, 1998, p. 12.

2-49. J.B. McCall, "Dieselization of American Railroads: A Case Study," in *Essays in Economic and Business History*, Edwin Perkins, ed., Vol. III, Macmillan, Basingstoke, Hampshire, UK, 1984, p. 155.

2-50. "Report on Hall-Scott Motor Car Company, Berkeley, California," 1931, p. AA-9, unpublished report. Courtesy of Taylor Scott.

2-51. Francis Bradford, "A History of the Hall-Scott Motor Car Company," unpublished manuscript, 1989, p. 9. Courtesy of Bancroft Library, University of California, Berkeley, BANC MSS 93/104c.

2-52. J.B. McCall, "Dieselization of American Railroads: A Case Study," in *Essays in Economic and Business History*, Edwin Perkins, ed., Vol. III, Macmillan, Basingstoke, Hampshire, UK, 1984, p. 155.

2-53. "Report on Hall-Scott Motor Car Company, Berkeley, California," 1931, p. 25, unpublished report. Courtesy of Taylor Scott.

2-54. James Laux, "Diesel Trucks and Buses; Their Gradual Spread in the United States," in *The Economic and Social Effects of the Spread of Motor Vehicles,* Theo Barker, ed., Macmillan, Basingstoke, Hampshire, UK, 1987, p. 100.

2-55.   Mike Schafer, *Vintage Diesel Locomotives*, Motorbooks International, Osceola, WI, 1998, p. 12.

2-56.   J.B. McCall, "Dieselization of American Railroads: A Case Study," in *Essays in Economic and Business History*, Edwin Perkins, ed., Vol. III, Macmillan, Basingstoke, Hampshire, UK, 1984, p. 154.

2-57.   Mike Schafer, *Vintage Diesel Locomotives*, Motorbooks International, Osceola, WI, 1998, p. 19.

2-58.   *Commercial Car Journal*, March 15, 1917, p. 13.

2-59.   J.B. McCall, "Dieselization of American Railroads: A Case Study," in *Essays in Economic and Business History*, Edwin Perkins, ed., Vol. III, Macmillan, Basingstoke, Hampshire, UK, 1984, p. 152.

2-60.   Robert Pripps, *The Big Book of Caterpillar*, Voyager Press, Stillwater, OK, 2000, p. 75.

2-61.   Reynold Wik, *Benjamin Holt and Caterpillar*, American Society of Agricultural Engineers, St. Joseph, MI, 1984, p. 100.

2-62.   Robert Pripps, *The Big Book of Caterpillar*, Voyager Press, Stillwater, OK, 2000, p. 75.

2-63.   *Western Machinery World*, January and February 1922, reprint, p. 2.

2-64.   Ibid. p. 41.

2-65.   Lorry Dunning, *Ultimate American Farm Tractor Data Book*, Motorbooks International, Osceola, WI, 1999, p. 156. A more recent and more detailed look at the Holt 2 Ton and its Hall-Scott engine is provided in Lorry Dunning, "Simple Compact Crawler, Large Complicated History: The Story of Holt's 2 Ton," *Antique Caterpillar Machinery Owners Club*, Issue 54, March–April 2004, pp. 8–13.

2-66.   Letter from E. Hall to P. Holt, November 24, 1922, Holt Archival Collection, Haggin Museum/Archive, Stockton, CA. Found by Lorry Dunning, historical consultant.

2-67.   Letter from L. Scott to P. Holt, April 7, 1921, Holt Archival Collection, Haggin Museum/Archive, Stockton, CA. Found by Lorry Dunning, historical consultant.

2-68.   *Western Machinery World*, January and February 1922, reprint, p. 1.

2-69.   Letter from Mrs. E. Hall to T. Sharpsteen, June 15, 1969. Courtesy of Tom Sharpsteen.

2-70.   Letter from P. Holt to H. Preble, September 24, 1921, Holt Archival Collection, Haggin Museum/Archive, Stockton, CA. Found by Lorry Dunning, historical consultant.

2-71.   Lorry Dunning, *Ultimate American Farm Tractor Data Book*, Motorbooks International, Osceola, WI, 1999, p. 156. *Western Machinery World*, January and February 1922, reprint, p. 2.

2-72.   Letter from R. Springer to P. Holt, January 20, 1922, Holt Archival Collection, Haggin Museum/Archive, Stockton, CA. Found by Lorry Dunning, historical consultant.

2-73.   Letter from Hall-Scott official (name unclear) to Mr. Shepard (Holt official), July 13, 1922. Courtesy of Haggin Museum. Found by Lorry Dunning, historical consultant.

2-74.   Contract between Hall-Scott Motor Car Company and Holt Manufacturing, October 17, 1922, Holt Archival Collection, Haggin Museum/Archive, Stockton, CA. Found by Lorry Dunning, historical consultant.

2-75.   Lorry Dunning, "Simple Compact Crawler, Large Complicated History: The Story of Holt's 2 Ton," *Antique Caterpillar Machinery Owners Club*, Issue 54, March–April 2004, p. 8.

2-76.   Contract between Hall-Scott Motor Car Company and Holt Manufacturing, October 17, 1922, pp. 1, 5.

2-77.   Letter from J. Glidewell to G. Borgeson, July 5, 1984. Courtesy of San Diego Aerospace Museum.

2-78.   Eli Bail, "Fageol," *Motor Coach Age*, November–December 1991, p. 4. G.N. Georgano, ed., *Complete Encyclopedia of Commercial Vehicles*, Motorbooks International, Osceola, WI, 1979, p. 226. The Fageol name also appeared on trucks built by Twin Coach from 1950 to 1954.

2-79.   Francis Bradford, "A History of the Hall-Scott Motor Car Company," unpublished manuscript, 1989, p. 37b. Courtesy of Bancroft Library, University of California, Berkeley, BANC MSS 93/104c. *Automobile Magazine*, October 1999, p. 83.

2-80.   G.N. Georgano, ed., *Complete Encyclopedia of Commercial Vehicles*, Motorbooks International, Osceola, WI, 1979, p. 226.

2-81.   *The Motor Truck*, February 1922, p. 67.

2-82.   James Laux, "Diesel Trucks and Buses; Their Gradual Spread in the United States," in *The Economic and Social Effects of the Spread of Motor*

Vehicles, Theo Barker, ed., Macmillan, Basingstoke, Hampshire, UK, 1987, p. 101.

2-83.   Debra Brill, *History of the J.G. Brill Company*, Indiana University Press, Bloomington, IN, 2001, p. 198.   Discussions of early Fageol production can be found in Eli Bail, "Fageol," *Motor Coach Age*, November–December 1991, and in G.N. Georgano, ed., *Complete Encyclopedia of Commercial Vehicles*, Motorbooks International, Osceola, WI, 1979, pp. 226–227.

2-84.   Letter from J. Glidewell to G. Borgeson, July 5, 1984.   Courtesy of San Diego Aerospace Museum.

2-85.   *The Motor Truck*, March 1923, p. 27.   *The Motor Truck*, July 1923, p. 9.

2-86.   *The Motor Truck*, July 1923, p. 9.   This was a review of the Fageol Parlor Car, which also used the HSF-4 engine.

2-87.   *The Motor Truck*, January 1925, p. 17.

2-88.   *The Motor Truck*, February 1925, pp. 44–45.

2-89.   G.N. Georgano, ed., *Complete Encyclopedia of Commercial Vehicles*, Motorbooks International, Osceola, WI, 1979, p. 227.

2-90.   Debra Brill, *History of the J.G. Brill Company*, Indiana University Press, Bloomington, IN, 2001, p. 164.

2-91.   G.N. Georgano, ed., *Complete Encyclopedia of Commercial Vehicles*, Motorbooks International, Osceola, WI, 1979, p. 490.

2-92.   *Motor Boating*, April 1931, p. 100.

2-93.   Hall-Scott Motor Car Company Incorporated Marine Engines and Marine Installations, brochure, 1920.   The company could not help but add in the introduction Colonel Hall's Distinguished Service Medal, his "exceptionally meritorious and conspicuous service rendered in the designing of the Liberty engine," and that he was "reputed to be one of the leading mechanical engineers in this country and abroad," all of which would be a "guarantee to our prospective customers that they will receive a product entirely up to Hall-Scott standard."

2-94.   Stan Grayson, *Engines Afloat, From Early Days to D-Day, Vol. 1: The Gasoline Era*, Devereux Books, Marblehead, MA, 1999, pp. 83, 85.

2-95.   Ibid., p. 85.

2-96.   Ibid., p. 82.

2-97.   Hall-Scott Motor Car Company Incorporated Marine Engines and Marine Installations, brochure, 1920. Stan Grayson, *Engines Afloat, From Early Days to D-Day, Vol. l: The Gasoline Era*, Devereux Books, Marblehead, MA, 1999, pp. 81–83.

2-98.   Stan Grayson, *Engines Afloat, From Early Days to D-Day, Vol. l: The Gasoline Era*, Devereux Books, Marblehead, MA, 1999, pp. 82–83.

2-99.   Type HSR-6–Model A/Type HSR-4–Model A, brochure, circa 1925.

2-100. Medium Duty HSM Type/Heavy Duty HSR Type, brochure, circa 1927.

CHAPTER THREE

ACF's NEW ENGINE DIVISION

For its first 15 years of operation, Hall-Scott introduced a variety of engines with very different performance objectives, usually stayed profitable (most years just barely, and a couple of years greatly), and ventured into some new markets and out of others. The path of the young company can be described as rather unpredictable and perhaps even impulsive. In the 1920s, though, the adolescent Hall-Scott settled down considerably when it became tied to an older and more established company. Under this new connection to a larger enterprise, Hall-Scott enjoyed making products of great historical impact, recorded a few years of high financial returns, lost the leadership of its founders, and committed itself to serving a handful of markets that would last through the remainder of its years as an engine company.

The marriage of ACF and Hall-Scott can be inferred from this emblem.

Hall-Scott Motor Car Company Is Purchased

The rise of Hall-Scott in the 1910s and 1920s made it attractive for purchase by any number of companies looking to cash in on the growing truck, bus, boat, and engine fields. It should not be surprising that on September 4, 1925, *The New York Times* reported that railcar maker American Car and Foundry (ACF) had purchased Hall-Scott. [3-1] Apparently, ACF was in the market to obtain an engine maker, and while "speculative gossip linked the names of the Mack Truck Company and White Motors" to ACF, the conspicuous successes of Hall-Scott had also made it an enterprise to watch. The new owner of Hall-Scott was quite a substantial company, operating 19 rail-car plants and 18 foundries, plus additional facilities across the Midwest and the East. In the 1923–1924 fiscal year, the company reported building 45,645 new rail cars and rebuilding 11,902. [3-2] Hall-Scott was a firm of some import; its stock value totaled an impressive $4 million, a tangible indication of how successful Hall-Scott had become in 15 years of operation. [3-3] ACF leadership envisioned purchasing Hall-Scott and Fageol and then combining the two companies, which would make a truck/bus/engine division to complement the primary ACF enterprise of making rail cars. Although Fageol and Hall-Scott had a marketing relationship, and the Fageol name was placed on the Hall-Scott engines it ran in its trucks, *The New York Times* article on the purchase of Hall-Scott noted that ACF executives stated that no corporate connections existed between Hall-Scott and Fageol. Even if the two companies had no publicly acknowledged corporate connections, a degree of the success that each company enjoyed was linked to the other.

ACF installed this plaque in one of its buses, underscoring the connection between Hall-Scott and ACF.

Actually, ACF was looking for more than just an engine maker to purchase in the mid-1920s. ACF underwent vigorous vertical and horizontal integration in this period, dramatically expanding the size and scope of the company, and Hall-Scott amounted to a critical part of that process. Managers at ACF felt compelled to tell *The New York Times* that its company was not "endeavoring to acquire control of companies which are customers of the Hall-Scott Motor Car Company," mitigating the appearance of an ACF feeding frenzy. [3-4] The ACF wheeling and dealing was far from over when it purchased Hall-Scott, however. The ACF product range embraced vehicles and craft, broadly speaking. ACF also entered the luxury boat market, producing upscale cruisers and yachts that often featured Hall-Scott engines, not coincidentally. Back to wheel-driven craft, ACF looked to broaden its rail offerings more into the light rail segment, too. Thus, in 1925, ACF and J.G. Brill, a Philadelphia-based streetcar and trolley maker, entered into a complicated relationship. [3-5] Brill had been engaged in some aggressive corporate maneuvering of its own, acquiring firms and planning to do more. For example, during this period, Brill had picked up a large block of stock in the White Motor Company, a maker of trucks and truck engines. Brill bought a large share of stock in Hall-Scott, Fageol Motors of Ohio, and ACF Motors for $24 million, finishing this fit of horizontal integration. [3-6] Now the ACF umbrella would also have Brill residing under it. Interestingly, the West Coast branch of Fageol was not part of the deal. When the dust settled in early 1926, American Car and Foundry Company (a holding company) controlled the Brill Corporation (another holding company), which operated two separate wings, one being overseen by the American Car and Foundry Motors Company (ACF Motors, owned 100% by Brill), which in turn owned 100% of the stock of the Hall-Scott Motor Car Company and 90% of Fageol Motors (of Ohio). American Car and Foundry Company was the parent company and made nothing, but American Car and Foundry Motors Company, through its Hall-Scott and Fageol divisions, made engines and vehicles. Here, Hall-Scott retained some token of self-control: Bert Scott assumed one of the nine director positions on the board of ACF Motors, and Elbert Hall (described in the *San Francisco Chronicle* as a "collaborator with Colonel Jesse G. Vincent in designing the Liberty motor") became vice president of engineering. The Brill Corporation also kept another wing of its business under its corporate umbrella, the J.G. Brill Company, which controlled the American Car Company, Kuhlman Car Company, Wason Manufacturing, and CIE J.G. Brill, companies it possessed when it linked itself with ACF. [3-7] The firms overseen by American Car and Foundry Company changed over time, but Hall-Scott resided under this corporate mantle for nearly 30 years.

This arrangement with ACF provided Hall-Scott some much-needed protection in an industry marked by an ominous mortality rate. The Hall-Scott business arrangement with Fageol benefited the Berkeley engine maker in several significant ways. As witnessed in any number of relationships between distant leaders and those being led, Hall-Scott personnel sometimes chafed under orders or management figures from ACF; thus, the marriage between Hall-Scott and ACF was not without problems. [3-8] Regardless, the relationship seemed positive overall for the small engine maker. Hall-Scott had achieved some success with its own engines while it was independently owned, but now as part of a conglomerate, it secured what was likely to be a reliable "in-house" buyer for its products. ACF continued producing Fageol buses after the purchase but built its own, too, which usually used Hall-Scott engines. Also, being part of a large business afforded Hall-Scott cover from economic downturns, which became more than a hypothetical point in the 1930s with the Great Depression. Its new parent company likewise did not require that Hall-Scott move its location. Production facilities for the parent company and related firms included Berkeley, Detroit, Kent, and Philadelphia, with ACF headquartered in New York City. The Hall-Scott purchase in 1925 also might further explain the departure of Hall-Scott from making aircraft engines, as ACF more closely refocused Hall-Scott to serving its need for engines. The purchase of Hall-Scott by ACF ranks as one of the most significant single events for the engine maker in the post-World War I era.

Hall-Scott products powered buses that rode on the cutting edge of industry, an association that aided both Hall-Scott and the companies with which it was now related. The Fageol Safety Coach, powered by a Hall-Scott engine, was such a vehicle. ACF and Fageol also each introduced gasoline-electric coaches around 1926, and both companies picked Hall-Scott units to drive the electric motors in their new vehicles. [3-9] These gas-electric coaches delivered power to their wheels basically like some contemporary smaller locomotives, in which an internal combustion engine turned an electric generator that fed current to electric motors attached to the wheels of the vehicle. This gasoline-electric arrangement obviated the need for a transmission and thereby simplified coach operation, with no gears to change or clutch to depress. With the frequent stops in urban conditions and the heavy weight of buses, conceivably driver and vehicle fatigue could be greatly lessened by this type of drivetrain. Even with possible drawbacks factored into the picture, such as technical complication and questionable fuel mileage, the idea was reasonable. ACF used the Hall-Scott 90-hp, 4-1/4 × 5-1/2-inch, 468-cubic-inch Model HS-6 to power this unusual vehicle. Although the ACF and Fageol units were early examples of gasoline-electric coaches, a number of makers introduced similar vehicles around 1926, from the universally known Mack, to the popular Twin Coach (led by William and Frank Fageol acting independently of ACF), to the never noticed Liberty Motor Vehicle Company. [3-10] Gasoline-electric drive in large people-movers enjoyed a brief period of popularity, but ultimately the

The Gas-Electric Q.C.f. Coach

THE Q.C.f. Coach is very successfully adapted to gas-electric operation. The engine requirements for gas-electric work are quite severe, imposing a greater amount of continuous operation at full power output than is required for the operation of a coach with mechanical transmission. The engine must be able to withstand the heat of such continuous operation without losing its lubricant and must be able to keep it up for a long time.

These requirements are quite similar to those of aviation work. The Hall-Scott Engine follows very closely the principles of design used in the Liberty aeroplane engine, and comes closer to the ideal for gas-electric service than any other commercial vehicle engine built. It reaches its torque peak at very moderate speed.

Inasmuch as gas-electric units impose heavy stress on certain portions of the chassis frame, the Q.C.f. frame is strongly reinforced so it can absorb these stresses and distribute them throughout the long section of the frame. The side members of the frame where the maximum stresses are thrown are reinforced with a ⅜" channel tightly pressed into place, giving a maximum frame section at this point measuring 11" deep with a 3" flange, and the combined thickness of the main channel and reinforcement is ⅞". The reinforcing channel extends for several feet both in front of and behind the point of maximum stress.

The rear axle arch is built up of two channels pressed from ¼" stock, giving a maximum section 6" deep, with 3" flange and ½" thickness of material.

American Car and Foundry set and followed the major trends in bus making in the 1920s and 1930s, as seen in its Hall-Scott-powered gas-electric bus.

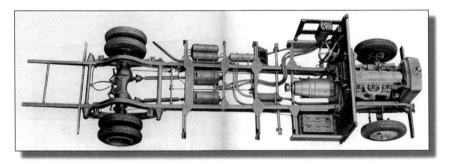

This chassis shot of the ACF gas-electric bus shows the Hall-Scott Model 160.

automatic transmission displaced it as a preferred drive system, with the first automatics appearing in the late 1930s.

Another ACF bus innovation appearing around this time was the snub-nosed 40-passenger Metropolitan Coach, which ACF announced in 1927. It presented a whole new platform that Hall-Scott had to power. [3-11] ACF engineers created a coach constructed somewhat like a streetcar, a product with which ACF was abundantly familiar. Even today, the Metropolitan Coach has a fairly modern appearance because many urban buses have a roughly similar body design as did this ACF bus of the 1920s. *Commercial Car Journal* described the all-steel Metropolitan as being "frameless," with "no chassis frame, the various chassis units, such as rear and front axles and engine, etc., being directly attached to the various parts of the body." [3-12] The efficiencies arising from this type of construction yielded a "weight per passenger seat with full passenger load...over 100 pounds per seat less..." than a standard coach. [3-13] From a visual standpoint, the ACF Metropolitan Coach achieved its modern look in large part through its smooth front, lacking the traditional hood covering the engine. More and more new coaches came out with their engines not in front of the driver but elsewhere on the vehicle, drastically changing the appearance of the buses, the way they were fabricated, and the way they accommodated passengers. The ACF Metro also hastened the demise of wood as a critical material in bus manufacture.

The first series of Metropolitan buses placed their Hall-Scott engines just forward of the rear axle, nestled low in the vehicle. Later models moved the engine to another interesting location. In a later edition of the Metro bus appearing in 1933, engineers canted the Hall-Scott power plant over on its side, fixing

140

Another modern design, the Hall-Scott-powered ACF Metropolitan Coach.

it underneath the bus floor. [3-14] Tipping the engine, which previously had been "vertical," in this manner made it "horizontal." This was a new way to fit an engine into a bus, but it proved popular with manufacturers in the decades ahead. Innovations such as this kept ACF on the forefront of bus manufacture. The fact that ACF announced this major engineering move during the depths of the Great Depression, committing sizable resources in the process, makes it all the more impressive.

This view of the chassis of the early series Metropolitan shows the unusual placement of the Hall-Scott 468-cubic-inch Model 160.

The Hall-Scott horizontal engine used in the later Metropolitan Coach was not an all-new engine *per se*, and it is not to be confused with a horizontally opposed engine. Instead, Hall's horizontal engine was an in-line, vertical engine tipped 90 degrees. To reduce costs, rather than build a new engine from the ground up, Hall-Scott engineers took an existing engine and modified it to run on its side. For the first horizontal Hall-Scott engine, the Model 180, engineers used the Model 175 as the base engine from which the new one emerged. [3-15] Hall-Scott built horizontal engines, which were always altered versions of an existing vertical engine, from the 1930s until the company closed. With Hall-Scott's parent company leading the coach industry down this new design path, and with ACF using Hall-Scott engines in its products, Hall-Scott became well versed in building horizontal engines.

The Model 175 was a road-tested, popular truck and bus engine for Hall-Scott, so it provided a good basis for the new horizontal unit. It was an all-new engine, not derived from another model, and was first sold around 1930. [3-16] The Model 175 boasted of many heavy-duty features common to Hall-Scott engines, such as alloy iron block, seven main-bearing crankshaft, connecting rods twice as heavy as those on most competitors' other trucks (those of the Model 175 weighed 113.5 ounces, whereas those in the Ford V-8 weighed 16.5 ounces), dual ignition system, five piston rings (other independent engine makers commonly used three or four, with the Ford V-8 using three), hemi head, and overhead camshaft with cross-flow cylinder head. [3-17] As Hall-Scott did with many of its engines, the company took the base Model 175 (5 × 6-inch bore and stroke, 707 cubic inches) and then released slightly modified versions, the Model 176 (increasing the bore to 5-1/4 inches, 779 cubic inches) and the Model 177 (increasing the bore to 5-1/2 inches, 855 cubic inches).

The Hall-Scott 707-cubic-inch Model 175.

An exploded view of the Hall-Scott Model 175, showing the unit construction.

Hall-Scott found some sales to buses, fire trucks, and even a few long-haul trucks, both as OEM equipment and as "repowers." Unlike bus engines that ACF coveted for its own vehicles, the truck engines could be sold to other makers, and the West Coast-based Kenworth used the Hall-Scott Model 175 in its 38,500-lb gross vehicle weight Model 385 in the 1930s. [3-18]

When ACF announced its first (short-lived) truck in 1931, it featured a choice of two Hall-Scott engines: the 110-hp Model 160 and the 186-hp Model 175. Until that point, Hall-Scott land vehicle engines had powered primarily buses, so when *Commercial Car Journal* introduced the new ACF truck, it noted, "While the Hall-Scott engines used are quite familiar in the bus field, these particular types are not well known to the truck operator." [3-19]

The engines may have been little known outside bus circles, but they were fine performers. The Models 175, 176, and 177 engines developed 186, 191, and 203 hp, respectively, and healthy torque numbers of 570, 630, and 690 ft. lb., respectively. [3-20] These enormous figures, two or more than three times the torque generated by the first Hall-Scott truck engines, actually tested the limits of contemporary driveline components.

With the ability of the Model 175 and its derivatives to tax many truck transmissions then available, Hall-Scott began production of transmissions hefty enough to handle the enormous power available. Hall-Scott had the engineering talent to design and build a quality transmission, as it had built successful engines for other engine builders and completed projects such as the Ruckstell

When ACF released its ill-timed and short-lived truck, the Highway Express, around 1931, it offered two engines—the Hall-Scott Model 160 or Model 175.

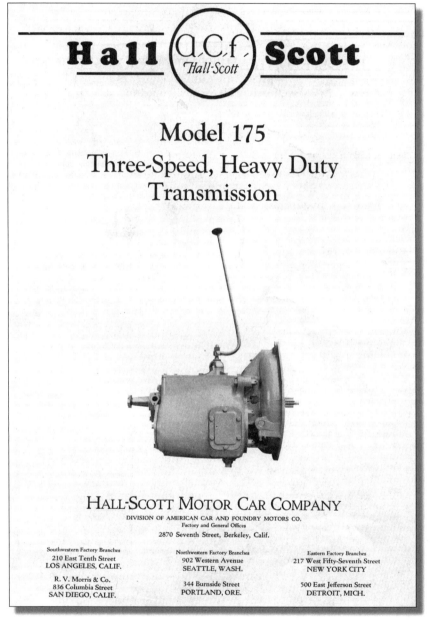

Hall-Scott management believed there was demand for this heavy-duty transmission, but the market demonstrated otherwise.

axle. The heavy-duty, three-speed transmission of the Hall-Scott Model 175 used nickel alloy heat-treated gears and shafts, ground shaft splines, heavy oversized bearings throughout, and it had a power takeoff opening. [3-21] The transmission did not enjoy great popularity, however, and began to collect dust in warehouses, leading to Hall-Scott soon ending the production of it. Likewise, Hall-Scott realized fairly disappointing production numbers for its Models 175, 176, and 177, with 415, 31, and 173 units built, respectively. [3-22] In spite of the low number of units sold, the Model 175 could still be viewed as a success, especially if the popularity of its horizontal derivatives is considered.

Quite a bit of modification was needed to transform the Model 175, as tough as it was, into the Model 180. [3-23] For example, engine mounts had to be changed. The Model 180 had to be attached to the frame with engine parts that were strong enough to support its weight. To accomplish this, the Model 180 had a one-piece block, instead of the two-piece upper and lower block found in the Model 175, which better accommodated the different stresses in the horizontal mounting. Ensuring proper lubrication was of prime concern to engineers when designing a horizontal engine. A vertical engine typically has its oil reservoir at its bottom, in a sump below the crankshaft in the crankcase or oil pan, from which oil is pumped throughout the engine, allowing it to flow back down to the reservoir by gravity. But in a horizontal engine, the sump is no longer below the crankshaft and therefore is no longer the lowest place on the engine, so another collection point had to be made. What's more, in a vertical engine turned on its side, oil might pool in undesirable places, such as around the valve guides, while oil starvation may occur at the same time in other parts. To solve these problems, Hall-Scott engineers fashioned a separate "dry sump" to collect the oil, and an interesting stack of three gears at both ends of the engine that would carry oil to the other end. Engine accessories such as the generator and oil filter had to be moved. Likewise, the placement of several components had to be altered to make them accessible for servicing in this new configuration. The Model 180 posted a higher maximum engine speed than the Model 175 (2200 rpm in the Model 180 versus 2000 rpm in the Model 175), but both were rated basically as having the same horsepower, with the Model 175 having an inconsequential 2-hp edge over the 184 hp of the Model 180. [3-24]

Hall-Scott successfully engineered solutions to all these challenges, and two horizontal versions of the Models 175, the Models 180 and 190, soon emerged, with a few others appearing in the years ahead. The Model 180 had the

Berkeley, Wilmington, Calif.
Seattle, Wash.

Portland, Ore.; Vancouver, B.C.
New York, N. Y.

Model 180 (Horizontal)

For Bus, Truck and Industrial Service

CONDENSED SPECIFICATIONS

General—Cylinders horizontal with overhead camshaft and valve mechanism.

Size—5" bore; 6" stroke; 706.8 cu. inches displacement.

*Horsepower—175 at 2200 R.P.M.

Weight—1868 pounds with all accessories, excepting compressor.

Suspension—4 point with rubber mountings.

Accessory Drive—4 strand 1/2" pitch roller chain.

Ignition—Dual, battery, 12 volt.

Carburetor—2" S.A.E.

Sump Capacity—7 gallons.

Crankcase—Cast iron.

Cylinder Block—Cast integral with crankcase, fitted with removable sleeves.

Cylinder Head—Single chrome nickel iron casting.

Crankshaft—7 main bearings chrome nickel alloy heat treated.

Connecting Rods—Chrome nickel alloy heat treated.

Main Bearings—3 1/4" diameter.

†Main Bearing Lengths—2-3/16", 1-9/16", 1-9/16", 1-9/16", 1-9/16", 1-9/16", and 2-9/16".

†Connecting Rod Bearings—2 3/4" diameter, 2" length.

Camshaft Bearings—1 3/8" diameter, 1 3/4", 1 5/8", 1 5/8", 1 5/8", 1 5/8", 1 5/8", 1 3/4" long.

Rockerarms—Curved shoe follower.

Pistons—Aluminum alloy.

Piston Pin—1 3/8" diameter floating in piston and rod.

Retainers—Aluminum alloy Hall-Scott type.

Cooling—Centrifugal pump.

Exhaust Manifold—3-piece special alloy

Intake Manifold—Hot spot controlled single carburetor, with provision for gas eliminator valve.

Flywheel Housing—Heat treated aluminum S.A.E. No. 2 S.A.E. standard.

Spark Plugs—12 plugs metric standard thread.

Additional Equipment—Oil cooler, oil filter, Evans fuel pump, 6 cu. ft. engine driven and oiled air compressor, generator mounted on chassis and belt driven, distributor, power take-off, clutch, transmission.

*Hall-Scott engines are rated at their actual net horsepower with full accessory equipment; no deductions are necessary.

†Bearing lengths are actual and do not include length of fillets or rounded edges.

A brochure for the Hall-Scott Model 180.

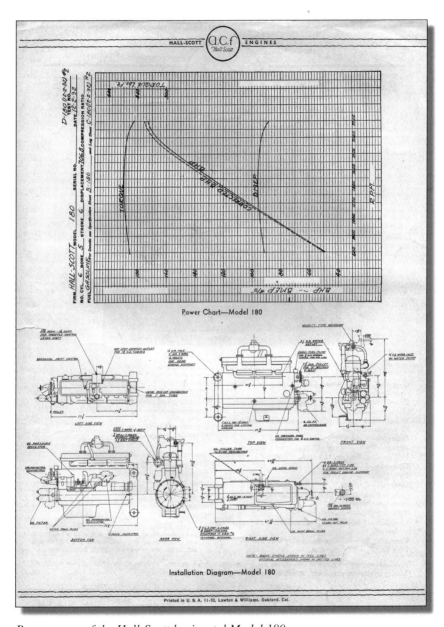

Power Chart—Model 180

Installation Diagram—Model 180

Power curve of the Hall-Scott horizontal Model 180.

149

5 × 6-inch cylinder measurements of the Model 175, but the Model 190 developed more horsepower, coming from its slightly larger bore of 5-1/4 inches, a higher compression ratio of 6:1 (which needed higher octane fuel to prevent "knocking" or pre-detonation), and a different intake manifold and carburetion. [3-25] The Model 190 provided extra power (211 hp and a locomotive-like 600 lb. ft. of torque at only 1000 rpm) for buses to negotiate steeper hills, carry larger loads, and reach higher speeds. Buses with a Model 190 engine could beat almost any other buses on the road. According to one driver who navigated coaches over the daunting grade between Bakersfield and Los Angeles that was dubbed the "Grapevine," his older bus used to be regularly passed there by more powerful Greyhounds, but with his new Hall-Scott Model 190-powered Brill, "We can now blow the 'Hounds' off the road." [3-26]

ACF took advantage of the new Hall-Scott Models 180 and 190 engines, powering many hundreds of its buses with Berkeley-made products but perhaps not taking full advantage of their sales potential in the larger bus market. As can be gleaned by looking at ACF sales literature, the company viewed offering Hall-Scott engines in its buses as a distinct sales advantage and a prime reason to buy an ACF coach as opposed to some other brand. Therefore, Hall Scott sales to outside bus makers as original equipment engines were sharply limited. Consequently, only minor bus makers such as Kenworth and Wentworth and Irwin used Hall-Scotts. In fact, bus specification charts from trade magazines of the 1930s do not show any other bus makers, which sometimes excluded nominal brands, using Hall-Scott engines as original equipment. Bradford said that because of the covetous relationship of ACF with the products of its engine division, "Opportunities abounded for sales but could not be accepted." [3-27] Even with the constricted sales of these new engines, the Models 180 and 190 were successful by company standards, and Hall-Scott ultimately produced 1,200 Model 180 engines and almost 2,500 Model 190 engines. [3-28] The Models 180 and 190 found market acceptance in ACF buses and in other vehicles, such as new fire trucks, and in repowering vehicles that originally used other motors. In the inter-war period, other horizontal models, some of which were not derivative of the Model 175, included the Model 95 (4 × 5 inch), the Model 130 (4-1/4 × 5 inch), the Model 131 (a slight revision of the Model 130), the Model 135 (4-1/2 × 5 inch), the Model 136 (a slight revision of the Model 135), and the Model 504 (4-5/8 × 5 inch). Production for these six horizontals totaled about 6,250 units (the most popular being the Model 136, with about 2,500 made), and a couple of the models continued to be sold into the early post-World War II period. [3-29]

While most Hall-Scott horizontal engines powered buses, a few ended up in trucks, as seen in this Model 190-equipped Kenworth built for the Los Angeles Fire Department.

This ACF 26-S bus has a horizontal Model 95 Hall-Scott engine, highlighted with bright paint. (Courtesy of Motor Bus Society.)

Prevented from selling to major bus makers, some Hall-Scott engines powered buses from smaller competitors such as Wentworth and Irwin, which called its buses Wentwin.

Hall-Scott was early among American engine makers to option its engines to burn butane, propane, and liquefied petroleum gas (a combination consisting mostly of butane and propane in some ratio, often abbreviated LPG) in the late 1920s. [3-30] Although these fuels have several qualities that can make them more desirable than gasoline as vehicle fuel (e.g., their reduced tendency to foul engine oil, their naturally high octane level and thus higher horsepower, and their cleaner exhaust), their lower operating cost was the most attractive feature to spurring their use in trucks and buses. Hall-Scott had to purchase most of the equipment needed for its engines to burn gasified fuel, such as regulators, heat exchangers, and special carburetors. Hall-Scott engineered several other changes into its butane-, propane-, and LPG-fueled engines, such as hard-faced exhaust valves and valve seats, chrome-faced top piston rings, and cooler-rated spark plugs. [3-31] As with the horizontal configuration, Hall-Scott throughout the remainder of its history offered many of its engine models with the option of using these fuels. Providing butane, propane, or LPG capability in so many of its models partially offset the cost disadvantage of not offering another lower-cost alternative to engine buyers—a diesel.

Another Hall-Scott-powered Wentworth and Irwin unit, this one using a Kenworth chassis.

Hall-Scott Makes a Serious Marine Engine

Marine applications became essential to Hall-Scott in the 1930s and 1940s. Hall-Scott entered the marine market right after World War I and, while attracting great press from some high-profile customers, sold only a few dozen engines each year. Those first Hall-Scott marine models—the LM, HSM, Navigator, and Explorer—were derivatives of land engines, but they did not make Hall-Scott into a leading marine power provider. With larger boats in the 1920s already looking into diesel, Hall-Scott had greater possibility to achieve success in powering smaller speedboats, yachts, and workboats. To become more than a ripple in the marine market, the company needed to make an engine of at least 250 hp, with reasonable weight, cast en-bloc of iron or iron alloy, and delivering smooth power. After 1925 and as part of ACF, Hall-Scott finally had the financial wherewithal to pull it off. The new engine that made Hall-Scott more visible in the marine market was the Invader.

If the Liberty motor was the best-known engine with which Hall-Scott was linked, then the Invader was possibly the best-known engine Hall-Scott ever built. Ironically, this might be true in spite of the fact that a little more than half of all Invaders ever produced came out of the factory of another company (as will be discussed in Chapter 4). The Invader enjoyed a production run of 23 years, with derivative models being produced for about another dozen years. In its heyday of the 1930s, the Invader was prized by boat owners and hailed by writers in the marine press as one of the great engines available. Hall-Scott

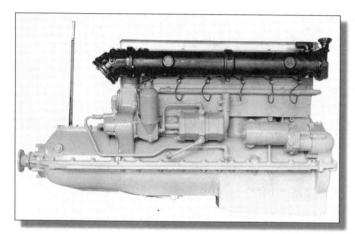

The exhaust side of the successful Hall-Scott Invader.

The intake side of the Hall-Scott Invader.

quickly pinned a great deal of hope that the Invader would achieve market success, and after 1931, references in Hall-Scott literature or boating magazines could not be found of the LM, HSM, and HSR models being sold.

Given the serious boats that most Invaders powered, war boats, the lineage of this engine might seem less than totally serious—pleasure boating and racing. However, recreational endeavors such as these are taken seriously by the participants, who invest enormous amounts of money and time in pursuit of speed and victories.

Elbert Hall and Bert Scott both owned boats and enjoyed racing them, making their company's postwar move into marine power at least partially personal. In fact, Bert and Leland Scott and two other men were involved in a serious boating accident shortly after Christmas in 1926. [3-32] It appears that gasoline had spilled on the deck, and a match ignited the fuel, the gas fumes below deck, and the fuel tank, causing a massive explosion. The blast destroyed the boat and hurled all four men into San Francisco Bay, with Bert and Leland Scott suffering burns on their faces and hands. Danger aside, high-speed powerboat races were popular in the West during the first half of the twentieth century, with a common site being Lake Tahoe, high in the Sierra Nevada Mountains on the Nevada–California border. This pastime was dangerous, thrilling, expensive, and, in its own way, glamorous. During this era, powerboat racing on Lake Tahoe attracted many luminaries from across the region. [3-33] From business circles, the names included truck and bus maker Louis Bill of Fageol, auto executive Norman De Vaux, and industrialist Henry J. Kaiser and his sons. From the entertainment world, band leader Guy Lombardo was a regular on the lake. Given the relative proximity of Tahoe to the San Francisco Bay Area, it would be natural for boat lovers Hall and Scott to spend time at Tahoe and to care very much about the racing success of Hall-Scott there.

Bert Scott's son Edward wrote a two-volume book, *The Saga of Lake Tahoe*, in which he mentioned Hall-Scott-powered boats and his family's time on the lake. The presence and reputation of Hall-Scott on Lake Tahoe appears to have been significant. For a period of time, the company even kept personnel on the lake to support Hall-Scott-powered boats and owned at least one boat that raced—the 28-foot-long mahogany *Mohawk*, a tangible, potent, floating advertisement for Hall-Scott prowess on the water. [3-34] Naturally, Hall-Scott was not the only performance engine maker on Lake Tahoe. Boats powered by Packard, Van Blerck, Scripps, Miller and "marinized" Liberties and other engines battled fiercely in ostensibly friendly contests for the checkered flag in the 1920s and 1930s. Edward Scott wrote that fanciers of given engine makes would make unflattering comments and spread rumors about the failures and supposed shortcomings of other engines, a practice that the Hall-Scott factory not only tolerated but actively engaged in doing. Scott recollected that "rumors were spread that the Hall-Scott engines would drop through the bottom of their mahogany hulls. The company retaliated that by assuring the marine minded that...Scripps power plants were throwing con-rods..." [3-35] This marine mudslinging continued far from the peaceful and scenic waters of Lake Tahoe. Stan Grayson wrote of "an undeniable rivalry emerged between" Sterling, the leading name in the premium end of the pleasure marine engine market, and newcomer Hall-Scott. [3-36] This marine historian continued, "In 1922 ads clearly aimed right at Hall-Scott, Sterling began touting its admittedly heavier (by some 700 pounds) en bloc cylinder castings, and suggested that the design prevented 'weaving and distortion.' Hall-Scott responded by suggesting that a modern pistol was more efficient than a stone axe, and that its engines were 'products of scientists and artisans.' It began adding a little tagline to ads, 'The most highly developed Marine Engine in America.' Sterling coined its own phrase: 'The Engine of Refinement for the Finest Boats That Float.'" Racing and pleasure boating was serious business, and after World War I, Hall-Scott set out to be a major player in that market. The LM and HSM engines charted a winning course for Hall-Scott in marine power, and the Invader built upon it.

The specs of the Invader were impressive. The all-new Hall-Scott marine motor displaced 998 cubic inches, with each of its six cylinders having a bore of 5-1/2 inches and a stroke of 7 inches. A chain-driven camshaft resided above the cylinders and actuated two large valves for each "hole," which, combined with the usual Hall-Scott unit construction, allowed for easier maintenance. The twin ignition did not simplify maintenance, but it did increase reliability. Invaders weighed around 1 ton, with reduction-gear-equipped models tipping the scales at about 3300 pounds, roughly twice what the first LM-6s weighed. But one prominent marine magazine called the Invader "light in weight." [3-37] Depending on the intake manifold, carburetion, and compression ratio used, within a few years the various Invader models developed 190–275 hp, a power range that could potentially find favor with a large number of customers. [3-38] Hall-Scott engineers made the Invader suitable for service in salt water by fashioning the heads and block from chrome nickel iron alloy to resist rusting and electrolysis, which *Motor Boating* magazine called "the best available material for salt water use" when introducing the Invader to its readers in its February 1931 issue. [3-39] Around 1928, Hall-Scott had moved from semi-steel to chrome nickel iron alloy across its engine line, finding that the latter

HALL-SCOTT

THE INVADER
Model 168-169

Price $3000.00

F. O. B. Factory or Factory Branches

The INVADER, a direct drive 250 to 275 H.P. engine, is built for fast express cruisers, water taxis, scout boats and cruisers. It *is the latest design from the Hall-Scott engineering staff* and combines the fine points of the line and the most modern improvements. Compact and powerful, it can be placed where engines of much lower horsepower formerly were installed. It has such refinements as an oil cooler of special design, a reverse gear giving 100% reverse and capable of transmitting 400 H.P. It is furnished in either *right or left hand rotation* with an option of high or medium compression ratio depending on the service for which it is intended. *This model also has been used extensively by the U. S. Coast Guard.*

SPECIFICATIONS

250-275 H.P., 5½″ bore, 7″ stroke, 6 cylinder, 997.8 cu. in. displacement, furnished in either right or left hand rotation with optional compression ratio for various services. Seven main bearings, counterbalanced crankshaft. Reverse gear giving 100% propeller speed. Weight 1950 pounds.

STANDARD EQUIPMENT: Starter, generator, distributor (dual), battery (12 volt), coils, oil gauge, ammeter, motometer, switches, oil filter, force-feed lubrication, dual fuel system, oil cooler.

OPTIONAL EQUIPMENT at added cost: Tachometer, bilge pump and power takeoff.

For installation dimensions and horsepower chart see pages 14 and 15 respectively.

The Invader came in left- and right-hand rotation, with a number of carburetion, compression, and gearing options. Shown here are the Models 168 and 169.

HALL-SCOTT

THE INVADER
Models 183-184

Price $2700.00
F. O. B. Factory or
Factory Branches

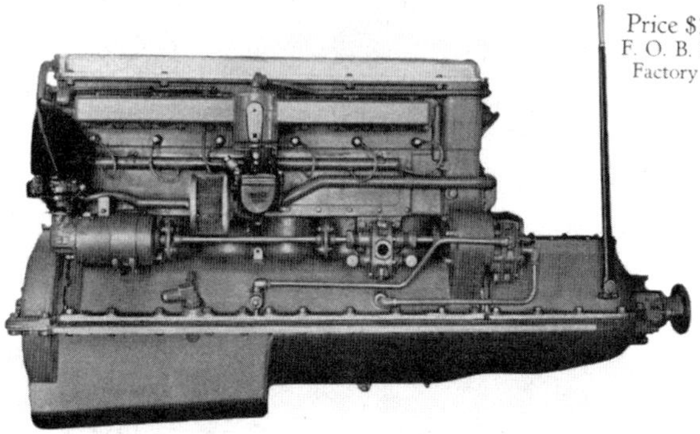

Hall-Scott has designed the single carburetor INVADER to propel boats of heavier draft and slower speeds where a fairly large propeller is required. This engine develops 180-190 horsepower at 1500 R.P.M. This INVADER is basically the same as the INVADER 250-275, the difference being in carburetion and compression. Having been designed for the higher horse-power and speed, this model has added life and economy. The same features are incorporated as in the INVADER 250-275 and can be supplied in either right or left hand rotation.

SPECIFICATIONS

180-190 H.P., $5\frac{1}{2}$" bore, 7" stroke, 6 cylinder, 997.8 cu. in. displace-ment, furnished in either right or left hand rotation. Reverse gear with 100% propeller speed. Weight 1950 pounds.

STANDARD EQUIPMENT: Starter, generator, distributor (dual), battery (12 volt), coils, oil gauge, ammeter, motometer, switches, oil filter, force-feed lubrication, dual fuel system, oil cooler.

OPTIONAL EQUIPMENT at added cost: Tachometer, bilge pump and power takeoff.

For installation dimensions and horsepower chart see pages 14 and 15 respectively.

Another page from the same Invader brochure. Shown here are the Models 183 and 184.

made more durable blocks and valve seats and lowered machining costs. [3-40] Of special interest to boaters, *Motor Boating* added, "As in all Hall-Scott engines, no bolt or stud holes are drilled through into the water jacket in order to eliminate the rusting of studs." [3-41] With seven main bearings and large counterbalances on the crankshaft, the Invader was unusually smooth all the way through its speed range, which initially was limited to 1800 rpm. As with new Hall-Scott models introduced after 1915, the Invader had semi-spherical combustion chambers. This was exactly the kind of engine for which many operators were looking.

The Invader was even a pleasure to look at, a factor for some customers when they selected a power unit. Smooth and long, it could be described as being "sleek" in appearance. For example, editors at *Motor Boating* characterized the Invader as having an "extremely compact and neat design." [3-42] The Invader had a minimum of what Hall-Scott engineer Bradford called "gingerbread hung on it," lacking external accouterments such as a governor, air compressor, power takeoff, or exhaust gas recirculation (EGR). [3-43] This was the impressive engine Hall-Scott needed to stay on the forefront of fast-moving currents in the crowded marine engine market.

The official launch of the Hall-Scott Invader came at the highly visible, extensively covered, and heavily attended New York Boat Show in 1931. Such an introduction to the boating world would maximize recognition and sales, which perhaps was especially important during the Great Depression. The timing for Hall-Scott to introduce the Invader as the country sank deeper into the economic morass of the Depression might seem dubious. Hall-Scott suffered similarly as other companies did across America, and the company flirted with closure. A measure of the magnitude of this catastrophe can be seen in the fact that in 1932, Macaulay Foundry shipped Hall-Scott only 10% of the iron it had in 1929, the year the stock market crashed. [3-44] With engine production free-falling from 3,971 units in 1929 (of which 3,245 were International Harvester engines) to only 145 units in 1932, the early 1930s were dark days at Hall-Scott. [3-45]

In spite of the widespread unemployment, a dismal lack of economic activity, and the contracting prices and wages that characterize this period, some elements of the marine industry weathered the storm pretty well. Given the investment Hall-Scott had made in the Invader, that is a point worth making. For example, across America in 1931, in stark contrast to the many breadlines and foreclosed farms, thousands of wealthy Americans still had money to buy some yachts, cruisers, and race boats. In addition to that, thousands of like-minded wealthy people in other countries purchased big American boats and engines. In March 1931, *Motor Boating* reported on some good times in its industry in a short article titled "Widespread Interest in Boating Throughout 1930." [3-46] In the article, Warren Ripple of the Johnson Motor Company, a maker of boats and outboard engines, said, "More persons wanted to buy motors and boats in 1930 than ever before... More inquiries were received by our sales department during 1930 than any twelve-month period for three years preceding." Ripple did not provide any sales figures (wanting to buy a boat is not the same as actually buying one), and Hall-Scott powered different boats than the small craft built and powered by Johnson. But that must have been encouraging news for Hall-Scott nonetheless. More directly relevant to the Hall-Scott enterprise, which through its history maintained a strong marketing bias for the American West, was another article in *Motor Boating*, this one from May 1931, "Western Yards Working at Capacity." [3-47] In the article, the writers noted, "Yacht building yards on the West Coast are speed-ing up their production in order to take care of the unprecedented demand at the present time." In a 1931 article providing a few industry sales numbers, *Motor Boating* revealed, "The number of motor boats registered with the Department of Commerce has been increasing steadily at the rate of from ten to twelve thousand per year for at least a ten-year period. The total number of boats registered at the close of the year 1930 was 248,448." [3-48] Not all of these people were Hall-Scott customers, much less buyers of Invader engines, but the general pool of boaters might have been healthier than the nation's economy as a whole. What's more, this same article reported that boat and engine exports remained strong, with 2,000 gasoline marine engines, 900 diesel marine engines, 7,200 outboard engines, and 497 boats with engines exported overseas in 1930. All in all, these were promising signs for the launch of the Invader in 1931. With the Invader price tag being more than $3,500, that market of well-heeled buyers needed to be there.

Bringing a new marine engine to market in the depths of the Great Depression certainly was not desirable timing, but Hall-Scott worked to sell Invaders. Hall-Scott could pitch the engine to a wide array of customers, which helped. Wealthy pleasure boaters looked to the Invader for sophisticated, smooth, and reliable power for their cruisers, yachts, and race boats. Some of these cus-tomers with a need for speed were more colorful than others. The Invader's instant reputation for performance led to the engines being purchased by some law enforcement agencies in the 1930s, as well as people on the other side of the law. With the nation living through the Prohibition of alcohol from 1919 to 1933, some law-breaking entrepreneurs tried to satisfy the nation's thirst by sneaking illegal alcohol into the country from offshore. Successful selling of "hootch" obviously depended on eluding law enforcement. These alcohol

The Invader and some typical installations, from an Invader brochure.

traffickers were often called "rum runners." According to Hall-Scott engineer "Speed" Glidewell, "one day a rum runner came into the plant and looked over some new engines just being run in on the test blocks. He decided on one and said he would take this one—how much? The Sales Manager told him '$3600.00'—so he immediately peals [*sic*] four one thousand dollar bills off his fat roll and hands it over. The Sales Manager had to do some scrambling to find $400.00 in change, especially when he could have said '$4000.00' in the first place and saved himself some trouble." [3-49] Hall-Scott's name for producing engines well suited for rum runners appears to have been widespread. For example, Herschel Smith, an aviation historian, wrote that Hall-Scott gained "some reputation for good rumrunner engines." [3-50]

A more reputable customer for the new Hall-Scott Invader was the U.S. Coast Guard, which took delivery of its first Invaders during the same year that the engines made their appearance. Hall-Scott wisely did not promote in its ads the attractiveness of the Invader to bootleggers, but the company crowed about the federal government buying the Invader. In 1931, the Coast Guard bought Invaders for 15 of its picket boats, which were roughly 100-foot-long craft that had patrol duties. According to one such ad, Hall-Scott engines had proven themselves superior over other engines in their "dependability, power, smooth running and economical operation" to be "far superior to the slower running, heavier and sluggish power units heretofore used" in these vessels. [3-51] In the 1930s, Hall-Scott could legitimately claim that its engines were more smooth, reliable, lightweight, and fast-turning than the engines of most of its competitors. As long as Hall-Scott produced engines that maintained that edge of superior performance, the company could remain competitive. Of course, there was tremendous market pressure on other manufacturers to possess these same qualities in their engines, too, so the target at which Hall-Scott aimed kept moving. But in 1931, Hall-Scott had a winner in the Invader, so additional (modest) government orders for Hall-Scott engines followed in the 1930s, as did the proud ads. ·

Through the 1930s, Hall-Scott realized acceptable but not great sales of the Invader. [3-52] The company delivered 97 Invaders in 1931, a decent enough first year but, unfortunately, a figure not topped until the advent of war. As the Depression grew worse, so did Invader sales, with Hall-Scott delivering 39 Invaders in 1932, and then only 23 in 1933. In fact, Invader sales roughly paralleled the American economy, with deliveries tanking in 1933 and then experiencing a slow and unsteady recovery through the remainder of the decade. Invader sales even mirrored the nation's late-1930s economic

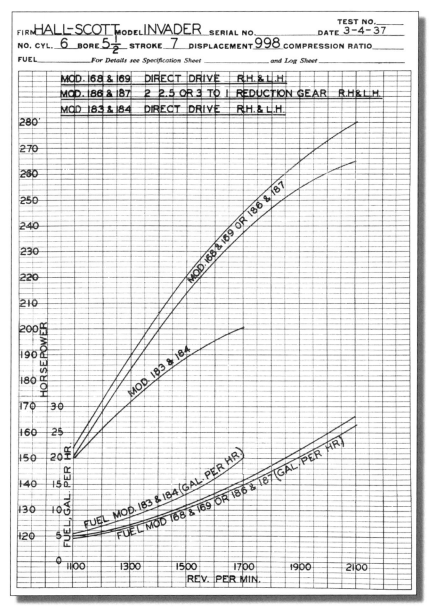

FIRM HALL-SCOTT MODEL INVADER SERIAL NO._____ DATE 3-4-37

NO. CYL. 6 BORE 5½ STROKE 7 DISPLACEMENT 998 COMPRESSION RATIO_____

FUEL_____ *For Details see Specification Sheet* _____ *and Log Sheet* _____

TEST NO._____

MOD. 168 & 169	DIRECT DRIVE	R.H. & L.H.
MOD. 186 & 187	2 2.5 OR 3 TO 1 REDUCTION GEAR	R.H & L.H.
MOD. 183 & 184	DIRECT DRIVE	R.H. & L.H.

Power curves of various Invader models.

A 1939 ad for the Invader. Although the Invader was designed to power pleasure and work craft, Invader sales did not reach high levels until wartime.

downturn, sometimes referred to as the "Roosevelt Recession," when engine deliveries dipped from 48 in 1936 and 1937 down to 44 in 1938.

But even if Invader sales did not transform Hall-Scott into a household name with thousands of sales in the 1930s, the new model instantly became a significant proportion of the marine engine production by the company. [3-53] The Invader suddenly accounted for 59.5% of Hall-Scott marine engine deliveries in 1931, a percentage that varied little through the remainder of the 1930s, spanning a low of 44.4% to a high of 64.5%. While it is impossible to say how many Invader customers would have purchased engines from other companies had this model not been available, it is safe to say that the Invader brought new customers to Hall-Scott.

The Invader continued to bless Hall-Scott with good press for the remainder of the interwar period. A decade after the launch of the Invader in 1941, *Pacific Motor Boat* described it as an "engine that in 10 years has become widely used..." and "...has given an exceptionally good account of itself in all types of craft: cruisers, motor yachts, commuters, runabouts, general utility boats, and commercial vessels. In the exceptionally exacting service of powering water-taxis, where power, reliability and economy are equally imperative, Hall-Scott Invaders have set outstanding operating records." [3-54] In describing other engines in this issue, *Pacific Motor Boat* writers provided only engine statistics and bare descriptions; the effusive praise was saved for only a few engines, such as the Hall-Scott Invader. For the small Berkeley engine maker, the Invader was an impressive achievement. By the end of its production run in the mid-1950s, Hall-Scott had produced roughly 3,300 to 3,500 copies of the Invader in its various model numbers (Models 168, 169, 183, 184, 186, and 187, not including the derivative truck engines, the V-12 Defender, or the 4,000 Invaders built by Hudson during World War II). [3-55] The Invader powered work boats, race boats, and war boats, proving to be a multipurpose engine.

The Invader was arguably the single most important engine model the company produced. In fact, this engine released in 1931 would be the second-to-last entirely new engine the company ever introduced. What's more, the Invader was the basis for two later engines, the Model 400 series truck and industrial engine, and the V-12 marine and industrial engine, both of which were actually produced into the 1960s after Hall-Scott had folded. This unusually long market life was a testimony to the essential strengths of the Invader as an engine, the amazing technical foresight of E.J. Hall, and the inability of the Hall-Scott Motor Car Company to introduce new engines and to remain in the forefront of innovation after the departure of its brilliant cofounder.

The U.S. military found the Invader a useful engine for its fleet, and its peculiar demands for power steered the development of the Invader in a new direction. The military used Invaders to propel many of its smaller craft, often using two or three in a single boat (a common practice) to obtain sufficient power. But for some boats, the U.S. Navy also needed engines with greater output. Therefore, in 1937, it contracted with Hall-Scott to build such an engine. [3-56] The LM, HSM, and Invader engines had firmly established Hall-Scott as a marine engine leader after World War I, so it was natural for the Navy to ask Hall-Scott for an important new engine as the country strengthened its defense in the late 1930s. By 1937, though, Hall-Scott no longer enjoyed the luxury of having the in-house engineering genius of E.J. Hall to build a new engine from scratch because the cofounder had departed several years ago. So Hall-Scott engineers had to make due with what equipment and know-how they already had around the Berkeley factory. The Invader was still in production, but it was not big enough to meet the Navy request; thus, Hall-Scott engineers used the Invader as a beginning point for the new motor. In a flippant way, it can be said that engineers more or less took two in-line six-cylinder Invaders and hooked them together around a common crankshaft, making a single V-12 engine. The two banks of six-cylinders were configured at a 60-degree angle to each other, making this the first V-engine Hall-Scott had built since the A-8 aircraft engine of 1917. The resulting goliath power plant was called the Defender, and it proved to be exactly what the Navy wanted. Although the market for such an engine would not be huge, there was at least modest interest in the engine through the early 1960s. By far its greatest demand came from the American and foreign governments during World War II. Hall-Scott did not produce a larger-displacement power plant for the remainder of its history as an engine maker.

The V-12 Defender and the Invader shared many parts, features, and internal dimensions but retained some important differences. [3-57] For example, both engines began with the same 5-1/2 × 7-inch cylinder dimensions. The Invader Models 1268 and 1269 had a displacement of 998 cubic inches, and the first Defender had a displacement of 1996 cubic inches, which was twice the volume of the Hall-Scott big six. So much engine would necessarily be quite heavy, and the Defender weighed an impressive 2 tons, ranging from 3600 to 4600 lb, depending on accessories such as reduction gears, and was about twice the weight of the Invader. The Defender had the typical Hall-Scott features of an overhead camshaft, hemi head, twin spark plugs, aluminum pistons, iron alloy block, and so forth. One significant difference between the two was that some versions of the Defender had a higher compression ratio than that of the Invader. Select versions of the V-12 had compression ratios up to 7:1,

The Hall-Scott Defender, a spin-off of the Invader.

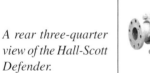

A rear three-quarter view of the Hall-Scott Defender.

while the six-cylinder engine usually had compression ratios around 5.2:1. Having twice as many cylinders as the Invader, plus the higher compression ratio, meant that cranking over the Defender would be quite a chore for any starting motor, making a challenge for engineers, too. This need for greater cranking power meant that the Defender came wired with a 24-volt charging system as opposed to the more common 12-volt system on the Invader. The Defender also had a separate upper block and crankcase, unlike the integrated block in the Invader. [3-58] Aside from these differences, it is still fair to say that had there not been an Invader originally, the Defender would never have been born, even if the two were not carbon copies of each other.

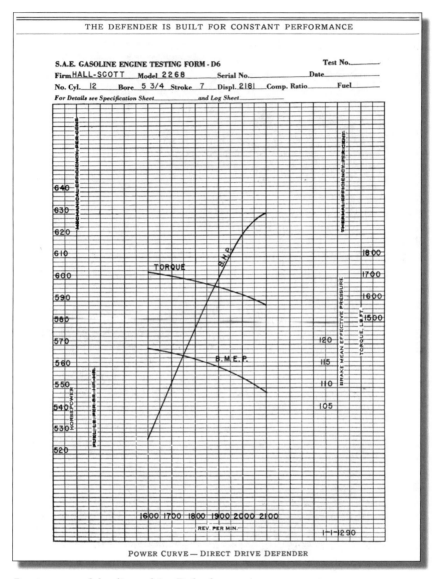

THE DEFENDER IS BUILT FOR CONSTANT PERFORMANCE

S.A.E. GASOLINE ENGINE TESTING FORM - D6   Test No._____

Firm HALL-SCOTT   Model 2 2 6 8   Serial No._____   Date_____

No. Cyl. 12   Bore 5 3/4   Stroke 7   Displ. 2181   Comp. Ratio_____   Fuel_____

For Details see Specification Sheet_____and Log Sheet_____

POWER CURVE — DIRECT DRIVE DEFENDER

Power curve of the direct-drive Defender.

Hall-Scott engineers made their new V-12 amenable to as many applications as possible. The Defender came available as either right- or left-hand drive, with direct drive or reduction gears. Thus, it was flexible enough

168

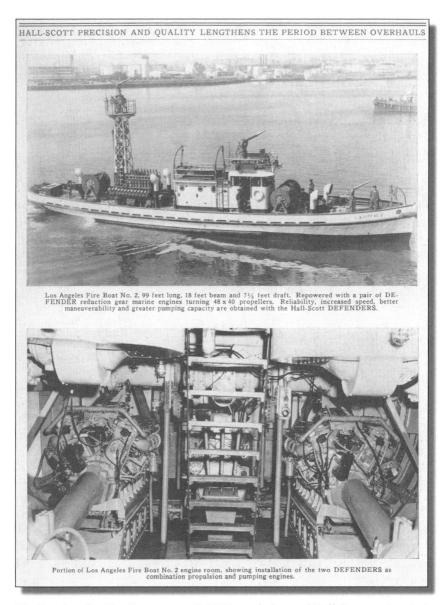

HALL-SCOTT PRECISION AND QUALITY LENGTHENS THE PERIOD BETWEEN OVERHAULS

Los Angeles Fire Boat No. 2, 99 feet long, 18 feet beam and 7½ feet draft. Repowered with a pair of DE-FENDER reduction gear marine engines turning 48 x 40 propellers. Reliability, increased speed, better maneuverability and greater pumping capacity are obtained with the Hall-Scott DEFENDERS.

Portion of Los Angeles Fire Boat No. 2 engine room, showing installation of the two DEFENDERS as combination propulsion and pumping engines.

The Los Angeles Fire Department (LAFD) used plenty of Hall-Scott engines in its trucks and boats. Shown here is the installation of two Defenders in an LAFD fire boat.

and powerful enough to move target boats, patrol boats, and aircraft patrol boats for the U.S. military and the military of other countries. The U.S. Navy took delivery of its first Defender in 1938, an impressive turnaround time from ordering to production. [3-59] More on the wartime uses and changes to the Defender can be found in Chapter 4.

The Defender was a hugely powerful engine in all its forms. The first Defenders displaced 1996 cubic inches and had 5-1/2 × 7-inch bore and stroke, good for about 575 hp at 2000 rpm. When the Navy asked for more power, Hall-Scott bored out the cylinders to 5-3/4 inches. [3-60] This increase translated into a displacement of 2181 cubic inches and about 630 hp. During the war, the Hall-Scott 2281-cubic-inch V-12 came in a supercharged version that developed even more power. [3-61] The Hall-Scott V-12 might not have been all new, strictly speaking, but its performance was so potent that it became highly respected. Stan Grayson wrote that the Defender was "considered by some to be the most outstanding marine engine of its class." [3-62] After the war, Hall-Scott began marketing the Defender for non-marine applications, mostly as an industrial engine to power pumps and generators. The Defender was too big to become a regular production truck engine. Defender production even outlasted the demise of the Hall-Scott company.

The Evolution of the Invader Continues

The Invader was too good to remain in the sole possession of boaters. Therefore, in 1940, Hall-Scott "de-marinized" the engine to make a power plant for trucks, buses, and industrial applications. Hall-Scott had been making engines for one type of application into engines for other different types of applications since the inception of the company, but the Invader seems to have been the only example of a Hall-Scott marine engine evolving into one for use on land. The outcome of this Darwinian-like transformation was the Model 400 series engines, a handful of closely related and derivative motors. The Model 400 was the most powerful Hall-Scott truck engine built to that point, a distinction previously held by the Model 177. The Model 400 engine had bore and stroke measurements of 5-3/4 × 7 inches, displacing 1090.6 cubic inches (sometimes rounded down to 1090 or rounded up to 1091), and it developed 295 hp at 2000 rpm and 940 lb. ft. of torque at 1350 rpm. [3-63]

In a rather confusing nomenclature policy, Hall-Scott applied the "400" label to a series of Invader-based engines with various number designations, at first having a number in the 400s, such as the Models 440 and 441, plus to one

The Hall-Scott Model 400.

particular model named the Model 400. Years later, Hall-Scott adopted two other systems that did not use 400-based numbers, though. Because all of these engines were hewn from the same basic design, differing chiefly in carburetion, manifold design, or cylinder dimensions, they shared the same weight of roughly 2200 lb, which is virtually the same as the weight of the Invader with its marine gear removed.

The 400-series engines also came with a number of features that made them attractive to truckers, and many of those features were seen on the Invader, such as unit construction for an easily replaceable head and block, chain-driven overhead camshaft, alloy block, hemi head, dual oil filters, an oil cooler, the intake and exhaust manifold located on opposite sides of the engine for easy access, a low engine speed for long life, and, most importantly, outstanding power. Large, heavy, and thirsty for fuel, the Model 400 was also strong and reliable. Consequently, even though Hall-Scott had not been a major presence in the OEM truck engine sector before 1940, a handful of prominent truck

HALL-SCOTT *Series 400 Engine*

In the **Hall-Scott Model 400** it is believed our company is offering to the trade the most powerful, dependable and efficient power unit ever designed for heavy transportation service.

Thoroughly tested for more than a year's period over snow-capped Snoqualmie Pass and into sun-baked valleys, with capacity loads, one of these engines logged over 100,000 miles with no maintenance cost; in fact, not even a valve grind. After careful inspection of every part, it was found there was no appreciable wear.

The tremendous power delivered at low revolutions with properly selected gear ratios permits the hauling of road-limit loads at maximum speeds, over grades as well as on the level. This results in faster schedules and economical operation costs that have not been obtainable in the past from smaller engines.

The design of this engine is exceptional as to its simplicity, ruggedness and size.

A Model 400-powered Kenworth, on which the company pinned a great amount of hope, in front of the Hall-Scott business office on 7th Street and Heinz in Berkeley, California.

Early 400-series sales literature shows the engine and features.

builders quickly added the Model 400 to their lists of power plants, including Autocar, International, Kenworth, Mack, and Peterbilt. [4-64]

As with other Hall-Scott products, company engineers tailored the engine to meet the needs of different customers as much as possible, given budgetary and engineering constraints. Thus, the Model 400 was available from 1940 to burn gasoline or gasified fuel. Not only were these gaseous fuels often cheaper than gasoline by several cents per gallon and produced more power, but they burned cleaner and produced a less noxious exhaust, a consideration for customers with sensitive cargo such as milk or fruit. Sales of the Model 400 engine began at a snail's pace, with only three engines delivered in 1940 and six engines in 1941, but this changed dramatically with the advent of war and the unquenchable need for engines, followed by the pent-up postwar demand for civilian engines. [4-65] Bradford estimated production for the base Model 400 and its later derivative Models 400, 400-0, 440, 441, 442, 450, 470, 480, 855, 935, 1091, and 1091-02 at more than 5,200 units. [3-66] However, because this figure does not include later versions such as the 6156 and 6182, this is a conservative estimate. Hall-Scott company data roughly yield this number through 1954. Subsequent production probably pushed this figure to more than 6,500 by 1958.

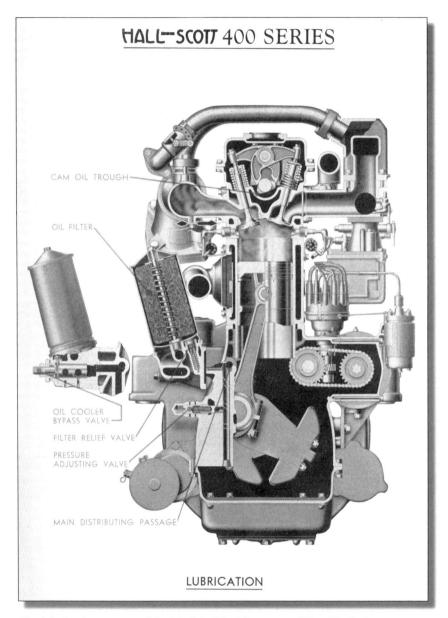

The lubrication system of the Model 400. (Courtesy of Tom Shafer.)

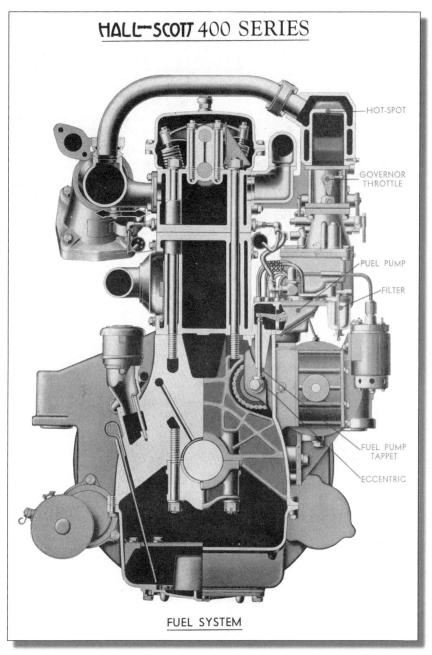

HALL-SCOTT 400 SERIES

HOT-SPOT

GOVERNOR THROTTLE

FUEL PUMP

FILTER

FUEL PUMP TAPPET

ECCENTRIC

FUEL SYSTEM

The fuel system of the Model 400. Note the long bolts that secure the head, and the lower and upper crankcase. (Courtesy of Tom Shafer.)

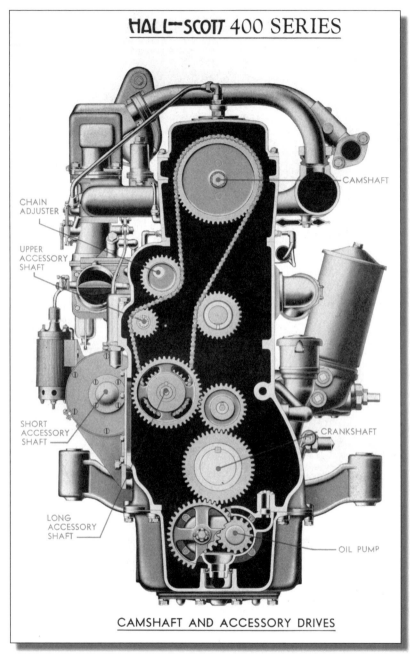

The camshaft and accessory drive of the Model 400. (Courtesy of Tom Shafer.)

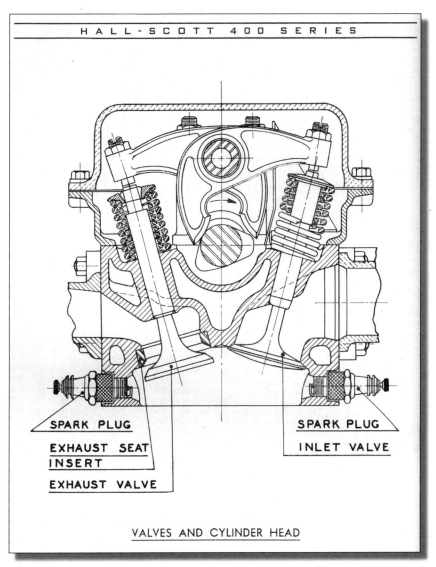

HALL-SCOTT 400 SERIES

SPARK PLUG

EXHAUST SEAT INSERT

EXHAUST VALVE

SPARK PLUG

INLET VALVE

VALVES AND CYLINDER HEAD

Drawing of the valves and cylinder head of the Model 400. (Courtesy of Tom Shafer.)

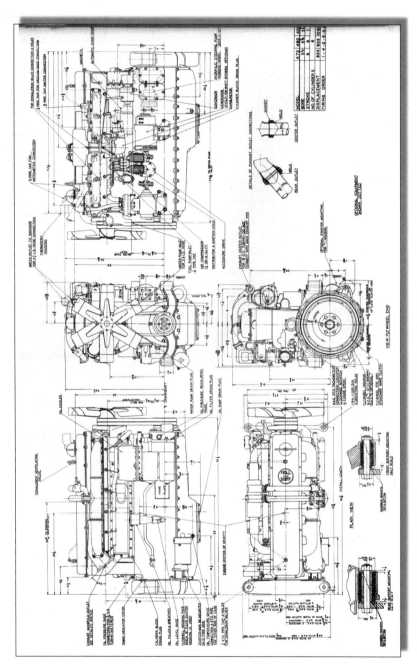

Drawing of the Model 400 series engine. (Courtesy of Tom Shafer.)

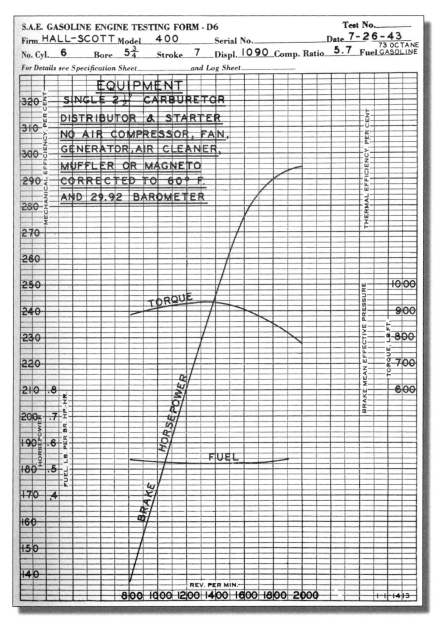

Power curve of the gasoline-fueled Model 400. Note the 73 octane gas. (Courtesy of Tom Shafer.)

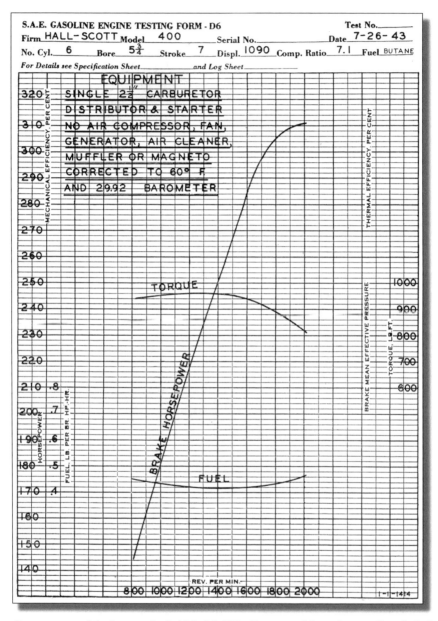

Power curve of the butane-fueled Model 400. Compare this to the gasoline-fueled model. (Courtesy of Tom Shafer.)

Hall-Scott Gets Burned with Diesel

The first Hall-Scott diesel engine, and its only marine diesel model, began life as a bus engine project in the early 1930s. With the demand for diesel power growing in stationary, rail, tractor, truck, bus, and marine uses, and with Hall-Scott's parent company being a leading bus maker and a minor producer of luxury boats, it is little wonder that ACF turned to its Hall-Scott division to develop a diesel. As ACF determined that Hall-Scott needed to make a diesel and applied some pressure on the company to achieve that goal, increasing numbers of newspapers and trade publications reported stories of bus companies experimenting with diesel power. Such an example came in 1929 when *Commercial Car Journal* reported that the Public Service Coordinated Transport in New Jersey fitted a bus with a Mercedes-Benz compression ignition engine. [3-67] That same journal reported in another article that while no U.S. builder of trucks or buses "is ready to introduce a Diesel engine at the present time, a majority of them admit that they are experimenting with engines of this type." [3-68] An engineer writing in the same *Commercial Car Journal* article pointed out that building a successful diesel for a truck or bus was a substantial project, one not taken lightly, and that "any company undertaking it must be prepared to spend money running probably into six figures." [3-69] But did ACF have that kind of money? Outside the truck and bus field, for reasons of economy and safety, marine customers had begun to adopt diesel as well. The U.S. Navy was such a customer, a major one, and had begun a much-discussed "dieselization" of its vessels. Indeed, Bert and Leland Scott's 1926 boating accident underscores the danger of using gasoline on the water. [3-70] Diesel engines still had a number of hurdles to overcome in order to become widely attractive to American operators in land and marine applications. Nonetheless, the promise of tremendous savings in operating costs and greater safety kept diesel development a topic of considerable interest. Being one of America's leading bus makers, and at least a minor boat maker, ACF was one of these interested firms and perhaps had the deep pockets required to undertake such an expensive project.

Building a successful new diesel engine cannot be reduced to slightly altering an existing gasoline engine, a salient point that sometimes is overlooked. Gasoline and diesel engines both use internal combustion, but the two have fundamentally different ways to ignite fuel. Because heat from compression is used to ignite the fuel in diesel engines, the engines generate much higher cylinder pressures. Compression ratios for gasoline engines were often around 5:1 at this time period, but in diesel engines of that era, compression ratios could reach 20:1 because of the tremendous heat needed. These greater pressures necessitated sturdier engine components, which made diesel engines heavier than gasoline engines. By the end of the 1920s, diesel power had already made serious inroads into the yacht, work-boat, and military segments of the marine market, and had made its promising appearance in rail. Stationary power, such as for electric generation and drilling, also saw diesel coming on strong in the 1920s. In America, truck and bus operators wanted engines to respond quickly to frequent throttle changes, to have the flexibility that comes with high engine revolutions per minute, to produce a minimum of exhaust, and to be lightweight. Thus, diesels were only beginning to conform to market demands. Regardless, the trend in the 1920s to increased and wider use of diesel was clear.

In an effort to further understand this fast-moving engine technology, in 1930 ACF president William H. Woodin sent Brill's vice-president of engineering Charles O. Guernsey across the Atlantic to study European diesel production. [3-71] Diesel power traces its development to Europe, with Rudolf Diesel receiving his first engine patent in 1892. Many of the subsequent important advances in diesel technology took place there, too, along with much greater public acceptance of diesel. Guernsey visited 22 European diesel engine makers in his seven-week trip to see in what directions engine development was heading and to explore possible marketing, technology-sharing, and licensing possibilities. At some firms, Guernsey was welcomed as a valued colleague and potential partner, literally "wined and dined." At others, he was barely allowed in the door. He looked at plans, inspected engines on test benches, talked with engineers (Guernsey apparently spoke only English), took detailed notes, and rode in diesel-powered vehicles. He noted the exhaust, odor, fuel consumption, weight, reliability, roughness, development, production, and other items of interest to ACF management. In virtually every category, ACF's engineer reviewed Europe's diesels favorably. Although he found diesels rougher, somewhat heavier, and having lower top engine speeds than commercial gasoline engines, those traits were more than offset by the superior fuel economy and reliability of diesels.

The trip sold Guernsey on diesel, and upon his return, he wrote a report for his superiors. In this report, Guernsey argued the need for his company to begin work immediately on its own compression ignition engine. He seemed to have no doubt about the need for this development, writing, "I recommend the six cylinder, four cycle type, although eventually the two cycle may be better." [3-72] He liked much of what he saw in Europe, especially from Sauer, A.E.C., and M.A.N., and suggested working with a European firm if time was of the essence. After all, this was the path taken by Hall-Scott competitors Buda, Hercules, and Waukesha. But, Guernsey continued, "If more time can be taken, then we should develop our own designs, with the help of such outside

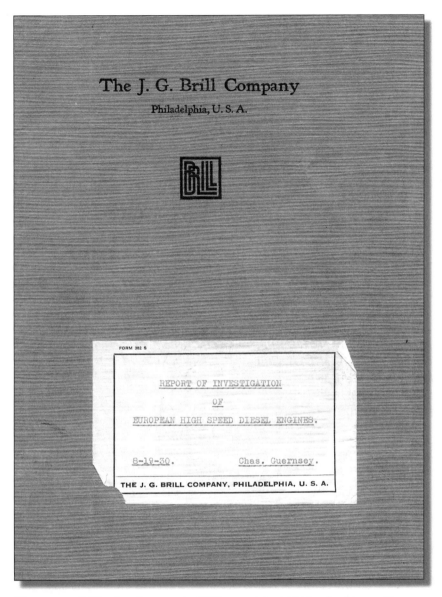

The cover of Charles Guernsey's 1930 report to ACF leadership on European diesel development.

talent as we might require." Although barely mentioning Hall-Scott by name in his initial report, Guernsey must have had Hall-Scott in mind for making the projected ACF diesels. An addendum to his report dated December 21, 1932, a full two years after filing his first assessment, was titled "Literature on Diesel Engines Being Sent Hall-Scott." [3-73] It contained more than 100 pieces of diesel-related literature—sales, descriptive, and engineering. Upon seeing this, Hall-Scott engineers no doubt felt they viewed their marching orders.

While generating a strong reaction, it does not appear that ACF and Brill management read Guernsey's report carefully. Unfortunately for Hall-Scott, around the time in 1930 that managers committed themselves to beginning the development of a diesel, the company had lost the engineering expertise of E.J. Hall, hardly a favorable sign for the chance of success of the project. The Invader was the last successful engine project that Hall spearheaded at Hall-Scott.

Eager—a little too eager—to get Hall-Scott into the ranks of America's diesel makers and soon after reading Guernsey's report, Hall-Scott general manager Alcock signed a contract with the Golden Eagle Bus Company of Los Angeles to deliver 10 diesel engines of 180–190 hp. [3-74] What's more, Alcock signed a deal obligating his company to deliver the first of these diesel engines within 60 days. Prodded from "upstairs," the ACF Hall-Scott division initiated what Francis Bradford described as "panic development of a diesel engine." [3-75]

Alcock's commitment to making Hall-Scott a contender in the diesel engine field was commendable. Hall-Scott sorely needed this commitment, but Alcock's company did not possess such an engine. Sixty days would have been enough delivery time if Hall-Scott had 10 such engines sitting in Berkeley that had to be trucked to Los Angeles for installation, or if Hall-Scott had temporarily run out of these engines from its regular production line and therefore had to "back-order" some units. But Hall-Scott did not even have such a model in its lineup that it could ship. Worse yet, the company had not even designed, let alone built, the first example of this engine when Alcock signed the contract! Hall-Scott management appreciated the larger point that Guernsey made of the desirability of diesel, but the management missed another critical point that he made: diesel engines are difficult to design and build well. In his report, Guernsey observed, "All builders emphasized the extent and difficulty of development. Some builders have been experimenting as long as eight years. The average [time for new diesel engine development] seems to be about two years." [3-76] Casting aside Guernsey's caution, Alcock demanded that his engineers compress a typical two-year gestation period into a few weeks. Even with Hall-Scott's impressive record of making good engines—and some very quickly, such as the Holt tractor engine—it would have been difficult to design and build a new and successful diesel from scratch in the time asked. It is doubtful that even E.J. Hall could have pulled off such a feat.

Facing this impossibility, Hall-Scott engineers altered and cannibalized as many existing designs and components as they could, cobbling together a "new" diesel power plant for Golden Eagle. The Hall-Scott six-cylinder, 707-cubic-inch Model 175 served as the basis for this four-stroke diesel. After all, the Model 175 had served as the platform for the first Hall-Scott horizontal engine, too. The new diesel weighed 2180 lb, compared to the 1830 lb of the Model 175. [3-77] Connecting rods from the Model 175 were drilled out to make a narrow oil passage that would spray the piston undersides for cooling for the higher-compression diesel. Crankshaft journals were enlarged, as were wrist pins. The crankshaft of the Model 175 was entirely too light for the rougher service it would encounter as a diesel, and the engineers did not think they could sufficiently strengthen it. Therefore, the new engine was governed at only 1800 rpm, as opposed to the 2000 rpm of the Model 175, in part to keep the crankshaft from breaking. [3-78] The new Hall-Scott oil burner produced a maximum of 133 hp at 1800 rpm and 420 lb. ft. of torque at 1200 rpm, numbers roughly in line with competing diesel engines of similar displacement at the time. For example, the Hercules truck, bus, industrial, and marine six-cylinder, 707-cubic-inch Model DHXB diesel produced 176 hp at 1800 rpm and 635 lb. ft. of torque at 1400 rpm, while the Waukesha truck and bus six-cylinder, 648-cubic-inch Model 6D-125 diesel produced 125 hp at 2000 rpm and 360 lb. ft. of torque at 1200 rpm. [3-79] Combustion chamber design was particularly vexing for Hall-Scott engineers and was not worked out satisfactorily before the first few engines were rushed to their expectant customers.

These challenges notwithstanding, Hall-Scott engineers worked overtime every day for weeks and all day on Saturdays to deliver the engines to Golden Eagle on time. They dubbed the engine the Model 140. But the engines that Hall-Scott delivered had not spent the usual time in working out the bugs at the factory—Golden Eagle buses would be the "test mules" for these modified gasoline engines passing as diesels. Maybe this was considered a reasonable risk to take; after all, Hall-Scott had built terrific bus engines in the 1920s. Upon installation, the buses, filled with people and luggage, set out from Los Angeles to Yuma, El Paso, and Kansas City. Not surprisingly perhaps, these unproven engines did not enjoy trouble-free journeys. Bradford described the

Model 140 engines as "not a success in any sense of the word," and therefore the engines "were pulled out of vehicle service at the first opportunity," with their weaknesses including having "broken crankshafts and burned pistons." [3-80] Simply put, the first Hall-Scott experiment with diesel amounted to a striking failure.

For this small company that had enjoyed a history of building winning engines, the Model 140 amounted to a rare embarrassment and a setback. Hall-Scott

Pre-production example of the intake side of a Hall-Scott Model 140 diesel.

The exhaust side of the same pre-production Model 140 diesel.

certainly did not need the bad reputation in the sales-starved 1930s, and the failure of the Model 140 did not make selling any future Hall-Scott engines, especially another diesel, any easier. Fortunately for ACF and Hall-Scott, the engine received little press, and references made to the Model 140 diesel are hard to find. Rare examples include an inauspicious entry in a diesel engine comparison chart in *Automotive Industries* in 1936, and a piston and ring specification chart for truck engines in *Commercial Car Journal* in 1937. [3-81] The Model 140 has been largely forgotten, and many people otherwise familiar with the Hall-Scott story have assumed that the company never made a diesel engine for buses or trucks. Hall-Scott expended little effort to disabuse people of that assumption.

But the story of the hapless Model 140 did not end with the engines being ignominiously yanked from Golden Eagle buses. Some limited engineering development continued on the Model 140 engine, and while Hall-Scott engineers could not satisfactorily modify it to stand up to the particular stresses of truck and bus service, with the constant changes in throttle demand, lugging, and engine braking, they did feel that it would be suitable for marine service. According to one diesel engine expert in the 1930s, marine compression ignition engines usually ran at lower revolutions per minute and endured more hard continuous service than their land-based cousins. [3-82] Thus, Hall-Scott engineers "tweaked" the Model 140 to serve marine customers. Hall-Scott rechristened the Model 140 bus engine as the Model 142 "Chieftain" and in 1936 or 1937 began marketing it as a marine diesel engine, priced at a rather sizable $4,500. [3-83]

Meanwhile, the Model 140 almost immediately disappeared from engine review charts in truck and bus publications, suggesting that Hall-Scott quickly retracted the troubled engine from its initial market. Hall-Scott made fairly high-profile reference to its marine diesel in ads, though, and even invested money in some splashy marketing, including full-color brochures, which were rare for Hall-Scott at the time. Maybe the bright colors would erase any dark association of the Model 140. The Chieftain benefited automatically from the established Hall-Scott reputation for quality, whether deserved or not for this engine. The 100-hp Model 142 weighed some 3300 lb, making it rather chubby compared to competing marine diesels such as the Cummins 100-hp Model AMR-4 that weighed 2000 lb, and the Kermath 113-hp Model 6-474 that weighed 2100 lb. [3-84] Thus, it is questionable how attractive the new Hall-Scott diesel would have been to boaters. It is not known how many Model 142 engines were sold, but their market life was only a few years; therefore, production more than likely did not top a couple dozen examples. Ads

Even in full color, this bright Chieftain brochure failed to spark much interest in the Hall-Scott compression ignition engine.

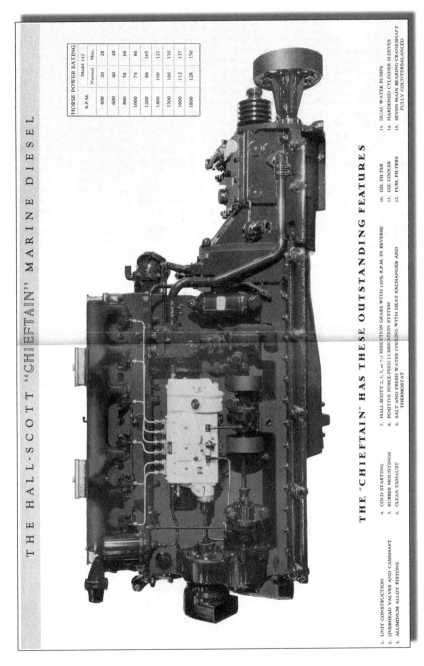

THE HALL-SCOTT "CHIEFTAIN" MARINE DIESEL

HORSE POWER RATING		
	Model 142	
R.P.M.	Normal	Max.
400	20	28
600	40	48
800	58	68
1000	74	86
1200	88	105
1400	100	121
1500	106	130
1600	112	137
1800	128	150

THE "CHIEFTAIN" HAS THESE OUTSTANDING FEATURES

1. UNIT CONSTRUCTION
2. OVERHEAD VALVES AND CAMSHAFT
3. ALUMINUM ALLOY PISTONS

4. COLD STARTING
5. RUBBER MOUNTINGS
6. CLEAN EXHAUST

7. HALL-SCOTT 2, 3, 5, or 7:1 REDUCTION GEARS WITH 110% R.P.M. IN REVERSE
8. POSITIVE FORCE-FEED LUBRICATION SYSTEM
9. SALT AND FRESH WATER COOLING WITH HEAT EXCHANGER AND THERMOSTAT

10. OIL FILTER
11. OIL COOLER
12. FUEL FILTERS

13. DUAL WATER PUMPS
14. HARDENED CYLINDER SLEEVES
15. SEVEN MAIN BEARING CRANKSHAFT FULLY COUNTERBALANCED

Fold-out from the same Chieftain brochure, showing some of the features of the Model 142.

found in *Pacific Motor Boat* as late as 1945 show Hall-Scott still advertising diesel engines for sale, without mentioning the Model 142 specifically, and company records indicate that three diesels were sold in 1946, the last year of any diesel deliveries. Thus, it appears that the Model 142 limped along for about 10 years. [3-85] With its heavily compromised origins and less-than-spectacular performance, this engine clearly could not have been the basis for a line of successful Hall-Scott diesel engines.

To the credit of management, the embarrassing failure in the Model 140 did not snuff out the ember burning at ACF and Hall-Scott to build a winning diesel. The clatter for diesel power was simply too strong for Hall-Scott or its parent company to ignore. Still, it did not take long for the setback of the Model 140 to be put aside and a new project initiated—one that was not related to the Model 140 or 142. Referring to this all-new engine, Bradford wrote that in the mid-1930s, Hall-Scott embarked on a program "to design and develop a suitable 125 H.P. horizontal [diesel] engine for under-floor mounting" for buses, with an eye for the promising South American export market. [3-86] Although the Model 142 marine engine struggled to swim on its own, development on another smaller and all-new Hall-Scott diesel began. Hall-Scott and ACF management seemed serious about developing its own diesel engine.

Hall-Scott's second effort at making a diesel was totally different than its first. Thankfully, the next attempt lacked an impossible deadline for completion. Also, the second program was not based on a converted gasoline engine. These two facts alone were positive signs for the chance of success for the project. The new engine would be a real compression ignition engine from oil pan to valve cover.

Without an E.J. Hall or comparable talent on the payroll, management sought diesel advice from outside the company, suggested as a "back-up" strategy by Charles Guernsey in his 1930 report. Hall-Scott obtained assistance from a successful diesel-building company, a competitor. In an unusual example of domestic intra-industry cooperation, Hall-Scott turned to Hercules Motors for help in developing a new compression ignition engine, hiring O.D. Treiber of Hercules and Hans Fisher of the Lanova Corporation. [3-87] Not surprisingly, this outside engineering input produced an engine that looked different from any other Hall-Scott product. These engineers did not use existing Hall-Scott blocks, pistons, or other parts for the new engine, which had been a common practice at Hall-Scott over the years. Therefore, the measurements of the new motor were not like those of any other Hall-Scott engine. The four-cycle, six-cylinder horizontal engine had a 4-5/8 inch bore and 5-1/2 inch stroke,

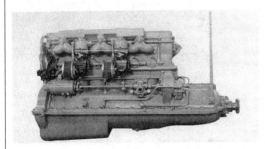

Hall-Scott leaders figured that connecting the Chieftain to the respected Invader couldn't hurt sales of the diesel. Note the price differences between the two engines.

THE HALL-SCOTT "CHIEFTAIN" MARINE DIESEL

CONDENSED SPECIFICATIONS

GENERAL—Hall-Scott Model 142; 6 cylinder direct injection Diesel type marine engine; 5" bore, 6" stroke; piston displacement 706.9 cubic inches; horsepower ratings based on 70 to 95 lbs. B.M.E.P.; net weight 3330 lbs. with 2 or 3:1; 4090 lbs. with 5 or 7:1 reduction gears.

UPPER CRANKCASE AND BLOCK—Cylinder block and upper crankcase cast integral from nickel chromium iron; removable wet cylinder sleeves; main bearings heavily ribbed and located 3⅝" above flange face; seven main bearings with heavily ribbed caps; removable steel backed copper lead bearing shells.

LOWER CRANKCASE—Cast iron; contains the oil sump and screen only; no moving parts or pipes attached; bolts to engine bed through rubber bushed bosses.

CYLINDER HEAD—Nickel chromium iron casting; carries the camshaft, valves, springs, rockerarms, rockerarm shaft, injectors, camshaft driving sprocket and compression release mechanism. Can be removed as a unit and valves ground on the bench; 2½" O. D. intake valves; 2" O. D. exhaust valves; cams run in pool of oil making mechanism practically noiseless; rockerarm cover of cast aluminum with bolted flange.

CRANKSHAFT—Chrome nickel molybdenum steel forging with seven main bearings 3⅛" diameter; 2⅞" diameter crankpins; heavy section webs; drilled for pressure feed lubrication; fully counterbalanced.

CONNECTING ROD—Con rod "I" beam section chrome nickel steel forging; each end balanced within ⅛ ounce; heat treated alloy steel connecting rod bolts and nuts; replaceable shells; piston pin bronze bushed 2" diameter.

PISTONS—Aluminum alloy trunk type; four compression rings; one oil control ring, one skirt ring; piston pin bearing in piston and rod; special keyed plug type piston pin retainers.

REDUCTION GEAR—Engine supplied with either 2:1 or 3:1 reduction gear; 5:1 or 7:1 gearing at additional cost. All reduction gears supplied with integral propeller shaft brake; water jacketed gear case; heavy-duty multiple disc clutch; 110% propeller R.P.M. in reverse.

INSTRUMENT PANEL — Furnished with engine; has oil pressure, oil and water temperature gauges; ammeter and tachometer; indirectly lighted.

ACCESSORY DRIVES—Accessories are chain driven with a quadruple strand half inch pitch roller chain driving the fuel injection pump, oil pump, water pumps and camshaft; an adjustable idler sprocket is used for chain adjustment.

OIL PUMP—Mounted on the intake side of the engine; gear type with pressure regulating valve conveniently located in the cover; pump can be removed and replaced without disturbing any other accessories.

OIL CIRCULATION SYSTEM — The oil pump takes oil from the sump through the screen, forces it through drilled passages in block to oil filter then oil cooler, through cooler to main oil lead in case to main bearings, through drilled holes in crankshaft to con rod bearings, from drilled holes in connecting rods to piston pins. Drilled oil passages carry oil from main oil line to all accessory shaft bearings. Chain drive mechanism lubricated by overflow from cylinder head.

WATER PUMPS—Bolted to cylinder block and driven off accessory shaft; one gear type with stainless steel gears and one centrifugal type; both provided with grease cups to grease shaft bushings.

WATER CIRCULATION SYSTEM — Sea water is drawn from scoop through strainer to gear type water pump; from pump through heat exchanger to oil cooler; from oil cooler through passages around reduction gear to exhaust elbow; through elbow into exhaust pipe and overboard. Fresh water is pumped from expansion tank through heat exchanger to centrifugal pump; from pump through cylinder block and exhaust manifold to cylinder head; through head and thermostat back to expansion tank.

GENERATOR—Seven hundred fifty watt generator; thirty-two volt with voltage regulation.

STARTER — Thirty-two volt arranged for remote control through two-stage switch.

OIL FILTER — Hall-Winslow replaceable cartridge type, mounted on the intake side of the cylinder block; has built-in by-pass valve to insure continued operation, should element become clogged.

PRESSURE REGULATING VALVE—Located in oil pump cover.

OIL COOLER—Bolted to block above water pump; multiple copper tube type.

FUEL INJECTION — Bosch or Ex-cell-O fuel pumps with built-in governors.

NOZZLES—Standard Bosch Pintle type.

FUEL FILTERS—Cleanable edge type to install in fuel line, also Hall-Winslow replaceable cartridge type mounted on engine.

HALL-SCOTT MOTOR CAR COMPANY

DIVISION OF AMERICAN CAR AND FOUNDRY MOTORS COMPANY

FACTORY AND GENERAL OFFICES

2850 SEVENTH STREET, BERKELEY, CALIFORNIA

FACTORY BRANCHES: SEATTLE, WASH.   PORTLAND, ORE.   LOS ANGELES, CALIF.   NEW YORK CITY

Specifications of the Hall-Scott Model 142.

An engine identification plate from the marine Model 142. (Courtesy of Michael Axford.)

measurements not shared with any other Hall-Scott model. What's more, it did not have an overhead camshaft, but rather came with overhead valves operated by pushrods, the first such valve configuration in a new Hall-Scott power plant built since its rail engines of the 1910s.

Hall-Scott engineers had not worked out an entirely suitable combustion chamber design with the Models 140 and 142. Thus, the new engineering team decided to purchase the rights to use an existing design, the so-called "Lanova" process, which promised to increase efficiency of operation and improve drivability. The Lanova system consisted of an hourglass-shaped pre-combustion chamber called an "energy cell" at the top of the cylinder that first accepted the fuel for partial combustion. When the fuel was shot into the pre-chamber, only partial combustion took place, the explosion of which then spewed the remaining fuel/air mixture into the cylinder with great turbulence for final ignition. This added swirl and partial burn enhanced efficiency and promoted cleaner burning of the fuel. The Lanova process answered the problem of starting diesels without resorting to some cumbersome system such as cranking over the engine with gasoline and then switching to diesel, and trying to tackle the long-standing diesel problem of producing excessive smoke. For the 1930s, the Lanova process was an acceptable system, and its use made the new Hall-Scott diesel engine workable.

The engineering team built a working example of the new engine, named it the Model 125, installed it in a bus and then a truck for testing, and found it to perform entirely satisfactorily. A Model 125-powered truck pulled a 26,800-lb load from Berkeley to Seattle, averaging 9.37 mpg; it then carried 15,000 lb on the way back, registering 10.6 mpg on the return leg, enviable numbers. [3-88] The test truck registered impressive economy numbers, validating the reputation of the diesel for fuel stinginess. More importantly, this latest Hall-Scott diesel did not snap, twist, or burn internal parts while on the road.

Given the growing media attention that diesel engines were receiving in the 1920s and 1930s, the Hall-Scott experiment in compression ignition was newsworthy. In its financial section, *The New York Times* reported in 1935 that Hall-Scott was dabbling in diesel, with a brief story titled "Brill Reports Progress. Small Diesel Motor, Getting Tryout on a Bus, Is Being Made." [3-89] The article reported on a Brill stockholders meeting in which one of the items of business discussed was that "the Hall-Scott Motors Company [*sic*], another subsidiary, was making a small Diesel motor, that the first one produced had been installed in a large omnibus and that this company's export business was picking up." The leadership of the innovative ACF and Brill companies had no intention of being left behind in a cloud of blue diesel exhaust.

The Model 125 could have been the basis of a long-overdue introduction of a successful Hall-Scott diesel, but the project suffered from the company refocusing its production for the government. In 1937, shortly following the report of testing the Model 125 diesel truck and bus engine, the U.S. Navy approached Hall-Scott with its lucrative plan to build thousands of V-12 gasoline motors. [3-90] The small size of Hall-Scott made concurrent development of a V-12 and the Model 125 not feasible. Ironically, after the war ended, the demand for diesel grew ferociously, but the Model 125 found itself too small to be competitive in the truck and bus market. The Model 125 was a viable and road-tested engine, but by the postwar era, Hall-Scott management determined that its relatively limited horsepower would make it unattractive to truck and bus owners. [3-91] The Model 125 engine died stillborn after its initial development phase; no evidence could be found that it saw regular production.

Even if few truck or bus operators would have purchased a 125-horsepower diesel engine from Hall-Scott, perhaps company engineers could have used the basic technology in the Model 125, or some of its parts, as the basis for a larger engine of six or eight cylinders. After all, Hall-Scott certainly had shown no aversion to taking an evolutionary approach to expanding its number of engine models in the past. The Invader serving as the basis for the Defender and Model 400 was a recent example. Here in the Model 125 was a working example of an engine technology, diesel, which obviously enjoyed a growing demand. By the postwar era, trucks and buses would embrace diesel as trains and boats had earlier, much to the detriment of Hall-Scott, which found itself without a diesel engine as the market became ever more dominated by them. Sadly, development of the Model 125 was a path not taken. This amounted to a costly, perhaps even fatal, decision by Hall-Scott leadership going into the 1940s, a decade that proved how workable the modern diesel had become.

"What Is Wrong with Hall-Scott?"

ACF purchased Hall-Scott in 1925 with the hope that the growth and profitability of the engine maker would continue, but that did not happen. As it turned out, Hall-Scott struggled to keep its doors open until the outbreak of World War II, its own financial difficulties actually predating the Great Depression by several years. The marriage to ACF almost seemed to be a kiss of death, and Hall-Scott immediately began to lose great sums of money after the 1925 purchase. Kept afloat largely by revenue from the highly profitable Ruckstell axle program, Hall-Scott reported net earnings from 1924 to 1926, totaling some $2.03 million for those three years (reversing four years of losses totaling $560,000). [3-92] ACF sold the Ruckstell axle line to Eaton in 1925, and once carryover from axle sales discontinued in 1926, persistent losses again returned to Hall-Scott. [3-93] ACF management was so troubled with this sorry and unexpected state of affairs that it conducted an in-depth analysis of the Hall-Scott operation in March 1931, with the report repeatedly posing the question, "What is wrong with Hall-Scott?"

The ACF investigation of the Hall-Scott operation revealed a large number of problems, many of them quite serious. Only occasionally naming B.C. Scott specifically, and E.J. Hall only in passing, the ACF audit suggested that Hall-Scott had always been a rather poorly led company and basically was lucky to be open in 1931. In terms of management structure, the report concluded, "The executive control is remote...the organization, particularly the active administrative branches are not definitely set up. Responsibilities are divided and obscure... The policy or objective of the business is not apparent... The sales and marketing branch has no head or no policy." [3-94] This lack of planning, clarity of vision, and aggressiveness went way back in company history. Not mincing words, the report said company founders had "only a vague precon-ceived idea of the product to be manufactured" when it opened, Hall-Scott's early success attributable to a combination of the "fortuitous circumstances" of growing markets and a world war, but also the founders' "business acumen and engineering skill" maneuvering in a "virgin field," acknowledging some limited positive aspects of Hall's and Scott's leadership. [3-95] But the report also said that Hall-Scott management became swamped by the growing breadth and scope of the company, so by the 1920s, the Hall-Scott evolution from a tiny startup operation, compounded with the aforementioned problems, resulted in the precarious situation in which the company found itself in 1931. Those early years of success and having a trailblazing product lingered in the minds of Hall-Scott leaders, however, to the detriment of the company, convincing these men to believe the company was more powerful, influential, and successful than it really was. Hall-Scott still made a good product but now operated "in a keenly competitive field, which is controlled by inherent values and selling price." [3-96] It was clear to ACF management that a successful diesel had to be introduced.

Hall-Scott management had failed the company in a multitude of ways. When it came to bringing out new products, Hall-Scott managers had failed "to intel-ligently survey the market before launching a new model of engine." Thus, tooling costs were high, sales were slow, and inventories and depreciation on under-used equipment and parts were a killer to company finances. [3-97] The report stated, "The method has been to offer product at cost plus a profit regard-less of the competition...to mould [sic] the market to the product instead of the reverse," what the report called a "delusion." [3-98] Similarly, "Managers have not bargained to get good prices for materials and have not priced engines well." Management had also failed the company when it came to buying parts, and the maintaining of outrageous inventories "perhaps represents the worst situation in the plant's management." [3-99] This included engines, parts (e.g., they sat on piles of obsolete LM-6 gears), and the Model 175 transmission, which was just introduced and had proven to be a slow seller. This again was tied to the marketing and sales issues of the company and was a tangible and costly manifestation of poor leadership. The report accused Hall-Scott of "living in the glamour of the past," and any performance superiority of its products simply was not worth the price, making them unattractive to buyers. [3-100] In other words, the industry had changed greatly in 20 years, but Hall-Scott's attitudes about itself and its products had not. While outside the control of Hall-Scott leaders, the West Coast plant location was not terribly cost efficient for serving ACF-Brill production, tacking on $22 to $45 per engine (and that did not even address the low-volume, high-weight Model 350). [3-101] The Berkeley plant was not terribly efficient anyway, having been expanded over the years in a piecemeal fashion, thus being saddled with high costs for routing of product. Therefore, the report did not suggest that keeping the Berkeley plant was a benefit to the company. These factors, and many others of lesser importance, led to Hall-Scott selling a high-priced, and thus poorly selling, engine line.

How expensive were the Hall-Scott engines, comparatively speaking? After surveying the field, the ACF report discovered that Hall-Scotts typically cost 25–75% more than comparable engines, with some portions of the Hall-Scott line being more competitive than others. [3-102] While marine engines as a

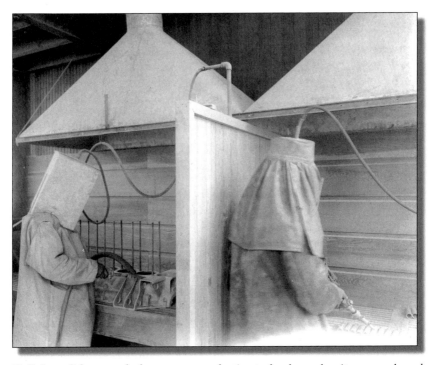

Hall-Scott did not use the latest mass-production technology when it was purchased; hand labor and small production numbers continued to characterize its manufacture. This photo was taken circa 1920. (Courtesy of Taylor Scott.)

Numerous pictures have been found of men carrying and lifting by hand at the Hall-Scott plant in the 1920s and 1930s. This photo was taken circa 1920. (Courtesy of Taylor Scott.)

line had not been good sellers or money makers because of their high cost and low volume, the Model 350-based engines, used first in rail and then moved into marine and industrial applications, were even more of a disappointment. In fact, the large-displacement models, with high tooling and transportation costs and low sales, had become a liability to the company. [3-103] The report concluded that the Model 350 was an engine built with no market and no demand. This report was written in 1931 during the early years of the Great Depression, which was a particularly difficult time to be selling a product deemed by customers to be too expensive. Almost the entirety of the 100-page report was scathing.

The ACF report found plenty of things wrong with Hall-Scott, and it laid most of the blame at the door of the front office. It appears that Hall-Scott management did not believe that it had to strike hard bargains for materials or

Hall-Scott did not use assembly lines, at least not in the "Big Three" automotive sense, in the manufacture of its engines. This photo was taken circa 1920. (Courtesy of Taylor Scott.)

services to keep a lid on costs, that it did not have to find customers through an aggressive sales program, and that it could simply make engines that it thought the market demanded. After all, Hall-Scott made a top-quality engine, with the best construction and methods; therefore, customers would find Hall-Scott and pay the price, regardless of the competition. Much needed to be addressed at Hall-Scott in terms of running a modern industrial enterprise in a successful manner—in fact, so much that was basic, that the ACF report reads it was as if Hall-Scott managers needed an introductory college business course.

But the report did find a few things about which to be positive at Hall-Scott. The International Harvester line was "vital" to the health of the company, with its high volume, low tooling cost, and consistent profitability, and it was "the only product in the plant that is based on modern commercial ideas." [3-104] It was held up as a template for the introduction and production of other models.

Hall-Scott was blessed with general labor harmony and a highly skilled work-force. The location of the plant in Berkeley was a handicap, inasmuch as ACF production was so far away. But at least Hall-Scott was poised to take advantage of the West Coast market, and the report did express high hopes for more of that in the future. The Berkeley plant did not provide for smooth throughput of product, but it was served well by highway and rail, energy costs were low, and it had no shortage of room to grow. Not surprisingly, given the long stay of E.J. Hall, the report found, "The engineering and kindred branches are satisfactory, in fact for a business of this size it is unusually well equipped." [3-105] Although little was positive about the marine line, two of the twelve models had at least some hope of commercial success: the Fisher Jr. (which was based on a low-cost International Harvester engine) and the Invader. The new Model 175 truck engine would be the basis for even larger models that hopefully would be competitive. If these models could be built in enough volume, they could bring profits. Overall, the writers of the report summed up that the future for Hall-Scott was "not too encouraging, but is not hopeless." [3-106]

ACF implemented an aggressive regime to counter the pressing problems at its struggling engine division. Employees took a cut in pay, the highest coming from management ranks, and overtime was cancelled for hourly workers. Strenuous efforts were made to move parts, engines, and transmissions laying around the factory and at branch offices. Some branch offices were closed, and others were scaled back. The leadership structure of Hall-Scott was streamlined. Goals were set to boost production, with a target of 3,300 engines annually of a favorable model mix. ACF leadership and Hall-Scott personnel all seemed committed to saving the operation. But what saved Hall-Scott were not these efforts to save dollars, but larger issues—ones of international scope—that revived engine demand in the late 1930s through the first half of the 1940s.

As America entered the war in 1941, the Hall-Scott line of marine power included five gasoline models, covering a range of 38 to 900 hp. The single Hall-Scott example in the marine diesel category, the six-cylinder, 110- to 130-hp Chieftain, was omitted in the *Automotive Industries* 1942 annual diesel engine review. [3-107] This suggests that by the early 1940s, Hall-Scott had possibly, although not positively, terminated marketing of its troubled diesel. By that time, diesel marine engines were common, though, and Hall-Scott's lack of a successful diesel development program was worrisome. Regardless, even if Hall-Scott suffered under a yoke of pressing problems, by 1941 it was still an established and respected marine engine maker, making some contributions to engine development and powering many hundreds of boats, large and small, in the span of only 20 years.

Hall-Scott engines for trucks, buses, and equipment in 1941 had even greater breadth in the number of models offered, 13, spanning a range of 60 to 286 hp. The Models 151 and 152 engines Hall-Scott had made for International Harvester had been discontinued in the early 1930s, which pared down the line a bit, and a couple other short-lived models had disappeared. The good name of Hall-Scott in bus engines was established by the early 1940s, with ACF maintaining a reasonable share in the bus market. But Hall-Scott still needed to forge a reputation for itself in powering trucks and equipment. The company had brought out some potent models, all with heavy-duty features, thoughtful construction, and high output, which it hoped would address that lack of recognition. While ACF prohibited Hall-Scott from selling engines to other bus makers of any size, Hall-Scott engines, even if they were 25–75% more expensive than competing products, were starting to appear in more trucks as OEMs, including major names such as International, Kenworth, and Peterbilt. Management held out promise for the new Model 400 engine to crack into the heavy-duty truck market in a major way. To its credit, the company had experimented with diesel, albeit unsuccessfully.

Hall-Scott Motor Car Company entered World War II without the presence of the two men who had launched the company and had led it through its first several formative decades. Bert Scott served as president of Hall-Scott from 1910 until 1938 when he "severed his connection with the company," working for several years in the wake of the blistering 1931 analysis from "upstairs." [3-108] Doubtless he felt significant pressure from ACF to lead his firm in a different manner and to turn profits. It is unknown what kind of relationship Scott had with ACF officials, or if that relationship led to his retirement while he was only in his mid-50s. In a letter from Bert Scott to Speed Glidewell dated 1956, the cofounder of the company did not betray his reasons for leaving.

The full story behind E.J. Hall's departure likewise is unclear. The *National Cyclopaedia of American Biography* stated that Hall served as "vice-president and factory manager" of Hall-Scott until 1926 when ACF purchased it, at which point Hall became "vice-president and general manager" of the company, while simultaneously holding other managerial positions with ACF and Fageol, until 1930. [3-109] A brochure written by the next venture he joined, De Vaux-Hall Motors Corporation, corroborates that date, saying that Hall left Hall-Scott to work with Norman De Vaux in June 1930. [3-110] Speed Glidewell offered another date for Hall leaving, 1928, and two reasons: the offer from De Vaux and "not liking [ACF] company policies." [3-111] The 1931 ACF analysis of Hall-Scott mentioned Hall by name only once or twice, and even then in only the most offhanded way, which supports the possibility that Hall and ACF

De Vaux-Hall Motors Corporation

In 1930, predictions by politicians, businessmen, and others that American economic recovery was just around the corner were commonplace, and all were wrong. Elbert Hall and Norman De Vaux's project to commence auto making in that year was such a quixotic statement of hope. Hall and De Vaux might have misread the tea leaves about an economic turnaround, but they correctly sensed the need to offer great value to car buyers. Thus, the De Vaux 6-75 had unusual performance and features for a car "in the low price field." One ad listed prices starting at $545 for a base phaeton, extending to $785 for the custom coupe or sedan (with six wire wheels). All De Vaux models used the same engine. That power plant seems to have been based on, or at least shared some parts with, the Continental 22A (Continental built the engines for De Vaux). The 214.7-cubic-inch six cylinder had 3-3/8 × 4-inch bore and stroke, a four main-bearing crank, and an L-head, which was less costly to manufacture. It produced 65 hp at 3100 rpm, which *Automobile Trade Journal* called "exceptionally high output." It also

Norman de Vaux

Col. Elbert J. Hall

reported that the block and manifolds "were specifically designed by Col. Elbert J. Hall"; the name "Hall" was indeed cast into the side of the block. In addition to having a fine engine, many noted the car's handsome lines, which were the work of noted stylist Count Alexis de Sakhnoffsky. Regular production began in the spring of 1931 in Grand Rapids, Michigan; the Oakland, California, plant never reached volume production. Attractive pricing, thoughtful engineering, smart styling, and a large dealer network (assembled by former auto executive De Vaux) were not enough to overcome the profound undercapitalization of the company, much less the worsening national economy. Almost immediately facing a serious cash-flow problem, De Vaux-Hall slipped into receivership in late 1931. Continental was owed almost a half-million dollars by De Vaux-Hall and could not recover much cash, so it assumed production, altered and renamed the line, and stayed at it until 1934. For the successful Hall (who is shown standing to the left of the car in the above photo) and De Vaux (who is shown standing to the right of the car in the above photo), the De Vaux-Hall experiment was a conspicuous failure. (Photos courtesy of Howard Reinke.)

leadership did not have the best relationship. The remainder of Hall's engineering career was marked by not staying at any one place more than a few years, his 18 to 20 years at Hall-Scott being by far the longest time he spent at one job. Perhaps the impatient creative genius of E.J. Hall needed some fresh surroundings by 1930.

Settling the precise date of Hall's departure from Hall-Scott is not terribly consequential. The critical thing is that Hall did indeed leave, and with him left not only an engineering leader, one of America's most talented in the automotive field, but the single most powerful explanation behind the otherwise inexplicable technical leadership, critical acclaim, racing victories, and any degree of sales success that Hall-Scott had enjoyed in engine building. As long as E.J. Hall led the engineering team of the company, Hall-Scott could be counted on to create power plants that pushed the state of the art in gasoline engines—products that "set the bar" by which other engines would be compared. In the years after Hall left, the Hall-Scott Motor Car Company largely coasted on the last engines that E.J. Hall had designed. Instead of creating new engines in the two decades after Hall left, the Hall-Scott engineering department kept busy improving and altering the existing models of the company, fashioning "new" motors largely from what Hall had left with the company, and working on non-engine projects. The fact that Hall's engines were able to keep the product line of the company viable for decades after 1930 is an impressive testimony to his amazing abilities.

As the United States and other nations geared up for World War II, the Hall-Scott Motor Car Company found itself busier than it had ever been. The number of engines produced soared, but the mix of what kinds of engines were made changed dramatically. As orders from Uncle Sam and foreign governments began to swell, the percentage of Hall-Scott production going to buses shrank considerably from about 80% in the mid-1930s, and the percentage going to boats topped 50%. (It would climb to more than 80% in 1942.) Hall-Scott truck engine deliveries also increased in raw number and percentage of their output. Belligerent nations around the world in these years did not have a dire need for buses; they were busy building ships and trucks for war. Just as it had done in World War I, Hall-Scott throttled up production in World War II to meet the power demands of many nations.

An aerial photo of the Hall-Scott plant and its surroundings. Note San Francisco Bay to the left (west).

205

References

3-1.   *The New York Times*, September 4, 1925, p. 32.

3-2.   Debra Brill, *History of the J.G. Brill Company*, Indiana University Press, Bloomington, IN, 2001, p. 164.

3-3.   Ibid., p. 165.

3-4.   *The New York Times*, September 17, 1925, p. 31.

3-5.   Debra Brill, *History of the J.G. Brill Company*, Indiana University Press, Bloomington, IN, 2001, pp. 164–165.

3-6.   *San Francisco Chronicle*, March 23, 1926, p. 12.

3-7.   Debra Brill, *History of the J.G. Brill Company*, Indiana University Press, Bloomington, IN, 2001, pp. 164–165.

3-8.   "Report on Hall-Scott Motor Car Company, Berkeley, California," unpublished report, 1931, pp. 37–38. Courtesy of Taylor Scott. The report said, "The Hall-Scott Company as compelled seller is by this circumstance always on the defensive," and ACF Motors "complains loudly of lack of cooperation and the excessive price paid for the exclusive right to use Hall-Scott engines in their buses."

3-9.   *Commercial Car Journal*, March 15, 1926, p. 42. *Commercial Car Journal*, October 15, 1926, p. 7.

3-10.   *Commercial Car Journal*, October 15, 1926, p. 7. *Commercial Car Journal*, September 15, 1926, p. 9. G.N. Georgano, ed., *The Complete Encyclopedia of Commercial Vehicles*, Krause Publications, Iola, WI, 1979, pp. 631–632.

3-11.   *The Motor Truck*, December 1927, p. 13.

3-12.   *Commercial Car Journal*, August 15, 1928, p. 26.

3-13.   *The Motor Coach*, December 1927, p. 13.

3-14.   *Automotive Industries*, June 17, 1933, p. 728.

3-15.   This Model 175 is not to be confused with the Hall-Scott marine engine designated as the H.D. 175, also referred to as Models 132 and 133. Francis Bradford, "A History of the Hall-Scott Motor Car Company," unpublished manuscript, 1989, pp. 34, 59–61. Courtesy of Bancroft Library, University of California, Berkeley, BANC MSS 93/104c.

3-16. *Commercial Car Journal*, April 1937, p. 23.

3-17. Ibid., pp. 61–63. *Commercial Car Journal*, August 1937, pp. 108–109.

3-18. *Commercial Car Journal*, July 1930, p. 98.

3-19. *Commercial Car Journal*, May 1931, p. 38.

3-20. Horse Power Chart—Hall-Scott Engines, specifications sheet, n.d.

3-21. Hall-Scott Model 175 Three-Speed, Heavy-Duty Transmission, brochure, n.d.

3-22. Francis Bradford, "A History of the Hall-Scott Motor Car Company," unpublished manuscript, 1989, p. 41. Courtesy of Bancroft Library, University of California, Berkeley, BANC MSS 93/104c.

3-23. Ibid., pp. 59–61.

3-24. Horse Power Chart—Hall-Scott Engines, specifications sheet, n.d.

3-25. Francis Bradford, "A History of the Hall-Scott Motor Car Company," unpublished manuscript, 1989, p. 60. Courtesy of Bancroft Library, University of California, Berkeley, BANC MSS 93/104c. Horse Power Chart—Hall-Scott Engines, specifications sheet, n.d.

3-26. Francis Bradford, "A History of the Hall-Scott Motor Car Company," unpublished manuscript, 1989, p. 61. Courtesy of Bancroft Library, University of California, Berkeley, BANC MSS 93/104c.

3-27. Ibid.

3-28. Ibid.

3-29. Ibid., pp. 66–69, 147–159.

3-30. Ibid., pp. 23–25.

3-31. Ibid., p. 25.

3-32. Ibid., p. 77. *San Francisco Chronicle*, December 29, 1926, p. 1. The men all suffered burns, especially to the face. The article called the accident "spectacular."

3-33. Francis Bradford, "A History of the Hall-Scott Motor Car Company," unpublished manuscript, 1989, p. 77. Courtesy of Bancroft Library, University of California, Berkeley, BANC MSS 93/104c. Mark Foster, *Henry J. Kaiser; Builder in the Modern American West*, University of

Texas Press, Austin, TX, 1989, pp. 271–272. Edward Scott, *The Saga of Lake Tahoe, Vol. I*, Sierra-Tahoe Publishing, Crystal Bay, NV, 1957, pp. 67–68, 439, 441. Edward Scott, *The Saga of Lake Tahoe, Vol. II*, Sierra-Tahoe Publishing, Crystal Bay, NV, 1973, pp. 115, 295.

3-34.   Edward Scott, *The Saga of Lake Tahoe, Vol. I*, Sierra-Tahoe Publishing, Crystal Bay, NV, 1957, p. 439. Edward Scott, *The Saga of Lake Tahoe, Vol. II*, Sierra-Tahoe Publishing, Crystal Bay, NV, 1973, p. 304.

3-35.   Edward Scott, *The Saga of Lake Tahoe, Vol. I*, Sierra-Tahoe Publishing, Crystal Bay, NV, 1957, p. 440.

3-36.   Stan Grayson, *Engines Afloat, From Early Days to D-Day, Vol. I, The Gasoline Era*, Devereux Books, Marblehead, MA, 1999, p. 83.

3-37.   *Motor Boating*, February 1931, p. 123.

3-38.   *Pacific Motor Boat*, February 1941, p. 42.

3-39.   *Motor Boating*, February 1931, p. 123.

3-40.   *Commercial Car Journal*, April 1930, p. 10.

3-41.   *Motor Boating*, February 1931, p. 123.

3-42.   Ibid.

3-43.   Francis Bradford, "A History of the Hall-Scott Motor Car Company," unpublished manuscript, 1989, pp. 80–81. Courtesy of Bancroft Library, University of California, Berkeley, BANC MSS 93/104c.

3-44.   Anthony Kirk, *Founded by the Bay; The History of Macaulay Foundry, 1896–1996*, Macaulay Foundry, Berkeley, CA, 1996, p. 48.

3-45.   William Nelson, Hall-Scott binder, financial section, p. 13. Courtesy of William Nelson. Nelson was the last president of Hall-Scott and kept many handwritten or typed company records in a binder. "Report on Hall-Scott Motor Car Company, Berkeley, California," unpublished report, 1931, pp. AA-7. Report courtesy of Taylor Scott.

3-46.   *Motor Boating*, March 1931, p. 160.

3-47.   *Motor Boating*, May 1931, p. 114.

3-48.   *Motor Boating*, July 1931, p. 34.

3-49.   J.E. "Speed" Glidewell, "A Brief History of Hall-Scott Motor Company," unpublished address, 1956, p. 2.

3-50. Herschel Smith, *Aircraft Piston Engines; From the Manly Balzer to the Continental Tiara,* Sunflower University Press, Manhattan, KS, 1986, p. 48. William Nelson, ACF-Brill executive and the last president of Hall-Scott, wrote, "The entry into the marine design was logical thru [*sic*] the demands of bootleggers for a vessel which could outrun government boats... It did give Hall-Scott the best opportunity for its existence." William Nelson, autobiography, unpublished manuscript, 1963, p. 266. Latter source courtesy of William Nelson.

3-51. *Motor Boating,* June 1931, p. 163.

3-52. William Nelson, Hall-Scott binder, financial section, p. 13. Courtesy of William Nelson. Nelson was the last president of Hall-Scott and kept many handwritten or typed company records in a binder.

3-53. Ibid.

3-54. *Pacific Motor Boat,* February 1941, p. 40.

3-55. William Nelson, Hall-Scott binder, financial section, p. 13, and material section, pp. 2–10. Courtesy of William Nelson. Nelson was the last president of Hall-Scott and kept many handwritten or typed company records in a binder. The Nelson source gave a figure of 3,337. Francis Bradford, "A History of the Hall-Scott Motor Car Company," unpublished manuscript, 1989, pp. 79, 83. Latter source courtesy of Bancroft Library, University of California, Berkeley, BANC MSS 93/104c. Bradford gave a figure range of 3,456–3,497.

3-56. J.E. "Speed" Glidewell, "A Brief History of Hall-Scott Motor Company," unpublished address, 1956, p. 3. Hall-Scott Power/Electronics, brochure, 1955, p. 4.

3-57. *Pacific Motor Boat,* February 1941, p. 42.

3-58. Francis Bradford, "A History of the Hall-Scott Motor Car Company," unpublished manuscript, 1989, p. 84. Courtesy of Bancroft Library, University of California, Berkeley, BANC MSS 93/104c. The Defender, brochure, 1938. The Invader, brochure, 1937.

3-59. Hall-Scott Power/Electronics, brochure, 1955, p. 4.

3-60. Francis Bradford, "A History of the Hall-Scott Motor Car Company," unpublished manuscript, 1989, p. 84. Courtesy of Bancroft Library, University of California, Berkeley, BANC MSS 93/104c.

3-61. Ibid., p. 89. *Pacific Motor Boat,* February 1941, p. 42.

3-62.   Stan Grayson, *Engines Afloat, From Early Days to D-Day, Vol. I, The Gasoline Era*, Devereux Books, Marblehead, MA, 1999, p. 87.

3-63.   *Automotive Industries*, June 15, 1947, p. 28.

3-64.   Ibid.

3-65.   William Nelson, Hall-Scott binder, financial section, p. 13. Courtesy of William Nelson. Nelson was the last president of Hall-Scott and kept many handwritten or typed company records in a binder.

3-66.   Francis Bradford, "A History of the Hall-Scott Motor Car Company," unpublished manuscript, 1989, p. 104. Courtesy of Bancroft Library, University of California, Berkeley, BANC MSS 93/104c.

3-67.   *Commercial Car Journal*, November 1929, p. 54.

3-68.   Ibid., p. 60.

3-69.   Ibid.

3-70.   *San Francisco Chronicle*, December 29, 1926, p. 1.

3-71.   Francis Bradford, "A History of the Hall-Scott Motor Car Company," unpublished manuscript, 1989, p. 43. Courtesy of Bancroft Library, University of California, Berkeley, BANC MSS 93/104c. Chas. Guernsey, "Report of Investigation of European High Speed Diesel Engines," 1930, unpublished report. Europe's leadership in diesel is discussed in James Laux, "Diesel Trucks and Buses: Their Gradual Spread in the United States," in *The Economic and Social Effects of the Spread of Motor Vehicles,* Theo Barker, ed., Macmillan, Basingstoke, Hampshire, UK, 1987, pp. 99–101.

3-72.   Chas. Guernsey, "Report of Investigation of European High Speed Diesel Engines," 1930, unpublished report, p. 3.

3-73.   Ibid., addendum to unpublished 1930 report, titled "Literature on Diesel Engines Being Sent to Hall-Scott," dated December 21, 1932.

3-74.   Francis Bradford, "A History of the Hall-Scott Motor Car Company," unpublished manuscript, 1989, p. 43. Courtesy of Bancroft Library, University of California, Berkeley, BANC MSS 93/104c.

3-75.   Ibid.

3-76.   Chas. Guernsey, "Report of Investigation of European High Speed Diesel Engines," 1930, unpublished report, p. 3.

3-77.   *Automotive Industries*, February 22, 1936, pp. 274, 294.

3-78. Ibid., p. 294. Francis Bradford, "A History of the Hall-Scott Motor Car Company," unpublished manuscript, 1989, p. 44. Latter source courtesy of Bancroft Library, University of California, Berkeley, BANC MSS 93/104c.

3-79. *Automotive Industries*, February 22, 1936, p. 294.

3-80. Francis Bradford, "A History of the Hall-Scott Motor Car Company," unpublished manuscript, 1989, pp. 44, 72. Courtesy of Bancroft Library, University of California, Berkeley, BANC MSS 93/104c.

3-81. *Automotive Industries*, February 26, 1936, p. 294. *Commercial Car Journal*, August 1937, p. 109.

3-82. J.W. Anderson, *Diesel Engines*, McGraw-Hill Book Company, New York, NY, 1935, pp. 24–50.

3-83. *Yachting*, February 1937, p. 93. Hall-Scott Model 142 ad, 1936, publication unknown.

3-84. *Pacific Motor Boat*, February 1942, p. 52.

3-85. *Pacific Motor Boat*, February 1945, p. 65. William Nelson, Hall-Scott binder, financial section, p. 13. Latter source courtesy of William Nelson. Nelson was the last president of Hall-Scott and kept many handwritten or typed company records in a binder.

3-86. Francis Bradford, "A History of the Hall-Scott Motor Car Company," unpublished manuscript, 1989, p. 72. Courtesy of Bancroft Library, University of California, Berkeley, BANC MSS 93/104c.

3-87. Ibid.

3-88. Ibid., p. 73.

3-89. *The New York Times*, May 4, 1935, p. 25.

3-90. J.E. "Speed" Glidewell, "A Brief History of Hall-Scott Motor Company," unpublished address, 1956, p. 3.

3-91. Francis Bradford, "A History of the Hall-Scott Motor Car Company," unpublished manuscript, 1989, p. 73. Courtesy of Bancroft Library, University of California, Berkeley, BANC MSS 93/104c.

3-92. "Report on Hall-Scott Motor Car Company, Berkeley, California," unpublished report, 1931, loose sheet. Courtesy of Taylor Scott.

3-93. Ibid., p. 6 and loose sheet.

3-94.   Ibid., p. 1-C.

3-95.   Ibid., p. 2.

3-96.   Ibid., p. 3.

3-97.   Ibid., p. 36.

3-98.   Ibid., pp. 2-B, 2-C, 17.

3-99.   Ibid., p. 35.

3-100. Ibid. p. 19.

3-101. Ibid., p. 8.

3-102. Ibid., p. 18.

3-103. Ibid., p. 25.

3-104. Ibid., p. 29.

3-105. Ibid., p. 15.

3-106. Ibid., p. 39.

3-107. *Automotive Industries*, March 15, 1942, pp. 94, 102.

3-108. J.E. "Speed" Glidewell, "A Brief History of Hall-Scott Motor Company," unpublished address, 1956, p. 1.

3-109. *National Cyclopaedia of American Biography, Vol. XLIII*, University Microfilms, Ann Arbor, MI, 1967, p. 493. For more information from the period on De Vaux-Hall, see *Automotive Industries*, December 20, 1930, pp. 899, 903, and *Automobile Trade Journal*, March 1931, pp. 33, 81.

3-110. The Men Behind the De Vaux, brochure, n.p. J.E. "Speed" Glidewell, "A Brief History of Hall-Scott Motor Company," unpublished address, 1956, p. 1. Years later, in 1956, Speed Glidewell gave a 1928 departure date.

3-111. Letter from J. Glidewell to G. Borgeson, July 5, 1984. Courtesy of San Diego Aerospace Museum.

CHAPTER FOUR

HALL-SCOTT GOES TO WAR

World War II was among the most important events in human history, and it marked a turning point for the Hall-Scott Motor Car Company. On one level, the war was beneficial for Hall-Scott, creating a voracious demand for heavy-duty engines that the company could sell at favorable prices. But at the same time, the war threatened the success of the company because it profoundly and permanently changed the market in which Hall-Scott operated. If Hall-Scott had also correspondingly changed the basic products that it sold, then these market changes would not have been so harmful. But those changes from the company did not come. Compounding the woes at Hall-Scott, serious problems in the corporate structure of American Car and Foundry (ACF), which had simmered below the surface of widespread attention during the 1930s, finally boiled over during the war years. To borrow a well-used phrase, World War II was both the best of times and the worst of times for Hall-Scott.

Mobilizing America and Hall-Scott for War

The Japanese attack on American forces stationed in Hawaii on December 7, 1941, led President Franklin Roosevelt to ask for and receive from Congress a declaration of war against Japan the following day. On the heel of these events, days later Italy and Germany declared war on the United States. Thus, by the middle of December, America was embroiled in a two-front war pitted against highly aggressive foes. To defend the homeland and vanquish the enemies of America, the federal government began coordinating the economy as it had never done. Such a massive federal effort would have many long-reaching consequences for individuals, businesses, and nearly every aspect of American life.

Hall-Scott workers form a "V" for victory, making a patriotic symbol for the cover of an issue of the company's wartime newspaper, the Invader Exhaust.

During World War II, the federal government placed severe restrictions on American production to ensure that the military received what it needed when it needed it and, concurrently, that the consumer market was not ignored. To oversee this effort, President Roosevelt created the Office of Production Management in January 1941 and then replaced it with the War Production Board in January 1942, to "exercise general responsibility" over the economy "by curtail[ing] nonessential civilian activity and...implement[ing] a system of preferences and priorities." [4-1] These federal restrictions on industrial and consumer goods affected the lifestyles of Americans in many and profound ways. For example, American auto and light truck production all but ended in February and March of 1942, save for a tiny output earmarked for a few military and high-priority non-military customers. Vehicle manufacturers turned from making sedans and semi-trucks to churning out massive numbers of attack planes and amphibious landing craft. Companies that had made components for civilian vehicles before the war began producing war vehicles or components for them.

For Hall-Scott, Washington's wartime production mandates meant a restriction on or, viewed another way, a refocusing of its engine lineup. After these restrictions became fully felt in 1942, Hall-Scott concentrated its efforts on two models: the six-cylinder 400 series truck engine and the twelve-cylinder Defender marine engine, both of which were based on the Invader. New ACF buses would no longer soak up the large percentage of Hall-Scott production as they had during the 1930s because the company suspended bus making late in 1942 to commence war work. But a Hall-Scott company binder listed some 4,500 engines, over and above the Model 440 and the Defender, which were delivered (as opposed to "produced") in the five years spanning 1941 to 1945. [4-2] These engines possibly were built before government edicts took effect and were stored at the plant; their production is unclear. Interestingly, Hall-Scott soon handed over the manufacture of its Invader to an auto company, which relieved the Berkeley plant of trying to meet the great demand for that versatile motor. [4-3] Certainly there could have been additional Hall-Scott sales had the company possessed more capacity. For example, Hall-Scott was considered to be a supplier for horizontal engines to FMC for an amphibious troop carrier it was building, but the Berkeley plant had all the production it could handle in the 400 series and the Defender. [4-4] Whatever the specifics on the Hall-Scott models produced and delivered, government restrictions lasted from 1942 until 1945, making an artificial marketplace in which Hall-Scott sold all the engines it could manufacture and still could not fully satisfy demand.

GET THERE FASTER...

with a new

HALL SCOTT
ENGINE!

Hall-Scott Model 177 engine for fire truck service has 6 cylinders, 5½" x 6", a piston displacement of 855 cubic inches, a maximum torque of 755 foot-pounds at 1200 r.p.m., and develops 243 h.p. at 2200 r.p.m.

Save for their inability to hold high *average* road speeds, by accelerating quickly after each enforced slowdown, many pieces of old apparatus are still very serviceable in fire fighting. Repowered with modern Hall-Scott engines, such units will give you 1943 efficiency, at a fraction of the cost of new equipment.

Designed especially for use in fire apparatus, Hall-Scott engines have unusual power in the lower engine r.p.m. ranges. This gives faster acceleration after every traffic slowdown, or corner rounded – saves precious minutes on the run to the fire!

Rugged and simple, the Hall-Scott engine will deliver its full horse-power for hour after hour if necessary. When servicing is needed, its unit-assembly design allows any given unit of the engine to be removed quickly, a substitute unit installed, and the apparatus returned to duty while repairs are made at the bench.

Hall-Scott has prepared a bulletin outlining in some detail the desirability of modernizing your older equipment by repowering. A copy is yours on request. Fire departments that once repower with a Hall-Scott engine, usually call for more Hall-Scotts to modernize other old units. They are also very apt to start specifying Hall-Scotts in any new equipment they may order. Let us know your requirements.

American LaFrance fire engine, owned by the city of Los Angeles, and repowered and modernized with a Hall-Scott Model 177 engine.

American LaFrance aerial truck operated by the Fresno Fire Department, Fresno, California, repowered and modernized with a Hall-Scott Model 177 engine.

HALL-SCOTT MOTOR CAR COMPANY

DIVISION OF AMERICAN CAR AND FOUNDRY MOTORS COMPANY

FACTORY AND GENERAL OFFICES: 2850 SEVENTH STREET, BERKELEY, CALIFORNIA
FACTORY BRANCHES: SEATTLE, WASH. • PORTLAND, ORE. • LOS ANGELES, CALIF. • NEW YORK CITY

Only a few high-priority, non-military customers could secure new engines during the war, and Hall-Scott could attract them with the promise of great speed.

The new Hall-Scott Model 400 engine had the brutish power to fit a number of military uses. However, American military planners had a specific application in mind for the Model 400 engine. The U.S. Army Ordinance Department oversaw the introduction of a new heavy-duty wrecker, one that could move loads up to 100,000 pounds. That vehicle appeared as two closely related models, the M26 and M26A1 tractor tank retrievers. The two truck models were functionally similar and will be referred to interchangeably here as the M26. There was a notable difference between the M26 and M26A1, though. The M26 had light steel armor bodywork and a rigid metal roof, tipping the scales at more than 45,000 lb, whereas the M26A1 had a thin skin of sheet steel and a soft canvas top but still weighed about 30,000 lb! [4-5] Often, the M26 and M26A1 tractor and its trailer attached have been collectively referred to as the M25, a further source of some confusion. [4-6] Model numbers aside, according to one military vehicle historian, the M26 was "one of the largest trucks designed, built and used by the Army in World War II," while another called it "one of the most remarkable and easily remembered vehicles to come out of W.W. II." [4-7] Clearly, the big Hall-Scott six-cylinder engine powered a highly capable war machine. Any doubters of the war credentials of the M26 would have been dissuaded of this notion by the serious weaponry of the truck, which included a 0.50-caliber machine gun, making it the most awesome tow truck ever constructed.

The armored Hall-Scott-powered M26.

Another view of the M26.

The unarmored M26A1.

The task of this impressive truck was to lift and pull tanks and other heavy vehicles in the field, which would be a Herculean task even in the best of situations. The M26 transported broken vehicles that could not move under their own power, as well as working vehicles near the front so they could enter fighting fully fueled with cooler motors. To tow an immense disabled tank in unpredictable battle conditions, the M26 possessed three axles, all of which transmitted power to its wheels, making it a so-called "6 × 6." Naturally, such a rig would be heavy, and even the lighter M26A1 was imposing in its dimensions. [4-8] Everything on this truck was huge. In fact, each wheel (tube, tire, and rim), of which there were 18 plus a spare, weighed about 900 lb. [4-9] Geared low to increase pulling power, the M26 had a final drive ratio of 7.69:1; therefore, unloaded it could reach a top speed of only 28 mph. [4-10] Picking up vehicles was accomplished by winches, one mounted to the front under the bumper and two mounted on the back behind the cab on the frame. A folding wrecker boom resided inside the frame rails when not in use. The M26 also had a highly adjustable fifth wheel mounted on the rear frame rails for towing a trailer. [4-11] With its 120-gallon fuel tank, the Hall-Scott-powered M26 boasted a cruising range of 120 miles, not exactly making it a fuel-economy champ. [4-12]

Being one of the largest trucks used by the United States in the war, the M26 needed an exceptional power plant to move it and its load adequately. The Hall-Scott 400 series was a modern, powerful, sophisticated, heavy-duty, spark-ignition engine fully up to that task. The engine, with its overhead camshaft, twin ignition, aluminum pistons, and hemispherical combustion chamber construction developed the enormous power required for this tough assignment. Specifically, the version of the 400 series used in this rig was the Model 440. The 1091-cubic-inch Model 440 had cylinder dimensions of 5-3/4-inch bore by 7-inch stroke, which also were seen in some Defenders. It developed 240 hp at 2100 rpm, using relatively low 5.4:1 compression. [4-13] Engineers sat the Model 440 engine atop the front axle of the M26, in the middle of the cab, which propelled the M26 through a transmission with twelve forward and three reverse gears. The transmission routed power to the rear axles via chains, a common setup in early twentieth-century big trucks. Such exposed drive chains needed regular lubrication, so the M26 had automatic oilers placed over the rear sprockets that dripped lubricant on the spinning chains. This method adequately lubricated the chains but left a telltale oil trail behind the giant tank retriever.

The most substantial differences Hall-Scott made to the Model 400 to prepare it for service in the wartime tank retriever were external to the engine itself. A visually obvious addition to the Model 400 was fitting it with a hydraulic pump needed to actuate the power steering of the M26. Trying to wrestle control of the retriever by its steering wheel without some assist, even without having a Sherman tank in tow, would have been a fierce fight for the strongest soldier. Therefore, the military ordered the truck equipped with power steering. Without doubt, power steering was not a luxury feature on this beast of a vehicle, and the M26 was one of the few U.S. military trucks so equipped. Fitting the pump to the Model 400 took some minor modification of the engine for mounting and accommodating a drive system for the pump. Another distinction between the standard Model 400 and the wartime Model 440 was the addition of a larger-diameter radiator fan and a strengthened water pump shaft. [4-14] A positive crankcase valve, popularly known in automotive circles as a PCV, was added by order of the military. The PCVs made their way into automobile usage, and thus widespread public familiarity, through California and federal legislation in the early 1960s as a means to combat engine emissions. These devices collect fumes in the crankcase, largely unburned gases that make their way past the pistons and piston rings (all six of them in the case of the Model 440!) into the crankcase, and then route these gases back to the intake manifold for combustion. These substances have deleterious effects on the environment, hence the government edicts in the 1960s. But these gases also are highly corrosive and are harmful to internal engine parts, as well as the oil medium in which they function. It has been known since the early twentieth century that scavenging unburned gases from the crankcase, through a simple and passive tube or a PCV, has positive effects on the longevity and effectiveness of oil, and thus engine life; this motivated the government to add this fixture to the Model 440 in

the 1940s. A last difference separating the Model 440 and base Model 400 was in the oil filter, altered in the wartime Model 440 to accommodate a manual bypass valve.

Originally designed by Knuckey Truck Company of San Francisco (Mr. Knuckey previously had been associated with Fageol), a company engaged in

The intake side of the U.S. Army-modified Model 440.

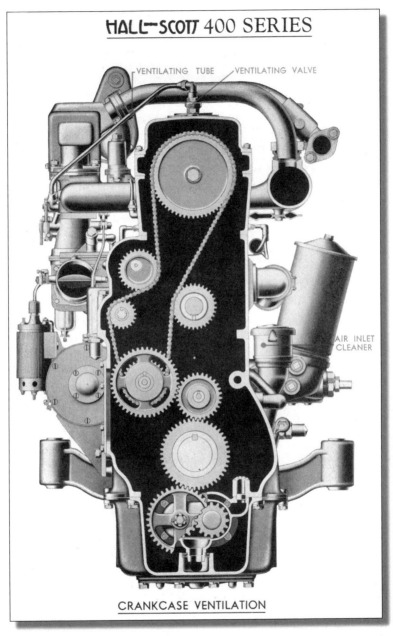

HALL-SCOTT 400 SERIES

VENTILATING TUBE   VENTILATING VALVE

AIR INLET
CLEANER

CRANKCASE VENTILATION

A cutaway view of the Model 400 through the chain housing, showing the standard ventilation of the engine, to which the U.S. Army added more for the crankcase.

The Pacifics of France

Several decades after Hall-Scott ended production, it is not an everyday occurrence to run across one of its motors still in operating condition today. This is true even on the West Coast, the base of Hall-Scott marketing. So how unlikely is it to find functioning Hall-Scotts in another country? It is hard to believe, but a handful of Hall-Scott-powered World War II-era trucks (M26 and M26A1, often called Pacifics) are still running in Europe. Rouhalde "Willy" Wilfried of France is among the small number of people who can claim to own an M26. (In fact, he owns four in various conditions.) Says Willy unapologetically, "I love this truck and I love its engine, the marvelous Hall-Scott 440." And Willy is not alone. MVCG Paris-Ile de France, a non-profit group of some 130 members, provides a home to about 30 old military vehicles, including two M26s and an M15 trailer. The members of this dedicated band of war vehicle collectors restore, maintain, drive, clean, and care for these gigantic machines. The men involved have an intense affection for the trucks and their engines. This group's trucks are not kept for static display purposes either; these are fully functioning machines, still

driving on streets, pulling loads and slogging through mud, and appearing amazingly capable some 60 years after the war ended. Member Pierre Phliponeau believes that "the real challenge facing us in the years to come is really the maintenance...especially the small parts around the engine," along with the graying of the organization. Individuals such as Willy and Pierre and groups such as MVCG have no shortage of commitment, and their tireless work keeps the memory of this impressive chapter of the Hall-Scott story alive. (Photos and information courtesy of Pierre Phliponeau and Rouhalde Wilfried.)

making off-road, heavy-duty trucks, this small Hall-Scott neighbor failed to win the contract to build the M26. [4-15] Ultimately, a much larger company with sufficient capacity for volume production won this distinction. Pacific Car and Foundry, headquartered in Renton, Washington, was a truck and equipment maker better known for building Peterbilts and Kenworths. The company also used Hall-Scott engines in some of its civilian trucks and landed the contract to produce the tank retriever. The truck maker produced 1,372 examples of the transporter; the armored M26 saw production in 1943 and 1944, and the unarmored M26A1 in 1944 and 1945. [4-16]

Because of its gigantic size and amazing capabilities, the M26 garnered a great amount of attention from the civilian press. Companies that made components for the M26 placed pictures of the enormous vehicle in their ads. This was a common advertising practice, seen in firms that provided the radiator, hydraulic pump, and lubricants for the truck. Hall-Scott likewise could not resist the marketing tactic.

The Model 440 engine proved to be rugged and dependable in military service. Hall-Scott engineer Bradford noted that only two serious problems in the Model 440 required additional attention from engineers back in Berkeley during the war. [4-17] Both of these—failure of the power steering pump driveshaft and the water pump driveshaft—were on items new to the Model 440, which did not benefit from the slightly longer "shake-down" period enjoyed by the basic Model 400 that was in production since 1940. When Hall-Scott engineers strengthened both of these weak links, failures in the field ceased being reported. The Model 440 turned out to be the most popular of the many iterations of the basic Model 400 engine, with 1,701 examples delivered during the war. [4-18] The success of the Model 440 and the prominence of the M26 became a source of enormous pride for Hall-Scott. The company's wartime newsletter, the *Invader Exhaust*, wrote, "The M-25 Tank Retriever has the most powerful gasoline engine ever developed for this type of work." [4-19] This internal company promotion was targeted to boost employee morale, not engine sales. *Invader Exhaust* writers reined in their horn blowing ever so slightly, saying, "Hall-Scott has given the M-25 Tank Retriever a reliable motor. The men who operate them in tight pinches can trust them. We would like credit for that, but it's far more important that the job is done right. That's good enough for us."

Late in the war, 1945, in another American wartime big rig, an experimental model received Hall-Scott power: the T-8 tank transporter built by Mack Truck. Having a mission similar to that of the M26—hauling tanks and other

Several companies that supplied parts for the M26, including Hall-Scott, used images of or references to the trucks in their ads. (Courtesy of Taylor Scott.)

heavy vehicles—this Mack also used a variation of the 400 series engine, the Model 441. The Model 441 shared the displacement and power rating of the Model 440, and as far as can be surmised, all of its other capacities and dimensions as well. [4-20] The only difference between the Models 440 and 441 was the mounting location of the power steering pump, as the T-8 had assisted steering similar to that of the M26. On the Model 441, Hall-Scott engineers placed the hydraulic unit on the flywheel housing. The Model 441 was a "one-off" engine model that did not see application in any other vehicle. Mack produced perhaps only one of these vehicles, and Hall-Scott produced only two of the Model 441 engines that powered it. [4-21]

The impressive T-8 looked much different than the M26, even if the two trucks had similar tasks. The T-8 weighed 95,000 lb unladen, stretching 60 ft from bumper to bumper, and boasted a carrying capacity of 80,000 lb. [4-22] The Mack transporter was a cab-over-engine design, with a much smaller passenger compartment than that of the M26 and a drastically shorter wheelbase, its two axles spaced close together, leaving the front of the cab to hang outward in front of the forward axle by several feet. The Pacific Car and Foundry M26 could accommodate a crew of about a half dozen, plus provide space for provisions, and even give them some room to fight if necessary. Not so with the Mack T-8, which had a more snug passenger compartment with only enough room for crew seating. But the thing really making the T-8 different from the M26 was that the T-8 was a "double-ender," with the truck having two cabs, one at each end of the truck, a Hall-Scott engine under each cab, and the bed located

between them. The T-8 was fairly obscure, so some military vehicle guides do not list it. Although the T-8 did not make anywhere near the public impression made by the M26, the fact that Mack chose a Hall-Scott for its giant retriever points to the rapid recognition Hall-Scott picked up after introducing the 400 series in 1940.

The intake side of the Model 441 for the Mack T-8. Note the visual similarities to the Model 440.

The experimental Hall-Scott-powered T-8.

The interesting "bogie" that transmitted power in the T-8.

The American Army, unlike the Navy, remained quite receptive to gasoline engines in World War II, much to the benefit of Hall-Scott. Army leaders decided to use gasoline engines to power almost all of the vehicles in its fleet, from jeeps to tanks and tank wreckers, with the exception of a few large transporters. This was due, in part, to reasons of logistics. [4-23] Stocking gasoline and diesel for different engines would have been cumbersome and expensive. Thus, having both gasoline and diesel engines would have complicated parts, supply, and technical support. Therefore, during World War II, Hall-Scott and other producers of large gasoline engines could still find markets for their products with the U.S. Army, such as for use in the M26, M26A1, and T-8.

While gasoline engines powered almost all U.S. Army vehicles during World War II, diesel had made much deeper inroads into the U.S. Navy fleet by the 1940s. The Navy had begun serious "dieselization" of its fleet in the early 1930s, but there was still call for gasoline power in a few specific American military craft in the 1940s.

Driving this switch to diesel was the recognition by Navy planners of the same reasons that drove increasing numbers of civilians in the marine sector to opt for compression ignition. The superiority of diesels over gasoline engines in fuel economy was a real issue for Navy policy makers. In combat situations, transporting fuel is a costly use of resources—whether men, money, or hardware—and can greatly hinder the mobility of fighting forces. Simply stated, the less refueling that has to be done in combat, the better. The high volatility of gasoline was another other reason behind the government adoption of diesel. What makes gasoline desirable as fuel also makes it a highly dangerous substance around which to work. Storing, fueling, transporting, and using gasoline expose fighting forces to danger in an already dangerous environment. Likewise, the accumulation of gasoline vapors under deck made gasoline-powered boats more hazardous than diesel-powered boats, a safety issue much discussed in the marine private sector and the Navy. The fact that Navy craft usually carried some kind of munitions on board only underscored the need to make fuel systems as fire safe and incombustible as possible.

Even with these serious drawbacks to the gasoline engine, some proponents in the Navy called for continued specific use of these motors. Most importantly, the exceptional power-to-weight ratio of high-performance gasoline engines made them desirable in high-speed applications such as torpedo, landing, patrol, and rescue craft. It is true that by 1940, diesels had dropped their power-to-weight ratios from numbers often around 100:1 seen during World War I to many examples being under 20:1 (except for old-style, low-speed marine diesels such as those made by Atlas-Imperial), with a few even reaching ratios under 10:1 (such as some two-stroke models released by General Motors in the late 1930s). But most diesels still had power-to-weight ratios several times greater than leading gasoline engines. For example, the Hall-Scott Model 3389 Defender, creating 900 hp and weighing about 4000 lb, had a power-to-weight ratio of about 4.4:1, a good figure for a 1940-era marine gasoline engine. By comparison, the Gray Model 66 diesel developed 165 hp and weighed 2750 lb, for a power-to-weight ratio of about 16.7:1, a good figure for a 1940-era marine diesel. [4-24] Engine producers Chrysler, Gray, Lycoming, Packard, and Hall-Scott all found military marine applications during World War II for high-performance gasoline power plants that they could fill.

With the many racing victories, widespread admiration, and relative commercial success of the Hall-Scott Invader, it was natural for the U.S. government to equip some of its war vessels with these brawny, reliable, and tested engines. Uncle Sam had purchased Hall-Scott marine engines from the 1920s and greatly expanded its purchasing in the late 1930s. In fact, demand was so great for this particular six-cylinder marine motor that the small and fully occupied Hall-Scott factory could not satisfy it. Invader output shot up from a couple of dozen delivered yearly in the mid-1930s to 139 in 1940, and then peaked at 1,692 in 1942. [4-25] Hall-Scott proved it could deliver sizable quantities of its Invader, but there were also demands on the company to make greater numbers of its V-12, plus its Model 400 truck engine. Even running at 100% capacity and enlarging its workforce, the little plant could churn out only so many engines, and a tough decision was made. In 1942, the Hudson Motor Car Company of Detroit was picked to produce Invaders under license during the war. [4-26] Hudson was a major corporation in the 1940s, and its prodigious engineering and production capacity allowed it to undertake a number of wartime projects, from assembling anti-aircraft guns, to airplane wing and fuselage construction, to making engines and engine parts. Hudson could certainly produce the Hall-Scott Invader in the quality, quantity, and speed demanded.

The Hudson-built Invader was little different in construction and performance than the Hall-Scott-built Invader, and the two appear identical from a distance. The Navy called for 250 hp to be developed from the engine, and Hudson tested it at 263.7 hp, providing a margin of surplus. [4-27] In terms of differences, this wartime Invader had a Navy-mandated heat exchanger added to better regulate the temperature of the coolant, and it used fresh-water cooling as opposed to the sea-water cooling that had been standard on Invaders made before the war. [4-28] Those were meaningful differences, but they were not huge. A closer inspection revealed conspicuous and numerous external labeling differences. The wartime Invader had "Invader 168" with the trademark Hudson triangle symbol embossed on its aluminum valve cover. Not satisfied

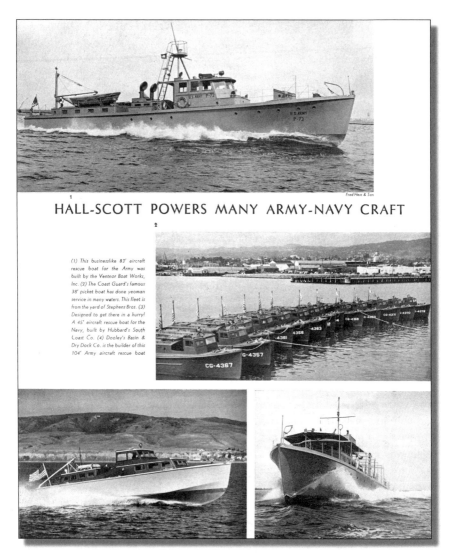

A page from a reprint of an article showing the major World War II marine applications for Hall-Scott engines.

with this single distinction sufficiently differentiating its version of the famous Hall-Scott model, Hudson also cast "Hudson Invader 168" into each of the two exhaust manifolds, affixed the Hudson triangle and Hudson Motor Car Company name onto the aluminum coil cover, and did the same on the top of

(5) Another view of the 104'
Army aircraft rescue boat reveals
many interesting features, note the
U. S. aircraft insignia on the awn-
ing top. This one is from the yard
of the Casey Boat Building Co.
(6) The Miami Shipbuilding Corp.
is the builder of this interesting
craft. Sixty-three feet o.a. and
having a family resemblance to the
PT hull, she is designed for the
Navy's aircraft rescue flotilla. (7)
A sidewise launching on the East
Coast. An 83' aircraft rescue boat
for the Army, built by Cambridge
Shipbuilders, Inc., starts her maiden
voyage with a mighty splash. (8)
This highly efficient aircraft rescue
boat for the Army is from Chris-
Craft. She is 42' o.a. (9) One of
the Royal Canadian Navy's famous "Fairmiles." She is designed
for offshore anti-submarine duty.

The Hall-Scott Motor Car Co., veteran manufacturer of marine engines, is today equipping a wide variety of Army and Navy craft,
and the excellence of its wartime record has
been confirmed by the award of the coveted
Army-Navy "E."

The Hall-Scott powered vessels here shown
are representative of types constructed and
equipped by many other builders and engine
manufacturers.

*Another page from the same reprint of an article showing the major World War II
marine applications for Hall-Scott engines.*

the gear box. [4-29] With all the effort poured into making it clear that this
Invader was not a Hall-Scott, it appears that Hudson management wanted to
claim as much responsibility for producing this engine as possible.

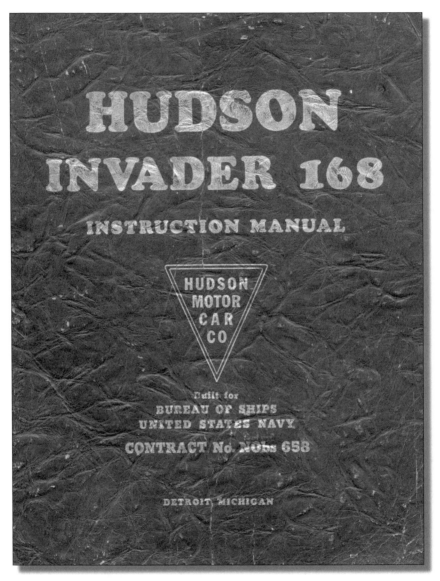

The cover of the Hudson repair manual for its Invader.

Considering the enormous feat required in moving across America the tools for making the Invader, Invader production quickly resumed in Michigan, even if did not last long. According to one Hudson historian, to build these engines

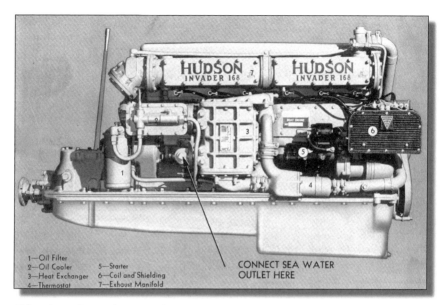

Taken from the Hudson Invader repair manual, this image shows only a few of the places where Hudson put its name on the engine. Note the Hudson name appearing twice on the exhaust manifold and in the small Hudson triangle on the coil cover.

the auto maker had to install some 6,000 special tools, gauges, jigs, and fixtures in its plant, where months before that time, only automobiles had emerged. Thus, the change to build the Invader amounted to a major undertaking. [4-30] Another Hudson writer credited the rapid startup to "the ingenuity and skill of Hudson engineers and toolmakers, who converted more than 800 machine tools that had been used for car production, saving much expense as well as time in waiting for equipment to be designed and built by the overburdened machine tool industry." [4-31] Hudson received its first orders for Invader engines in October 1942 and reached volume production by May 1943, an impressive setup time. [4-32] Invaders left the Hudson plant in a quantity greater than they could have in Berkeley. The last wartime Invader left the Hudson assembly line in Detroit in late 1944, meaning that in about a year and a half, Hudson produced 4,000 engines, a rate that reached the Hall-Scott total yearly production highpoint in the 1930s. [4-33] Put into a more long-term perspective, the brief production by Hudson accounted for about 55% of all the Invaders ever made. Given the other commitments of Hall-Scott, farming out Invader production meant that these important marine motors would arrive at boatyards in a timely manner. The Hall-Scott Model 168 Invader saw duty during the war by powering 36- and 45-foot picket boats and Hickman-built rescue craft, among other applications. The wartime reliability record of the Invader could not be found, but anecdotally, the number of Hudson Invaders finding their way into pleasure and commercial boats after the war suggests that the automaker enjoyed success in producing the big marine power plant in 1943 and 1944, as had Hall-Scott before the war.

The twelve-cylinder Defender probably made a bigger name for itself during the conflict than any other Hall-Scott engine. In fact, the Defender was an original power plant for what was to become one of the most celebrated small craft in the war—the Higgins boat. Dwight Eisenhower described the unusual little vessel as the "boat that won the war," a powerful phrase from an influential figure that has contributed to the boat's place in history and public imagination. The Navy had spawned the Hall-Scott development of the V-12 engine in 1937 precisely for a boat such as this—fast, small, and ocean-going. The British Navy also purchased quantity numbers of the Defender. The U.S.S.R. (America's

Here, a Hall-Scott V-12 assembly crew visits with a colleague back from the fighting.

erstwhile foe turned temporary ally in the war), as well as Holland, Canada, and Australia, among others, operated craft with Hall-Scott V-12s. [4-34]

At the behest of the U.S. government, Hall-Scott released two more versions of the Defender to increase the horsepower of the engine. With its 1996 cubic inches (having 5-1/2-inch bore by 7-inch stroke), the first Defenders developed about 575 hp at 2100 rpm. These initial Defenders were given the model number 1268 if equipped for right-hand rotation and the model number 1269 for left-hand rotation units. Five hundred horsepower sounds like a good deal of power, and it is; however, it was not sufficient for all fast war-boat applications. The Navy asked for more punch from the V-12 engine, so Hall-Scott introduced the Models 2268, 2269, 2286, and 2287 (direct-drive right-hand rotation, direct-drive left-hand rotation, reduction-gear right-hand drive, and reduction-gear left-hand drive, respectively), which swept 2 181 cubic inches, obtained by enlarging the bore 0.25 inches. That small increase, multiplied by the long 7-inch stroke of the engine and spread over twelve cylinders, added a substantial 185 cubic inches to the displacement of the Defender and approximately another 130 hp.

The bored-out 2181-cubic-inch Defender found an appreciative customer in the British government, which wanted the bigger V-12 engine to power its Fairmile patrol boats. [4-35] In 1943, the Hall-Scott *Invader Exhaust* described the Fairmile as a wooden boat made of oak, teak, mahogany, and plywood, 112 feet long and having a 20-foot beam—an "unsung hero" of the war, used by Great Britain and nations of the Commonwealth, such as Canada and Australia. [4-36] The British navy had used Italian-made Isotta-Fraschini engines before picking the Hall-Scott V-12 for this popular boat, which was often employed as a submarine chaser. The earlier Italian marine engines were particularly impressive, in that they created 1100 hp but weighed a scant 2699 lb, making for only 2.45 lb per horsepower. But when Italy and Britain found themselves on opposite sides in the war, the British had to look elsewhere for powering their Fairmile. [4-37] The Brits ordered the Hall-Scott V-12 equipped with reduction gears, and with the great power developed by the engine, the heat generated in the transmission would reach dangerous levels. Therefore, these beefed-up V-12s came with water cooling in the transmission. Bradford reported that a number of the engines that set sail from Berkeley bound for Great Britain did not survive the trip, being sunk by German submarines en route. [4-38] The ones that made it across the Atlantic Ocean and were installed in a Fairmile could propel the patrol boats at 18 to 20 knots and, according to one British marine writer, "gave outstanding service in many theatres." [4-39] Britain ordered its first Defenders in 1939. [4-40] Hall-Scott bragged, "All other marine engines

IN PERFORMANCE . . . HALL-SCOTT DEFENDERS SET THE STANDARDS

This 70-foot Motor Torpedo Boat was built by the Higgins Industries, Inc. Powered by three Hall-Scott Supercharged Defenders.

Close to 3,000 B.H.P. is installed in this compact engine room consisting of three Hall-Scott Supercharged Defenders.

A Defender installation in a war boat. The superchargers can be seen on the top of the engines.

which the British operate at similar piston speeds have a standard overhaul period of 500 hours, compared to the 1,500 hours for the Hall-Scotts." [4-41] Each Fairmile housed two Defenders in its engine room.

But Navy men wanted still more power than 630 hp, which prompted Hall-Scott to develop an even more potent iteration. To coax more output from the already impressive engine, Hall-Scott engineers installed a supercharger, often called a "blower," to the bigger 2181-cubic-inch V-12. These blown engines received the designations Models 3368, 3369, 3386, and 3387 (corresponding to direct-drive right-hand rotation supercharged, direct-drive left-hand rotation supercharged, reduction-gear right-hand drive supercharged, and reduction-gear left-hand drive supercharged, respectively). [4-42] Thus equipped, this ultimate Defender got up and roared with about 900 hp at 2100 rpm. [4-43] To drive the blower, Hall-Scott engineers rigged a shaft turned by bevel gears on the front end of the crankshaft. The supercharger sat above the intake manifold of the engine and was a relatively small package that yielded a substantial increase in horsepower. Hall-Scott produced some 482 supercharged V-12 engines during World War II. [4-44]

Superchargers can dramatically increase horsepower, as they did on the Defender, but their installation requires engine alterations so that the units themselves do not cause premature failure of the motors they are intended to improve. Superchargers add both horsepower and stress to an engine. With the added cylinder pressure coming from the blower, Hall-Scott engineers compensated by lowering the compression ratio a bit. The additional horse-power also correspondingly boosted the amount of heat produced, so engineers increased the amount of coolant flow by adding a second water pump. [4-45] The reverse gears likewise were strengthened to handle the 50% increase in horsepower brought about by the supercharger. It appears that the minor fix kept the drive acceptably cool, as suggested in a story kept alive for decades by Hall-Scott employees. According to a verbal account, a supercharged Defender-powered British patrol boat had its prow shot off while on duty in the Mediterranean. In spite of the damage, the crew somehow managed to retain limited control of the vessel and successfully coaxed it all the way back to England in reverse. [4-46] Stories such as this gave Hall-Scott workers tremendous pride in the engines they made.

Beyond the changes performed to increase the horsepower of the Defender, during the war years the engine also went through a number of less dramatic improvements. [4-47] Some of these upgrades included the government request to install radio shielding to the ignition wires. This order was rescinded when a later one instructed engineers to fit Defenders with four distributors rather than two. More fuel pumps, now electric, were added to supplement the standard mechanical units in order to combat vapor lock. Vapor lock occurs when fuel boils in the fuel lines, carburetor, or filter, resulting in fuel starvation

A World War II-era magazine ad, showing the Hall-Scott supercharged V-12. (Courtesy of Jack Alexander.)

in the cylinders. Non-supercharged Defenders received two such pumps; the supercharged versions received four. A power take-off unit, often called a "PTO," was added so that the Defender could power equipment on deck or on the dock near the ship. Cleanouts were added so that the exhaust manifolds could be purged of salt accumulation in seawater-cooled units. It appears that the Defender underwent a few more wartime changes than did the Invader.

The many alterations the Defender experienced, plus its relative newness, were reflected in a small number of problems that Hall-Scott engineers needed to rectify. [4-48] For example, some engines developed problems with the crankshaft and connecting rod bearings, no doubt arising from the higher power developed by the newer Defender models. Early starters sometimes failed after struggling to turn over the large-displacement, relatively high-compression engine. The accessory drive chain, which drove components such as the generator, developed the serious problem of sometimes breaking, requiring engineers in Berkeley to shuffle the mounting and driving of the engine accessories. Hall-Scott engineers also needed to alter the oil pumps of the Defender. But this handful of shortcomings did not sully the enviable reputation of the Defender, and there is every indication that these V-12s served Allied forces well. No doubt a chief reason behind the Defender's reputation for reliability and toughness was that Hall-Scott went to amazing lengths to ensure that the highest quality was built into each Defender. [4-49] Many of its critical parts such as connecting rods, wrist pins, and crankshafts had to pass a "Magnaflux" inspection, a process that magnetically checked for cracks and other imperfections. After each Defender finished assembly, it received a ten-hour test run. More impressive yet, if it passed that examination, then Hall-Scott personnel completely disassembled the engine and inspected it for defects. Finally came the last reassembly and two-hour test run, and, upon completion of which, the engine was shipped. Although bumped from ultimately powering Higgins boats, Hall-Scott engines powered thousands of other vessels for the American military and its allies. Deliveries of the V-12 began in 1938 with only 4 units and then accelerated rapidly, peaking at 1,855 units in 1943 and arriving at a cumulative a total of 6,514 units by the end of 1945. [4-50] In some years after the war ended, Defender deliveries could be measured in single digits, which dramatically underscores the unusual market conditions presented to Hall-Scott by World War II. But during that war, the Defender clearly was a Hall-Scott superstar.

Defender demand so strained Hall-Scott production that engineers had to change their machining procedures to manufacture enough in the quantity required. With crankshaft production forming a bottleneck in engine output, Hall-Scott personnel designed massive lathes that could machine the complicated, heavy, and cumbersome crankshaft for the big V-12 in fewer steps and using fewer machines. Before engineer Ralph Harrison and others in the Hall-Scott tool room created the machine, five separate lathes were needed to perform this same function. These impressive machines enjoyed a long life, being sold when Hall-Scott went out of business and then used to carve out more heavy-duty crankshafts into the 1960s. [4-51] Hall-Scott men also designed a special device that could machine all six of the journals of the V-12 crankshaft on one setup. [4-52] No evidence could be found that Hall-Scott built machining tools, or any other manufactured products outside of engines, for sale during the war. But the Hall-Scott reputation for outstanding machining practices, established decades earlier, continued to be recognized through the war years. The trade journal *Machinery* reviewed the Hall-Scott production procedures in a 1942 issue, noting the close tolerances Hall-Scott parts needed to meet—sometimes as small as 0.00025 of an inch. The author observed that the Hall-Scott marine engines "have been produced by manufacturing methods that were developed

Hall-Scott workers take a minute from their work to commemorate building the 5,000th V-12 during the war, early 1945.

over a long period of years and that are comparable with the best practice anywhere." [4-53]

The American and other allied governments targeted Hall-Scott for wartime fundraising and encouragement to extract ever-greater production, as they did with other important purveyors of war materiel. Similar to other businesses across America during the war, Hall-Scott sponsored war bond sales and blood drives among its employees. Hall-Scott received visitors at its Berkeley factory that helped keep output humming at a feverish rate. In July 1941, five months before the Pearl Harbor attack, Britain's Lord Halifax visited the Berkeley plant and "praised the good work done by Hall-Scott and urged us on to bigger and better production," according to Francis Bradford. [4-54] Halifax came to Berkeley to laud Hall-Scott employees for their labors that created the outstanding V-12 engines used by his nation's navy. The British people also benefited from a lower-profile relief effort by company employees. Bradford remembered that employees packed the empty spaces of some wooden crates containing Defender engines bound for England with non-perishable food items, such as canned goods, for workers in English boatyards. [4-55] Not all of this food

Because Hall-Scott performed defense work for the government during the war, employees had to carry an identification card at the plant. This is the front of the card for one employee, Anton Bedney.

The back of Mr. Bedney's Hall-Scott identification card.

During the war, Hall-Scott employees also had to wear a pin to work, such as this one for Mr. Bedney.

reached its intended recipients, though. When Hall-Scott employees heard that British dock workers had begun to pick the crates clean of these non-engine items, the practice of stuffing food into crates promptly ended.

In a long and bloody war that created countless tragedies, one story resonated particularly deeply with the American public—the deaths of the Sullivan brothers. These five siblings served on the same ship, and all were killed in the 1943 Guadalcanal campaign. Their parents turned their painful loss into a powerful promotion presented to war workers and others, and they brought their message to the Berkeley factory. Said Bradford who heard Mr. and Mrs. Sullivan speak, "Their presentation was a moving experience and everyone returned to their duties more determined than ever to do his or her best." [4-56] Such a response was exactly what Navy leaders had hoped to accomplish by bringing the Sullivans to Berkeley, of course, and the impressive production record of Hall-Scott suggests that the government promotional effort succeeded.

Numerous Hall-Scott employees served in the armed forces during World War II, and their visits and correspondence served as a basis for greater pride and motivation. The Hall-Scott *Invader Exhaust* featured a regular column titled "News from the Front." A common feature in the *Invader Exhaust* was to have a returning serviceman, either a former Hall-Scott employee or a relative of a current employee, standing next to a workman. For example, former Hall-Scott ignition wire assembler Don Van Horn, who the *Invader Exhaust* described in its November 1943 issue as an 18-year-old "kid" who "grew up and joined the Navy," wrote home to "'Tell all the boys...at the factory hello and that they are doing a fine job.'" [4-57] While stationed in the South Pacific, Van Horn's "landing barge was shot up and sunk... A later letter stated that he's got a new one, also powered with a Hall-Scott motor. He writes that of all his contacts with our motors he has not seen one fail yet." Ab Abbadie returned home in early 1944 for a visit from his Navy duty, stopping by his old place of employment. Abbadie told of "long patrols in northern waters in the engine room of a sub chaser. Yes, it was equipped with twin Hall-Scott V-12

Religious teaching is deeply rooted in American life. Basic to this is the belief in immortality—a life beyond the flimsy environs of earth.

And so it must be that a young American who gives his life for his country, fighting a righteous cause, *must*, perhaps in ways we cannot know now, achieve a rich compensation for his sacrifice.

With this in mind, we tell you of the death of First Lt. Preston Richardson, pilot of a B-17 bomber, awarded posthumously the Purple Heart and the Air Medal with Oak Leaf Cluster. On his 11th mission in the African campaign his plane was forced down in the sea.

His home was in Oakland. Preston worked in the shop on the nightshift, left early in 1942, died in May, 1943.

Defenders, and the performance was swell." [4-58] Stories such as these filled the company newsletter through the war years. Hall-Scott employees were immensely proud of their contribution to the war effort.

The greater production of high-performance engines was exactly what the American and other Allied governments needed, and received, from Hall-Scott. Impressive an engine as the Defender was, it was not able to hang onto its initial assignment in the engine compartment of the Navy Higgins boats. Early versions of the Higgins craft built in their Louisiana boatyards carried a single Hall-Scott V-12 in their hulls, but the U.S. Navy soon reconsidered this application. Remembered Richard "Mac" McDerby, who trained servicemen to pilot the new landing craft, "I was training marines in Hall-Scott powered boats in 1941... But later, the Navy wanted diesel. It had better fuel consumption and less fire hazard." [4-59] By the time the Higgins boats appeared for their legendary assignment in France on D-Day, June 6, 1944, the dieselization of that particular fleet had been made, and each of the American Higgins boats delivering Allied soldiers

The Hall-Scott Invader Exhaust *covered when the company's men left for war, when they came back to visit, and sometimes when they died in combat.*

243

on the Normandy coast that day was powered by a six-cylinder, two-stroke, 225-hp General Motors diesel that had been "marinized" by Gray Marine. [4-60] Hall-Scott had another one of its gasoline engines displaced by the diesel of a competitor. This was not the first time, nor would it be the last, that Hall-Scott would face such a rejection.

The engine that replaced the Hall-Scott Defender was a version of the General Motors 6-71, which turned out to be an important power plant and arguably even revolutionary. An unquestioned success on the water, after the war in its *terra firma* form, the 6-71 went on to dominate the American bus market, a niche that Hall-Scott highly prized and unequivocally needed for its survival. Rugged, economical, safe, powerful, and reliable, the 6-71 also had an incredible power-to-weight ratio; therefore, it was little wonder that this oil-burning engine was such a success.

Hall-Scott actually was stung in two ways by the 6-71. Not only did the General Motors-designed diesel replace the Defender from its prestigious assignment of powering Higgins boats, but the 6-71 familiarized thousands of men with modern high-speed diesel operation. This exposure to the qualities of the latest diesel engines changed the opinions of many people about compression ignition. According to more than one engine historian, this acquaintance was the "main impact the Second World War had on the spread of diesel engines." [4-61] Because of its amazing performance in the war, the General Motors 6-71 prepared the way for diesel to move into even more boat, truck, bus, and industrial engine compartments after the war, much to the detriment of the Hall-Scott Motor Car Company.

Hall-Scott's Parent Company Begins a Protracted Break-Up

In July 1944, as Allied forces solidified their position in France a month after the D-Day invasion, the complicated relationship between American Car and Foundry, J.G. Brill, ACF Motors, and its many divisions such as Hall-Scott shifted when company directors voted to merge the Brill Corporation and American Car and Foundry Motors Company. [4-62] The parent company formed in this action, known as ACF-Brill, oversaw a new division known as ACF-Brill Motors, a subsidiary that controlled the Hall-Scott Motor Car Company. Among the company names that disappeared when these changes took effect on August 1, 1944, were American Car and Foundry Motors, J.G. Brill, and the Fageol Company. Hall-Scott Motor Car Company was the only branch under the ACF umbrella that was not refigured, renamed, or removed in this first restructuring of ACF. Hall-Scott not being changed in this shuffle should not be construed as a sign of its vigor, independence, or resilience, however.

Efforts to break up the corporate arrangement of ACF had been simmering in and out of its boardroom dating back to the early 1930s. What bothered some in the ACF organization, such as Charles Hardy of bus and rail car manufacturer Brill Company, was that several entities under the ACF roof no longer produced anything, some produced almost nothing, and some consistently lost money, which pulled down the financial well-being of those parts that made money and dragged on the entire ACF company. Moreover, ACF clearly benefited from the success of its profitable divisions, but what did these divisions get in return from ACF? For example, ACF Motors, which oversaw Hall-Scott, funneled about $300,000 per year to its parent company, in spite of the fact that ACF Motors lost money for ten years straight (from 1927 to 1936), showed a profit briefly in 1937, and then slipped back into the red again for 1938 and 1939. [4-63] The Brill Company was one of those money-making divisions of ACF, but the poor performance of its related firms undermined its own success during the desperately lean 1930s. Hall-Scott, another division that sometimes operated profitably (especially during the war), was greatly hurt by the limitations imposed on it against making sales outside of ACF, as it was by the disappointing bus sales of ACF.

Hardy had tried several efforts at reorganizing during the interwar period, only to run up against determined opposition. After all, just as Brill might have been stung financially with the existing corporate arrangement, other companies in the ACF organization would have benefited from it. Because of the consistent losses reported by ACF Motors, which worked against the financial health of J.G. Brill, in 1940 executors of the Frederic Brill estate demanded in court to inspect the closed books of the company. These members of the Brill family charged the company with mismanagement of funds, squandering the earnings of the company their patriarch had built. While the court denied the Brill motion, the call for change was growing louder and was picking up more support from other people associated with ACF. No evidence could be found of how Hall-Scott leaders reacted to this palace coup, but the fact that it was not led or visibly supported by Hall-Scott personnel suggests that in Berkeley, these intercompany machinations were more likely viewed with dread rather than with glee.

Clearly, ACF-Brill needed to put its financial house in order. The changes brought about in 1944 to alter the structure of ACF were an attempt to address some of these long-standing grievances, but they did not solve the many deep problems of the company, nor did they silence the calls for more changes. What this struggle would mean for the Hall-Scott Motor Car Company was unclear, but there is no written evidence that Hall-Scott was able to affect these changes in any substantial way. Shortly after the war ended, this fight within ACF for its future and how that future would look would begin anew.

The War and Hall-Scott's Position as an Engine Maker

On several occasions, the U.S. Army and Navy departments publicly recognized Hall-Scott for its important contributions to the war effort. [4-64] During both world wars, the U.S. government gave awards to recognize and encourage efficiency and output in war production, and in both global conflicts, Hall-Scott won this accolade. Hall-Scott received its first World War II "E" pennant and star in 1942, and subsequent years and continued successes brought three additional stars. The government's 1945 letter marking the fourth star cited the "untiring efforts" of the company at maintaining production. [4-65] Army-Navy "E" pennants and stars hung on the company flagpole below the Stars and Stripes and adorned a wall in the plant cafeteria, demonstrating the proud participation of the company in the war effort. Marking the award of the fourth star to the "E" pennant, the *Invader Exhaust* observed, "We haven't forgotten that the men in the service are called upon to face the enemy. Our part has been relatively trivial, compared with theirs. But we're mighty glad of our part in the war."

Wartime (1941–1945) engine deliveries from the Berkeley factory totaled some 12,226 units, a record figure for a five-year period at Hall-Scott. [4-66] Distributed over five years, that comes to some 2,445 engines annually, which even with complete prewar production numbers unavailable, can safely be estimated as being at least twice as great as usually reached in the 1920s and 1930s. This expanded output necessitated the engine maker to operate at full capacity with additional workers, which reached an all-time high figure of 900. [4-67] One company executive described Hall-Scott as becoming "fantastically efficient" in the war years. [4-68] In turn, the greater production had positive effects on the company ledgers. The ACF 1943 annual report declared that after ringing up expensive costs in gearing up for the war in 1938 and 1939, losing $150,000 in the process over those two years, four successful years followed, with Hall-Scott earning $951,000, $877,000, $656,000, and $507,000, respectively. [4-69] Given the meager earnings picture in the 1930s (Hall-Scott earned money only two years in that decade, 1936 and

Excellence IN PRODUCTION!

Excellence IN PERFORMANCE!

....TEAMED WITH

ARMY · "E" · NAVY

We are, naturally, very proud that Hall-Scott has been honored by the Army-Navy Production Award. It is a source of deepest satisfaction—and of highest inspiration—to every member of our organization.

But we all also take deep pride in the war-proved performance of Hall-Scott INVADER and DEFENDER engines, themselves. Performance of a caliber that made our receipt of this award possible. Performance—across the seven seas—which now so imperatively calls for production of these engines in ever greater numbers.

To those of you who knew and enjoyed the service rendered by Hall-Scott engines in days of peace, the achievements of Hall-Scott powered naval and military craft will make a most stirring story—when it can be told!

HALL-SCOTT MOTOR CAR COMPANY

DIVISION OF AMERICAN CAR AND FOUNDRY MOTORS COMPANY, 2850 7TH STREET, BERKELEY, CALIFORNIA, U.S.A. · 254 WEST 31ST STREET, NEW YORK CITY · LOS ANGELES, CALIFORNIA, 5847 SANTA FE AVENUE · SEATTLE, WASH., 607 WESTERN AVENUE · IN NEW ENGLAND, MARINE EQUIPMENT COMPANY, 126 STATE STREET, BOSTON, MASS.

An advertisement noting the Hall-Scott "E" award.

Hall-Scott also contributed to the war effort by operating a training facility in Berkeley. Shown here is a Hall-Scott-engined boat tied to the dock. (Courtesy of David Linley.)

1937, a paltry $33,000 and $26,000, respectively), these wartime figures were truly outstanding. In fact, Hall-Scott engine making was a fabulous boon to ACF; the only reason why ACF made any money at all in some war years was because of the profits realized at Hall-Scott! The earnings and losses picture for ACF and Hall-Scott generally mirrored each other. Thus, for example, when Hall-Scott lost big money in 1938 and 1939, so did the parent company. Conversely, when Hall-Scott reported fantastic earnings in 1940–1945, so did ACF. In terms of engine output, profitability, and employment levels, as the war ended Hall-Scott appeared to have been in good shape, certainly in as strong a position as it had been in a decade. If Hall-Scott managers had taken some of the cash their company generated and used it to improve its product line and modernize its facilities, it would have made a smooth transition to peacetime production and situated itself to address the postwar market.

But during this same period, serious fissures appeared in the foundation of Hall-Scott, with the internal struggles of ACF-Brill threatening its stability.

The Hall-Scott engineering department in the early 1940s. Francis Bradford is on the right side, second desk from the front, sitting, next to a standing associate. Speed Glidewell is located two desks in back of them, wearing a dark coat.

The efforts to break up ACF-Brill that were initiated by Charles Hardy did not satisfy calls for additional and more penetrating changes. This intracompany conflict sapped the strength of Hall-Scott by compromising its institutional continuity and putting the finite resources of ACF in flux. This desperate need for money would tempt ACF-Brill leaders to take whatever revenue they could from their divisions, including Hall-Scott.

Unfortunately for the company, Hall-Scott management did not plow the monies earned in the first half of the 1940s into new engines or improvements to the Berkeley plant. ACF-Brill executive and future Hall-Scott president William Nelson observed, "no post-war planning had been done by Hall-Scott although funds were readily available to carry on both planning and design work. Further, Hall-Scott undertook no rehabilitation of its plant which would have made matters easier in the post war period. And since Hall-Scott Motor Company [*sic*] was a wholly owned subsiderary [*sic*] of Brill, Philadelpphia [*sic*], the money that had been made during the war had been siphoned off for use by Brill. By itself, Brill did little or nothing during World War II. Hall-Scott was left after the war without designs or plans on which to build." [4-70] This short-sighted strategy soon would come back to haunt ACF-Brill executives.

Even more serious than any fissures in the edifice of unity in the ACF-Brill facade came with some deep and lasting changes in the engine market brought by the war. In a telling quote that forecast the future of heavy-duty engine development, Admiral E.L. Cochrane, who had served as the Navy Chief of the Bureau of Ships, pointed out, "The United States, in this last war, built thousands of ships and 90% of them were diesel powered... The whole landing craft program was diesel powered, and these ships worked under the most strenuous conditions. In many an emergency, when a ship was bombed, diesel engines saved the day. Not a single one failed us in a critical operation." [4-71] In terms of numbers produced, diesel engines jumped tenfold in the years from 1940 until 1945, with Cummins, General Motors, and Mack building most of them. [4-72]

In the same way that the performance of gasoline-powered trucks proved their superiority over horse-powered wagons in World War I, paving the way for a greatly enhanced market presence of gasoline engines following that conflict, the outstanding performance of diesel engines in World War II likewise paved the way for their enhanced market presence after the second global conflict. Hall-Scott had a history of leaving markets that changed rapidly, as the company had done in rail and aviation in the 1920s. With much-improved diesel engines poised after World War II to move aggressively into truck, bus, marine, and industrial applications, there would be new and even more pressure on Hall-Scott to bring out engines that had much lower operating costs, weight, and size. In terms of marketing strategy for Hall-Scott, if the company again elected to retreat from rapidly changing markets rather than alter its products to meet new consumer demand, it had few, if any, new markets into which it could move, given the kind of engines it made—large displacement, heavy duty, and spark ignition. The post-World War II period would require fresh thinking inside Hall-Scott, with the company needing to introduce products as sparkling and industry-leading as its engines had been in the 1910s and early 1920s, or the firm would likely fail. After 1945, Hall-Scott desperately needed the genius of its cofounder E.J. Hall. However, Hall had already departed the company some years prior to this time, and if another person of vision and imagination could not fill those shoes at Hall-Scott, the company would face a contest for its survival against great odds.

Colonel E. J. Hall, one of the founders of the Hall-Scott Motor Car Company, visited the shop recently. In the last war Colonel Hall received the Congressional Medal of Honor for his achievements in engine design and production. He and test foreman Oliver Thorgerson are observing an experimental motor. He was pleased with news of the 4-star E pennant.

A newsworthy item—E.J. Hall (left) visits the Hall-Scott plant, 1945.

References

4-1. Allan Winkler, *Home Front USA; America During World War II*, Harlan Davidson, Arlington Heights, IL, 1986, p. 6.

4-2. William Nelson, Hall-Scott binder, financial section, p. 13. Courtesy of William Nelson. Nelson was the last president of Hall-Scott and kept many handwritten or typed company records in a binder.

4-3. Francis Bradford, "A History of the Hall-Scott Motor Car Company," unpublished manuscript, 1989, pp. 82–83. Courtesy of Bancroft Library, University of California, Berkeley, BANC MSS 93/104c. Don Butler, *The History of Hudson*, Motorbooks International, Osceola, WI, 1992, p. 260.

4-4. Francis Bradford, "A History of the Hall-Scott Motor Car Company," unpublished manuscript, 1989, p. 61. Courtesy of Bancroft Library, University of California, Berkeley, BANC MSS 93/104c.

4-5. Thomas Berndt, *Standard Catalog of U.S. Military Vehicles, 1940–1965*, Krause Publications, Iola, WI, 1983, p. 126. Fred Crismon, *U.S. Military Wheeled Vehicles*, Motorbooks International, Osceola, WI, 1994, pp. 383–384.

4-6. Fred Crismon, *U.S. Military Wheeled Vehicles*, Motorbooks International, Osceola, WI, 1994, pp. 383–384.

4-7. Thomas Berndt, *Standard Catalog of U.S. Military Vehicles, 1940–1965*, Krause Publications, Iola, WI, 1983, p. 126. Fred Crismon, *U.S. Military Wheeled Vehicles*, Motorbooks International, Osceola, WI, 1994, p. 383.

4-8. Fred Crismon, *U.S. Military Wheeled Vehicles*, Motorbooks International, Osceola, WI, 1994, p. 384.

4-9. *Invader Exhaust*, December 1943, p. 2.

4-10. Thomas Berndt, *Standard Catalog of U.S. Military Vehicles, 1940–1965*, Krause Publications, Iola, WI, 1983, pp. 26, 28.

4-11. Fred Crismon, *U.S. Military Wheeled Vehicles*, Motorbooks International, Osceola, WI, 1994, p. 283.

4-12. Thomas Berndt, *Standard Catalog of U.S. Military Vehicles, 1940–1965*, Krause Publications, Iola, WI, 1983, p. 128.

4-13. Francis Bradford, "A History of the Hall-Scott Motor Car Company," unpublished manuscript, 1989, p. 96. Courtesy of Bancroft Library, University of California, Berkeley, BANC MSS 93/104c. Thomas Berndt, *Standard Catalog of U.S. Military Vehicles, 1940–1965*, Krause Publications, Iola, WI, 1983, p. 126. Berndt cites the maximum engine speed of the Model 440 as 2000 rpm and its compression ratio as 5.7:1.

4-14. Francis Bradford, "A History of the Hall-Scott Motor Car Company," unpublished manuscript, 1989, p. 101. Courtesy of Bancroft Library, University of California, Berkeley, BANC MSS 93/104c.

4-15. David Doyle and Pat Stansell, *Dragon Wagon, A Visual History of the U.S. Army's Heavy Tank Transporter 1941–1955*, Ampersand Publishing, Delray Beach, FL, 2004, p. 3. Fred Crismon, *U.S. Military Wheeled Vehicles*, Motorbooks International, Osceola, WI, 1994, p. 283.

4-16. David Doyle and Pat Stansell, *Dragon Wagon, A Visual History of the U.S. Army's Heavy Tank Transporter 1941–1955*, Ampersand Publishing, Delray Beach, FL, 2004, p. 3. Bart Vanderveen, *Historic Military Vehicles Directory*, Battle of Britain Prints, London, UK, 1989, p. 381.

4-17. Francis Bradford, "A History of the Hall-Scott Motor Car Company," unpublished manuscript, 1989, p. 101. Courtesy of Bancroft Library, University of California, Berkeley, BANC MSS 93/104c.

4-18. William Nelson, Hall-Scott binder, financial section, p. 3. Courtesy of William Nelson. Nelson was the last president of Hall-Scott and kept many handwritten or typed company records in a binder. Page 13 in Nelson's binder cited 2,116 total Model 440s built, while Bradford reported 2,115 (Francis Bradford, "A History of the Hall-Scott Motor Car Company," unpublished manuscript, 1989, p. 104. Courtesy of Bancroft Library, University of California, Berkeley, BANC MSS 93/104c), virtually a corroboration. Perhaps the discrepancy of 400 engines (between 2,116 Model 441 engines built and 1,701 Pacifics built) was spares or units delivered after 1945.

4-19. *Invader Exhaust*, December 1943, p. 2.

4-20. Francis Bradford, "A History of the Hall-Scott Motor Car Company," unpublished manuscript, 1989, pp. 102, 157. Courtesy of Bancroft Library, University of California, Berkeley, BANC MSS 93/104c.

4-21. Ibid., p. 102.

4-22. Fred Crismon, *U.S. Military Wheeled Vehicles*, Motorbooks International, Osceola, WI, 1994, p. 291.

4-23. James Laux, "Diesel Trucks and Buses: Their Gradual Spread in the United States," in *The Economic and Social Effects of the Spread of Motor Vehicles*, Theo Barker, ed., Macmillan, Basingstoke, Hampshire, UK, 1987, p. 105.

4-24. *Pacific Motor Boat*, February 1942, pp. 42, 52.

4-25. William Nelson, Hall-Scott binder, financial section, p. 13. Courtesy of William Nelson. Nelson was the last president of Hall-Scott and kept many handwritten or typed company records in a binder.

4-26. Francis Bradford, "A History of the Hall-Scott Motor Car Company," unpublished manuscript, 1989, pp. 82–83. Courtesy of Bancroft Library, University of California, Berkeley, BANC MSS 93/104c. Don Butler, *The History of Hudson*, Motorbooks International, Osceola, WI, 1992, p. 260.

4-27. Don Butler, *The History of Hudson*, Motorbooks International, Osceola, WI, 1992, p. 267. *Hudson Invader 168*, repair manual, n.d., p. 7. The Hudson World War II Invader repair manual cited 250 hp at 2100 rpm.

4-28. Francis Bradford, "A History of the Hall-Scott Motor Car Company," unpublished manuscript, 1989, p. 83. Courtesy of Bancroft Library, University of California, Berkeley, BANC MSS 93/104c.

4-29. Letter from D. Keister to R. Dias, November 27, 2002. Keister owns several Hudson Invaders. These Hudson symbols can be seen in the repair manual that Hudson made for the Invader in World War II.

4-30. John Conde, *The Cars That Hudson Built*, Arnold-Porter, Keego Harbor, MI, 1980, p. 127.

4-31. Don Butler, *The History of Hudson*, Motorbooks International, Osceola, WI, 1992, p. 264.

4-32. Ibid., pp. 260, 264.

4-33. Ibid., p. 267.

4-34. Francis Bradford, "A History of the Hall-Scott Motor Car Company," unpublished manuscript, 1989, p. 91. Courtesy of Bancroft Library, University of California, Berkeley, BANC MSS 93/104c.

4-35. Francis Bradford, "A History of the Hall-Scott Motor Car Company," unpublished manuscript, 1989, pp. 84–85. Courtesy of Bancroft Library, University of California, Berkeley, BANC MSS 93/104c. The increased bore gave the Defender Models 2268 and 2269 the same 5-3/4-inch bore as that of the Models 440 and 441.

4-36. *Invader Exhaust*, October 1943, p. 2.

4-37. Francis Bradford, "A History of the Hall-Scott Motor Car Company," unpublished manuscript, 1989, p. 85. Courtesy of Bancroft Library, University of California, Berkeley, BANC MSS 93/104c. Peter Du Cane, *High-Speed Small Craft*, second edition, Philosophical Library, New York, NY, 1957, p. 149.

4-38. Francis Bradford, "A History of the Hall-Scott Motor Car Company," unpublished manuscript, 1989, p. 85. Courtesy of Bancroft Library, University of California, Berkeley, BANC MSS 93/104c.

4-39. Peter Du Cane, *High-Speed Small Craft*, second edition, Philosophical Library, New York, NY, 1957, plate 6b.

4-40. Hall-Scott Power/Electronics, brochure, 1955, p. 4.

4-41. *Invader Exhaust*, October 1943, p. 2.

4-42. Defender as Supplied to the United States Navy, repair manual, n.d., p. 4.

4-43. *Pacific Motor Boat*, February 1942, p. 42.

4-44. Francis Bradford, "A History of the Hall-Scott Motor Car Company," unpublished manuscript, 1989, p. 92. Courtesy of Bancroft Library, University of California, Berkeley, BANC MSS 93/104c. This may be an incomplete production figure, as Bradford did not list the Model 3369 in his breakdown of V-12 production.

4-45. Ibid., pp. 89–90.

4-46. Ibid., p. 90.

4-47. Ibid., pp. 85–91.

4-48. Ibid., pp. 84–87.

4-49. Charles Herb, "Hall-Scott Marine Engines Aid Invasion and Defense," *Machinery*, Vol. 49, No. 1, September 1942, pp. 121–134.

4-50. William Nelson, Hall-Scott binder, financial section, p. 13. Courtesy of William Nelson. Nelson was the last president of Hall-Scott and kept many handwritten or typed company records in a binder.

4-51. Francis Bradford, "A History of the Hall-Scott Motor Car Company," unpublished manuscript, 1989, p. 57b. Courtesy of Bancroft Library, University of California, Berkeley, BANC MSS 93/104c.

4-52. *Invader Exhaust*, November 1943, p. 2.

4-53. Charles Herb, "Hall-Scott Marine Engines Aid Invasion and Defense," *Machinery*, Vol. 49, No. 1, September 1942, p. 122.

4-54. Francis Bradford, "A History of the Hall-Scott Motor Car Company," unpublished manuscript, 1989, p. 131. Courtesy of Bancroft Library, University of California, Berkeley, BANC MSS 93/104c.

4-55. Ibid., pp. 131–132.

4-56. Ibid., p. 131.

4-57. *Invader Exhaust*, November 1943, p. 4.

4-58. *Invader Exhaust*, May 1944, p. 4.

4-59. Stan Grayson, *Engines Afloat; From Early Days to D-Day, Vol. II: The Gasoline/Diesel Era*, Devereux Books, Marblehead, MA, 1999, p. 166.

4-60. Ibid., pp. 166–167.

4-61. For example, see James Laux, "Diesel Trucks and Buses: Their Gradual Spread in the United States," in *The Economic and Social Effects of the Spread of Motor Vehicles*, Theo Barker, ed., Macmillan, Basingstoke, Hampshire, UK, 1987, p. 105.

4-62. Debra Brill, *History of the J.G. Brill Company*, Indiana University Press, Bloomington, IN, 2001, p. 211.

4-63. Ibid.

4-64. J.E. "Speed" Glidewell, "A Brief History of Hall-Scott Motor Company," unpublished address, 1956, p. 3. *Invader Exhaust*, April 1945, p. 4. ACF Motors Annual Report, n.d., n.p.

4-65. *Invader Exhaust*, April 1945, p. 4.

4-66. William Nelson, Hall-Scott binder, financial section, p. 13. Courtesy of William Nelson. Nelson was the last president of Hall-Scott and kept many handwritten or typed company records in a binder.

4-67. *Berkeley Gazette*, February 1, 1946, p. 1.

4-68. William Nelson, autobiography, unpublished manuscript, 1963, p. 266. Courtesy of William Nelson.

4-69. ACF Motors Annual Report, 1943, n.p.

4-70. William Nelson, autobiography, unpublished manuscript, 1963, pp. 266–267.

4-71. Stan Grayson, *Engines Afloat; From Early Days to D-Day, Vol. II: The Gasoline/Diesel Era*, Devereux Books, Marblehead, MA, 1999, pp. 168–169.

4-72. James Laux, "Diesel Trucks and Buses: Their Gradual Spread in the United States," in *The Economic and Social Effects of the Spread of Motor Vehicles*, Theo Barker, ed., Macmillan, Basingstoke, Hampshire, UK, 1987, pp. 104–106.

CHAPTER FIVE

SHUFFLED AROUND, BLED DRY, AND SPUN OFF

Having operated at full capacity during World War II, Hall-Scott faced a sudden reversal of fortunes when the conflict ended. By early 1946, employment at Hall-Scott had plummeted 50%, falling from its wartime high of 900 to only 450 as the nation's economy transitioned erratically to peacetime. [5-1] Bus engine sales, which had been a staple at Hall-Scott before the war, proved to be unreliable in the postwar period. The bus market roared off with record sales right after peace came, only to crash shortly thereafter. This complicated the financial outlook of Hall-Scott and its parent company, both of which depended heavily on bus production. Truck engine sales also failed to meet expectations. The ever-growing demand for diesel power, which was seen across the truck, bus, marine, and industrial engine markets, continued to vex Hall-Scott and ACF managers. The early postwar period was characterized by great change in the engine market, but it also was a time in which Hall-Scott continued to make the same basic type of product that it had made since the post-World War I period. Hall-Scott was becoming increasingly out of step with its customers. Since its purchase in 1925, Hall-Scott fell from being the ACF prized engine-producing division, to becoming a critical revenue provider, to finally being only an unwanted and underperforming asset.

More Changes in the Leadership of Hall-Scott

From the 1940s through the 1950s, the Hall-Scott Motor Car Company struggled with wrenching instability in its leadership. For years, Hall-Scott had nestled under the corporate umbrella of a larger firm. Considering the difficulty faced

ACF-Brill had a Canadian arm, Canadian Car and Foundry, which produced buses, often powered by Hall-Scott engines. Note the similarities between the American brochure (these two pages) and the Canadian brochure (next two pages).

258

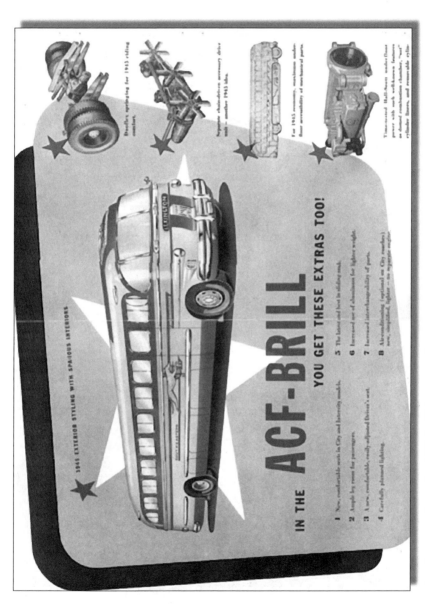

Another page from the ACF-Brill American brochure.

Brochure for Canadian Car and Foundry, the Canadian arm of ACF-Brill. Compare this brochure with the American brochure showon the preceding two pages.

Another page from the brochure for the Canadian arm of ACF-Brill.

by engine makers to remain solvent in the twentieth century, such an arrangement provided some benefit for Hall-Scott. Then in the 1940s, American Car
and Foundry (ACF) underwent a confusing succession of names and configurations. The struggle within ACF that had made its way into national newspapers
during World War II continued to rage in the years that followed.

The long-time control of Hall-Scott by ACF came to an end shortly after World
War II. In late January 1946, the company broke up, resulting in the emergence
of two new firms: American Car and Foundry and ACF-Brill Motors. The former American Car and Foundry, its managers perhaps having the clairvoyance
to see certain disaster looming, wanted to divorce the company from trolley,
bus, and engine making and instead focus solely on making and repairing rail
cars. As of this writing (2006), this firm, known today as ACF Industries, is
still a leader in non-passenger rail car production. In hindsight, the managers of the former American Car and Foundry might have made the correct
financial decision when they moved their stockholders' money into other safer
and more lucrative fields. The other major corporate entity emerging from
the breakup, ACF-Brill Motors Company, was snapped up quickly that same
year by Consolidated-Vultee Aircraft Corporation, a major aviation firm, for
$7.5 million. [5-2]

An ACF-Brill Motors Company stock certificate.

The purchase of ACF-Brill Motors by Consolidated-Vultee affected Hall-Scott because the Berkeley engine maker was a wholly owned subsidiary. Not surprisingly, the sale of a hometown firm earned the story a place on the front page of the *Berkeley Gazette*. The *Gazette* seemed optimistic about the purchase, inasmuch as it "is expected that the transaction eventually will mean an expansion of the Hall-Scott plant...," which would be welcomed, given the recent slashing of the company workforce. [5-3] The deal did not come as a complete surprise, however; *The New York Times* had reported rumors circulating about this deal shortly before Christmas 1945. [5-4] The desire of American Car and Foundry to sell ACF-Brill Motors, and by extension Hall-Scott, was a poorly kept industry secret.

The new owner of Hall-Scott was a large and influential company, more than ACF had ever been. Consolidated-Vultee was actually part of Aviation Corporation, usually referred to simply as AVCO or Avco. Consolidated-Vultee had been created in 1943 from the merger of Vultee Aircraft and Consolidated Aircraft. During the war, Consolidated-Vultee had made quite a name for itself; thus, it enjoyed wide name recognition. [5-5] In fact, Consolidated-Vultee became one of the largest aircraft producers on the planet during World War II. In total, Consolidated-Vultee made some 37,000 planes for the U.S. Army and Navy for training, reconnaissance, combat, and transport purposes. [5-6] Some of its better-known aircraft include the B-24, BT-13, Vengeance, and Catalina. While busy making planes for the government, Avco executives had speculated about various products their company could make when peace returned. In fact, in January 1944, the Avco board of directors considered a proposal titled "Postwar Continuation Program for Consumer Goods." [5-7] As was true with many American companies, Avco managers kept one eye to the future while the war was being fought. The great success of the company during the war allowed management to use the accumulated cash, new industrial capacity, and recently acquired expertise as a foundation to manufacture a wide variety of commercial and consumer goods. War production brought a flood of talented people to Avco, who then could be refocused on making these goods. At the top of this list, no doubt, was William B. Stout, one of the most gifted, successful, and famous industrial designers in America. [5-8] Avco seemed well situated for peacetime.

By 1946, making good on its plans for postwar expansion, Avco positioned its divisions to strike the civilian market on a number of fronts. These divisions included firms such as the Crosley Corporation, well known for its highly popular radios and refrigerators. (Crosley also made cars for a while, but its auto division was not part of the Avco acquisition.) Also included were Spencer

Heater, which made commercial and residential heating units, and New Idea, which made farm implements. [5-9] ACF-Brill Motors would figure into this assault by manufacturing surface transportation products. The postwar plans of Avco called for Consolidated-Vultee to begin mass-producing civilian goods at its large factory in Nashville, Tennessee, where it had assembled bombers during the war. In the closing months of 1945, Consolidated-Vultee management announced that the Nashville facility "will be converted immediately" to produce a host of new products, first gas and electric kitchen ranges and later New Idea farm implements. [5-10] Shortly thereafter, buses would be added to the expanding product mix. ACF-Brill Motors had controlled up to 12% of the American bus market in recent years, and management hoped the new Nashville-made buses would allow the company to grow that share considerably. [5-11]

Avco and Consolidated-Vultee managers charted an ambitious postwar course for their burgeoning surface transportation operation. Being part of Aviation Corporation, Consolidated-Vultee enjoyed access to the highly sophisticated Avco plant in Williamsburg, Pennsylvania, home of its Lycoming engine facility, which it purchased from the War Assets Administration of the federal government for a half-million dollars. Actually, by picking up ACF-Brill Motors in 1946, Avco then controlled two engine makers—Hall-Scott and Lycoming. Lycoming, which began making engines in 1908, had competed for several years with Hall-Scott. But the growing concentration by Lycoming on aviation mirrored the retreat of Hall-Scott from that same field. In fact, as of this writing (2006), Lycoming remains an industry leader in producing civilian airplane engines. The grand expectations of Avco management for its bus and engine-making arms meant that the Hall-Scott Berkeley engine plant could not possibly meet the demand. To adequately address the expected popularity of its vehicles, Avco expanded the Lycoming plant (charging the work to Hall-Scott) and gave it a target of producing 36 Hall-Scott engines per day, which would be shipped to Nashville for installation in ACF-Brill buses. [5-12]

Commencing engine and bus making, Avco ventured into territory not completely foreign to its personnel or beyond its capabilities. The Avco acquisition of ACF-Brill Motors marked what the *Berkeley Gazette* reported was "the first entrance by a major aircraft producer in the field of automotive surface transportation." [5-13] But the company had plenty of experience with metals and vehicle construction, which is shared with making planes, buses, and engines. Consolidated-Vultee board chairman Irving Babcock observed, "In the building of thousands of aircraft, Consolidated Vultee has acquired a knowledge of engineering and mass production which can be of tremendous value in the manufacture of buses and trolley coaches." [5-14] Aircraft engineers had great knowledge concerning "the load-carrying abilities of such metals as aluminum and magnesium," which was expertise in metals that perhaps could have benefited Hall-Scott.

The Avco bus experiment certainly was bold and caught the attention of industry journals. *Automotive Industries* titled a 1947 article on the Avco bus building project "A Radically Different Method of Building Motor Coaches." [5-15] Avco leaders wanted to bring the latest, most cost-effective methods of mass production to the manufacture of buses, lessons it had learned from making massive numbers of war planes. The government had kept a close guard on the "master tooling dock" and "geometric mastering system" used during the war in manufacturing large military aircraft in amazing volume. But with the end of the fighting came a relinquishing of this control and the spread of these techniques to many types of large-scale peacetime manufacturing, such as at the Nashville bus plant. With this information now available for civilian uses, Avco engineers could finally bring mass production to bus making. Hitherto, buses had been assembled in place, fashioned slowly by skilled metal workers. Given that Hall-Scott had abandoned trailblazing engine making years earlier when E.J. Hall left the company, at least its engines could power cutting-edge vehicles.

As it turned out, though, Consolidated-Vultee did not hold its interest for long in ACF-Brill Motors nor in Hall-Scott. Barely allowing the ink to dry on the ACF-Brill Motors deal, Consolidated-Vultee transferred its non-aviation firms (including its bus and engine-making companies) to its newly formed Nashville Corporation division. [5-16] The intracompany sale was announced in September 1947. Avco and Consolidated-Vultee did not terminate their connection to Hall-Scott; they merely distanced it and insulated themselves from it. Old-timers at the Berkeley plant no doubt noticed one further change that occurred to their company in November 1947. In what might have seemed more like a semantic shell game to anyone outside of Hall-Scott, in December 1947, ACF-Brill Motors Company announced that the company known as Hall-Scott Motor Car Company since 1910 would henceforth be the Hall-Scott Motor Division. [5-17] Because Hall-Scott had not assembled a rail motor car in nearly 30 years by that point, the change made sense, and it accurately reflected the dependent relationship of Hall-Scott with ACF-Motors, Nashville Corporation, Consolidated-Vultee, and Avco.

In spite of the money, planning, technology, and expertise applied to this project, Avco's road to becoming a provider of surface transportation proved to be filled with potholes. The converted factory in Tennessee got off to an unsure start with the first 1947 model year buses, which endured innumerable problems and never reached quantity production. Having an existing supplier of proven bus engines within the corporate family did not seem to help the launch of the new enterprise. For reasons of logistics and finances, moving Hall-Scott production from the West Coast to Pennsylvania made some sense. Likewise, the decision by Avco engineers to increase the power developed by the Hall-Scott Model 136 also was not unreasonable. How Avco engineers pulled off the modifications, however, was wanting. When Avco engineers proposed changes to the Hall-Scott Model 136 horizontal bus engine, those modifications were not undertaken in Berkeley. The resulting engines proved to have serious problems, but addressing them promptly and effectively was made more difficult by the decentralization of engineering. For example, to coax a bit more power from the Model 136, engineers in Pennsylvania fitted the engines with a new intake manifold, called an "octopus" type, that would increase airflow. This and other minor alterations of the Model 136 rendered the Model 477. When fitted to the engine, though, the new manifold significantly lowered the temperature at which air entered the cylinders, causing early buses fitted with the Model 477 to misfire badly. [5-18] If this manifold issue had been the only problem encountered with the Model 477, that would have been easy to overlook, but it was not. Because these new Hall-Scott engines would be produced in Pennsylvania, new parts suppliers had to be found. But the company that was chosen to produce the rocker arms for the Model 477s "did not have the skill to do the job," according to Bradford, resulting in these critical valvetrain components failing. Similarly, Model 477 cylinder head studs stripped when machinists cut into them. These failures led to the engines being returned to Berkeley for proper assembly, which was an expensive and time-consuming process. [5-19] Considering the high level of technological sophistication of the Nashville plant, the mistakes and bad judgment encountered when "improving" the Hall-Scott engines were surprising. This decentralization of engineering and testing of Hall-Scott engines proved to be a costly error in judgment.

These were only the problems experienced with the re-engineered (or mis-engineered) motors. The bus manufacturing side of the process suffered through its own parade of disasters. The innumerable small mistakes and problems resulted in customer dissatisfaction, canceled orders, and, compounded with the sudden collapse of the American bus market, the failure of the Nashville bus-building experiment. Pictures of the facility appearing in a 1947 magazine article show a plant stuffed with tools, parts, and buses in various states of construction, but few workers. True, one of the advantages of the Avco master tooling dock and geometric mastering system was that fewer and less skilled workers could do more of the construction. However, photos of a plant not teeming with workers suggested that little production was actually occurring. Because of this avalanche of problems, Bradford stated that the Nashville plant installed only 52 engines, Models 477 and 504, in buses during its short tenure. [5-20] The ACF-Brill Motors 1949 annual report did not even mention bus or engine production at the Williamsburg or Nashville facilities, only pointing to notes payable to the Nashville Corporation. The corporate history of Avco written in the 1970s barely mentioned the bus venture, stating, "The same growing middle class market that had created a demand for some of Avco's other products was also the cause of one of the company's failures: the buses and trolleys built by ACF-Brill Motors... The expanding, sprawling suburbs had created a demand for cars, not buses." [5-21] By the end of 1948, the promising bus venture had failed. ACF-Brill Motors executive and future Hall-Scott president William Nelson explained, "Then Brill had to take the Nashville inventory and the Hall-Scott Division had to take the Lycoming inventory... [ACF-]Brill was heavily in debt and had no means of rescuing anything from the major mistakes made..." [5-22] The bottom falling out of the bus market in 1948 drove the nails into the coffin of the Nashville debacle.

A Model 504 bus engine, a few of which ended up in Nashville-built ACF-Brill Motors buses. (Courtesy of Tom Shafer.)

The demise of the Tennessee bus program was mercifully quick, and evidence of it is hard to find half a century later. In a historical and spelling oversight that points to the abject failure in Nashville and how unimportant Hall-Scott was to Aviation Corporation, Avco's 1979 corporate history stated, "Hall-Scott's operations were removed from Berkely [*sic*], California to Lycoming in Pennsylvania." [5-23]. That is simply incorrect. A few Hall-Scott engines were indeed assembled in Pennsylvania, but the company did not remove the Hall-Scott operations from Berkeley and begin them in Pennsylvania. Avco management stated that it wanted to move the Hall-Scott operations to Pennsylvania, but announcing plans to move is not the same as actually doing it. Indeed, the harsh 1931 ACF assessment of Hall-Scott suggested that the plant was not perfectly outfitted nor geographically situated to supply bus production in the East efficiently; thus, such a move would not have been totally unreasonable. Misspelling Berkeley only underscores the distance Avco put between itself and the bus venture, then and in the years that followed.

Given the poor return on the Avco investment in ACF-Brill Motors, it is little wonder that Avco managers soon wanted to shed the company of the new bus and engine-making divisions. Predictably, in June 1951, Avco Manufacturing Corporation sold its share of ACF-Brill Motors (which amounted to 48.6% ownership) to Allen and Company. [5-24] Almost nothing about the sale was mentioned in the ACF 1951 annual report; it was as if no one in the firm wanted to bring any attention to the deal. Led by well-known financier Charles Allen, Jr., the New York-based Allen and Company had men on its board with connections to various transportation companies. Thus, there were some obvious reasons behind the acquisition by Allen and Company. Brill production continued in Philadelphia, and Hall-Scott production continued in Berkeley, but the latest corporate shuffle did not suggest that Brill buses or Hall-Scott engines were manufactured by companies considered highly desirable. The bus and engine makers of ACF-Brill Motors seemed more like corporate "hot potatoes" that no one wanted to hold for long, so why should Charles Allen? Although a mass resignation of ACF-Brill Motors officers followed this latest transaction, Charles Perelle remained as president of ACF-Brill Motors, and he naturally managed to find an optimistic statement to issue, saying, "ACF-Brill intends to strengthen and augment its position in the bus and trolley coach manufacturing industries," and citing a $17 million backlog of civilian and military orders as evidence of the health of the company. [5-25] Few people placed much stock, literally or figuratively, in Perelle's words.

Corporate instability aside, the late 1940s through the 1950s also were trying times for Hall-Scott because of the changing demands of the heavy-duty engine market. Whether it was in trucks, buses, boats, or industrial applications, customers made new demands of their engines, and there were producers willing and capable of meeting those new demands. In the face of this deep change, however, Hall-Scott continued to produce engines that were essentially unchanged and represented only a narrow band of the market spectrum: heavy-duty, water-cooled, spark-ignition units of roughly 130 to 900 hp. Hall-Scott products were good for what they were, and Hall-Scott focused with unflinching and even slavish devotion on what it did well.

The blame for Hall-Scott being so uncompetitive in the postwar years cannot be laid entirely at the feet of company leaders or engineers in Berkeley; its parent company did much to torpedo its chances for success. In 1949, the new Hall-Scott division manager William Nelson found the company needed new machinery, new plant organization, and, of course, new engine designs. But even if Hall-Scott realized profits from its own production and sales, and it did in the 1940s, the success of the parent company remained the priority above all else. "I had to contend, however," explained Nelson, "that Brill must be pulled thru [sic] even if Hall-Scott suffered... So we set to make as much profit as possible [at Hall-Scott]... And all the cash generated was transferred regularly to Brill." [5-26] Whatever chances Hall-Scott might have had in surviving the fast-moving postwar market were undermined by the men who should have dedicated themselves to the success of the engine maker.

As managers looked for ways to generate revenue, Hall-Scott continued its practice of making specialty products and equipment in addition to engines. In earlier decades, these enterprises included the Ruckstell axle and heavy-duty transmissions. The ongoing Cold War, with its long-term military buildup punctuated by short-term flare-ups such as the Korean Conflict, presented Hall-Scott with revenue-generating government contracts. Not only could Hall-Scott sell engines to the federal government (which it did, similar to almost 300 V-12 marine engines in the early 1950s), but it could also perform the kind of close machining work that it had done for various customers. Hall-Scott's famous scrupulous attention to detail and use of specialized equipment, sometimes of its own manufacture, allowed the small company to win a number of private sector and military contracts in this era. In the early 1950s, Hall-Scott began to land government contracts to manufacture specialized items such as power generators, gears for equipment, helicopter transmissions, and gun mechanisms for large-caliber automatic weapons. [5-27] Around 1953, the company opened a 38,000-square-foot plant in nearby Richmond to produce ammunition, as well as a new plant in Oakland to package military goods. [5-28] Many struggling firms such as Hall-Scott benefited from the vigorous Pentagon spending during the Cold War. Not surprisingly, ACF also grew reliant on federal contracts.

Beginning in the 1940s, ACF-Brill Motors and its subsidiary Hall-Scott became much more dependent on federal contracts and on the regulatory actions of local governments. ACF-Brill Motors managers acknowledged that the early peacetime period was a difficult one, saying in the 1949 annual report, "Since the end of the war, bus operators have been faced with greatly increased costs without corresponding increases in operating revenues," only reaching profitability when "fare increases [had] been granted by regulatory bodies." [5-29] The company's short-term forecasts for recovery appeared "not encouraging" as the industry was "undergoing lean years." ACF-Brill Motors lost $2.1 million in 1949 on $13.5 million in sales, with total sales and the number of buses sold dropping more than 50% from the previous year. [5-30] But heftier Pentagon budgets came as the Cold War intensified, especially with the involvement of America in the decidedly non-cold Korean Conflict in the fall of 1950. This escalation in hostilities turned back the pessimistic prognostications at ACF-Brill Motors just as United Nations forces initially turned back the North Korean advance across the 17th parallel. The 1951 ACF-Brill annual report explained, "Due to the expanded requirements of the national defense program, a substantial portion of the Company's development activities have been directed toward special vehicles, special engines, and other equipment needed by the Government." [5-31] This included delivery of 1,037 buses. In fact, it took the infusion of federal defense spending to return ACF-Brill Motors to profitability after its early post-World War II slump. In 1951, ACF-Brill Motors reported a $2.5 million profit on sales of $23.6 million, following a $124,000 loss in 1950. The 1952 ACF-Brill Motors annual report acknowledged, "Defense contracts also accounted for an important share of Hall-Scott's production in 1952. The Navy Department recently placed a substantial order for marine engines which are an improved version of the Hall-Scott 'Defender'...." [5-32] Hall-Scott and ACF-Brill Motors also won contracts to rebuild military trucks and buses at its Philadelphia bus plant. On a worrisome note, though, while defense contracts increased from 1951 to 1952, "Sales of commercial buses and commercial engines remained at the reduced level which has prevailed for the last few years." [5-33] ACF-Brill Motors remained profitable in 1952, with a net income of $1.88 million. It was clear that by the early 1950s, the only reason why the company ledgers were not awash with red ink, and why the company sat on a multimillion-dollar backlog of orders, was because of the recent surge in defense work. The spending associated with the Korean Conflict came at a fortuitous time for the struggling company.

When the fighting in Korea ended in 1953, the drop in spending associated with the conflict exerted a negative effect on ACF-Brill Motors fortunes. Shortly after Dwight Eisenhower's inauguration as president, the principal parties in Korea signed an armistice. Not surprisingly, the ACF-Brill Motors 1954 annual report was decidedly gloomier than it had been the previous three years. Management could tell stockholders that ACF-Brill Motors recorded $944,335 of net income for 1954, but that was down from the $1.3 million figure posted in 1953, and sales had tumbled from $29.1 million in 1953 to only $18.3 million in 1954. [5-34] The reason behind this colossal dip in sales and profits was easy to explain: "The reduction from 1953 sales is due primarily to the discontinuance of bus manufacture and to reduced military business in the Philadelphia Division." Having government orders can be a lucrative portion of the income for a company. But relying on government contracts for profitability opens a company to a destabilizing rollercoaster ride of spending peaks and valleys. Because of postwar changes in the heavy-duty engine market, with new aggressive competitors and new consumer demands, other engine makers looked to Uncle Sam for salvation in the postwar period, too. Competitor Hercules, in an in-house written history, stated that since the end of World War II, it had become "evident that the independent engine manufacturer must depend more and more on the Armed Services for volume business." [5-35] True enough. ACF-Brill was on a government rollercoaster ride in the early 1950s, and it was questionable if the company could survive until the arrival of the next spending surge.

Hall-Scott Motor Division was able to generate some revenue in this period, and it did not suffer the oscillating highs and lows endured by ACF-Brill Motors' bus making. However, its figures were hardly robust. The engine maker's sales amounted to $7.3 million in 1949, remained flat in 1950 at $7.2 million, and then saw three years of modest increase. [5-36] In 1951, Hall-Scott rolled up $9 million in sales, a figure that increased in 1952 to $9.8 million and then jumped again to $12.4 million in 1953. ACF-Brill Motors' drop in sales in 1954 with the end of the Korean Conflict was replicated at Hall-Scott, with sales in Berkeley sliding sharply to $9.1 million. In most years during this six-year period, Hall-Scott racked up $7 to $9 million in sales. The company was, at best, treading water. The sales picture at Hall-Scott did not appear ruinous, but it was hardly encouraging, not realizing any growth in that six-year period. The net income of Hall-Scott over that same time period was reason for great concern, though. In 1949, Hall-Scott reported a net income of $353,000 and saw it double in 1950 to $734,000; however, doubling an unacceptably low figure only renders a low figure. In 1951, Hall-Scott reported a net income of $618,000, and $527,000 in 1952. But the banner sales year of 1953 saw net income actually stumble to $384,000, and 1954 brought in only $74,000. Through the early Cold War period, Hall-Scott management could claim that the company was a money-making operation. But the consistent inability of Hall-Scott to earn respectable profits meant that it would not remain greatly valued by its struggling parent company. Nor would this income history make Hall-Scott attractive to another firm looking to purchase it. In addition to that, net income levels of half to three-quarters of a million dollars left almost nothing for aggressive product development, the kind Hall-Scott badly needed to regain a competitive posture.

Four years of declining net income—from $734,000 in 1950 to $74,000 in 1954—represented a dangerous trend at Hall-Scott. The company simply could not survive with these depressed (and depressing) levels. The engines made by the company were not finding enough customers, but perhaps management could find other things to make and sell in sufficient quantity.

More Truck, Bus, and Boat Owners Discover Diesel

After the war ended and the government production restrictions lapsed, Hall-Scott re-entered the engine market with a leaner selection of models. In the marine sector, the company retrenched most dramatically. By the end of the war, the Voyager, Navigator, and Fisher Jr. had all disappeared from the lineup. In fact, Hall-Scott offered only two models for boaters in 1946: the Invader and the Defender. [5-37] Truck, bus, and industrial customers had many more models from which to choose: Models 130, 135, 136, 180, 190, 400, 470, and 480, at least for a short time. All of these truck and bus models had six cylinders. Additionally, in the early postwar years, Hall-Scott began marketing its V-12 as an industrial engine, at first designated the Model 2269-0. Although Hall-Scott offered horizontal and vertical models that burned CPG or gasoline, it did not offer any diesels, for land or water, and it no longer included any four-cylinder engines. The output of its engines stretched from 130 to 900 hp (although the 900-hp engine was not available for long) and was wide enough to cover a number of applications, but fewer than before the war.

Unfortunately for the health of Hall-Scott, in the postwar era the company did not bring out any new models that were substantially different from what it had settled on as its narrow engine niche. In fact, the number of models offered by Hall-Scott shrank through the 1950s. Not only did the company contract the number of engine models, but the "new" truck, bus, and industrial engines

272

The Hall-Scott 400 series engine, no matter the model, had plenty of power, and the company wanted customers to know that.

An example of how Hall-Scott argued that its engines could save owners money—by cutting transit time.

MORE POWER

to the city of Los Angeles

New 1,250 gallon pumpers

with **HALL-SCOTT "400" ENGINES**

The latest addition to the modern efficient fire-fighting system of the City of Los Angeles is eighteen 1,250 gallon pumpers built by Peter Pirsch & Sons. Top power performance is assured with Hall-Scott "400" engines. In getting to fires it means quick acceleration after traffic slow-downs, rapid hill climbing and unexcelled dependability. In fighting fires Hall-Scott provides steady pumping for 48 hours.

These precision built power plants develop from 250 to 300 B.H.P. at speeds below 2,200 R.P.M.—an important factor in extending motor life. Hall-Scott unit assembly design permits a part to be serviced while a duplicate is in the engine out fighting fires.

For added power and dependability make sure that your fire fighting equipment is powered with Hall-Scott engines.

HALL-SCOTT
MOTOR CAR COMPANY

Factory and General Offices: 2850 Seventh Street, Berkeley 2, California
Factory Branches: Seattle, Washington · Los Angeles · New York City
Division of ACF-Brill Motors Company

Hall-Scott made the same pitch to fire chiefs that it did to truckers when advertising the Model 400. (Courtesy of Taylor Scott.)

Hall-Scott never marketed its V-12 for trucks, but a few folks installed them on their own.

Hall-Scott experimented with a truck version of the V-12, as shown here.

A rear three-quarter view of the Hall-Scott industrial V-12. These engines often were used in oil and gas fields and in water pumping.

that it introduced in this era, save one, were all derivatives of the Invader. The high-water mark of Hall-Scott industry leadership had unquestionably passed decades ago.

In spite of a lack of truly new Hall-Scott engines, several exciting product and technology trends from other companies dominated the pages of truck and bus magazines in the postwar period. Wider use of lightweight metals in vehicles and trailers increased payloads. Trucks and buses must operate under weight limits imposed by state and local governments; therefore, truck and bus owners naturally wanted to carry as much cargo or passengers as possible to maximize profits. For owners, every pound saved in vehicle weight was another pound of money-making freight that could be carried. Hence, in the postwar years as competition in transportation heated up, a pronounced push came from the market for lighter vehicles. Trucks, buses, trailers, and engines were shrinking in weight, and by the postwar era, engine makers could boast of having heavy-duty engines with power-to-weight ratios that had been seen only in aircraft years earlier. Highway transportation became faster during this period, too, with more powerful and more efficient trucks, as well as improvements

Three Hall-Scott industrial V-12s at work pumping.

in roads, such as the advent of the interstate highway system in the late 1950s. Following World War II, states across America boosted their weight limits, and many western states allowed some tractor-trailer combinations up to 70,000 lb, with stretched trailer length limits to 45 ft. [5-38] This steady improvement made to trucks and engines, and more generous legislation favoring larger loads, allowed trucks to overtake trains in carrying most of America's freight during the postwar period.

Heavy-duty vehicle owners found new types of transmissions they could order. Basically, two main developments were receiving the most attention: improved manual transmissions with greater numbers of gear ratios and better shifting, and automatic transmissions. Automatics, hitherto seen only in cars, were slowly making inroads into select heavier-vehicle applications, led by the General Motors Allison Division, and the industry looked forward to technical advancements and greater industry acceptance. Improved transmissions could boost vehicle fuel economy, cut delivery times, reduce driver fatigue, and lead to other benefits. Hall-Scott did not produce truck transmissions in the 1950s as it had in the 1930s when its products were unusually powerful, so much so that the company felt compelled to make transmissions strong enough to handle them.

New power plants also received a great amount of ink in trade publications after 1945. Not surprisingly perhaps, given wartime development, people pondered the possibilities of small jet engines powering land vehicles. Ford, General Motors, and Kenworth were some of the companies exploring this exciting technology, with Kenworth placing a jet engine in one of its trucks in 1950. [5-39] Jets, also known as turbine engines, found their way into numerous test commercial vehicles and even cars after World War II. But ultimately, they failed to make a positive impression in the truck and bus engine market. Lightweight, powerful, and compact, at first turbine engines seemed like a modern solution to the old challenge of moving things economically. The high fuel consumption inherent in jets made them unattractive to truckers, but they nonetheless fired people's imagination.

Truck and bus operators wanted more power from their engines, and they demanded lighter weight, which, in spite of how it might seem, is not a contradiction in a heavy-duty engine. To meet this demand, more efficiently constructed gasoline engines, using the compact "V" design, began to appear in greater numbers. With a shorter length than a straight-six of similar displacement, a V-8 could fit into shorter-nosed trucks, allowing the vehicle to be lighter, too. In the 1950s, modern, lighter, high-compression, more powerful, overhead-valve V-8s appeared from the established "Big Three" auto makers and a handful of the independents, such as Continental, Le Roi, and Reo. Even Hall-Scott announced plans to develop a V-8, and a diesel at that, although the company never sold one. [5-40] Sketchy references to a Hall-Scott V-8, such as in a company annual report, document Hall-Scott's interest in such an engine and acknowledge the popularity of this industry trend.

Also in this period, a growing number of engine makers sought to squeeze more power from their engines through supercharging and turbocharging. Supercharging had a long history in racing and had some proven working examples in commercial and light-duty vehicles. Turbocharging, on the other hand, was still being developed and finding market approval in the 1940s and 1950s. Turbos normally use wasted energy, exhaust gas, to spin one end of a two-sided vane that charges more air into the engine. In the postwar years, engineers hoped this device could extract more power without incurring the fuel economy penalty attached to superchargers, which are mechanically driven by gear or belt. Hall-Scott had incorporated a turbo-like technology into its marine LM-6 after World War I, with its clever, albeit barely effective, "semi-supercharger." But E.J. Hall was still engineering for Hall-Scott then, so it is understandable that this nascent technology was abandoned after he left. Hall-Scott did fix turbochargers onto later engines, though. The obscure (even for Hall-Scott) Model 442 was a Model 400 with a turbocharger and fuel injection, sold to the military in the postwar period for large trucks such as snow blowers. [5-41] The company perhaps made 159 examples of the Model 442. Then there is a reference in a Hall-Scott repair manual to a Model 6182 GT, also a fuel-injected and turbocharged Model 400, which developed 450 hp and 1312 lb. ft. of torque. [5-42] The photo of the blown engine was dated 1956, but it is unclear if any 6182 GTs were sold, and if so, when, for how much, and so forth. But neither the Model 442 nor the Model 6182 GT, which could have been the same engine, left much of a paper trail in ads, brochures, or annual reports. Although Hall-Scott participated in this new and increasingly popular technology, for unknown reasons it did not expend great effort to alert engine buyers.

By far the most talked-about engine development in the postwar period was the continuing evolution of the diesel engine. By the mid-1940s, no longer was the compression-ignition engine the ponderously heavy, large, slow-turning technology it had been at the opening of the twentieth century. By 1945, with rail and marine leading the way in acceptance, diesels were getting ever lighter, smaller, more powerful, and simpler to maintain. One source reported that the total number of diesel-powered trucks and buses in America jumped from fewer than 1,000 in 1938 to some 30,000 in 1948. [5-43] In the truck sector, diesel powered one of every twenty new trucks made in 1945, one of every ten made in 1950, and one of every five made in 1957. [5-44] The greater efficiency of diesels allowed them to compete well in the changing postwar truck market, with higher speeds being attained and greater weights being carried. In turn, the growth of diesel engines fed this increase in truck tonnage

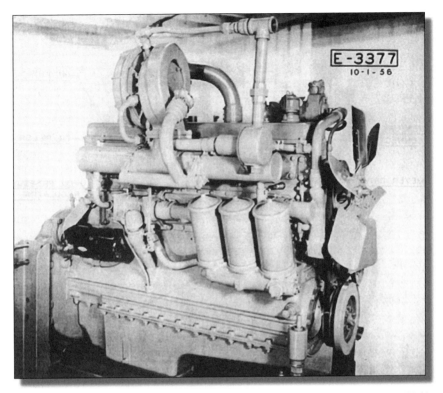

This image, dated 1956, of the exhaust side of a 6182 GT was taken from a 1960s Hercules-printed Hall-Scott repair manual but shows a turbocharged 400 series engine.

and speed. Improved roads and trucks allowed average truck speeds to climb from 42.8 mph in 1948 to 48 mph in 1959. [5-45] Trucks also were carrying more of America's freight after the war. From 1948 to 1959, intercity freight increased 143%, from 81 billion ton-miles in 1941, to 115 billion ton-miles in 1948, to 279 billion ton-miles in 1959. The healthy gain in acceptance of diesel certainly was helped by the lower price of diesel fuel, about three-quarters the price of gasoline in the early postwar period. [5-46] Not only did diesel fuel require less refining, but it was still exempt from the same high taxation of the federal and most state governments that gasoline faced. With heavier loads and higher speeds driving up fuel consumption per mile in the late 1940s through the 1950s, adopting diesel power for buses and trucks made perfect sense.

Plenty of people inside the engine industry in the mid-1940s predicted that the growth of diesel in trucks and buses would continue even more rapidly after the end of World War II. For example, managers at Continental Motors Corporation foresaw this trend and "decided late in 1944 to begin manufacture of four- and six-cylinder models from 25 h.p. up as soon as government restrictions on manpower and materials could be lifted." [5-47] A builder of diesels since the early 1930s, Continental expanded its diesel offerings more into the truck and bus markets. But having diesel engines was not enough to ensure success, as Continental discovered in the 1950s. Continental engineers stuck with the Lanova principle of combustion, as Hall-Scott had used with its Model 125 diesel in the 1930s. Continental historian Wagner described Lanova technology as "relatively poor in performance when judged against later developments, [but] these diesels were adequate for their day." [5-48] By the 1950s, this method was proving itself inferior to the "open chamber" principle increasingly used by other makers, so competitors "drew off much of the available business" in diesel sales from Continental. Wagner argued that the compromised performance of the Lanova process was one reason why more than 90% of sales by Continental in the early postwar period were gasoline-powered engines. As of this writing (2006), Continental still builds engines, including diesels; however, it did not predicate its success in the postwar period on having diesels. But Continental stayed in the diesel game and improved its products.

A measure of the strength of this growing postwar interest in diesel power can be gleaned from reading issues of the popular trade publication *Commercial Car Journal*. The January 1951 edition listed the articles that appeared in its 1950 issues, giving an idea of those topics of most interest to the editors of *Commercial Car Journal* and, presumably, its readers, too. That index listed two 1950 articles on jet engines, six on automatic transmissions or torque converters, and at least twelve on diesel engines, clearly making diesel power the most popular single topic that publication addressed in 1950. A few of these diesel-related articles carried names such as "Buda Develops Three New Diesels," "American Fleetmen Eye British Diesels," "Truck and Bus Operators Favor Diesel Vehicles," and "Important Assets of Diesels." [5-49] Other issues of *Commercial Car Journal* around these years only replicated this same overwhelmingly positive and hopeful interest in diesels. In 1954, *Commercial Car Journal* printed an article titled "Operation Switchover Saves Money for Busmen," in which *Commercial Car Journal* editor Bart Rawson wrote on the many bus lines across America that had chosen to repower their vehicles with diesel engines when their existing gasoline units wore out. [5-50] While the conversion cost upward of $3,500 for the engine and $500 for installation, the superior fuel mileage of the diesel (sometimes 50% greater than gasoline power plants) and cheaper fuel (usually several pennies per gallon) resulted in bus lines being able to pay for the expensive conversion in only two years of normal operation with the new engines. Ominously for readers in Berkeley, managers from one of these bus lines happily exchanged their Hall-Scott gasoline engines for British-built Leyland diesels. With this widespread conversion to compression ignition engines in all sorts of buses, Rawson concluded that it "appears to be just about final proof that diesel is here to stay."

The parent company of Hall-Scott offered no protection to the engine maker from the volatile postwar marketplace. Bus sales figures in part explain this failure. As mentioned, after a brief surge of bus sales in the United States when the war ended, the numbers dropped off sharply. In 1946, sales of buses in the United States totaled 10,000. [5-51] That number soared to 19,100 in 1947, and then sales dried up just as suddenly, dropping to 12,000 in 1948, 5,500 in 1949, and 4,900 in 1950, about one-quarter of the 1947 figure. ACF-Brill Motors bus production numbers fell as precipitously, tumbling from 1,004 units shipped in 1948, to 414 in 1949, to only 375 in 1950. [5-52] Given these numbers, the timing for Avco to open its Nashville bus plant could not have been much worse. And given the fact that more and more of the buses sold after World War II came with diesel power meant that ACF-Brill Motors would have a harder time selling its Hall-Scott power as an attractive feature to customers.

This troubling scenario did not paralyze ACF managers into inaction. To their credit, ACF leaders remained at least somewhat responsive to market changes and offered new products to meet altered demand. In 1947, ACF brought out two smaller transit models under the Brill name and broke from its practice of exclusively using Hall-Scotts by equipping the buses with International gasoline engines. [5-53] ACF kept up with the growing popularity of automatic transmissions by offering Spicer hydraulic units. But these changes did not halt skidding bus figures at ACF. Linked to the free-fall in the number of buses sold came the related slide in ACF-Brill Motors finances; total sales figures plummeted from $27.3 million in 1948, to $13.5 million in 1949, to $12.6 million in 1950. [5-54] Management tried to console its stockholders by pointing out, "While the outlook for the bus and trolley coach manufacturing industry as a whole is not encouraging, it is significant that ACF-Brill has maintained its position in the industry." [5-55] That was something of a silver lining, probably the best management could muster.

A few other bus makers used Hall-Scotts, but all were minor producers; the old ACF policy of monopolizing Hall-Scott bus engines left the Berkeley firm to wither as ACF-Brill Motors sales sank. One lesser bus maker that

Johnston's Fuel Liners

Right after World War II, Eldon Johnston, Wilson Burnette, and Merrill Tate formed a trucking company called Johnston's Fuel Liners (JFL). Headquartered in Newcastle, Wyoming, the firm hauled petroleum products from a refinery located there to customers in several states. The men built the venture into a successful company, with a growing fleet of trucks, dozens of employees, and a handful of branch offices. The JFL fleet, which was usually kept very clean, had cabs painted a distinctive black and white. The drivers even wore ties

and caps, at least for a few years. And through the 1940s and 1950s, JFL exclusively used Kenworth conventionals with gaseous-fueled Hall-Scott engines. (A small oval "Hall-Scott Power" plate could be found on the truck hoods shown here.) Johnston's had ready

access to propane, and it was cheap to buy. Tate was in charge of the fleet hardware and, according to former JFL driver, dispatcher, and terminal manager Jim Dixon, was "very very adamant" about using Hall-Scott 400s. To stretch engine life and fuel economy, Tate demanded that drivers limit engine speed to only 1700 rpm, which meant about 45 to 47 mph in top gear. To ensure that drivers observed that ceiling, management installed "tach charts" in the trucks. The devices, popular with fleets at one time, created a hard copy of engine revolutions per minute over time. The seemingly low engine (and road) speed caused drivers little grief, though. Dixon remembered that with a Hall-Scott 400 under the hood, hauling a full load, even up steep mountains at high altitude, "You could pull your tach chart out at night and from here to Casper you pretty much had a straight line at the 45 mph mark." With the changing tax structure on propane and diesel fuel, though, and the steady improvement of diesel engines, by the mid 1970s the old Hall-Scotts didn't make much financial sense anymore. In one fell swoop, management pulled the last Hall-Scotts, either retiring the trucks or repowering them with Detroit Diesel. But until that point, with about two dozen Hall-Scott 400 engines in vehicles, Johnston's Fuel Liners was probably the last truck fleet to run Hall-Scotts. (Artifacts, photos, and information courtesy of Wayne McDougall, Cleo Bunette, Ronald Tate, and Jim Dixon).

placed Hall-Scotts in the engine compartments in some of its vehicles was Kenworth, which used Hall-Scotts for its new hybrid bus/truck vehicle, dubbed the "Bruck." They came in at least two closely related versions. Kenworth's novel three-axled Bruck first appeared in 1949, with capacity for 17 passengers up front, 1000 cubic feet of freight in the rear, and a horizontal Hall-Scott Model 136 engine underfloor powering it. [5-56] The rear deck over the freight compartment in this Bruck was elevated a couple of feet higher than the passenger compartment. Another series of Brucks emerged in 1951, having a 21-passenger capacity, a 24-foot-long rear freight compartment, and a larger Hall-Scott Model 190 engine underfloor. [5-57] A highly visible difference

An example of a Kenworth first-series Bruck, built for Northern Pacific Transport, and moved by a 477-cubic-inch, 157-hp, horizontal Hall-Scott Model 136 engine. Note the elevated cargo section in the rear. (Courtesy of Motor Bus Society.)

between the two models was the flush roof line of the latter model; volumetric measurements of the newer Bruck could not be found. It is interesting to note that the passenger/freight combination in the Bruck was similar to that of the first Hall-Scott product, the dual-purpose passenger/freight rail car sold to the Yreka Railroad in 1910. A handful of Brucks served local transit agencies, or as "feeders" for the Great Northern Railway Company's passenger rail service in the Pacific Northwest, primarily bringing freight and passengers to and from trains. Unfortunately for Hall-Scott, Bruck sales did not soar; thus, this new application did little to bolster Hall-Scott finances.

Kenworth's later Bruck used the 779-cubic-inch 220-hp horizontal Model 190 mated to a Fuller ten-speed transmission. Note the flat line of the roof. (Courtesy of Stumptown Historical Society.)

A later-series Bruck on display in Kalispell, Montana, a city it had served. The Stumptown Historical Society restored the vehicle. (Courtesy of Stumptown Historical Society.)

ACF-Brill Motors was selling fewer buses. The small number of minor bus makers that picked Hall-Scott power did not ring up many sales, and increasing numbers of bus buyers demanded diesel. According to one source, by the early 1950s about half of the new commercial buses sold in America had diesel engines. [5-58] In an attempt to remain relevant in the industry, in 1952 the bus maker introduced the Model IC-41 AD, which was not powered by an in-house Hall-Scott engine but rather by a six-cylinder, 200-hp, Model NHHB-600 Cummins diesel located horizontally under the floor. [5-59] If ACF-Brill Motors would not give Hall-Scott the money needed to develop a diesel, going outside the corporate family for power was the only option.

Perhaps it is fitting that a Cummins motor propelled the new ACF-Brill Motors IC-41 AD bus. This engine company, more than any other, represented the single most serious competitive challenge to the future of Hall-Scott as an engine maker. Cummins was the most aggressive and successful of the diesel makers in the post-World War II era, but it was not the first American engine maker to enter the diesel field. A number of other heavy-duty diesel makers,

Decades later, many still remember the ACF-Brill Motors IC-41, a popular intercity bus used by Greyhound, Trailways, and other bus companies. These buses often had Hall-Scott power.

such as Atlas-Imperial, had already come and gone by the 1950s. And a few firms such as Buda, Hercules, and Waukesha had all established themselves years before Clessie Cummins began to achieve any success. Buda tapped European technology as early as the 1920s, buying the rights to some products of the German M.A.N. company in 1926. [5-60] In spite of regularly releasing new models, Buda never became a major diesel builder. In November 1953, heavy-equipment-maker Allis-Chalmers bought the Illinois-based engine company, taking the Buda name off the market soon thereafter. [5-61] In fact, only months before the Allis-Chalmers purchase, Buda introduced another new diesel truck model—a supercharged, 165-hp, six-cylinder engine weighing about 1825 lb. [5-62] Having diesel models, even good and ostensibly modern ones, was no guarantee for success in the cutthroat engine business of the postwar era. Similarly, "old timers" Hercules and Waukesha cooperated with European firms to stay in the diesel game with marine, truck, and industrial models. However, none of these companies ultimately could compete effectively with Cummins, nor could they keep up with another successful diesel builder, industrial super-power General Motors, or with heavy-equipment-maker Caterpillar. Cummins, General Motors, and "Cat" became diesel leaders by continuously "pushing the envelope" through relentless programs to change and improve their products with ever-better performance and effective marketing.

Similar to how American bus line managers turned increasingly to diesel engines to power their vehicles in the 1940s and 1950s, so did boat operators. Even as Hall-Scott continued to target marine applications for its engines in the postwar period, the company found rapidly diminishing interest in that prized area, too. For one thing, Americans changed the types of pleasure boats they bought after World War II, with fewer, less expensive custom boats and more lower-priced production boats. Similarly, these were automotive-based boat engines. Auto engines "marinized" by Hercules, Cris-Craft, and Chrysler often powered these smaller craft. The engines now finding favor from boaters were lighter and cheaper, owing to the automotive origins of the engines. Another attractive element for these motors was that many of their parts were easy to obtain (i.e., from auto parts stores) and were inexpensive. According to marine historian Stan Grayson, despite the widely acknowledged quality of Hall-Scott, "the post-World War II era found the company unprepared to compete in a market that had forever changed." [5-63] Ironically, by the 1950s, Hall-Scott products had become what the company had accused its less successful competition of being in the 1910s to 1930s: heavy, slow-turning, and outdated. Except for small pleasure craft, the market for large boats, commercial, and military moved almost exclusively to diesel by the postwar era, and Hall-Scott had nothing to sell to those customers. Caterpillar, Cummins,

Fairbanks-Morse, General Motors, Hercules, and some other small diesel makers ably met the new market with engines that marine customers demanded. One popular book from the time period, *High-Speed Small Craft*, echoed this widespread sentiment in its 1957 second edition. The author argued that when it came to choosing a power plant for a high-speed small craft, which he defined as being less than 130 feet in length and capable of speeds exceeding 15 knots, for work, military, and pleasure applications, "It is probable that the Diesel engine cycle, provided power output, weight and reliability were acceptable, would undoubtedly represent the optimum for marine purposes." [5-64] He suggested that although diesel engines were "on the heavy side for the faster types" of boats, they still enjoyed several advantages over gasoline engines, such as being more efficient in transforming fuel into power. Plus, diesels did not burn an "unduly volatile fuel" such as gasoline. [5-65]

Reflecting this diminished interest by water-going customers after the war ended, sales for Hall-Scott marine engines simply vanished. Forty-four Invader deliveries in 1946 could be passed off as responding to the nation's transition to a peacetime economy, but deliveries of 16 engines in 1949 could not, nor could one engine being delivered yearly in 1952, 1953, and 1954. [5-66] Defender sales in this period were equally depressing, saved only by a one-time contract with the U.S. Navy for some 300 units. Not changing its products in response to different demand cost Hall-Scott dearly, as it had in other instances through the history of the company. For all practical purposes, Hall-Scott disappeared from the marine engine market at the end of World War II.

In response to the turbulent postwar engine market, with the greater use of V-8s, diesels, supercharging and turbocharging, lightweight construction, and other advances, Hall-Scott introduced four "new" engines in 1953 and 1954. Hall-Scott engineers were not exactly sitting on their hands in the postwar years. Unfortunately for Hall-Scott, these new motors were largely iterations of what the company had been making for many years. Hall-Scott introduced Models 855, 935, and 1091 in 1953 and Model 590 in 1954. [5-67] The model numbers of each corresponded to their cubic-inch displacement, making them typical of large engines by truck standards. On the positive side, each of the new models boasted of having high horsepower (205 to 285 hp) and very high torque (510 to 945 lb. ft.). They also contained the usual Hall-Scott features, including overhead camshaft; unit construction; hemi head; the choice of burning butane, liquefied petroleum gas (LPG), or gasoline; and blocks cast of long-wearing alloy iron. Unfortunately, three of the models were heavy; the Models 855 and 935 shared the same weight of 2150 lb, and the Model 1091 was very close. Being derivatives of the Invader, these three new models

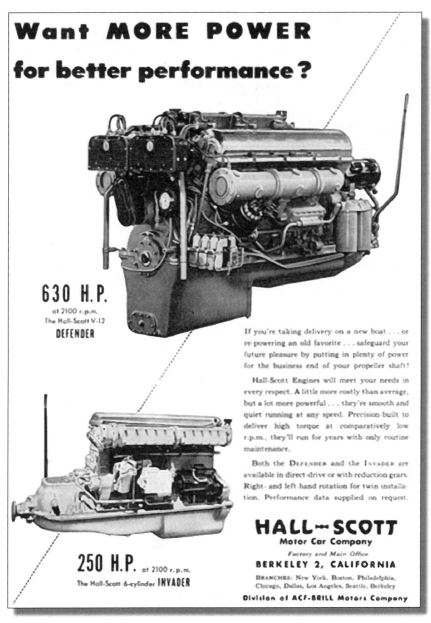

Want MORE POWER
for better performance?

630 H.P.
at 2100 r.p.m.
The Hall-Scott V-12
DEFENDER

250 H.P. at 2100 r.p.m.
The Hall-Scott 6-cylinder INVADER

If you're taking delivery on a new boat . . . or re-powering an old favorite . . . safeguard your future pleasure by putting in plenty of power for the business end of your propeller shaft!

Hall-Scott Engines will meet your needs in every respect. A little more costly than average, but a lot more powerful . . . they're smooth and quiet running at any speed. Precision-built to deliver high torque at comparatively low r.p.m., they'll run for years with only routine maintenance.

Both the DEFENDER and the INVADER are available in direct-drive or with reduction gears. Right- and left-hand rotation for twin installation. Performance data supplied on request.

HALL~SCOTT
Motor Car Company
Factory and Main Office
BERKELEY 2, CALIFORNIA
BRANCHES: New York, Boston, Philadelphia, Chicago, Dallas, Los Angeles, Seattle, Berkeley
Division of ACF-BRILL Motors Company

Similar to the Hall-Scott 400 series truck engine ads, Hall-Scott marine engine ads in the postwar period stressed the great power available.

naturally shared the roughly 1-ton weight of the Invader. All four of the newly announced models were six-cylinder spark-ignition engines. Given the directions in engine making at that time, with industry prognostications for future development going down several new paths, and with the flagging fortunes of Hall-Scott from selling engines such as these, the proposition of introducing these models in the 1950s was dubious at best.

Shortcomings aside, the Model 590 deserves special attention. It was an entirely new engine, the first from Hall-Scott in more than 20 years. It achieved some measure of market acceptance, and it was the last entirely new engine designed and marketed by the company. Chief engineer J.E. "Speed" Glidewell created the Model 590 because, according to Francis Bradford, there was "demand for a cheaper, higher [speed] and more powerful" engine, and Hall-Scott was losing "lots of sales to our competitors." [5-68] Glidewell departed from a long-accepted Hall-Scott engineering tradition when he gave the Model 590 "square" cylinder measurements—the same dimensions for bore and stroke—of 5 inches

The exhaust side of the Hall-Scott Model 590.

by 5 inches. Almost every Hall-Scott engine built from 1910 to 1954 had used a longer stroke than bore measurement (sometimes referred to as being "under square"). Engines with larger stroke than bore tend to maximize the amount of torque produced, but their long piston travel hinders the maximum revolutions per minute that can be achieved, which puts some limits on horsepower. Glidewell governed the engine speed of the Model 590 at 2800 rpm, compared to the 2200 rpm of the Invader derivatives, owing in part to the shorter stroke of the new engine. That gave the Model 590 perhaps the highest maximum engine speed rated on a Hall-Scott model. Recognizing, or perhaps bowing, to market pressures, the chief engineer rejected the usual Hall-Scott practice of emphasizing big torque development over higher revolutions per minute, moving the Model 590 in a more automobile engine-like direction. Another factor that made the Model 590 less like a truck engine was its lighter weight. The new engine, which in its various forms over the next few years developed 192 to 245 hp and 465 to 530 lb. ft. of torque, weighed only 1300 to 1400 lb. [5-69]

The intake side of the Hall-Scott Model 590.

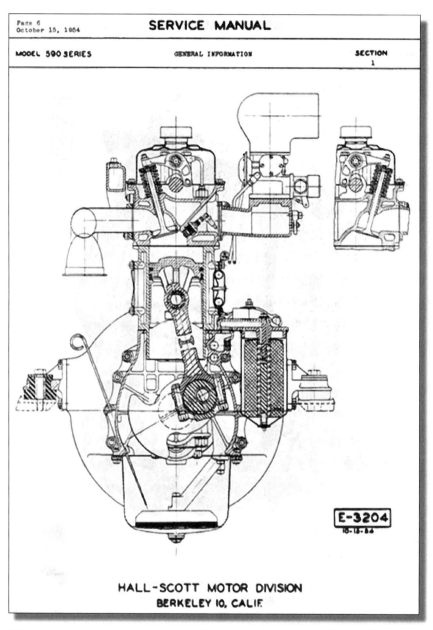

E-3204
10-15-53

HALL-SCOTT MOTOR DIVISION
BERKELEY 10, CALIF.

This line drawing from a 1954 Hall-Scott manual shows that this Model 590 did not have a true hemispherical head as seen in earlier Hall-Scotts but could also be described as having a "wedge head."

About 700 lb lighter than its recently introduced stable mates, the Model 590 still produced horsepower that was at least in the ballpark with the other new engines, even if its torque numbers lagged.

The prime advantage of the Model 590 over other Hall-Scott engines was its lower weight, its dimensions, and its fuel consumption. The Model 590 measured 49.5 inches front to back, some 13 inches shorter than descendents of the Hall-Scott Invader. It also measured 26.25 inches wide, about 4 inches narrower than the others. Therefore, Hall-Scott had reason to claim in a Model 590 ad that it now had a powerful engine available "to fit your trucks," unlike its other engines that were heavier and larger, sometimes even needing frame modification on trucks to accommodate them. [5-70] Another ad splashed the number "6" across the page—the 6:1 power-to-weight ratio of the Model 590. [5-71] The advertisement proclaimed that the Model 590 had "more power per pound than any other truck engine." This was a not-so-subtle reference to customers that the Model 590 was a different kind of engine from Hall-Scott, more modern and competitive, giving them the lighter, smaller, higher-speed, more economical characteristics that they demanded.

Designing and building a new engine of any type is prohibitively expensive. Cost ranked as the main reason why it was easier for big firms such as General Motors, or larger independents such as International Harvester or Continental, to produce new engines, stay competitive, provide customers with the features and performance they demanded, and remain viable. Hall-Scott ranked as a tiny firm, comparatively speaking, and ACF was no General Motors either. Without the capital available from a well-financed parent company to underwrite new engine development (or in the case of Hall-Scott, without having significant money siphoned off by its parent company, which would have been a boon), or without having a sizable cash flow to secure a large loan, Hall-Scott clearly operated at a disadvantage in this respect. Glidewell saved money where he could when designing this new engine. One advantage of the Model 590 from the perspective of management was its low manufacturing cost. For example, producing the Model 590 was simplified, and thus made more economical, by grouping together most accessories such as the water pump and distributor drive, by using the same size of valves for the intake and exhaust (at least on early units), and by securing the impellers of the water pump with a cross pin (later replaced by a more expensive woodruff key when the cheaper cross pin failed in use). [5-72] Economy in design and production led Glidewell to make the Model 590 strong enough to handle multiple fuels—gasoline, propane, and even diesel. Hall-Scott never released the Model 590 as a diesel, though. The

Hall-Scott ads argued that Model 590 customers could have it all—traditional Hall-Scott power and good fuel economy. (Courtesy of Commercial Carrier Journal, *formerly* Commercial Car Journal.*)*

Hall-Scott marketing was different with the Model 590, stressing that this engine was powerful but lightweight and efficient. (Courtesy of Commercial Carrier Journal.)

Model 590 was a good engine, evidenced by the fact that it continued to be produced by another firm after Hall-Scott closed its doors.

Obviously, Hall-Scott managers hoped the Model 590 would be different enough to lure more engine buyers, and company ads and press releases focused on the relative weight and size advantages of the engine. In its 1953 annual report, ACF-Brill management hoped aloud, stating, "All indications are that the new engine will meet with considerable consumer popularity as it is offered to the trade generally." [5-73] A year later, however, a more worried ACF-Brill Motors management obliquely pointed to disappointing sales for the new motor when it said that the Model 590 "is expected to find an expanding market as its excellent characteristics become more generally known in the trade." [5-74] To maximize its attractiveness to buyers, the Model 590 could be ordered to burn LPG, butane, propane, or gasoline, and it could be equipped to run vertically or horizontally. Therefore, the Model 590 could be used in those buses and fire trucks needing that configuration. Considering that the Model 590 was another

Similar to the 400 series, the Hall-Scott Model 590 was packaged as an industrial engine.

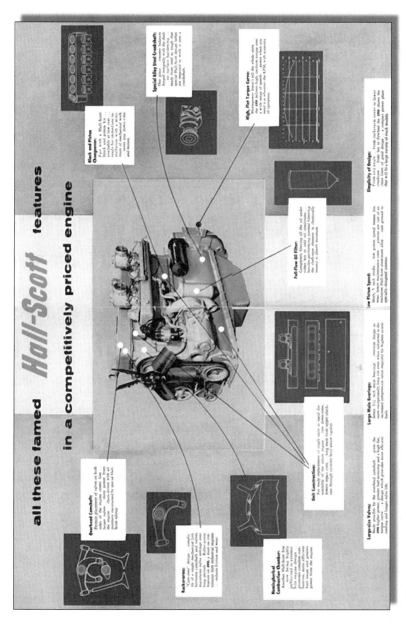

Although the small type is difficult to read, this fold-out brochure points out many of the features of the Hall-Scott Model 590.

spark-ignition, six-cylinder engine making around 200 hp, as were most Hall-Scott engines, Glidewell and his team tried to make the engine as attractive to as many potential customers as possible. Hall-Scott engine sales hovered in the hundreds of units per year in the postwar era—not the thousands—in spite of the promise briefly held by the new Model 590.

With demand growing for lighter-weight but still powerful gasoline truck engines (for those customers not choosing diesel, that is), engine makers tried to offer products that consumers wanted. The "Big Three" automakers—Chrysler, Ford, and General Motors—did so most successfully. Hall-Scott faced competition not only from other heavy-duty independent makers such as Cummins, International, Caterpillar, and Mack, but also from the colossal automakers. With their backgrounds in automobile manufacture, it is little surprise that the truck engines of the Big Three reflected automobile engine characteristics. In fact, many of the small-displacement engines that the Big Three fitted into their light trucks also saw double duty in powering cars. This dual application was true of both six- and eight-cylinder engines. The greater compactness of the V-8 was drawing considerable attention by engine builders and engine buyers in the postwar period; many looked upon it as a more modern design. By the mid-1950s, Chrysler, Ford, and General Motors each marketed V-8 gasoline truck engines that developed about 200 hp but weighed only 700 lb or less. These engines were smooth, efficient, reliable, and economical.

Several of the independents marketed one or more truck gasoline V-8 engines, too, but they did not look or perform much like those sold by the Big Three. Figures obtained from a 1957 *Commercial Car Journal* engine chart show that in the popular 200-hp range, the Le Roi Model TH 540 V-8 developed 206 hp and weighed 1355 lb, and the Continental Model V-8603 V-8 developed 240 hp and weighed 1786 lb. [5-75] Similarly, heavy-duty, in-line, six-cylinder gasoline engines in the 200-hp range similarly mirrored the differences seen among the V-8s produced by the independents and those of the Big Three. In an era when people in the truck and bus markets placed a premium on light weight, including in engines, this tendency on the part of independents to sell heavier engines had a predictable result on their sales.

Likewise, the maximum engine speed figures of the heavy-duty motors from the independents reported on that chart were significantly lower than those of Chrysler, Ford, and General Motors, which reflected the deeper engineering and marketing differences among them. The automotive firms governed their truck engines at higher speeds, as seen in their car engines. Chrysler commercial power plants were governed at an average of 3878 rpm, those of Ford were

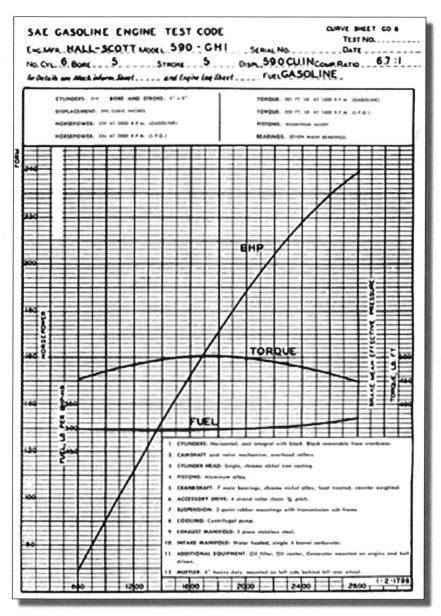

The power curve of the Hall-Scott Model 590.

governed at 4028 rpm, and those of General Motors were governed at 3833 rpm. Compare those numbers to the average maximum speeds of gasoline models made by the independents: Allis-Chalmers at 1800 rpm, Hall-Scott at 2472 rpm, Hercules at 2814 rpm, International Harvester at 2300 rpm, and Le Roi at 2733 rpm. The independents governed their engines at about 1000 rpm less than those of the Big Three. Not surprisingly, the gasoline engines from independents such as Hall-Scott, with their lower maximum revolutions per minute, put more emphasis on developing impressive torque numbers (i.e., the greatest torque is generated at lower engine speeds than maximum horsepower) than on developing big horsepower numbers (i.e., the greatest horsepower is generated at higher engine speeds). It was not unusual for engines from independents to develop more than twice as much torque as horsepower, whereas Big Three engines tended to have torque figures more similar to their horsepower figures. If the relationship of horsepower to torque is expressed as a ratio, the Big Three truck engines generated a ratio of horsepower to torque of about 1.5:1. Chrysler engines had a torque-to-horsepower ratio of 1.56, Ford of 1.5, and General Motors of 1.58. By comparison, Allis Chalmers engines had a torque-to-horsepower ratio of 3.29, Continental of 2.10, Hall-Scott of 2.43, Hercules of 2.52, International Harvester of 2.57, and Le Roi of 2.35. On paper and on the road, commercial engines from the Big Three and the independents looked and operated far differently.

Independents claimed with some pride (and defiance) that they sold heavier-duty products than the popular models produced by the Big Three, not only converted car engines. In one Reo advertisement appearing in a 1946 trade journal, the independent truck and engine manufacturer said, "In every detail and every dimension Reo is *all truck*." [5-76] Hall-Scott pointed to its engines having desirable heavy-duty features such as semi-steel blocks, larger crankshaft counterweights, heavier connecting rods, a stiffer block, and dual oil filters. Hall-Scott and its cohort in the independent ranks also argued that their low maximum engine speeds increased engine life and that the high torque could help big trucks pull heavier loads up longer grades, minimizing shifting, unlike the less heavy-duty engines offered by the Big Three. But engine buyers seemed less moved by these common-sense arguments as the years passed. The commercial engines made by the Big Three and the independents might have all had pistons, cams, and crankshafts, but they differed substantially in performance. Hall-Scott found itself in a postwar-era contest with rapidly changing rules. But in the face of this change, the Berkeley engine maker failed to appreciably alter its game plan.

A small and shrinking number of companies offered gasoline V-12s for the truck and bus market after World War II, such as Seagrave, shown here. It is doubtful that Hall-Scott would have realized many sales had it offered its V-12 to fire departments and other truck customers in this period.

Hall-Scott and Fire Trucks

Beginning in the 1930s, Hall-Scott began to focus on serving the power needs of fire departments. The company advertised in relevant publications, produced engines with performance favored by firefighters, and specially marketed engines targeted at that market, for both OEM and re-power customers. Hercules continued this special attention after purchasing the Hall-Scott Power Division. Even as diesel began to gain rapidly in popularity after World War II, plenty of fire department staff wanted to keep gasoline-fueled engines. One reason for this was the problem of smelly, oily, and noxious diesel exhaust accumulating in the truck and in the firehouse. Suction fans and other accommodations to firehouses came with adopting diesel. However, because demand continued for gasoline-powered fire equipment, Continental, American-La France, LeRoi, Seagrave, Waukesha, and Hall-Scott all offered big spark-ignition engines after the war. Jim Ryan, a fireman, engineer, and captain from California, looks back with great fondness to the tremendous "power and torque, the famous Hall-Scott sound with the blue flame coming from the exhaust pipe," which he said was "very impressive at night." Hall-Scotts could pull a heavy fire engine up hills, away from a traffic stop or slowdown (and thus not tempting the driver to avoid slowing at intersections, a safety consideration), and survive repeated long runs. For decades, the fleet in Los Angeles was mostly Hall-Scott powered. Says Don Brittingham, who for years did much of the fire equipment purchasing for Los Angeles, "The Hall-Scott was probably one of the best designed and manufactured heavy-duty spark-ignition engines ever built." In fact, Los Angeles bought so many Hall-Scotts that Brittingham and his colleagues would occasionally buy other engines solely because "we wanted to show we weren't married to Hall-Scott." Some fire departments hung onto their Hall-Scotts long after the Berkeley factory closed and even after Hercules stopped selling (and supporting) them. In the 1970s and beyond, fire departments had to cannibalize existing equipment, scrounge for parts, or even make their own parts to keep their beloved Hall-Scotts running. Difficulty in finding parts became a major reason why many Hall-Scotts were retired, not because they wore out or because competing engines, even diesels, performed better. It is in old fire equipment where it is most common to find running Hall-Scotts today. (Information courtesy of Jim Ryan and Bill West.)

HALL-SCOTT *FIRE* ENGINES

23

UNEQUALED IN PERFORMANCE

HALL-SCOTT
FIRE ENGINES

(Photos continued on next two pages)

Hercules builds that extra "fire horse" into Hall-Scott engines!

Old-time fire horses were always rarin' to go when the alarm clanged. The same is true of today's Hall-Scott engines.

The rugged 370 H.P., Model 6182 FES turns up instant torque for quicker starts. Packed with new power and performance, this eager brute gives you all the go and dependability a fire truck demands.

New materials, new machining techniques and advanced production procedures help to put a little more of that fire-horse into all Hall-Scott engines. That's why Hall-Scott is still the leader—still King of the Road—from coast to coast. America's top fire departments prefer Hall-Scott engines. You will, too.

We'll be happy to send complete literature and power curves on the Model 6182 FES engine and other sizes of Hall-Scott engines for fire trucks. Write today.

HUPP
CORPORATION

HERCULES ENGINE DIVISION ● CANTON, OHIO

Distributors in all major cities. Branches in Chicago, Philadelphia, Baltimore, Atlanta and Jacksonville.
For More Facts Circle 100 on Reply Card

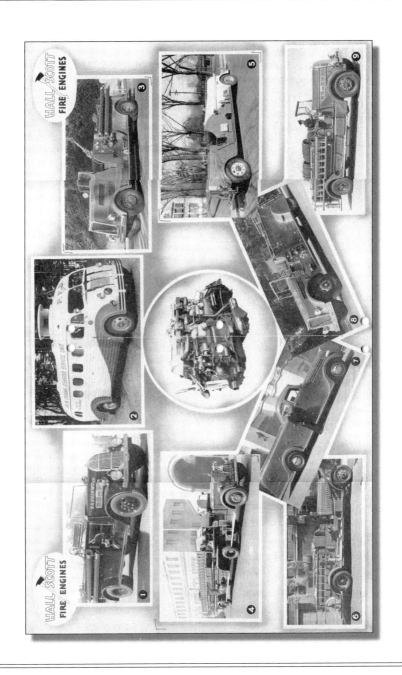

The ACF–Hall-Scott Split

The rough-and-tumble postwar economy was playing havoc on the fortunes of ACF-Brill Motors, which in turn directly impacted Hall-Scott. Brill company historian Debra Brill wrote that the bus "Business dropped off sharply through the latter part of the 1940s," with ACF-Brill Motors keeping its doors open as long as it did largely because of government contracts for buses and other equipment, leading to ACF-Brill Motors ceasing production "in early 1954." [5-77] Brill wrote that after terminating bus making, the company did not actually make anything: "ACF-Brill Motors Company was essentially a name on a bank account worth about $7 million." [5-78] Charles Allen considered dissolving ACF-Brill Motors and distributing the cash to stockholders, but instead chose to sink ACF-Brill Motors finances into a number of Midwest grocery stores such as Piggly Wiggly. Company executives made a clean break from industrial production; selling hamburger and milk at grocery stores would be the new "cash cow" for ACF-Brill Motors. Hall-Scott, its function of late primarily being a source of capital to keep the moribund ACF-Brill Motors limping along, was for sale. ACF-Brill Motors executive William Nelson remembered, "We were continuously on the look out [*sic*] for a buyer to take Hall-Scott. There were several individuals that looked at the set up but there were very few that did more than glance at it and walk away. The reason, no doubt, rested in the fact that Hall-Scott had no Diesel engine on which to capitalize." [5-79]

In early 1954, ACF-Brill Motors executives and stockholders rejected bus making as a means of making money. Later that same year, they decided to terminate engine making. In October 1954, ACF-Brill Motors stockholders voted to "spin-off" the Berkeley engine maker, a move that came as no surprise. [5-80] The new, independent engine-making firm emerging from this change took the name of Hall-Scott Motors Company. The action did not amount to a financial windfall for either company. Hall-Scott Motors received the "business and assets" of its engine-making business in exchange for "1,003,434 shares of its common stock and $1,003,434 of its debentures." ACF-Brill Motors management offered little in the way of commentary on dropping Hall-Scott. This is surprising, if for no other reason than it had controlled the engine maker for nearly 30 years. In its 1954 annual report, ACF-Brill Motors management simply said, "It is believed that operation as separate companies will enable each to conduct and develop its own business in the most efficient and profitable manner." [5-81] Given the feeble financial position of ACF-Brill Motors, with management looking for any means to generate greater sales and profits, Hall-Scott proved to be more of a liability than an asset, suggesting how bleak the position of Hall-Scott really was. If Hall-Scott had been a consistently substantial money maker in the late 1940s and early 1950s, ACF-Brill Motors would have clung to it like a drowning man grasping a life preserver. But the plain fact was that both ACF-Brill Motors and Hall-Scott were quite weak, selling products that fewer and fewer customers wanted.

References

5-1.   *Berkeley Gazette*, February 1, 1946, p. 1.

5-2.   *The New York Times*, February 1, 1946, p. 31.

5-3.   *Berkeley Gazette*, February 1, 1946, p. 1.

5-4.   *The New York Times*, December 22, 1945, p. 23.

5-5.   This deal is discussed in *Automotive Industries*, February 15, 1943, p. 48. *Automotive Industries*, April 1, 1943, p. 48.

5-6.   *Automotive Industries*, December 1, 1945, p. 93. *The New York Times*, November 2, 1945, p. 16.

5-7.   *Avco Corporation; The First Fifty Years*, Avco Corporation, Greenwich, CT, 1979, p. 28.

5-8.   *Automotive Industries*, July 1, 1944, p. 85.

5-9.   *The New York Times*, November 2, 1945, p. 16. *Automotive Industries*, July 1, 1945, p. 48.

5-10. *Automotive Industries*, December 1, 1945, p. 93.

5-11. 1951 ACF-Brill Motors Company Annual Report, p. 3.

5-12. Francis Bradford, "A History of the Hall-Scott Motor Car Company," unpublished manuscript, 1989, p. 68. Courtesy of Bancroft Library, University of California, Berkeley, BANC MSS 93/104c.

5-13. *Berkeley Gazette*, February 1, 1946, p. 1.

5-14. Ibid., p. 2.

5-15. *Automotive Industries*, October 1, 1947, pp. 24–25. See also *Automotive Industries*, January 15, 1949, p. 38, which discusses the retooling of the Lycoming plant to build Hall-Scott engines, including the addition of a novel "turntable engine block testing machine." Second article courtesy of John Perala.

5-16.　*The New York Times*, September 6, 1947, p. 21.

5-17.　*The New York Times*, December 25, 1947, p. 38.

5-18.　Francis Bradford, "A History of the Hall-Scott Motor Car Company," unpublished manuscript, 1989, p. 61–62, 69. Courtesy of Bancroft Library, University of California, Berkeley, BANC MSS 93/104c.

5-19.　Ibid., p. 69.

5-20.　Ibid.

5-21.　*Avco Corporation; The First Fifty Years*, Avco Corporation, Greenwich, CT, 1979, p. 39.

5-22.　William Nelson, autobiography, unpublished manuscript, 1963, p. 256. Courtesy of William Nelson.

5-23.　*Avco Corporation; The First Fifty Years*, Avco Corporation, Greenwich, CT, 1979, p. 30.

5-24.　*The New York Times*, June 12, 1951, p. 46.

5-25.　Ibid.

5-26.　William Nelson, autobiography, unpublished manuscript, 1963, p. 259. Courtesy of William Nelson.

5-27.　1951 ACF-Brill Motors Company Annual Report, p. 5. 1952 ACF-Brill Motors Company Annual Report, p. 3. 1953 ACF-Brill Motors Company Annual Report, n.p.

5-28.　1953 ACF-Brill Motors Company Annual Report, n.p. Hall-Scott Power/ Electronics, brochure, 1955, n.p.

5-29.　1949 ACF-Brill Motors Company Annual Report, p. 4.

5-30.　Ibid., p. 5

5-31.　1951 ACF-Brill Motors Company Annual Report, p. 4.

5-32.　1952 ACF-Brill Motors Company Annual Report, p. 3.

5-33.　Ibid., p. 2.

5-34.　1954 ACF-Brill Motors Company Annual Report, p. 3.

5-35.　Hercules Motors Corporation, "History, Growth & Expansion of the Hercules Motors Corporation," unpublished manuscript, 1963, p. 20. Courtesy of Charles Balough Family Collection.

5-36. Francis Bradford, "A History of the Hall-Scott Motor Car Company," unpublished manuscript, 1989, p. 116. Courtesy of Bancroft Library, University of California, Berkeley, BANC MSS 93/104c. All of the Hall-Scott financial data offered in the remainder of this paragraph are taken from this source.

5-37. *Automotive Industries*, March 15, 1946, p. 134. For several years, or through February 1945 anyway, Hall-Scott regularly ran a small ad in *Pacific Motor Boat* that said the company sold "gasoline and diesel power for all types of boats." But claiming diesel power was available in 1945 possibly was a stretch because engine lineup charts in industry publications could not corroborate this availability.

5-38. Ron Adams, *Big Rigs of the 1950s*, MBI Publishing, Osceola, WI, 2001, p. 8.

5-39. Peter Davies, *The World Encyclopedia of Trucks*, Lorenz Books, London, UK, 2000, p. 19.

5-40. 1955 Hall-Scott Annual Report, p. 5. J.E. "Speed," Glidewell, "A Brief History of Hall-Scott Motor Company," unpublished address, 1956, p. 4. *Commercial Car Journal*, August 1955, p. 206. *Commercial Car Journal* article found by John Perala.

5-41. Francis Bradford, "A History of the Hall-Scott Motor Car Company," unpublished manuscript, 1989, pp. 103–104. Courtesy of Bancroft Library, University of California, Berkeley, BANC MSS 93/104c. William Nelson, Hall-Scott binder, loose sheet. Courtesy of William Nelson. Nelson was the last president of Hall-Scott and kept many handwritten or typed company records in a binder. A loose sheet in the binder, indicating the models that were made and in what quantities, listed 159 Model 442s built. The Pickering report on Hall-Scott operations cited an interview with a customer who said he had several Hall-Scott Model 590s with factory-installed fuel injection. The Pickering Agency, "Hall-Scott Incorporated Power Division Total Marketing Analysis and Plan," unpublished report, 1957, p. 8.

5-42. *Hercules Engines, Inc., Operations and Maintenance Manual for Models 855-935-1091-1091-OS-6156-6182*, Hercules Engines, Inc., Canton, OH, 1969, pp. 10, 11, 24.

5-43. *Commercial Car Journal*, May 1950, p. 70.

5-44. *Commercial Car Journal*, July 1957, p. 68.

5-45. James Laux, "Diesel Trucks and Buses: Their Gradual Spread in the United States," in *The Economic and Social Effects of the Spread of Motor Vehicles*, Theo Barker, ed., Macmillan, Basingstoke, Hampshire, UK, 1987, p. 106.

5-46. Ibid.

5-47. William Wagner, *Continental! Its Motors and Its People*, Aero Publishers, Fallbrook, CA, 1983, p. 107.

5-48. Ibid., p. 151.

5-49. *Commercial Car Journal*, January 1951, p. 64.

5-50. *Commercial Car Journal*, December 1954, pp. 74–75, 127.

5-51. *Commercial Car Journal*, April 1951, p. 128.

5-52. 1951 ACF-Brill Motors Company Annual Report, p. 3.

5-53. G.N. Georgano, ed., *Complete Encyclopedia of Commercial Vehicles*, Krause Publications, Iola, WI, 1979, p. 24.

5-54. 1949 ACF-Brill Motors Company Annual Report, p. 3. 1951 ACF-Brill Motors Company Annual Report, p. 2.

5-55. 1949 ACF-Brill Motors Company Annual Report, p. 5.

5-56. Robert Ayer, "Kenworth," *Motor Coach Age*, Vol. XXXIII, Nos. 8 and 9, August–September 1981, pp. 31–32.

5-57. *Commercial Car Journal*, October 1951, p. 180.

5-58. James Laux, "Diesel Trucks and Buses: Their Gradual Spread in the United States," in *The Economic and Social Effects of the Spread of Motor Vehicles*, Theo Barker, ed., Macmillan, Basingstoke, Hampshire, UK, 1987, p. 105.

5-59. *Commercial Car Journal*, March 1952, p. 154. 1951 ACF-Brill Motors Company Annual Report, p. 4.

5-60. Stan Grayson, *Engines Afloat, From Early Days to D-Day, Vol. II: The Gasoline/Diesel Era*, Devereux Books, Marblehead, MA, 1999, p. 30.

5-61. *Commercial Car Journal*, December 1953, p. 146.

5-62. *Commercial Car Journal*, March 1953, p. 96.

5-63.   Stan Grayson, *Engines Afloat, From Early Days to D-Day, Vol. II: The Gasoline/Diesel Era*, Devereux Books, Marblehead, MA, 1999, p. 87.

5-64.   Peter Du Cane, *High-Speed Small Craft*, Second Edition, Philosophical Library, New York, 1957, p. 150.

5-65.   Ibid., p. 159.

5-66.   William Nelson, Hall-Scott binder, financial section, p. 13, and material section, pp. 2–10. Nelson was the last president of Hall-Scott and kept many handwritten or typed company records in a binder.

5-67.   *Commercial Car Journal*, February 1953, p. 177. *Commercial Car Journal*, June 1953, p. 165. *Commercial Car Journal*, January 1954, p. 18. *Automotive Industries*, March 15, 1954, p. 278.

5-68.   Letter from F. Bradford to R. Dias, August 19, 2002.

5-69.   *Automotive Industries*, March 15, 1954, p. 278. Model 590 Truck Engine, brochure, 1954.

5-70.   *Commercial Car Journal*, April 1954, p. 282.

5-71.   *Commercial Car Journal*, September 1954, p. 199.

5-72.   Francis Bradford, "A History of the Hall-Scott Motor Car Company," unpublished manuscript, 1989, p. 124–125. Courtesy of Bancroft Library, University of California, Berkeley, BANC MSS 93/104c. Letter from F. Bradford to R. Dias, August 19, 2002.

5-73.   1953 ACF-Brill Motors Company Annual Report, n.p.

5-74.   1954 ACF-Brill Motors Company Annual Report, p. 5.

5-75.   *Commercial Car Journal*, April 1957, p. 128.

5-76.   *Motor Truck & Coach*, June 1946, p. 18.

5-77.   Debra Brill, *History of J.G. Brill Company*, Indiana University Press, Bloomington, IN, 2001, pp. 212–214.

5-78.   Ibid, p. 214.

5-79.   William Nelson, autobiography, unpublished manuscript, 1963, p. 262. Courtesy of William Nelson.

5-80.   *The New York Times*, October 21, 1954, p. 45.

5-81.   1954 ACF-Brill Motors Company Annual Report, p. 4.

CHAPTER SIX

OLD ENGINE MAKERS
JUST FADE AWAY

In late 1954, for the first time in almost three decades, Hall-Scott was on its own in the marketplace, not controlled by a parent company. Thrust into this environment with little capital, heavy debt, and a product line of limited (and shrinking) appeal, it was not long before management began looking for a larger company to buy Hall-Scott. That large owner soon was found, a rapid transfer of production took place, and the last decade of Hall-Scott engines emerged from a factory some 2,000 miles away from Berkeley, where the first Hall-Scott product was built.

The New Path of Hall-Scott as an Independent Company

After its newly found, although hardly beneficial, freedom, Hall-Scott quickly changed its name to Hall-Scott, Incorporated. Behind this subtle wordsmithing was something substantial, though: diversification. No longer having a parent company to shield its operation from the ups and downs of the engine market, Hall-Scott managers wisely decided to broaden operations. Looking at trends in American business and society, which a Hall-Scott brochure from 1955 described as a "new era—a time when supersonic and atomic weapons, missiles, and complicated electronic devices form an integral part of our present life and promise to have a more and more significant place in our future," the old company opened an Electronics Division. [6-1] Hall-Scott purchased and then combined several existing firms into its new arm. Headquartered in Burbank, California, the new division consisted of the former Bardwell &

McAlister; Dynamic Analysis, Inc.; Douglas-Roesch, Inc.; and Rosan Locking Systems. [6-2] With these acquisitions, Hall-Scott added desktop electronic computers, metal housings for electronic equipment, wiring harnesses, and thread locking inserts to its product line. Adding this new division also brought to Hall-Scott the ability to fashion sophisticated sheet metal. A 1955 Hall-Scott brochure describing its products referenced something not mentioned in other Hall-Scott literature—photographic lighting. [6-3] Eight different lights were pictured in the brochure, including spot lights, lights hung on booms, and sky pans. The many and varied products sold by the Electronics Division would find buyers in both the private and public sectors. Cold War spending by the federal government promised a bonanza for many companies across America, such as Hall-Scott, Inc. Because these four companies were operating firms, they brought with them a dowry of buildings and equipment, some 300 employees, and current contracts. In fact, the new division accounted for half of the sales volume of Hall-Scott during its first year of operation. As an added plus, with its products so far removed from the core line of Hall-Scott, the new division would be safe from the mercurial fortunes of the engine market and therefore could potentially offer some protection for the beleaguered Hall-Scott investors.

As important as this new addition was to Hall-Scott, it could have been more beneficial in breathing some life into the tired products of the old company. The Electronics Division could have been the catalyst for introducing new ideas and industry-leading technology, which were so lacking in Hall-Scott engines in the postwar period. Unfortunately, it did not. Hall-Scott might have made quality engines, but at the same time, the company did not represent the cutting edge of its field in the mid-1950s as it had done decades earlier. In the 1910s, Hall-Scott engines boasted of high power-to-weight ratios and unusual features that set, rather than followed, industry trends. There were plenty of exciting engine trends in the 1950s, but Hall-Scott had not seriously embraced, let alone led, a single one of them. The new Model 590 made only a feeble attempt to answer the call for lighter-weight engines. There is no evidence of any interaction between Hall-Scott engine and electronics personnel. They probably would have had little to say each other, given the recent timing of the acquisition, the geographical distance between them, and the great difference in the products that each made. But the Hall-Scott Power Division suffered from such stale thinking that even the possibility of cross-pollination or inspiration from the Electronics Division made any lack of working together a missed opportunity.

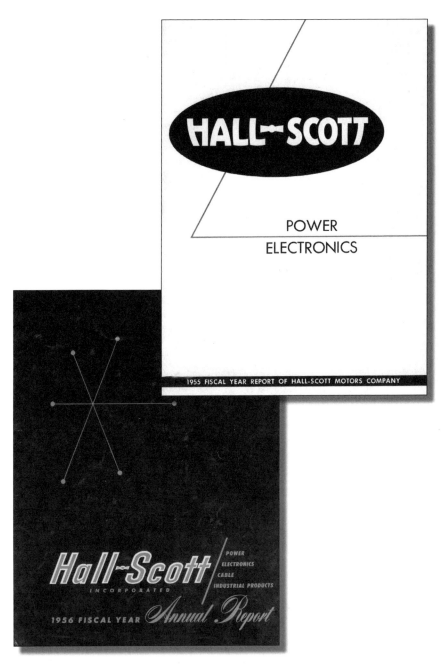

The covers of the first two annual reports of Hall-Scott as an independent company, 1955 and 1956, showing some of the new Hall-Scott product lines.

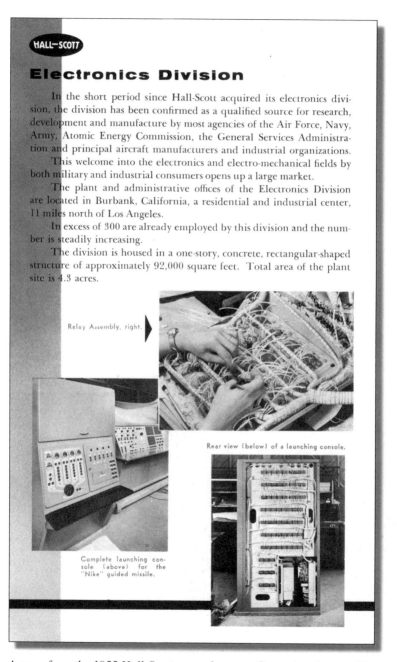

Electronics Division

In the short period since Hall-Scott acquired its electronics division, the division has been confirmed as a qualified source for research, development and manufacture by most agencies of the Air Force, Navy, Army, Atomic Energy Commission, the General Services Administration and principal aircraft manufacturers and industrial organizations.

This welcome into the electronics and electro-mechanical fields by both military and industrial consumers opens up a large market.

The plant and administrative offices of the Electronics Division are located in Burbank, California, a residential and industrial center, 11 miles north of Los Angeles.

In excess of 300 are already employed by this division and the number is steadily increasing.

The division is housed in a one-story, concrete, rectangular-shaped structure of approximately 92,000 square feet. Total area of the plant site is 4.3 acres.

Relay Assembly, right.

Rear view (below) of a launching console.

Complete launching console (above) for the "Nike" guided missile.

A page from the 1955 Hall-Scott annual report, discussing the new Electronics Division.

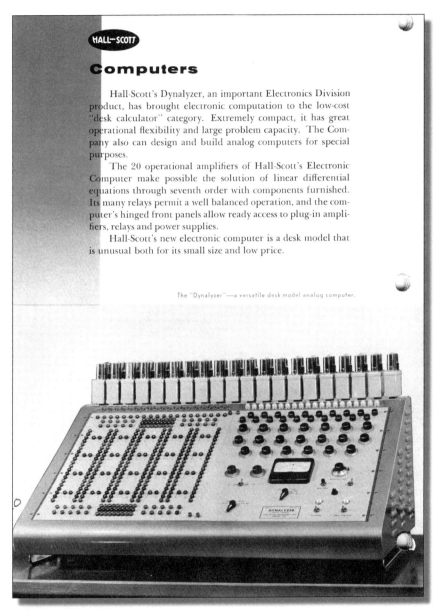

HALL—SCOTT

Computers

Hall-Scott's Dynalyzer, an important Electronics Division product, has brought electronic computation to the low-cost "desk calculator" category. Extremely compact, it has great operational flexibility and large problem capacity. The Company also can design and build analog computers for special purposes.

The 20 operational amplifiers of Hall-Scott's Electronic Computer make possible the solution of linear differential equations through seventh order with components furnished. Its many relays permit a well balanced operation, and the computer's hinged front panels allow ready access to plug-in amplifiers, relays and power supplies.

Hall-Scott's new electronic computer is a desk model that is unusual both for its small size and low price.

The "Dynalyzer"—a versatile desk model analog computer.

Products of the Hall-Scott Electronics Division spanned a broad range, including items outside of electronics specifically. This page from the 1955 Hall-Scott annual report highlights computers.

Precision Sheet Metal Products

The sheet metal activities of our Electronics Division are two-fold.

First, as a precision sheet metal fabrication unit, capable of working with all types of metals, it serves as an important supplemental source to numerous large manufacturing companies.

Secondly, as an integral part of our electronics production, it fabricates and assembles the housing for complete electronic units.

The division is actively engaged in designing, developing and manufacturing diversified packages for the electronics and electro-mechanical fields. A high degree of accuracy and quality is essential in this diversified type of production, and Hall-Scott's carefully selected personnel have the highest skills obtainable.

Typical of the devices designed, developed and manufactured by the Division is the radar scanning screen shown in this report.

Another of the electronic packages, now under construction for Douglas Aircraft Company, is a launching console assembly for the Nike, the Army's supersonic anti-aircraft guided missile.

The accompanying photos show some important phases of precision work in sheet metal.

The Electronics Division's sheet metal facility is capable of working with all types of metal. Building from raw stock —under one roof—permits an excellent control over all problems of design.

Radar scanning screen (right). This is one of the many precision products of the sheet metal activities of the company's Electronics Division.

Another page from the 1955 Hall-Scott annual report focuses on sheet metal products in the Electronics Division.

CABLE AND ELECTRONICS DIVISION

Sub-contracting to airframe, missile and automation manufacturers is the part being played by Douglas Roesch Cable Division, newest member of the Hall-Scott team. The Division is equipped to handle research, development and production of a large variety of cables, cable assemblies and harness items used in the general preparedness program. The more than 100 highly skilled technical and production personnel are qualified for this product's complex and exacting requirements.

In addition to serving most of the major Western aviation companies, they also do work for the internationally famous Jet Propulsion Laboratory at the California Institute of Technology; the United States Government Proving Grounds at White Sands, New Mexico; the Army Ordnance Department, Fort Bliss; and the Navy Testing Grounds at Inyokern, California.

At the date of acquisition in March 1956, the Roesch Company's backlog was confirmed by our auditors at approximately $365,000. It has since grown to almost $1,500,-000.

Much of the operation revolves around the Douglas Variable Pitch Planetary Cabler. This machine, over 8 feet high, 20 feet long, weighing approximately 8 tons, is capable of taking 48 spools of wire and at one time wrapping them into intricate cable assemblies. Associated with the cabler is a special process enabling the company to take cable assemblies and completely cover hundreds of feet of cable with neoprene, silicone, or thermoplast sheath.

The Douglas Variable Pitch Planetary Cabler

Missile Disconnect Connector for Either Electrical or Mechanical

Flat Cable Going into a Standard "Cannon" Connector

Included among the unusual cable assemblies are extremely flat cables designed to fit the specific space requirement and also provide extreme flexibility, hollow center cables, cables that are capable of carrying air, fuel, etc., through the center in addition to providing electrical conductors around cables with nylon or steel cores and special temperature and acid resistant cables.

A Hall-Scott Produced Jet Engine Fuel Analyzer

This page from the 1956 Hall-Scott annual report shows further diversification of the Electronics Division.

What was more detrimental to the short-term success of Hall-Scott, Inc., was that although its new Electronics Division might have pumped up the overall sales figures of the company, it did nothing for the dismal profit picture of the company. Not only did the Electronics Division fail to be profitable, but it soon became little more than another stone around the neck of Hall-Scott. William Nelson remembered, "The setup as a whole was operating at a substantial loss. It was quite evident that the business could not grow much for they had little that dozens of other Los Angeles small businesses" [did not also have]. "The competition was severe and would get worse." [6-4]

The new management searched for revenue-generating possibilities far outside of engine and parts sales, and outside of the new Electronics Division. More in keeping with the traditional skills of Hall-Scott, the company continued making and selling machining tools and doing close tolerance and complicated machining work. Hall-Scott had built made many of its own specialized tools for years; therefore, making similar machines for sale would utilize talents and resources the company already had. These specialized tools included cylinder boring machines, hypoid bevel gear and helical gear grinders, and cam grind-ers. [6-5] Even after being spurned by ACF-Brill Motors, Hall-Scott continued to do limited contract work for its previous parent company, such as making a geared assembly for a generator drive. Some contract work also continued for the federal government, even if the lucrative gravy train that had rolled out of Washington during the Korean Conflict had slowed. Perhaps the most interest-ing military project began around 1955 when Hall-Scott began the design and manufacture of the transmission for the futuristic-looking "Flying Platform" made by Hiller Helicopter, a military "personal helicopter" of sorts. [6-6] Hall-Scott, Incorporated was branching into a number of areas in the mid-1950s. Given the stagnant engine sales of Hall-Scott, management was wise to look elsewhere for projects. Regardless, placing engineers on non-engine projects was a use of talent that could have been spent on new or improved engines that customers were seeking.

After Hall-Scott became independent, it reduced the range of engine models it sold. Once a recognized provider of marine power that sold more than half a dozen different models at any one time, after being spun off by ACF-Brill Motors, Hall-Scott marketed only one, the V-12. Although that engine could be ordered with left- or right-hand rotation, having 605 or 630 hp, a supercharged version was no longer available. [6-7] Because of the rapidly changing nature of the marine market, 1954 was the last year for the Invader, concluding a respectably long 23-year production run. True, offspring from that engine lived on in the Model 400-based 935 and 1091 plus the V-12, but

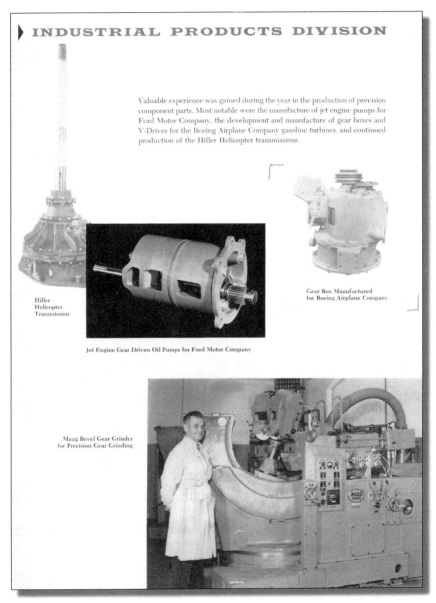

▶ INDUSTRIAL PRODUCTS DIVISION

Valuable experience was gained during the year in the production of precision component parts. Most notable were the manufacture of jet engine pumps for Ford Motor Company, the development and manufacture of gear boxes and V-Drives for the Boeing Airplane Company gasoline turbines, and continued production of the Hiller Helicopter transmissions.

Hiller
Helicopter
Transmission

Gear Box Manufactured
for Boeing Airplane Company

Jet Engine Gear Driven Oil Pumps for Ford Motor Company

Maag Bevel Gear Grinder
for Precision Gear Grinding

Hall-Scott never wanted for skilled workers and machines with the ability to perform close tolerance work, which certainly helped the company in the 1950s.

A close-up of the Hiller flying craft, shown in an image from the 1955 Hall-Scott annual report. The craft used a transmission made by Hall-Scott.

the demand for the kind of engines that Hall-Scott produced had shrunk to the point that continued marketing of the big six-cylinder gas marine engine made no sense. For truck, bus, and industrial customers in 1955, Hall-Scott offered the Models 180, 190, 400, 504, 590, 935, 1091, and 2268 (the V-12),

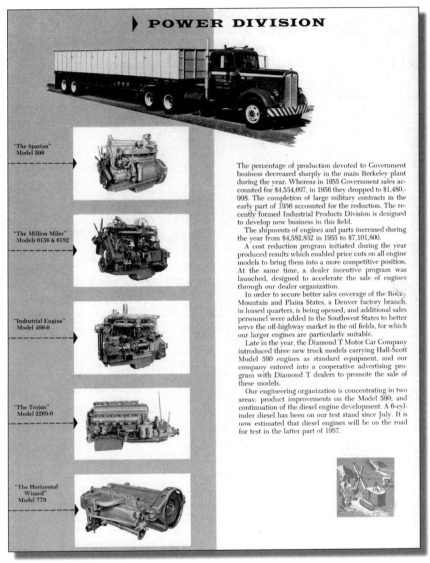

▶ **POWER DIVISION**

"The Spartan"
Model 590

"The Million Miler"
Models 6156 & 6182

"Industrial Engine"
Model 400-0

"The Trojan"
Model 2269-0

"The Horizontal
Wizard"
Model 779

The percentage of production devoted to Government business decreased sharply in the main Berkeley plant during the year. Whereas in 1955 Government sales accounted for $4,534,697, in 1956 they dropped to $1,480,998. The completion of large military contracts in the early part of 1956 accounted for the reduction. The recently formed Industrial Products Division is designed to develop new business in this field.

The shipments of engines and parts increased during the year from $4,582,832 in 1955 to $7,101,800.

A cost reduction program initiated during the year produced results which enabled price cuts on all engine models to bring them into a more competitive position. At the same time, a dealer incentive program was launched, designed to accelerate the sale of engines through our dealer organization.

In order to secure better sales coverage of the Rocky Mountain and Plains States, a Denver factory branch, in leased quarters, is being opened; and additional sales personnel were added in the Southwest States to better serve the off-highway market in the oil fields, for which our larger engines are particularly suitable.

Late in the year, the Diamond T Motor Car Company introduced three new truck models carrying Hall-Scott Model 590 engines as standard equipment, and our company entered into a cooperative advertising program with Diamond T dealers to promote the sale of these models.

Our engineering organization is concentrating in two areas: product improvements on the Model 590; and continuation of the diesel engine development. A 6-cylinder diesel has been on our test stand since July. It is now estimated that diesel engines will be on the road for test in the latter part of 1957.

The Hall-Scott, Inc. engine lineup for truck, bus, and industrial applications.

ending production of the Models 136, 470, 480, and 855. For the 1955 model year, Hall-Scott engines ranged from 162 to 630 hp, of either six or twelve cylinders, some horizontal, some vertical, and many could be chosen to burn gasoline or gasified fuel.

In the mid-1950s, Hall-Scott still enjoyed a reputation for producing quality engines, but its commitment to gasoline power was putting the company at a greater competitive disadvantage that only grew with time. And Hall-Scott managers knew it. By this time, high-speed diesels powered many tens of thousands of trucks in America, and a number of companies, including independents, produced them. Allis-Chalmers, Caterpillar, Continental, Cummins, Hercules, and Waukesha all sold such engines, as did automotive industry giant General Motors through its Detroit Diesel arm. With this long-term and irrefutable market trend toward diesel continuing, Hall-Scott's incremental moves into the fray were all the more overdue and ultimately futile. The 1955 Hall-Scott annual report stated, "A new six-cylinder diesel laboratory engine (160 h.p.) is scheduled for completion in April, 1956," and a "V-8 diesel (225 h.p.) is being developed and a laboratory engine is scheduled to be completed in August." [6-8] This was a noteworthy development and would be something truly new and important for Hall-Scott. Nothing out of the ordinary about these engines was betrayed in the skimpy annual report description, however. But at least Hall-Scott engineers were taking aim at a current, albeit fast-moving, target. The annual report also stated that other projects underway included fitting existing Hall-Scott motors, among them a truck version of the V-12, with turbochargers. Engineering imagination was showing some faint signs of life at Hall-Scott.

Around 1955, Hall-Scott management seemed intent about bringing a diesel to market, and ACF was no longer siphoning off the valuable Hall-Scott capital and stifling development. In a speech to the Berkeley Exchange Club in 1956, reiterating the diesel news shared in the annual report, Hall-Scott vice president of engineering sales J.E. "Speed" Glidewell, the designer of the Model 590, told his audience of local boosters, "A new automotive type 6 cylinder diesel engine is being designed and will be placed in production in 1956. This engine will be followed by a higher power V-8 type diesel which will round out Hall-Scott's line of engines to better cover the entire field of power requirements." [6-9] This was big news.

Although it appears that Hall-Scott management could marshal enough diesel commitment to issue a unified and clear message from the factory, any substantial progress beyond blueprints and pronouncements was less evident. There were no photos of these experimental engines included in the annual report, which does not support the possibility that these engines ever saw the light of day. Engineer Francis Bradford does not remember seeing any such power plants in the small Berkeley facility where he worked every day. Glidewell, speaking in 1956, announced a 1956 arrival date for the first of the new engines

"Our Diamond T 831 is a time saver, driver saver, and profit-maker. It's a terrific performer . . ."
Says Boyd Oliver, President
Dry Mix Products, Roseville, Calif.

NEW DIAMOND T MODEL 831

Light-weight powerhouse with

HALL-SCOTT 590 ENGINE

GAS—239 ACTUAL H.P. • LPG—256 ACTUAL H.P.

Want 1500 lbs. more payload every trip? Check the table at the right— it shows more usable power per pound than any comparable heavy-duty tractor. Model 831 is just what the headline says, a "light-weight powerhouse," outperforming big diesels and saving nearly a ton of chassis weight.

And the Hall-Scott 590 engine is as famous for endurance as performance. Minor adjustments are few and far between and overhaul periods are measured in the hundreds of thousands of miles. It is

first choice for long life, reliability and economy with maximum loads. It is available for LPG fuel as well as gasoline.

Every Diamond T "custom-built" Diamond T builds a complete line of heavy-duty motor trucks— gas and diesel—each "custom-built" to match the job precisely. See for yourself how much truck performance, economy and service you can buy right here. We are happy to quote on new trucks for you or give you top-notch shop service on your present units.

HALL-SCOTT 590

	Gasoline	L.P.G.
Fuel	Gasoline	L.P.G.
Max. Power	239 h.p. @	256 h.p. @
Governed Speed	2800 r.p.m.	2800 r.p.m.
Max. Torque	501 lbs. ft.	530 lbs. ft.
Bore & Stroke	5"x5"	5"x5"
Displacement	590 sq. in.	590 sq. in.
Camshaft	Overhead	Overhead
Crankshaft	3¼"	3¼"
Crankpin	3"	3"
Bearings	Precision	Precision
Oil Capacity	3½ gal.	3½ gal.
Weight	1275 lbs.	1275 lbs.

MODEL 831

	Gas	LPG
Base Chassis	Gas	LPG
Wgt. (Approx.)	9000 lbs.	9700 lbs.

DIAMOND T TRUCKS

Established 1905

The Diamond is for Quality

Hall-Scott, Inc. signed a deal with Diamond T to offer the Model 590 as an option on one of its new truck models. (Courtesy of Doug Gigstad.)

but used the present progressive tense when saying that the engine "is being designed." If Hall-Scott really planned to introduce a brand new engine that year, Glidewell probably should have said the engine "has been designed" and "is being tested." Company leadership must have had some optimism that the new engines would actually appear. Hall-Scott issued a short and vague press release that appeared in the August 1955 issue of *Commercial Car Journal*, announcing its "entrance into the diesel engine field with engines for bus, truck, industrial, and marine use." [6-10] The 1955 Hall-Scott annual report, Glidewell's address, and the 1955 press release all suggest that although Hall-Scott was in a precarious situation, at least the company had managers who knew what the company had to do to remain in business.

With Hall-Scott struggling for its life in the mid-1950s, the death of company cofounder E.J. Hall in 1955 seemed a bad omen for the future. The *San Francisco Chronicle* obituary for Hall described him as an "internationally known engineer and inventor." [6-11] Referring to him as "Colonel," the paper noted his World War I technical contributions and his Distinguished Service Medal, as well as a passing reference to the Hall-Scott Motor Company of Berkeley. Not included in the article was any reference to his many engineering successes after leaving the company he had largely propelled to its brief leadership position. In fact, Hall held engineering jobs on both sides of the Atlantic, and not always in the auto industry, which is not surprising, given his conspicuous early mechanical aptitudes. He left Hall-Scott in 1930 to start De Vaux-Hall with Norman De Vaux (see Chapter 3). [6-12] After leaving that short-lived auto enterprise, he traveled to France to work at Citroën for a few years. Hall helped the French firm with its technically interesting front-wheel-drive cars, improved factory operation, and oversaw changes to personnel management. Returning to the United States in 1935, he entered the oil industry and then briefly attached himself to the Reo Company. As war clouds began to gather in the late 1930s, Hall turned his focus to independent engineering projects, briefly working for companies such as the Joshua Hendy Iron Works in Sunnyvale, California. Independent projects largely occupied his time and talents until his death. Leaving an estate valued at $651,086 suggests that Colonel Hall achieved some level of monetary success as well. [6-13] There is no written record of Hall making any engineering contributions to the company that he helped found after he left. Indeed, the only record that could be found of his participation in Hall-Scott affairs after 1930 was a 1945 visit to the plant. This divorce was unfortunate. By the postwar period, the company desperately needed the kind of vision and imagination for which E.J. Hall had made his name.

With the engine-building situation appearing increasingly grim and sales remaining flat at around 500 to 700 units per year, in 1957 the Pickering Advertising Agency of Oakland was hired to assess the strengths and weaknesses of Hall-Scott and to make suggestions for its future. The consultant's report pointed out that while Hall-Scott needed to produce about 80 engines per month to turn a profit from making engines, and the company had set a goal to build 120, monthly production through the mid-1950s averaged closer to only 60 units. [6-14] In 1956, the most recent year that the consultants had full-year figures, Hall-Scott produced 673 engines, losing $256,862 in the process. On the other hand, selling parts yielded a profit of $465,688. Any company in the business of making engines should be able to make money from that primary activity. Indeed, in the case of Hall-Scott, the primary money-making enterprise of the company seemed to be killing it.

But why was Hall-Scott not selling 80 or 120 engines per month? It certainly was not because Hall-Scott produced engines that the buying public perceived as being of inferior quality. In fact, the opposite was true. The consultants had little trouble finding operators who raved about the performance of their Hall-Scott-powered machines. For example, Myron Pierce, shop foreman for the General Petroleum Company, told the consultants, "I have nothing but good to say about Hall-Scott motors." [6-15] Pierce listed a number of Hall-Scott engines his company operated, Model 480s and Model 935s, that each logged many hundreds of thousands of miles with a minimum of servicing required. The consultants found that the drivers they interviewed liked Hall-Scotts because the engines "were so responsive" and "possess outstanding torque characteristics." Mechanics reported that they liked Hall-Scott motors because "they are cleaner than diesels and because all parts of the engine are easier to get at than [is] the case with other engines." It was not tough to find users of Hall-Scott engines who believed that the engines were exceptional products.

Outside of this consulting report, independent evaluations during the "make or break" postwar period only corroborated consumers' positive impressions of Hall-Scott engines. Dick Brown recalled that drivers at his father's northern California trucking business in the 1950s used to fight over who would drive the Hall-Scott-powered rigs. "The drivers loved them," remembered Brown, referring to his father's Hall-Scott-powered Autocars and Peterbilts. [6-16] Compared to the other trucks in the fleet, those with Hall-Scott engines "could go up hills more than three m.p.h. faster when loaded. They all wanted to drive them." Similarly, an article appearing in *Western Motor Transport* in 1945 carried the title, "Save Eight Hours on L.A.–Salt Lake Run," which underscored the dramatic performance found in Hall-Scott engines. [6-17] According to this article, so great was the power in a Kenworth with a butane-burning Model 400 Hall-Scott engine that it could shave eight hours off the time needed for the 780-mile drive over that of trucks powered by other (unnamed) engines. The writer of the piece, W.J. Rellaford, a trucking company safety and personnel manager, argued, "Long line highway carrier operators must save time on over-the-road delivery of maximum loads to avoid losses. Saving of a few hours on each round trip means the difference between profit and loss." Rellaford acknowledged an unspectacular fuel mileage figure of 3.2 mpg (a good figure because many operators of full-sized trucks powered by a Hall-Scott engine reported getting 2 mpg) for the trip, but explained that the higher fuel consumption was offset by the savings reaped from completing the trip so much more quickly. Rellaford also noted that a Hall-Scott representative accompanied the truck to record the performance, thus making the article more of a Hall-Scott advertisement than an objective report. Hall-Scott understood that the strength of its product was in its great power, more than in its low cost of initial purchase or outstanding fuel mileage. Thus, the company chose to emphasize this aspect as a marketing point. But were these points attractive ones for engine buyers in the postwar era?

Regarding the kinds of applications that Hall-Scott engines powered, the Pickering report stated that by the mid-1950s, two-thirds to three-fourths were in highway trucks as newly manufactured vehicles—OEM (original equipment manufacturer). [6-18] That figure translated into roughly 300 to 500 new trucks with Hall-Scott engines per year rolling out of factories in the mid-1950s. That was a minuscule number, considering that American factories produced more than 100,000 buses and large trucks annually during that period. [6-19] By the time Pickering submitted its report in 1957, only 3 to 5 of every 100 truck buyers chose Hall-Scott for their power needs, for whatever reason. This was bad news for the Berkeley engine maker.

The company's narrow focus on the western market was another problem identified by the consultants. In fact, the first significant OEM truck and bus customer of Hall-Scott was the Oakland-based Fageol Company. (The last may have been the Los Angeles-based Crown Coach Company.) Hall-Scott did not even try particularly hard to market its engines outside the West. In the report, the consultants found that of thirty Hall-Scott dealers, only six were located east of the Mississippi River. Export sales were feeble, too—three overseas countries, and some Canadian western provinces. The lack of an aggressive sales program was exacerbated by the glaring problem that, at the time this report was written, Hall-Scott lacked a general sales manager and that "the

Operating a Hall-Scott

With more than three decades having passed since the last new Hall-Scott was made, plenty of enthusiastic Hall-Scott fans can be found today. Many remember the impressive pulling power, deep rumble, fiery exhaust, and occasional cannon-like backfires of the big engines. Those who operated heavy-duty trucks with Hall-Scotts are outspoken in their praises. Said California driver and mechanic Craig Smith, Hall-Scotts were "very torquey, incredible acceleration (for a large truck engine). They were very responsive and were especially appreciated here in the west with the very mountainous terrain… We used to call them 'Hop-Scotches' since they would generally 'hop around' any other truck pulling a long grade!" Similarly, Californian Jody Kirsan remembered the outstanding feature being "POWER! POWER! POWER! If you had Hall-Scott power under the hood, nobody could stay with you, gas or diesel. Smooth, almost no vibration when compared to the diesels of the time." But there were negative impressions, too. Among the most common was that Hall-Scotts seemed to generate more heat than other engines. Wayne McDougall (a mechanic, not a driver) of Wyoming observed, "The exhaust was very hot and in the summer would keep the cab of the truck very warm." This heat also became an issue if the engine was used for pumping purposes, such as in the case of a fire engine. Fuel costs for running a Hall-Scott, especially for owner-operators and particularly with the larger-displacement models, was also a real issue. Referring to a 400 series-powered truck he remembered from the early 1960s, back when gas stations used to entice customers with trading stamps, Al Outsen of Texas remembered, "The fuel stations nicknamed it 'The Green Stamper' because

of the vast quantities of fuel purchased." But the positives far outweighed the negatives in the minds of drivers, who loved their Hall-Scotts, as long as they didn't have to pay for the fuel. (Photo courtesy of Vern Racek. Information courtesy of Jody Kirsan, Al Outsen, Wayne McDougall, and Craig Smith.)

Working on Hall-Scotts

Mechanics seemed to be as fond of Hall-Scotts as drivers. They appreciated the thoughtful design, features, and construction in Hall-Scotts that made working on these engines a pleasure. Californian Craig Smith, who continued to sell

Hall-Scott parts long after even Hercules abandoned the line, "really liked the how the camshaft gear was mounted on a taper on the cam. You could remove a bolt, rap the camshaft sprocket with a hammer, the gear would disengage the cam and rest on a built-in support pedestal, allowing you to remove the complete cylinder head assy. [assembly] without losing timing or the chain going slack. Really neat!" Californian Jody Kirsan, who as a boy was a Hall-Scott fan and actually met "Speed" Glidewell, noted that replacing the timing chain or belt is a long and complicated job on most overhead cam engines, but "the same procedure can be performed on a Hall-Scott by an experienced mechanic in 10 minutes start to finish." Don Brittingham of the Los Angeles Fire Department liked how, in the 400 series, "The studs that clamped the head down ran clear thru [sic] the crankcase, providing a clamping force not obtainable with shorter head fasteners, making head gasket failures almost impossible." And unit construction allowed for cheaper rebuilding. "Hall-Scott provided rebuilding kits at a reasonable cost (around $300 in the late 1950s)." Rouhalde Wilfried of France, owner of four World War II-era 440s, said, "A Hall-Scott engine is a masterpiece," and he has familiarity with engines from Rolls-Royce and Ferrari. On the other hand, several mechanics remarked to us that the Hall-Scott twin-ignition models needed plenty of maintenance (e.g., plugs, plug wires, points, rotors, caps,

timing) to keep running well. But Hall-Scotts didn't seem to have a glaring problem or shortcoming that plagued mechanics. In fact, Wyoming mechanic Wayne McDougall (a winner of Wyoming's Mechanic of the Year) liked working on Hall-Scotts, and he remembered them being "very simple to work on," plus they were cleaner than diesel, which has "engine oil you can hardly wash off your hands." Kirsan spoke for many when he observed that the strongest suits of Hall-Scott were "quality and craftsmanship" with "the best castings, the best forgings, high quality fasteners [and] advanced design." ("48% less for Maintenance" brochure courtesy of Mike Lusher. Information courtesy of Jody Kirsan, Wayne McDougall, Craig Smith, Bill West, and Rouhalde Wilfried.)

quality and quantity of salesmen are open to questioning." [6-20] While an increasing number of engine buyers were looking for products different than those marketed by Hall-Scott, who knows how many potential sales were missed at Hall-Scott because of the lack of tenacity by the sales department to move the engines they had?

Another problem pointed out in the report was that Hall-Scott was competitive only in too small a part of the engine market. Hall-Scott had enough fairly large gasoline and liquefied petroleum gas (LPG) engines to compete in that sector, and those compared well against similar engines. But fairly large gasoline and LPG engines composed only a fraction of the whole engine market. Hall-Scott did not manufacture small gasoline engines that could power lift trucks, pumps, welders, electrical generators, and other equipment. Continental and Hercules sold tens of thousands of such small gasoline engines every year. Then there were large gasoline engines producing more than 1000 hp—a limited market admittedly, but one in which a few companies such as Fairbanks-Morse and Waukesha survived. Of course, there was the obvious lack of diesel engines in the Hall-Scott lineup. There was no question that Hall-Scott engines were good at what they were and that they had earned a great reputation with many operators, but those favorable impressions would not translate into increased or even adequate sales. The consultants concluded, "Whereas mechanics and drivers swear by Hall-Scotts, our interviews show that when these same men become superintendents, they find they cannot afford the larger engines. A 350 horsepower Hall-Scott that is a prize to drive and a dream to maintain becomes too expensive for the longer hauls." [6-21] Dick Brown remembers exactly the same situation facing his father's use of Hall-Scott engines. While his father's logging truck drivers loved the power of Hall-Scott engines, the "accountants did not like the high cost per mile. In the end, they [the Hall-Scott engines] were never replaced" with other Hall-Scott units. At Brown's company, as seen in trucking companies that had used or considered using Hall-Scott engines, "Diesel won the day." [6-22] With diesel-powered trucks achieving double the mileage on cheaper fuel than the 1 to 3 mpg realized in trucks using Hall-Scott gasoline engines, Hall-Scott faced a serious marketing problem. The consultants observed that Hall-Scott was making good engines, for which there was diminishing demand. The company simply had to change the kind of engines it offered if it wished to remain in business.

Hall-Scott, Inc. struggled to remain open and to spruce up its financial appearance as the new management led by William Nelson (who returned to the firm and became president in 1957) searched for another company to purchase it. Hall-Scott might have marched to its own drummer, but it did not wish to march alone. The company struggled under a heavy debt of some $3 million in 1957. [6-23] Cash levels were low, and the meager sales for the company meant that moving a few engines and desktop computers could not fund product development, and when income was realized, it went to pay down that debt. Around 1957, inventories had reached three times what they should have been because of unwise stockpiling by management earlier in the decade. However, through price slashing, the inventory was quickly reduced. [6-24] Efficiency in the Power Division had dropped about 50% by the middle of the decade, but that too was addressed through job cuts and changes in operations. Both divisions had products that suffered from significant competitive forces, but Nelson worked hard to make Hall-Scott profitable in the short term. While Hall-Scott did not face a rosy future by any means, management looked for the best possible outcome.

Captain William Nelson, Hall-Scott president from 1957 to 1960, was a graduate of the U.S. Naval Academy and Massachusetts Institute of Technology. During World War II, Nelson served as a division manager at Consolidated Aircraft and worked on the famous PPY Catalina "Flying Boat." This is a picture of Nelson during the war; he is shown at the left. (Courtesy of William Nelson.)

In August 1957, Hall-Scott president Nelson met with the board of directors and staked out a bold plan for the company. Looking around the company and seeing the awesome problems that it faced must have daunted him, but it also made his decision clear. Nelson remembered, "I made my report to the effect that one road only was open to Hall-Scott and that was liquidation." [6-25] His case was entirely convincing and "By unanimous consent they agreed with a plan of terminating Hall-Scott." With obligations to their stockholders to deliver returns on their investment, carrying a high debt-to-earnings ratio, facing a dim future for the Power Division, and forecasting only modest growth for the Electronics Division, the board made the obvious sound financial choice. Terminating the company did not mean simply turning off the lights and walking away; instead, it meant making the company as attractive as possible, in short order, and then selling it for as much as possible. Nelson's dramatic belt-tightening created the results he had hoped: a return to profitability. It was small, but the red ink quickly turned to black. Now he had to sell the firm.

Nelson went to the press to tout the company as a viable business investment. In April 1958, Nelson told the *Wall Street Journal* that the company was "making a small profit and we hope to increase it." [6-26] Hall-Scott reported earnings of $312,993 in 1956 and a loss of $555,036 in 1957. But with unit production "down about 20% from last year" and the workforce dropping from 775 to 575 in the same time period, Nelson remained optimistic for the future. A modest turnaround in Hall-Scott fortunes between 1957 and 1958 came largely through Nelson putting the financial house of the company in order—consolidating the separate Electronics and Power Divisions cut overheard, and laying off one-quarter of the workforce slashed labor costs and boosted productivity. Inasmuch as he was looking for a buyer, it is not surprising that he found a silver lining in the ledgers. While the Power Division had become mired in the economic malaise of the sharp downturn of the country in the late 1950s, the Electronics Division still "hasn't been affected by the recession to any great extent" and, in fact, enjoyed an increase in the number of inquiries in the last quarter. Nelson announced that his company was "receptive" to a merger because "it is necessary for us to have a broader product base in order to operate profitably." Nelson did not seem desperate; in fact, he placed conditions on any takeover. Hall-Scott would require any purchaser to "use our plants on the West Coast and utilize our engine." As the company limped along in 1958, the Hall-Scott headquarters on Seventh and Heinz was preparing for surrender.

The Hercules Years

After the desire (or need) of Hall-Scott management to sell was made public, which was underscored by the company board of directors axing engine making, suitors soon appeared. Several companies nibbled at the bait, only to lose interest, including Mack Truck. Then on May 7, 1958, Hercules Motors Corporation, an old competitor and sometimes partner, purchased Hall-Scott, Inc. [6-27] The *Wall Street Journal, The New York Times*, and other publications quickly reported the transaction to the public, but details of the deal were few, including the purchase price for Hall-Scott. The *Journal* article described Hercules' purchase of Hall-Scott as including "all inventory, certain machinery, tools and engineering data and use of the Hall-Scott name." Hercules president William Pringle told the *Journal* that Hercules would begin production of Hall-Scott engines at its plant in Canton, Ohio, as quickly as possible and that support of existing Hall-Scott products would continue to be handled through Hall-Scott and now Hercules distributors and dealers. In fact, Hall-Scott had promoted the spare parts program, which had remained a consistent money maker, as an especially attractive element of the sale. [6-28] The old Berkeley engine maker estimated that about 13,000 of its engines remained in service. While not being huge, that number still created a basis of sales for years to come. Then there was the making of new engines. The Hall-Scott large-displacement six- and twelve-cylinder units fit well into the diverse Hercules line of gasoline and diesel offerings. With the addition of the big Hall-Scott twelve-cylinder, Hercules extended its engine range from 5 to 600 hp. Picking up the Hall-Scott engine line also gave Hercules a product to sell to truckers. Pringle told the local Canton newspaper that Hercules had been focusing on industrial customers because it "did not have the type of engine required for present highway truck operation." [6-29] Hercules leadership believed that they would be able to make and sell the engines much cheaper than Hall-Scott had done. Pringle told the Canton Rotary Club in June 1958, "We can reduce the cost of these high-quality engines so truck manufacturers will be interested in installing them." [6-30] Thus, the

Hercules took the basic oval Hall-Scott hood plate and altered it slightly, which is reflective of how it approached the Hall-Scott product line. (Courtesy of Michael Axford.)

Hall-Scott acquisition was attractive to Hercules for several reasons. However, William Nelson's earlier condition that any buyer of Hall-Scott use its Berkeley plant and engines was either rejected, ignored, or forgotten.

Acting quickly to answer the many questions of stockholders, management issued a fairly illuminating one-page letter dated June 5, 1958. [6-31] Hall-Scott stockholders must have been desperate for more information, and this letter offered more details about the sale and management's plans for the immediate future. Company leaders naturally put a good face on the deal, calling Hercules "a respected name in the industry," reassuring those who worried about service to the company products that Hercules was "well able to service the many Hall-Scott engines in use, and to supply bus service parts to Brill bus operators. We feel that we are particularly fortunate to find a purchaser so admirably equipped to render service and at the same time to continue to make the famous Hall-Scott engines available to the many operators in the field." And finally, a price tag could be affixed to the sale: "about $1,800,000, part of which will be realized immediately in cash, part in notes, and the balance according to a formula related to future sales by Hercules..." Expanding the scope of the sale to Hercules, the letter reported that Hall-Scott sold its "engine inventory, service parts (engine and Brill bus parts), engineering data and tooling, and the branches located at Los Angeles, California and Upper Darby, Pennsylvania. Hercules will carry on the manufacture of the Hall-Scott engines at its Canton, Ohio plant. Certain special purpose machinery required in the manufacture of engines is also being sold to Hercules. In addition, it is planned that some of the Hall-Scott personnel will be transferred to Hercules to facilitate the transition." The fate of the Electronics Division was left up in the air, but management suggested that it also probably would be sold. "It is expected that it will serve its purpose best by making it a part of some larger enterprise." More sentimental stockholders might have been soothed to know that the Hall-Scott name would continue to be seen on products after the transaction, and Hall-Scott products would live on, at least for the time being. The 1958 Hall-Scott annual report, dated February 10, 1959, explained a bit more of the story. Near the top of the report, managers cited the Hall-Scott debt load of $1.35 million, "which was a heavy burden considering the modest earnings being attained." [6-32] Although Nelson's housecleaning had reduced debt considerably, the suffocating debt-to-earnings ratio of Hall-Scott and the expectation of realizing only meager profits in the future clearly had forced management's hand to sell.

It is difficult to pinpoint exactly when the Berkeley plant produced its last engine or shut its doors. Sadly, virtually all Hall-Scott records were relegated to landfills as employees gutted the 244,227-square-foot facility in 1958. It appears that Hercules did not keep these records long either. [6-33] The company kept Hall-Scott engineer Francis Bradford on the payroll for a short time to help oversee the closure of the Berkeley plant; he received his last Hall-Scott paycheck on March 21, 1958. [6-34] Without having a document indicating exactly when operations terminated, it can be estimated that the last new Hall-Scott engine was produced in Berkeley in late 1957 or early 1958, months before the actual sale of the company to Hercules in May.

Hall-Scott management had (wisely) begun to explore more revenue-earning possibilities outside engine making in the postwar period, and it appears that these were attractive to Hercules. A 1958 machine tool inventory showed 44 special tools designed at Hall-Scott, which showcased the considerable abilities of the company. [6-35] Hercules acquired the rights to the Hall-Scott tool-making machines; thus, it would be natural for it to seek avenues to use such equipment. In 1960, Hercules announced the opening of a Special Products Division to perform "custom machining and engineering for outside concerns." [6-36] Hercules official Joseph Rongitsch told the *Wall Street Journal* that the new division had "multi-million dollar potential" for the firm, a prognostication buffeted by the fact that Hercules could already point to a having a "several hundred thousand" dollar contract with a major auto company for volume production of components. So the machining and engineering activities and equipment of Hall-Scott had a market life beyond 1958, as was true of its engines.

Hercules was a much stronger company than Hall-Scott in 1958, but it hardly enjoyed an enviable market position. In 1958, the Ohio engine maker posted a

A photo, circa 1945, of part of the Hercules plant in Canton, Ohio, which was many times larger than the Hall-Scott plant. (Courtesy of the Wm. McKinley Presidential Library & Museum, Canton, Ohio.)

$114,525 loss, right after it had tightened its belt by cutting 48 of its 86 basic models. [6-37] Regardless, Hercules managers knew that they had to continue introducing engines that customers wanted, with competitive features, performance, and prices. The 1958 purchase of Hall-Scott was an attempt to accomplish that, as was the agreement Hercules signed in 1958 to sell the German-made "Jlo" line of air-cooled gasoline and diesel engines of 7 to 12 hp. [6-38] In 1957, Hercules purchased the rights from Avco, the previous owner of Hall-Scott, to make several small Lycoming industrial engines (a venture that soon failed). [6-39] The late 1950s brought the same crushing pressures to Hercules that had been witnessed at Hall-Scott, and Hercules scrambled to respond effectively. Similar to Hall-Scott, Hercules broadened what it sold, but unlike Hall-Scott, Hercules continued to focus on engine making. This would not be an easy path, however. Observed Hercules in an in-house company history about the engine market in the late 1950s, "Passenger car engines were improved to the point where they were becoming highly competitive to heavy duty engines such as manufactured by Continental, Hercules and others in the marine, agricultural and industrial fields. There was also a decided trend for manufacturers of end products to produce their own engines instead of purchasing them from non-captive engine manufacturers...General Motors, I.H.C., Caterpillar, Chrysler, Ford, Case, Deere, Allis-Chalmers all, while building engines for their own purposes, were competing with the independent engine manufacturers." [6-40] The future of the Hall-Scott engine line was by no means rosy or certain in 1958, even if that line would continue to be produced by a much larger company.

After divesting itself of its poorly performing Power Division, Hall-Scott, Inc. redoubled its efforts at reaping greater profits for its investors. To accomplish this goal, management moved its capital to areas far removed from engine manufacture that promised higher yields. The high-technology Electronics Division found itself on the seller's block, being sold on July 15, 1958 "for about $1,200,000 cash and an undisclosed amount of Mandrel common stock" to Mandrel Industries, a growing Houston-based firm that was expanding its electronics operations. [6-41] In the deal, Mandrel agreed to lease the Burbank plant for five years, beginning on August 1, 1958.

Hall-Scott had failed to make substantial money in the engine and high-technology areas, so where would it turn next? At the time of the Mandrel deal, William Nelson only told *The New York Times*, "A number of opportunities are being studied and investigated, but there is nothing definite at the present time." [6-42] Management was not looking to re-enter manufacturing specifically, but rather, according to Nelson, "acquiring a new business for

Hall-Scott, or at least finding a suitable investment vehicle." [6-43] They were open as to the field in which they invested their capital, but the good news for Hall-Scott was that after 1958, the company would no longer lose money by selling engines. Within a short time, a suitable company was found to purchase, one far removed from heavy-duty engines. Taking the money from the sale of its divisions, cash on hand, along with a loan from banks that covered some notes, Hall-Scott in October 1958 bought 50% of the capital stock in the Cincinnati-based DuBois Holding Company, a transaction totaling $7,500,000. [6-44] DuBois Holding Company controlled DuBois Company, which distributed and manufactured industrial soaps and detergents, as its president Lou Lerner described, to clean "everything from dishes to missiles." [6-45] In business since 1920, DuBois enjoyed a profitable and growing history. It had posted yearly profits averaging about $1.5 million for the last five years and was claimed in *Investor's Reader* to have "a 27-year unbroken chain of operating profits gains as well as an increase in sales every year but one since 1933." These were results Hall-Scott could not touch from its building of gasoline engines and thread lock fittings. This acquisition would form the basis of the Hall-Scott "planned expansion in the chemical industry," said Nelson. [6-46] With new modern plants coming on line, having a product line that is moved by direct sales to commercial customers as opposed to sales divisions and advertising to the market, benefiting from the fact that new products were relatively easy to develop, and possessing an amazing record of steady growth and profitability, DuBois made a solid choice for Hall-Scott.

At this juncture, Hall-Scott, Inc. really made nothing. It had its place on the New York Stock Exchange, it had a board of directors that met and made decisions involving investments, it continued making incremental progress selling its real estate in Berkeley, and it earned returns from its detergent-making and distributing subsidiary. While the Burbank land sold quickly, Hall-Scott could not find a buyer for its entire Berkeley plant, settling instead for making small piecemeal sales. Either Hall-Scott would expand its holdings to include other firms, or it would fade away. There was no real reason for it to remain separate from DuBois. The other shoe dropped in February 1960, when the boards of directors for Hall-Scott and the DuBois Holding Company voted to merge their concerns (DuBois Holding Company and DuBois Company along with Hall-Scott) and to name the resulting company DuBois Chemicals, Incorporated. [6-47] DuBois had turned in another successful year in 1959, with annual sales of $2,096,856 and net income of $1,866,000. This was a 17% increase in sales over the previous year, indicating the sound business decision Hall-Scott directors had made in washing their hands of engines and concentrating on soap. The merger took effect in April 1960, effectively

These DuBois executives are smiling for good reason—this was the first day that stock of the new DuBois Chemical Company traded on the Big Board, terminating the Hall-Scott corporate name and years of it enduring marginal financial performance. William Nelson is at the far left. (Courtesy of William Nelson.)

terminating any additional chemical company acquisitions by Hall-Scott that Nelson had predicted. With that merger, Hall-Scott as a corporate entity disappeared, 50 years after its birth in Berkeley in 1910.

About two years after the Hall-Scott name disappeared on official letterhead, another important remnant of the Hall-Scott Motor Car Company disappeared when company cofounder Bert C. Scott died. [6-48] After a short illness, the 80-year-old Scott passed away in July 1962. Scott left Hall-Scott and ACF in 1938, and it is unclear if he held another job after that. A member of the San Francisco Rotary, the Bohemian Club, and the Claremont Country Club, Scott remained connected to regional business leaders after leaving the engine company he cofounded, assuming a position as a retired Bay Area businessman of some stature. Sadly, Scott lived to witness the slow death of the company he formed with Al Hall.

The closing of the Berkeley engine plant and the deaths of both Hall and Scott did not spell the end of Hall-Scott engine production. Bradford and other Hall-Scott employees who were charged with turning out the lights at the Berkeley factory accomplished their massive task in short order. To resume Hall-Scott production, workers had to transport "more than 2,000,000 pounds of parts, machine tools and tooling equipment" from Berkeley to Canton. [6-49] In July 1958, Hercules announced it had produced its first Canton-built Hall-Scott engine, a horizontal Model 779, in large part from parts on hand, and sold it to Crown Coach, a faithful Hall-Scott customer. Not wanting to miss any potential sales, few as they might be, Hercules quickly began running ads for its newly acquired engine line, suggesting that it was business as usual for Hall-Scott customers. In such an ad appearing in the May 1959 issue of *Commercial Car Journal*, a crew of men surrounded a truck, hood up, exposing its Hall-Scott engine, which, according to the article, had just passed its one millionth mile with only $544 spent on parts. [6-50] The Hall-Scott name was in the ad, but the bold type and logo at the bottom of the ad were all Hercules.

After the 1958 purchase, Hercules sold four basic Hall-Scott six-cylinder engines for trucks, buses, and industrial applications, plus the V-12. Those five Hall-Scott engines that were born again as Hercules–Hall-Scotts, at least for a short time, were the 590-cubic-inch Model 590, the 779-cubic-inch Model 779 (the old Hall-Scott Model 190), the 935-cubic-inch Model 6156 (which Hall-Scott had called the Model 480 and then the Model 935, the new number referring to each of the six cylinders displacing about 156 cubic inches), the 1091-cubic-inch Model 6182 (the old Hall-Scott Model 1091, the new number referring to each of the six cylinders displacing about 182 cubic inches), and the 2181-cubic-inch V-12 Model 2269 (a designation Hall-Scott had used for years for the V-12). [6-51] Some of these models came in various versions over the next few years, and not all were on the market as long as others. Hercules seemed to drop the horizontal Model 779 and the V-12 Model 2269 early, while it continued to sell the other six-cylinder models.

Hercules was not interested in all Hall-Scott products nor did it have much interest to grow the line or to develop its engines. Joseph Scheetz, Cost Department manager at Hercules at the time of the Hall-Scott purchase, later vice president (1961–1976), and finally president (1976–1987), recalled that a prime reason for management to purchase Hall-Scott was selling parts for engines rather than solely selling the engines. [6-52] This decision merely reflected the reality that in many years, Hall-Scott made money by selling parts, while it lost money selling engines, and that situation was not likely to change. This was not an outlook that would make Hall-Scott a long-term prospect for the

Hercules carried over much of the Hall-Scott engine lineup, promotions, and targeted market. This continuity can be seen in the Million Miler Program, which was given to Hall-Scott owners who racked up a million miles of use on their engines. They received a couple of photos of the truck (above) and documentation (opposite page) of the service performed. (Courtesy of Bob Bronson.)

```
OWNER: Petrolane Gas Service, Inc.          TRUCK:  Cab & Chassis — Autocar
       1696 E. Hill Street                          Engine        — Hall Scott Model 480
       Long Beach, California                       Compressor    — Westinghouse
                                                    Tires         — U.S. Royal

                                            TRAILER:

                                                    Mfg. by       — Utility Trailer Co.
                                                    Insured by    — The Nelson Co.

SERVICE RECORD

    Placed in Service — Oct. 1, 1952
    Turned 1,000,000 miles — Feb. 14, 1959
    Truck & Trailer transports L.P. Gas (7650 Net Gallons)
    Number of loads hauled in 1,000,000 Miles — 2300
    Total Gallons Hauled — 17,595,000 Gallons
    Additional 3,564 hours on engine (Pump Oil Time)
    This truck operated a total of 186,000 miles the first 12 months in service.
    No "AT FAULT" Accidents
    This unit has never had a "major" overhaul . . .

        In this million miles, replacement parts for the truck totaled slightly over $2100.00 and
    $1,072.00 for the trailer unit.

                    This represents the following new parts & material:
                        2 Sets Exhaust Valve seats
                        2 Exhaust Valves
                        2 Water Pump shafts
                        2 Water Pump pulleys
                        1 accessary drive shaft
   TRUCK                4 Sets Rings & Gaskets
                        3 Sets — Clutch Plates
                        1 Cover Plate
                        2 Driver Hubs
                        3 Brake Drums (Note *)
                        1 Repaired Trans. Case

                    Driver Brakes relines — 19 times
                    Dolly Brakes relined — 6 times
                        1 Air Compressor Exchange (Note **)

   * — 2 of the brake drums were changed at 935,089 miles.
   ** — Original air compressor exchanged at 900,061 miles.

                        3 — Brake Drums
                        6 Sets Brake Lining
   TRAILER              8 Slack Adjustors
                        8 Brake Cams
                        1 Rebuilt 5th Wheel (*)
                    (*) Rebuilt at 785,069 miles.
    General Petroleum Lube Oils & Greases used throughout this period.
```

Documentation of the service record for a Petrolane Gas Service truck engine in the Million Miler Program. (Courtesy of Bob Bronson.)

Hercules operation, but it would generate revenue for a few years. Scheetz believed Hall-Scotts to be "well-built" and "very durable," as did many other observers and consumers outside of Hercules. But Scheetz also leveled a damning assessment of Hall-Scotts: they were simply "not competitive" with other products in the 1960s, plus they were "costly." Similarly, Jack Fidler, who worked from 1950 until 1970 as a technician in the experimental test department (in a career at Hercules that lasted from 1942 until 1987, broken only by a three-year stint in the Army), viewed the Hall-Scott as being a "well designed engine with very long engine life," that was "very reliable" and created "high horsepower." [6-53] But working against the success of the line was its "high cost to purchase" and the fact that "at this time the industry was going to mostly Diesels." Years later, Hercules personnel had only vague memories of the Hall-Scott line because it never became a significant part of the output of the Canton plant.

Although Hercules manufactured, serviced, sold, and promoted Hall-Scott engines, Hercules plowed very little capital into its newly acquired line. Comparing the specifications between one model engine over a 14-year span in trade journals and a service manual, the 1955 Hall-Scott Model 935 and the 1969 Hercules-Hall-Scott Model 6156, reveals how little evolution occurred. The horsepower of the big six-cylinder rose negligibly from 295 hp in 1955 to 300 hp in 1969, but torque remained the same at 800 lb. ft. [6-54] The valves had the same dimensions and were made of the same material. The pistons appear to have been the same, too. Both engines weighed 2150 lb. Carburetion changed from updraft Zenith to downdraft Holley over the years. The engine shrank 3/8 inch in width, grew 1-5/8 inches in height, and lost 3/4 inch in length. Overall, this cursory comparison suggests that for all practical purposes, this engine did not change appreciably from the year Hall-Scott became an independent company until the last years the engine was offered for sale. It also points to the generally static nature of Hall-Scott-branded engines after 1958. Worth pointing out is that Hercules continued to offer its big Hall-Scott engines with the LPG fuel option through the late 1960s. Writing in 1963, William Nelson observed the new Hercules–Hall-Scott enterprise and predicted, "Unless the effort is intensified, I doubt that anything important will ever come to pass." [6-55] He appears to have seen correctly into the future.

Hercules did not completely ignore the Hall-Scott line. Hercules service manuals for Hall-Scott engines (covering Models 855, 935, 1091, 1091-OS, 6156, and 6182) listed the 1091-cubic-inch Hall-Scott Model 6182 as being available with a "Schwitzer-Cummins Turbo-Charger." [6-56] One manual listed two 6182 models: the Model 6182 and the Model 6182 GT. The Model 6182 was rated at 332 hp at 2200 rpm and 960 ft. lb. of torque at 1200 rpm, while the Model 6182 GT was rated at 450 hp at 2200 rpm and 1312 ft. lb. of torque at 1400 rpm. Those kinds of specs made the Model 6182 GT potent indeed; however, with each passing year, the demand for high-output commercial gasoline engines shrank even more. Unfortunately, neither manual stated when this feature first became fitted on the Model 6182; it is unclear if Hall-Scott had introduced turbochargers to the Model 6182 before selling to Hercules. Available Hall-Scott literature dating from before the 1958 sale did not list turbochargers as regular features on any of its models, although there was plenty of experimental work with fitting turbochargers to Hall-Scotts beginning in the mid-1950s. [6-57] Those same service manuals also show that Hall-Scott Models 6182-GT and 1091-OS-GT did not have carburetors, but rather Simmonds SU fuel injection systems. Again, available Hall-Scott literature before 1958 did not list fuel injection as a regular feature, but it is known that company engineers tinkered with it, as seen in the rarely mentioned Model 442. Either Hercules continued offering fuel injection and turbochargers on the Model 6182 as Hall-Scott had introduced in the late 1950s, or it continued development work begun in Berkeley and began offering the Model 6182 with these features after 1958. A little more clear is some research and development work done in Canton on the Model 590. Jack Fidler worked on a project in the 1960s to convert the Hall-Scott Model 590 into a diesel. Indeed, J.E. "Speed" Glidewell had designed the Model 590 with this kind of dual fuel operation in mind. Fidler remembered, "The Diesel experimental engines were very clean burning and had very good fuel economy. However, we couldn't overcome cylinder head cracking." [6-58] The Model 590 was the only Hall-Scott engine with which Fidler remembered experimenting, and he was there during the years that any such work would have taken place; therefore, that probably was the only model to receive such expensive attention. While the Model 590 project did not yield a successful engine, this interesting story shows that there was at least some effort in Canton to breathe a little life into the old Hall-Scott name.

The exact number of Hall-Scott engines made by Hercules is unknown, as is when the company finally discontinued production. For a short time, Hercules continued to buy the castings for its Hall-Scotts from Macaulay Foundry in Berkeley, but the amicable relationship between the two companies did not match the one that had existed between Hall-Scott and Macaulay. In 1962, after what Macaulay's historian called "a year of marginal orders," Hercules discontinued its dealings with Macaulay and transferred its Hall-Scott patterns to a foundry in Indiana. [6-59] The Hall-Scott line was not exactly thriving. By 1969, *Commercial Car Journal* no longer carried a listing for a Hall-Scott product line in its annual gasoline engine review, nor were there any Hercules

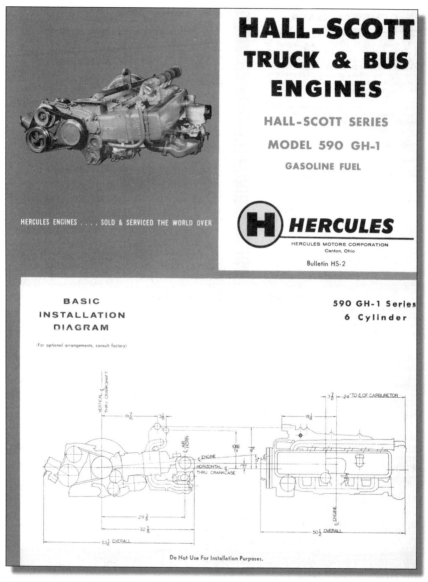

Hercules held some particular hope for the relatively new Hall-Scott Model 590; it was offered in multiple forms, including a gasoline-fueled horizontal model. (Courtesy of Rick Anderson and Doug Gigstad.)

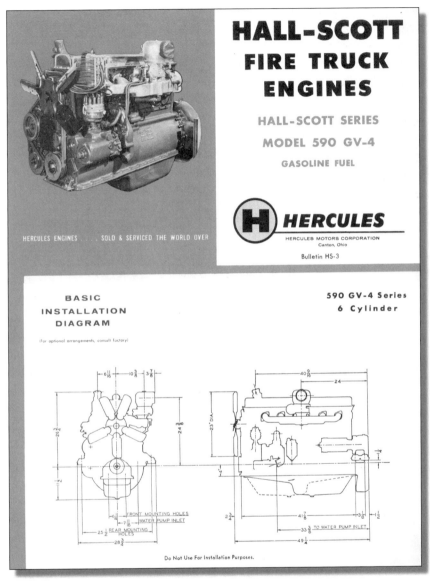

Hercules also offered the Hall-Scott Model 590 as a gasoline-fueled vertical model. (Courtesy of Rick Anderson and Doug Gigstad.)

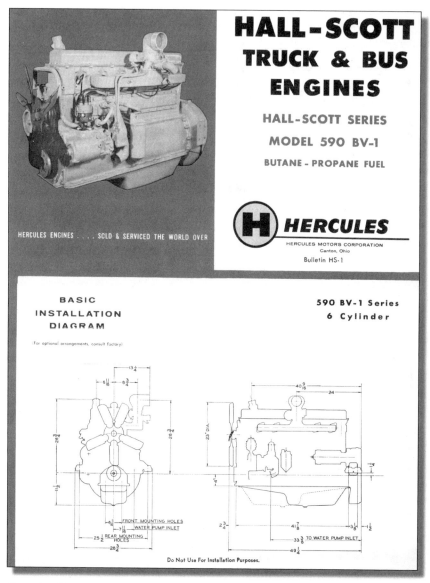

Hercules likewise offered the Hall-Scott Model 590 as a butane-fueled model. (Courtesy of Rick Anderson and Doug Gigstad.)

engines listed of Hall-Scott's dimensions. [6-60] But that same *Commercial Car Journal* reported that Los Angeles-based Crown Coach was still offering the Hall-Scott Model 590 as an option in its 1969 annual bus review. [6-61] By 1970, that lone Hall-Scott entry in Crown buses also disappeared from *Commercial Car Journal*. [6-62] *Automotive Industries* listed two basic models as "Hercules–Hall-Scott" in its 1969 gasoline engine review, the Models 6156 and 6182; only one in 1970, the Model 6182; and none in 1971. [6-63] In its annual bus review, *Automotive Industries* listed Crown as still offering the Model 590 as an option through the 1970 model year but not 1971. [6-64] Crown Firecoach collector Mike Britt reports that Crown installed its last Hall-Scott in a new truck in 1969, its 435th new-truck Hall-Scott installation since 1951, which corroborates with the trade journal data pointing to 1969–1970 as the end of the line for the old name. [6-65] Crown assembled buses, fire apparatus, and other specialty vehicles in Los Angeles starting in 1933, first using Hall-Scott engines in 1937, and probably was the last OEM to use Hall-Scott. Therefore, it appears that the last new engines to carry the Hall-Scott name in a bus or truck were sold as late as 1970, a dozen years after Hercules purchased the old Berkeley engine name. Unfortunately, correspondence with Hercules officials in 1993 was not able to yield any specific information on when that company built or sold its last Hall-Scott engines or even how many it made. [6-66] Joe Scheetz has no specific data listing the last year of production, but he remembers total Hall-Scott production being small. Ultimately, Hercules stopped making Hall-Scotts for one basic reason, which Scheetz curtly described as being a "lack of sales." [6-67]

Hercules itself became the target of a purchase—twice within the 1960s, in fact—and this complicates the last chapter of the Hall-Scott story. Hercules was in a stronger financial and market position than Hall-Scott was in the late 1950s, with a broader range of engines and vastly greater production figures, but the company often operated in the red or earned only meager profits. After reporting operating losses in 1958 and 1960 and only a small profit in 1959, Hupp Corporation, a former auto maker, purchased Hercules in 1961. [6-68] Only a few years later, Hercules went through another change in ownership. Long-time truck maker White purchased Hercules in 1966 and renamed the Canton engine maker White Motors. These sales allowed new Hercules engines and, by extension, new Hall-Scott engines to continue to power vehicles a while longer.

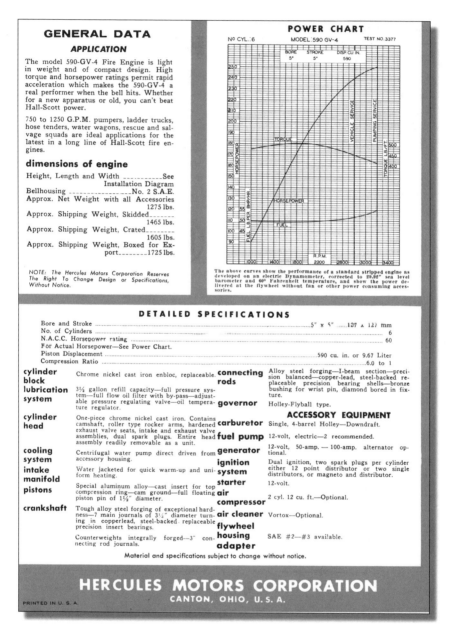

GENERAL DATA

APPLICATION

The model 590-GV-4 Fire Engine is light in weight and of compact design. High torque and horsepower ratings permit rapid acceleration which makes the 590-GV-4 a real performer when the bell hits. Whether for a new apparatus or old, you can't beat Hall-Scott power.

750 to 1250 G.P.M. pumpers, ladder trucks, hose tenders, water wagons, rescue and salvage squads are ideal applications for the latest in a long line of Hall-Scott fire engines.

dimensions of engine

Height, Length and Width _____ See
Installation Diagram
Bellhousing _____ No. 2 S.A.E.
Approx. Net Weight with all Accessories
1275 lbs.
Approx. Shipping Weight, Skidded _____
1465 lbs.
Approx. Shipping Weight, Crated _____
1605 lbs.
Approx. Shipping Weight, Boxed for Export _____ 1725 lbs.

NOTE: *The Hercules Motors Corporation Reserves The Right To Change Design or Specifications, Without Notice.*

POWER CHART

N° CYL.: 6   MODEL: 590 GV-4   TEST NO. 3377

The above curves show the performance of a standard stripped engine as developed on an electric Dynamometer, corrected to 29.92" sea level barometer and 60° Fahrenheit temperature, and show the power delivered at the flywheel without fan or other power consuming accessories.

DETAILED SPECIFICATIONS

Bore and Stroke .... 5" x 5" ...... 127 x 127 mm
No. of Cylinders 6
N.A.C.C. Horsepower rating 60
For Actual Horsepower—See Power Chart.
Piston Displacement .... 590 cu. in. or 9.67 Liter
Compression Ratio .... 6.0 to 1

cylinder block	Chrome nickel cast iron enbloc, replaceable.	**connecting rods** — Alloy steel forging—I-beam section—precision balanced—copper-lead, steel-backed replaceable precision bearing shells—bronze bushing for wrist pin, diamond bored in fixture.
lubrication system	3½ gallon refill capacity—full pressure system—full flow oil filter with by-pass—adjustable pressure regulating valve—oil temperature regulator.	**governor** — Holley-Flyball type.
cylinder head	One-piece chrome nickel cast iron. Contains camshaft, roller type rocker arms, hardened exhaust valve seats, intake and exhaust valve assemblies, dual spark plugs. Entire head assembly readily removable as a unit.	**carburetor** — Single, 4-barrel Holley—Downdraft. **fuel pump** — 12-volt, electric—2 recommended.
cooling system	Centrifugal water pump direct driven from accessory housing.	**generator** — 12-volt, 50-amp. — 100-amp. alternator optional.
intake manifold	Water jacketed for quick warm-up and uniform heating.	**ignition system** — Dual ignition, two spark plugs per cylinder either 12 point distributor or two single distributors, or magneto and distributor.
pistons	Special aluminum alloy—cast insert for top compression ring—cam ground—full floating piston pin of 1¼" diameter.	**starter** — 12-volt. **air compressor** — 2 cyl. 12 cu. ft.—Optional.
crankshaft	Tough alloy steel forging of exceptional hardness—7 main journals of 3¼" diameter turning in copperlead, steel-backed replaceable precision insert bearings. Counterweights integrally forged—3" connecting rod journals.	**air cleaner** — Vortox—Optional. **flywheel housing adapter** — SAE #2—#3 available.

ACCESSORY EQUIPMENT

Material and specifications subject to change without notice.

HERCULES MOTORS CORPORATION
CANTON, OHIO, U. S. A.

PRINTED IN U. S. A.

These are the performance and stats of the GV4 gasoline version of the Model 590. (Courtesy of Rick Anderson and Doug Gigstad.)

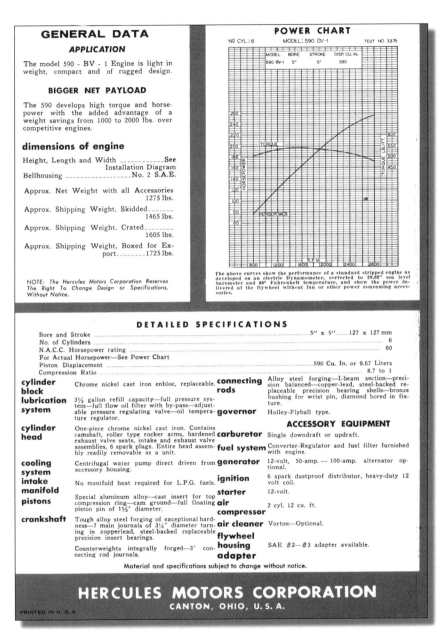

GENERAL DATA

APPLICATION

The model 590 - BV - 1 Engine is light in weight, compact and of rugged design.

BIGGER NET PAYLOAD

The 590 develops high torque and horse-power with the added advantage of a weight savings from 1000 to 2000 lbs. over competitive engines.

dimensions of engine

Height, Length and Width _____See
                                Installation Diagram
Bellhousing _____No. 2 S.A.E.

Approx. Net Weight with all Accessories
                                1275 lbs.
Approx. Shipping Weight, Skidded_____
                                1465 lbs.
Approx. Shipping Weight, Crated_____
                                1605 lbs.
Approx. Shipping Weight, Boxed for Ex-
                    port_____1725 lbs.

NOTE: The Hercules Motors Corporation Reserves The Right To Change Design or Specifications, Without Notice.

POWER CHART

NO CYL.: 6   MODEL: 590 BV-1   TEST NO 3375

MODEL	BORE	STROKE	DISP. CU. IN.
590 BV-1	5"	5"	590

The above curves show the performance of a standard stripped engine as developed on an electric Dynamometer, corrected to 29.92" sea level barometer and 60° Fahrenheit temperature, and show the power delivered at the flywheel without fan or other power consuming accessories.

DETAILED SPECIFICATIONS

Bore and Stroke ....5" x 5".......127 x 127 mm
No. of Cylinders 6
N.A.C.C. Horsepower rating 60
For Actual Horsepower—See Power Chart
Piston Displacement ....590 Cu. In. or 9.67 Liters
Compression Ratio .... 8.7 to 1

cylinder block — Chrome nickel cast iron enbloc, replaceable.

lubrication system — 3½ gallon refill capacity—full pressure system—full flow oil filter with by-pass—adjustable pressure regulating valve—oil temperature regulator.

cylinder head — One-piece chrome nickel cast iron. Contains camshaft, roller type rocker arms, hardened exhaust valve seats, intake and exhaust valve assemblies, 6 spark plugs. Entire head assembly readily removable as a unit.

cooling system — Centrifugal water pump direct driven from accessory housing.

intake manifold — No manifold heat required for L.P.G. fuels.

pistons — Special aluminum alloy—cast insert for top compression ring—cam ground—full floating piston pin of 1¼" diameter.

crankshaft — Tough alloy steel forging of exceptional hardness—7 main journals of 3¼" diameter turning in copperlead, steel-backed replaceable precision insert bearings.
Counterweights integrally forged—3" connecting rod journals.

connecting rods — Alloy steel forging—I-beam section—precision balanced—copper-lead, steel-backed replaceable precision bearing shells—bronze bushing for wrist pin, diamond bored in fixture.

governor — Holley-Flyball type.

ACCESSORY EQUIPMENT

carburetor — Single downdraft or updraft.

fuel system — Converter-Regulator and fuel filter furnished with engine.

generator — 12-volt, 50-amp. — 100-amp. alternator optional.

ignition — 6 spark dustproof distributor, heavy-duty 12 volt coil.

starter — 12-volt.

air compressor — 2 cyl. 12 cu. ft.

air cleaner — Vortox—Optional.

flywheel housing adapter — SAE #2—#3 adapter available.

Material and specifications subject to change without notice.

HERCULES MOTORS CORPORATION
CANTON, OHIO, U. S. A.

PRINTED IN U. S. A.

These are the performance and stats of the BV butane version of the Model 590. Compare them with those of the GV4 version on the preceding page. (Courtesy of Rick Anderson and Doug Gigstad.)

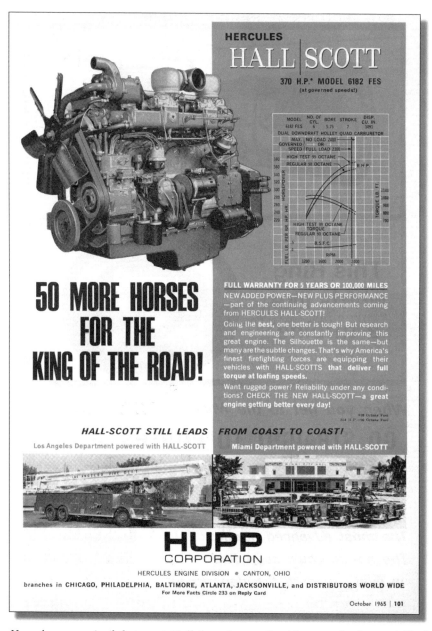

Hercules recognized that most Hall-Scott buyers (in this example, firemen) liked Hall-Scott engines for their big power. (Courtesy of William Nelson.)

This is another example of a Hercules ad pitching Hall-Scott power to firemen. (Courtesy of William Nelson.)

Even with parent companies, Hercules posted an uneven and modest profitability record through the 1960s. In fact, it earned money only because it relied greatly and successfully on winning U.S. military contracts. [6-69] Hercules was able to keep production numbers high—in the tens of thousands of engines yearly—so the company could lower its unit costs and remain competitive in landing government engine bids. White Motors had been gobbling up companies since the 1950s to become highly vertically and horizontally integrated by the time it picked up Hercules. For example, before acquiring Hercules, White had purchased truck makers Autocar, Diamond T, Sterling, and Reo, continuing some of these as separate labels, combining some, and dropping others. This empire-building strategy gave White Motors a range of trucks plus some engines, notably the Reo six- and eight-cylinder gasoline "Gold Comets," although these motors hardly represented cutting-edge design. In a related set of moves, in 1965 White had purchased agricultural tractor makers Cockshutt, Minneapolis-Moline, and Oliver; thus, the acquisitions by White were diverse. The 1966 acquisition of Hercules Engine Company gave to White the engines to use in its own trucks and other equipment or to sell to other companies if it wanted. But more importantly perhaps to White was the Hercules plant in which new engines could be developed and built. Hercules had been making about 300 engines per day at the time of the takeover, about half of which went to the military. Therefore, the Canton facility possessed decent production capacity. With its growing industrial holdings, White wanted to reap more of the benefits that come with economies of scale and to produce more of its own engines of new design. The Hercules facility therefore attracted White. White executive John Beck told *Commercial Car Journal* that when a truck maker's "sales volume exceeds about 15,000 units a year, it becomes considerably more economical to make [engines] than buy" them. [6-70] With the many truck and tractor divisions of White, the company had a "captive market in excess of 30,000 diesel engines a year, covering the range of 50 to 400 horsepower," plus whatever engines it could sell to other companies. White wanted to be self-sufficient in engines, and the Hercules plant was where management wanted to build. Therefore, the managers of White invested $60 million in a new line of gasoline and diesel engines, of six and eight cylinders, and expanded the Hercules plant. Beck promised that the new White engines would be up to date, weighing about six to eight pounds per horsepower. Furthermore, the manufacture of these modern motors would be accomplished by the latest in labor-saving machinery. Officials of White claimed that "only three workers would be required to oversee 14 machining stations on the engine block line and only four for the 12 stations on the engine head line." [6-71]

Crown perhaps was the best civilian customer of Hall-Scott outside of ACF, but Crown management was not blind to industry trends. Therefore, in the 1960s and 1970s, Crown solicited customers to exchange the gasoline engines (usually Hall-Scott engines if they were Crown vehicles) in their units for diesels. (Courtesy of Tom Shafer.)

But where would Hall-Scott engines figure into this new plan for White? The 14-year-old Hall-Scott Model 590 would still pass the new White weight requirement with its five- to six-pounds-per-horsepower figure. But the managers of White wanted to build a family of related engines, including diesels, and the stand-alone Hall-Scott Model 590 did not fit into this picture. Nor did the static and out-of-date remainder of the Hall-Scott line, which, after all, was based on the Invader. By 1968, that Invader design was 37 years old—a virtual relic from the Stone Age. With the takeover of Hercules by White in late 1966, it is little wonder that the Hall-Scott engine line rather quickly, and very quietly, faded away shortly thereafter. But even if Hercules would have continued producing the Model 590 for trucks and buses, the early 1970s brought an energy crisis and surging fuel prices, pushing many heavy-duty gasoline engines off the market.

By around 1970, when the last new Hall-Scott engine was made, the days of the large, heavy-duty, spark-ignition engine dominating the commercial engine field—the kind of engine on which Hall-Scott had concentrated its efforts for five decades—were over. The dieselization of the commercial engine market in America, a trend Hall-Scott had witnessed first growing before World War II, had changed the face of the engine industry worldwide. The later resurgence of natural gas and "bio gas" as fuels for commercial engines, such as in power generation and facilities heating, came too late for Hall-Scott to participate in it, although that was a technology the company had used since the 1920s. Perhaps the engine market had come back around to Hall-Scott after all. But by then, Hall-Scott had been unresponsive to the changing market for too many decades.

References

6-1.   Hall-Scott Power/Electronics, brochure, 1955, p. 3.

6-2.   Francis Bradford, "A History of the Hall-Scott Motor Car Company," unpublished manuscript, 1989, p. 114. Courtesy of Bancroft Library, University of California, Berkeley, BANC MSS 93/104c.

6-3.   Hall-Scott Power/Electronics, brochure, 1955, p. 26.

6-4.   William Nelson, autobiography, unpublished manuscript, 1963, p. 281. Courtesy of William Nelson.

6-5.   Hall-Scott Power/Electronics, brochure, 1955, p. 11.

6-6.   Ibid., p. 15.

6-7.   *Automotive Industries*, March 15, 1954, p. 278. *Automotive Industries,* March 15, 1955, p. 244.

6-8.   1955 Hall-Scott, Inc., Annual Report, p. 6.

6-9.   J.E. "Speed" Glidewell, "A Brief History of Hall-Scott Motor Company," unpublished address, 1956, p. 4. Nelson said that the Hall-Scott diesel program was axed in 1957 but "was by any measuring stick years away." William Nelson, autobiography, unpublished manuscript, 1963, p. 282. Courtesy of William Nelson.

6-10.   *Commercial Car Journal*, August 1955, p. 202. Courtesy of John Perala.

6-11.   *San Francisco Chronicle*, October 25, 1955, p. 33.

6-12.   *The National Cyclopaedia of American Biography, Vol. XLIII*, University Microfilms, Ann Arbor, MI, 1967, p. 493. Hall's life is drawn from this source unless otherwise noted. The connection of the De Vaux engine to Continental can be seen in William Wagner, *Continental! Its Motors and Its People,* Aero Publishers, Fallbrook, CA, 1983, p. 58. Primary sources include "De Vaux Develops 65 Hp.," *Automobile Trade Journal*, March 1931, pp. 33, 81, and "De Vaux Six—A New Car in the Lower Priced Field," *Automotive Industries*, December 20, 1930, pp. 899, 903.

6-13.   *San Francisco Chronicle*, April 10, 1957, p. 40.

6-14.   Pickering Advertising Agency, "Hall-Scott, Incorporated Power Division Total Marketing Analysis and Plan," unpublished report, 1957, p. 12. This is referred to in the text as the Pickering report.

6-15.   Ibid., pp. 8, 10.

6-16.   Letter from R. Brown to R. Dias, November 13, 2002.

6-17.   W.J. Rellaford, "Save Eight Hours on L.A.–Salt Lake Run," *Western Motor Transport*, reprint, March 1945, n.p.

6-18.   Pickering Advertising Agency, "Hall-Scott, Incorporated Power Division Total Marketing Analysis and Plan," unpublished report, 1957, p. 14. This is referred to in the text as the Pickering report.

6-19.   *Commercial Car Journal*, July 1958, p. 35. *Commercial Car Journal* reported American total truck production at 346,656 in 1957 and 511,092 in 1958. However, it is unclear exactly what kinds of trucks are included in these numbers.

6-20. Pickering Advertising Agency, "Hall-Scott, Incorporated Power Division Total Marketing Analysis and Plan," unpublished report, 1957, p. 13. This is referred to in the text as the Pickering report.

6-21. Ibid., pp. 10–11.

6-22. Letter from R. Brown to R. Dias, November 13, 2002.

6-23. William Nelson, autobiography, unpublished manuscript, 1963, p. 282. Courtesy of William Nelson.

6-24. Ibid., pp. 286–288.

6-25. Ibid., p. 285.

6-26. *Wall Street Journal*, April 14, 1958, p. 23.

6-27. *Wall Street Journal*, May 8, 1958, p. 47. *Commercial Car Journal*, July 1958, p. 35.

6-28. William Nelson, autobiography, unpublished manuscript, 1963, p. 289. Courtesy of William Nelson. Letter from J. Scheetz to R. Dias, November 8, 2003. Scheetz was the Hercules cost department manager at the time of the purchase and said that Hercules was much more interested in selling Hall-Scott spare parts than its engines.

6-29. *Canton Repository*, February 1, 1959, n.p. The newspaper article was photocopied and the page number not included. Courtesy of the Wm. McKinley Presidential Library & Museum, Canton, OH.

6-30. *Canton Repository*, June 21, 1958, n.p. The newspaper article was photocopied and the page number not included. Courtesy of the Wm. McKinley Presidential Library & Museum, Canton, OH.

6-31. Letter from F. William Harder and W. Nelson to Hall-Scott stockholders, June 5, 1958.

6-32. 1958 Hall-Scott, Inc. Annual Report, n.p.

6-33. Letter from R. Klotz to F. Bradford, September 1, 1993.

6-34. Francis Bradford paycheck stub, March 1958.

6-35. Francis Bradford, "A History of the Hall-Scott Motor Car Company," unpublished manuscript, 1989, p. 57b. Courtesy of Bancroft Library, University of California, Berkeley, BANC MSS 93/104c.

6-36. *Wall Street Journal*, August 26, 1960, p. 14.

6-37.   *Wall Street Journal*, December 17, 1957, p. 21. *Wall Street Journal*, November 4, 1958, p. 13.

6-38.   *Commercial Car Journal*, March 1958, p. C8. *Wall Street Journal*, September 3, 1958, p. 24.

6-39.   Hercules Motors Corporation, "History, Growth & Expansion of the Hercules Motors Corporation," unpublished manuscript, 1963, p. 19. Courtesy of the Charles Balough Family Collection. *Canton Repository*, July 8, 1958, p. 27. Courtesy of the Wm. McKinley Presidential Library & Museum, Canton, OH. A later White acquisition of Avco products (Avco was then under the control of Studebaker-Worthington, the same Studebaker of automaking fame) is covered in *Automotive Industries*, May 1, 1970, p. 88.

6-40.   Hercules Motor Corporation, "History, Growth & Expansion of the Hercules Motors Corporation," unpublished manuscript, 1963, p. 19.

6-41.   *The New York Times*, July 16, 1958, p. 41. 1958 Hall-Scott, Inc. Annual Report, n.p.

6-42.   *The New York Times*, July 16, 1958, p. 41.

6-43.   William Nelson, autobiography, unpublished manuscript, 1963, p. 292. Courtesy of William Nelson.

6-44.   *Wall Street Journal*, October 14, 1958, p. 10. *Investor's Reader*, December 21, 1960, p. 6. Second source courtesy of William Nelson.

6-45.   *Investor's Reader*, December 21, 1960, p. 7

6-46.   *Wall Street Journal*, October 14, 1958, p. 10.

6-47.   *Wall Street Journal*, February 25, 1960, p. 2. 1959 Hall-Scott, Inc. Annual Report, n.p.

6-48.   *San Francisco Chronicle*, July 22, 1962, p. 31.

6-49.   *The New York Times*, July 28, 1958, p. 30. *Canton Repository*, July 27, 1958, n.p. The information in the second source was taken from a photocopy that did not include the page number. Second source courtesy of the Wm. McKinley Presidential Library & Museum, Canton, OH.

6-50.   *Commercial Car Journal*, May 1959, p. 184.

6-51.   *Commercial Car Journal*, April 1959. p. 279. This lineup is confirmed in a sheet included in a Hercules manual, *Gasoline Diesel Air-Cooled and Liquid-Cooled Engines*, circa 1958, and spec sheets. Courtesy of Rick

Anderson. The *Commercial Car Journal* list does not include the V-12, but other sources do.

6-52.   Letter from J. Scheetz to R. Dias, November 8, 2003.

6-53.   Letter from J. Fidler to R. Dias, March 6, 2004.

6-54.   *Automotive Industries*, March 15, 1955, pp. 244–245. *Automotive Industries*, March 15, 1969, pp. 194–195.

6-55.   William Nelson, autobiography, unpublished manuscript, 1963, p. 290. Courtesy of William Nelson.

6-56.   *Service Manual Models 855–935–1091–1091-0S–6156–6182*, Hercules Engines, Inc., September 1969, pp. 10, 11, 20, 362–365.

6-57.   Bradford and other sources point to an obscure Model 442, made before the Hercules purchase, which was a turbocharged 400, and sold to the government for use in trucks. Francis Bradford, "A History of the Hall-Scott Motor Car Company," unpublished manuscript, 1989, p. 103. Courtesy of Bancroft Library, University of California, Berkeley, BANC MSS 93/104c. William Nelson, Hall-Scott binder, loose sheet. Courtesy of William Nelson. Nelson was the last president of Hall-Scott and kept many handwritten or typed company records in a binder. A loose sheet in the binder states only that 159 of the model were produced.

6-58.   Letter from J. Fidler to R. Dias, March 6, 2004.

6-59.   Anthony Kirk, *Founded by the Bay; The History of Macaulay Foundry, 1896–1996*, Macaulay Foundry, Berkeley, CA, 1996, p. 60.

6-60.   *Commercial Car Journal*, April 1969, p. 286.

6-61.   Ibid., p. 288.

6-62.   *Commercial Car Journal*, April 1970, p. 273.

6-63.   *Automotive Industries*, March 15, 1969, p. 194. *Automotive Industries*, March 15, 1970, p. 166. *Automotive Industries*, March 15, 1971, pp. 118–119.

6-64.   *Automotive Industries*, March 15, 1969, p. 163. *Automotive Industries*, March 15, 1970, p. 154; *Automotive Industries*, March 15, 1971, p. 99.

6-65.   Letter from M. Britt to R. Dias, August 19, 2003.

6-66.   Letter from R. Klotz to F. Bradford, September 1, 1993.

6-67.   Letter from J. Scheetz to R. Dias, November 8, 2003.

6-68.   *Wall Street Journal*, July 3, 1961, p. 4.

6-69.   *Wall Street Journal*, July 18, 1966, p. 4. The change took effect on December 30, 1966, so some sources cite the date as 1967.

6-70.   *Commercial Car Journal*, July 1968, pp. 113–114.

6-71.   *Automotive Industries*, April 15, 1969, p. 140.

CHAPTER SEVEN

CONCLUSION

Although much is known about the history of Hall-Scott, a great deal remains clouded in ambiguity. Vital information remains unknown, such as precisely how many engines were built overall and who in the company made many of its important decisions. Part of the explanation for the lacunae is that these events occurred some time ago and that Hall-Scott was a small company that did not attract wide attention. These answers ring more true with the birth of Hall-Scott, but they are less satisfying explanations about its demise. If the truth be told, as the company began to falter in the 1950s, few people outside the company took much notice. After all, Hall-Scott was hardly a household name. Many people today who are familiar with Hall-Scott are not even aware that Hercules produced Hall-Scott engines through the 1960s. Almost nothing is known about the Hercules years. Such was the low profile that Hall-Scott maintained through most of its history, especially as the years passed and competing companies grabbed more sales. Sadly, company management did not think enough of their own enterprise to save most of its records.

Between the bookends of the vague birth and death of Hall-Scott stands an impressive record of design and production. That Hall-Scott built products of high quality and thoughtful design is not questioned. Consumers who have operated or evaluated Hall-Scott products have been conspicuous in their praise. Hall-Scott's innovative use of overhead camshafts, hemi heads, aluminum pistons, oil filtration, unit construction, horizontal configuration, and gasified fuels are commonly found today. The outstanding performance of Hall-Scott engines—from the remarkable power-to-weight ratios of its aviation engines to the ground-pounding power of the 400 series truck engines—still raises eyebrows. The fact that Hall-Scott engines were produced for more than half a century might be one of the more impressive aspects of its history. This is not the story of failure so much as it is a story of success.

In fact, rather than ask why Hall-Scott failed, a more appropriate question to ask might be how this company of rather modest output lasted as long as it did in the rough-and-tumble engine marketplace. Hall-Scott did not need to build 100,000 engines per year to make money, or to satisfy its owners, or to be successful. Simply put, over the years, Hall-Scott produced engines for which there was some demand, and its products possessed qualities for which (a few) buyers were willing to pay more. Small companies can compete against large ones—even though they do not share the economies of scale that can allow giants to sell for less—if they can provide a product that commands a higher price in the marketplace. The trick is finding that niche to exploit. [7-1]

Hall-Scott remained flexible enough at a few critical junctures, especially in its early years, to respond quickly to changes in demand or to sell some new product. This can be seen in Hall-Scott turning to high-output aircraft engines in that up-and-coming field, producing two-speed rear axles for the incredibly

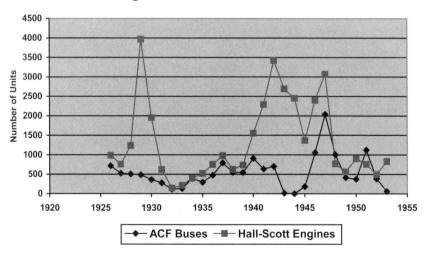

Hall-Scott Engine and ACF Bus Deliveries, 1926–1953

This graph demonstrates Hall-Scott's history of occasionally augmenting its dependence on ACF bus deliveries with high-volume, high-profit, short-term production of engines for International Harvester around 1930, and marine engines in the early 1940s.

popular Model T as sales of that car peaked, and transforming the Invader into a V-12 and a truck engine for World War II. It did not take Hall-Scott long or much of its own capital to augment engine making with axle making, or to take a terrific six-cylinder marine engine and transform it into a truck engine or a V-12. One thing management did right a few times was to find things that the company could make profitably with a minimum of setup costs and transition time. True, some of these products were produced for only a few years (sometimes called batch production), but they used existing space, machinery, and labor to keep the factory busy. Some yielded great profit, which could carry the company through leaner times until another product was found; another niche was exploited. Staying lean, responsive, and quick on its feet can be a recipe for success for a small company.

Although E.J. Hall and B.C. Scott can be faulted for some of their business practices, the two founders were good at using local networking to foster growth. After buying one of Hall's Comets in 1908, Scott enticed friends to do so, too. After joining forces with Hall, he found a buyer for the first product, the motor car, and lined up financing through his father, a leading business figure. Elbert Hall used his connection with a fellow World War I veteran to launch the lucrative Ruckstell project. The transition of the company from supplying power to rail and aviation, to tractor and truck, came through supplying neighbors, companies literally in Hall-Scott's backyard—Pliny Holt and the Fageol brothers. This approach of using local sources was more clearly evident when Hall and Scott were still leading the firm than after it was purchased by East Coast-based ACF. Little evidence could be found of Hall-Scott relying on local producers, using personal or family connections, to score big business deals in the 1940s, 1950s, and 1960s.

A number of independent American engine makers, outside of the Big Three auto firms, have continued operations from the early twentieth into the twenty-first centuries. In fact, most of these surviving firms at one time or another were competitors of Hall-Scott in the aviation, rail, truck, bus, marine, or industrial engine markets. Some of these are high-volume producers, and others are not. Among the leading names of this successful group are Caterpillar, Continental, Deere, Fairbanks-Morse, Cummins, International, Lycoming, Mack, Waukesha, and Wisconsin. Absent from this list is Hercules, also known through the years as White-Hercules or White Engines, the company that purchased the Hall-Scott Engine Division in 1958. Established in 1915, Hercules produced a couple million engines through its history, only to finally close its doors in 1999 after years of teetering on the brink of bankruptcy. [7-2] The list of companies still making heavy-duty engines is not nearly as long today as it was in the early twentieth century, but the market is not monopolized by the Big Three automakers or by one or two independent firms. There has always been room for independents of different sizes in this market.

The list of fallen independent American engine makers is long indeed—longer than the list of survivors. Therefore, Hall-Scott is not outstanding in this regard. Only some of the makers of truck, bus, and industrial engines that now have a headstone in that industry graveyard include Allis-Chalmers, American-La France, Brennan, Buda, Hercules, Hinkley, Le Roi, Herschell-Spillman, Murphy, P & H, Reo, and White (Truck). Many small vehicle makers in the early twentieth century made their own engines, too, such as Kissel and Whippet. A comprehensive list of truck and bus engine makers would be lengthy. The list of deceased marine engine makers is even longer. Some competitors of Hall-Scott on the water that are now gone include once formidable and/or respected companies such as Atlas-Imperial, Buda, Covic, Enterprise, Emperor, Gray, Hill, Hicks, Kermath, Lorimer, Palmer, Packard, Red Wing, Regal, Scripps, Sterling, Union, Universal, and Van Blerck. Failure has been the rule among American engine makers, not success.

Explaining how a few independent commercial engine makers managed to survive through the twentieth century is complicated, but the surviving firms almost always have been part of some larger entity. Often, this larger enterprise even has international scope. This is true of Continental, which has been part of the diverse Teledyne Industries since 1969. Likewise, Continental purchased Wisconsin in 1943, offering that even smaller engine maker some protection from the harsh engine market. This acquisition afforded Continental more breadth to its line to address the needs of more customers, especially those in the low-horsepower ranges. Similarly, Cummins Engine Company purchased Onan in 1986. Onan had been controlled by McGraw-Edison and then Cooper Industries before Cummins, so Onan management well appreciated the importance of being part of a larger company. Cummins found in Onan a company that made a different product, but one that would broaden its overall engine line. Another old-timer, Fairbanks-Morse, which made its first engine in 1893, became a division of Colt Industries and then part of Goodrich, which "spun off" elements of itself to form EnPro, a holding company, in 2002. Waukesha, an engine maker since 1906, has been part of the huge Dresser Industries since 1974. Lycoming has been controlled by several firms over the decades, including American Car and Foundry (ACF), linking it to Hall-Scott. Rather recently, Lycoming became part of Textron, a firm with diversified aviation and aerospace units. A few independent truck makers build engines today. Mack Trucks (of which Renault began to purchase increasing control in 1979) and

International are examples in this group. International (known as Navistar beginning in 1986 and then reclaiming its International name in 2000), which is not owned by another company, stands alone among independent heavy-duty truck makers that produce engines. The uniformity of current engine makers to be part of some larger company is not likely a coincidence.

Having such a joined relationship has been no guarantee of success, though. Allis-Chalmers purchased Buda in 1953 and then ceased selling engines with the Buda name shortly thereafter. The White purchase of Hercules failed to save that old engine builder (and by extension, Hall-Scott). These two examples notwithstanding, an engine maker having a large and diversified benefactor appears to be a critical component of success in this turbulent industry.

Of the companies that still operate and are concentrating on making commercial engines and relying on engine sales primarily as Hall-Scott did, only Cummins remains independent. This makes Cummins an exception to an otherwise pervasive trend. Cummins management considered linking with White (what company didn't?) in the 1960s, but that courtship proved to be more of a flirtation than a serious romance, and today Cummins remains a spinster.

There is little doubt that when Hall and Scott oversaw the purchase of their company to ACF in 1925, they pursued a wise course. Even as early as the 1920s, engine companies were failing left and right, so seeking protection through an association with a larger firm was a sound decision. In the 1920s, ACF was a large and forward-thinking company with divisions making products that used Hall-Scott engines. But ACF failed as a parent company on at least three major counts. First, ACF severely restricted Hall-Scott engine sales to competing companies. While ACF managers felt that having Hall-Scott engines exclusively would be a selling point for ACF buses, it appears buyers did not buy a bus only because of its engine. ACF arguably could have helped its engine division, and thus itself, by allowing Hall-Scott sales to other major bus makers. Demonstration of this path not taken by ACF is seen in General Motors and International Harvester, which have made trucks and buses for decades, and have sold engines to other truck and bus makers. In spite of Hall-Scott being a maker of premium bus and truck engines since 1921, *Commercial Car Journal* noted that when ACF introduced its first truck in 1931, which featured Hall-Scott power, these engines "are quite familiar in the bus field...[but] are not well known to the truck operator." [7-3] That surprising statement was not the fault of uninformed writers at *Commercial Car Journal*, but rather misguided managers at ACF. The second failing of ACF was in not giving Hall-Scott the stability that can come from having a larger company in charge. Better leadership at ACF would have kept its managers and stock-holders from seeking to dissolve that company in the 1940s and 1950s. Third, commandeering excessive profits from Hall-Scott, especially in the pivotal early post-World War II years, deprived Hall-Scott from being given a fighting chance of survival as the engine market changed radically in those years. Bleeding of the Hall-Scott coffers helped kill Hall-Scott prematurely through stifling the research and development that its managers knew was essential for the survival of the company.

Bus Engines as a Percentage of Total Hall-Scott Deliveries, 1926–1953

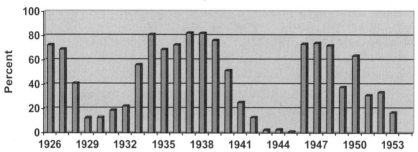

This graph illustrates the reliance of Hall-Scott on ACF bus production. However, ACF rarely sold enough units to allow Hall-Scott to reach profitability from building bus engines.

Did Hall-Scott have to go out of business? This question really cannot be answered with assurance; such a query is a "counter factual" (a "what if?") question that cannot be proven beyond doubt. But a reasoned conjecture as to whether or not Hall-Scott could have survived can be posed nonetheless. Given the body of successes that Hall-Scott compiled over its 48 years of independent operation, plus the fact that a handful of makers of heavy-duty engines have survived the engine business of the twentieth century, suggest that the answer to this question is yes, the company could have survived. But the survival of Hall-Scott to the present day would have necessitated that management would have made some very different decisions. And that story would not have been the Hall-Scott story. Therefore, given the leadership approach of Hall-Scott management, the outcome was indeed certain. Regardless, because other small-volume engine makers have succeeded into the twenty-first century means that Hall-Scott, as a small-volume producer, was not automatically doomed. Finding reasons why the company failed can tell us much about the American commercial engine industry.

What would have given Hall-Scott a fighting chance at survival would have been finding another parent company, before or following the implosion of ACF. The benefactor possibly could have been a truck maker, such as International, Mack (which did look into buying Hall-Scott after World War II), or Paccar (maker of Kenworth and Peterbilt, regular Hall-Scott users). [7-4] Any of these could have acquired Hall-Scott and maintained it as an engine making division. Perhaps then Hall-Scott would have had sufficient motivation, financing, and expertise to develop its own diesel line. Or another engine maker could have picked up Hall-Scott. Waukesha today makes a significant portion of its engines to run on liquefied petroleum gas (LPG), biogas, natural gas, and other alternative fuels, an option Hall-Scott began offering to customers in the 1920s. The purchase of Hall-Scott by Hercules, which in turn was later consumed by the insatiable White Motors, could have been the ticket to survival for Hall-Scott. But Hercules was not interested in buying the Hall-Scott company as much as it was interested in selling parts and moving a few Hall-Scott models to augment its existing line. Serious development of Hall-Scott products was never in the cards at Hercules, and the Hall-Scott line did not grow, evolve, or become the basis for new engines. Hercules, as ACF before it, failed to provide Hall-Scott the kind of management it needed to better ensure long-term success.

Surviving engine makers have found a specialized sector in the market for their products, and Hall-Scott did this pretty well, especially through World War II. Small-volume firms can understand their customers well, address their needs, and thereby remain competitive. For example, Waukesha, which in the early twentieth century powered dozens of truck models at any one time, got pushed out of the truck and bus market after World War II. But for the last few decades, it has been a dominant force in making large-displacement units, such as for drilling and power generation. Fairbanks-Morse never established a strong presence as Waukesha did in trucks and buses, but it was a major rail power provider for years. Today, Fairbanks-Morse remains a prime supplier of large-displacement engines, especially diesel, for power generation, drilling, and marine, with the U.S. Navy and Coast Guard being major customers. Wisconsin has taken refuge at the other end of the engine size spectrum. Long absent from the truck and bus market, Wisconsin plowed development into small gasoline engines and some diesel engines for welders, road machinery, pumps, and other modest horsepower applications. Today, rather than competing directly with Detroit Diesel and Cummins, Wisconsin squares off against Briggs & Stratton and Honda. Another old timer, Lycoming, at one time built engines for cars and trucks; however, in the mid-twentieth century, Lycoming narrowed its focus to airplanes. Today, the company purports that it is the world's largest supplier of engines for private aircraft, a sector in which Hall-Scott at one time claimed a leading position.

Likewise, Hall-Scott could have staked its claim of some part of the market—rail, civilian or military aviation, large drilling and pumping, welders and small road equipment, commercial or pleasure marine—and then stuck with it, providing engines that customers wanted. Indeed, Hall-Scott was primed for such a domination of one or another sector of the engine market, but management elected to pull the company out of those fields when customers began to change their demands. Leading up to World War I, Hall-Scott was one of leading aircraft engine makers in America, one of the few with anything approaching volume production and having rapidly evolving models that pushed industry development. One aviation historian, looking back at the role of Hall-Scott in helping that industry take off, wrote, "The Hall-Scott motor deserves a special place in the history of aviation and this is true not only for California but also for the nation as a whole." [7-5] But as the aviation engine market evolved in the 1920s, Hall-Scott halted aircraft engine development with the Liberty-based L-4 and L-6 models, in spite of its success. Similarly, Hall-Scott competed in the truck, bus, marine, and industrial engine markets vigorously for a while and then let its engines become outdated and unattractive to buyers. It was a deleterious trend seen repeatedly in the Hall-Scott story. Given the history of the company, Hall-Scott managers probably would have preferred to abandon the truck, bus, marine, and industrial markets, too. However, by the 1950s, there was no place left for the company to retreat. Instead of Hall-Scott abandoning those markets, those markets abandoned Hall-Scott.

Related to this last point was the inability of Hall-Scott to make and market a working line of diesel engines. It is incontrovertible that not having diesel engines in the post-World War II period cost Hall-Scott customers and, ultimately, its place as an engine maker for truck, bus, marine, and industrial applications. But Hall-Scott did not need to develop a diesel engine to remain in the engine business; Lycoming and Wisconsin are examples of engine makers that focused on gasoline engines and kept their doors open nevertheless. Briggs & Stratton, which was never a competitor of Hall-Scott, is another. However, note that neither Lycoming nor Wisconsin any longer sells its engines to trucks, buses, boats, and large equipment. Clearly, though, if Hall-Scott wanted to stay in the truck, bus, industrial, and marine markets, a line of diesels was an absolute requirement, not an option. The percentage of diesel engines powering trucks, buses, and boats grew steadily through the mid-twentieth century, and by the opening of the twenty-first century, even finding a gasoline-powered 18-wheeler, bus, or commercial boat is a rare occurrence. Customers looking for heavy-duty engines have increasingly demanded diesels, and Hall-Scott was passed over because the company simply did not give customers what they wanted. Relatively few American companies have produced popular and successful diesel engines—it is a difficult feat to pull off. The first oil-burning Hall-Scott models built before World War II failed. Whether or not the Hall-Scott postwar diesels would have been more successful, and possibly have allowed the company to keep its doors open, was settled when an automobile accident killed the project manager. [7-6] By the post-World War II period, and especially after being spun off by ACF, Hall-Scott was too small a company, with too limited a resource pool, to absorb that loss.

The high quality of Hall-Scott engines allowed the company to compete in a market for a few years and then abandon it, but this high quality did not allow Hall-Scott to stay in business with that approach much past World War II. In spite of the fact that the basic internal combustion engine design has remained more or less unchanged over the last 100 years, the particulars have changed dramatically. And keeping engines on the forefront of change has allowed

Invader-Based Engines as a Percentage of Total Hall-Scott Deliveries, 1931–1953

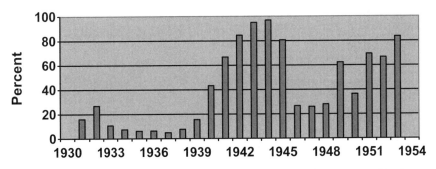

Marine, truck, and industrial derivatives of the Invader became a critical part of overall sales for Hall-Scott. By the early 1950s, this 20-year-old design often constituted more than 50% of all deliveries, demonstrating the lack of innovation at Hall-Scott after 1930.

a few to remain in business while many others have failed. In this context, change must be central to the ethos of any successful engine company, its "corporate culture." [7-7] The transportation industry is an environment every bit as harsh as the natural environment described by Charles Darwin: adapt or become extinct. Hall-Scott ultimately failed because change was not incorporated into its mission, a hubris shared by many now-defunct companies. In 1939, *Pacific Motor Boat* reported that the Lorimer Diesel Engine Company of Oakland, California, "feels that its line of slow speed heavy-duty marine diesels has reached perfection, based on practical work in the field, and they are announcing no new models or changes for 1939." [7-8] When was the last new Lorimer engine installed in a boat?

Behind keeping the products of a company attractive to customers is management. Perhaps here is where the prime reason behind the ultimate failure of Hall-Scott resides. In 1931, facing several consecutive years of dismal sales and financial performance at its Hall-Scott division, an ACF report pulled no punches when placing much of the blame at the feet of company leaders, saying that the company "has been working under a delusion." [7-9] Although years later, William Nelson, a Brill executive in the 1940s and 1950s and twice in charge of Hall-Scott (and its last president), similarly found little in the front office worth praising. "Hall-Scott management was generally weak anyway," wrote Nelson in his autobiography, "but there was a complete lack of secondary supervision." [7-10] He had little on which to stage a comeback for the company. On his coming to Hall-Scott shortly after World War II, Nelson picked up that "the organization had a reputation for being a country club. There were a few on which to build department heads. There were none with any aggressive spirit, and there was little to do other than to pull it out of the doldrums and trust to luck." [7-11] In fact, Nelson found a pervasive attitude that stymied attempts at change. In his words, "The top management was adept at convincing themselves that they were large, important and extraordinarily capable of producing substantial profits in the near future. Actually they believed their own invincibility which made matters worse." [7-12] The critical 1931 ACF-Brill report and Nelson's autobiography both addressed innumerable serious shortcomings with management, but these challenges also were obvious to people outside the company. One example was John Bodden, general manager of Peterbilt from 1963 to 1970, who remembered that by the time he took the helm at Peterbilt, Hall-Scott had been reduced to a "non-factor" in the industry. [7-13] He cited Hall-Scott's pricing, the lack of a diesel at Hall-Scott, ineffectual marketing, and distribution, much as others had pointed out. In fact, Bodden was unable to remember installing a single new Hall-Scott engine in a new "Pete" while he was at the company. "In the end," wrote Bodden, "one must blame mgmt [management]." So for years—decades, in fact—Hall-Scott drifted, buoyed by a solid product or two, making healthy profits for only a few of its 50 years, led by management incapable of taking the firm to the next level.

The founders of Hall-Scott show us that 100 years ago, a man with a good head on his shoulders and some good ideas, even though lacking substantial capital or extensive technical training, could make something and make something of himself in the American automotive industry. Elbert Hall and Bert Scott launched their firm with products that people wanted and for several years kept their products fresh and evolving, responsive to changes in the market. Had Hall-Scott continued to be led by managers who made change the basic tenet dominating the leadership "culture" of the company, perhaps tied Hall-Scott to a larger company, and then staked out a niche (or two) for their engines and other products that they steadfastly sought to satisfy, it is reasonable to believe that this impressive engine maker would still be in business today.

References

7-1.   For a review of how some business historians have looked at the history of small business in America, see Mansel Blackford, *A History of Small Business in America*, Twayne Publishers, New York, NY, 1991. See also Philip Scranton, *Endless Novelty, Specialty Production and American Industrialization, 1865–1925*, Princeton University Press, Princeton, NJ, 1997. Scranton observed that small firms can compete with large firms if detail, precision, and style, not price, dictate purchasing. This proposition seems to be supported by the Hall-Scott story.

7-2.   www.herculesengine.com, accessed October 29, 2002. Hercules Engine Company halted engine making in 1999, but several months after it closed, Hercules Engine Components opened in Massillon, Ohio, relying on a core of former Hercules employees to support Hercules engines and to market new power units using General Motors or other brand engines.

7-3.   *Commercial Car Journal*, May 1931, p. 38.

7-4.   William Nelson, autobiography, unpublished manuscript, 1963, p. 288. Courtesy of William Nelson.

7-5.   Kenneth Johnson, *Aerial California: An Account of Early Flight in Northern & Southern California 1849 to World War I*, Dawson's Book Shop, Los Angeles, CA, 1961, p. 75.

7-6.   Letter from F. Bradford to R. Dias, December 21, 1999. Francis Bradford, "A History of the Hall-Scott Motor Car Company," unpublished manuscript, 1989, p. 73. Courtesy of Bancroft Library, University of California, Berkeley, BANC MSS 93/104c.

7-7.   Jeffrey Cruikshank and David Sicilia, *The Engine That Could: Seventy-Five Years of Values-Driven Change at Cummins Engine Company*, Harvard Business School Press, Boston, MA, 1997.

7-8.   *Pacific Motor Boat*, February 1939, p. 31.

7-9.   "Report on Hall-Scott Motor Car Company, Berkeley, California," 1931, unpublished report, p. 17. Courtesy of Taylor Scott.

7-10.   William Nelson, autobiography, unpublished manuscript, 1963, p. 260. Courtesy of William Nelson.

7-11.   Ibid., p. 268.

7-12.   Ibid., p. 282.

7-13.   Letter from J. Bodden to R. Dias, March 14, 2005.

BIBLIOGRAPHY

Books

Adams, Ron, *Big Rigs of the 1950s*, MBI Publishing, Osceola, WI, 2001.

Anderson, J.W., *Diesel Engines*, McGraw-Hill Book Company, New York, NY, 1935.

Angle, Glenn D., *Airplane Engine Encyclopedia*, Otterbein Press, Dayton, OH, 1921.

Avco Corporation, *Avco Corporation, The First Fifty Years*, Avco Corporation, Greenwich, CT, 1979.

Berndt, Thomas, *Standard Catalog of U.S. Military Vehicles, 1940–1965*, Krause Publications, Iola, WI, 1983.

Bilstein, Roger, *The American Aerospace Industry; From Workshop to Global Enterprise*, Twayne Publishers, New York, NY, 1996.

Blackford, Mansel, *A History of Small Business in America*, Twayne Publishers, New York, NY, 1991.

Borgeson, Griffith, *The Golden Age of the American Racing Car*, SAE International, Warrendale, PA, 1998.

Bowers, Peter, *Boeing Aircraft Since 1916*, Funk & Wagnalls, New York, NY, 1968.

Breihan, John R., Stan Piet, and Roger S. Mason, *Martin Aircraft 1909–1960*, Narkiewicz-Thompson, Santa Ana, CA, 1995.

Brill, Debra, *History of the J.G. Brill Company*, Indiana University Press, Bloomington, IN, 2001.

Burness, Tad, *American Truck & Bus Spotters Guide, 1920–1985*, Motorbooks International, Osceola, WI, 1985.

Butler, Don, *The History of Hudson,* MBI Publishing, Osceola, WI, 1992.

Conde, John A., *The Cars That Hudson Built*, Arnold-Porter, Keego Harbor, MI, 1980.

Crismon, Fred, *U.S. Military Wheeled Vehicles*, Motorbooks International, Osceola, WI, 1994.

Cruikshank, Jeffrey L. and David B. Sicilia, *The Engine That Could; Seventy-Five Years of Values-Driven Change at Cummins Engine Company*, Harvard University Press, Boston, MA, 1997.

Davies, Peter J., *The World Encyclopedia of Trucks*, Lorenz Books, London, UK, 2000.

Decker, Wilbur F., *The Story of the Engine, From Lever to Liberty Motor*, Charles Scribner's Sons, New York, NY, 1920.

Dees, Mark, *The Miller Dynasty*, Second Edition, Hippodrome Publishing, Moorpark, CA, 1994.

Dickey, Philip, *The Liberty Engine 1918–1942*, Smithsonian Institution Press, Washington, DC, 1968.

Doyle, David and Pat Stansell, *Dragon Wagon; A Visual History of the U.S. Army's Heavy Tank Transporter 1941–1955*, Ampersand Publishing, Delray Beach, FL, 2004.

Du Cane, Peter, *High-Speed Small Craft*, Second Edition, Philosophical Library, New York, NY, 1957.

Dunning, Lorry, *Ultimate American Farm Tractors Data Book: Nebraska Test Tractors, 1920–1960*, MBI Publishing, Osceola, WI, 1999.

Eaton Corporation, *The History of Eaton Corporation, 1911–1985*, Cleveland, OH, 1985.

Foster, Mark, *Henry J. Kaiser: Builder in the Modern American West*, University of Texas Press, Austin, TX, 1989.

Georgano, G.N., ed., *The Complete Encyclopedia of Commercial Vehicles*, Krause Publications, Iola, WI, 1979.

Grayson, Stan, *Engines Afloat, From Early Days to D-Day, Vol. I: The Gasoline Era*, Devereux Books, Marblehead, MA, 1999.

Grayson, Stan, *Engines Afloat, From Early Days to D-Day, Vol. II: The Gasoline/Diesel Era*, Devereux Books, Marblehead, MA, 1999.

Gunnell, John, *Standard Catalog of V-8 Engines*, Krause Publications, Iola, WI, 2003.

Gunston, Bill, *World Encyclopedia of Aero Engines*, Patrick Stephens, Ltd., Newbury Park, UK, 1998.

Heilig, John, *The Cadillac Century*, Chartwell Books, Edison, NJ, 1998.

Jane, Fred, ed., *All the World's Air-Ships*, Sampson, Low, Marston & Co., Ltd., 1909, reprint, Johnson Reprint Corporation, New York, NY, 1968.

Johnson, Kenneth, *Aerial California: An Account of Early Flight in Northern & Southern California 1849 to World War I*, Dawson's Book Shop, Los Angeles, CA, 1961.

Kaminski, Edward, *American Car and Foundry Company*, Signature Press, Wilton, CA, 1999.

Keilty, Edmund, *Interurbans Without Wires*, Interurbans, Glendale, CA, 1979.

Kimes, Beverly Rae, ed., *Standard Catalog of American Cars 1805–1942*, Third Edition, Krause Publications, Iola, WI, 1996.

Kirk, Anthony, *Founded by the Bay; The History of Macaulay Foundry, 1896–1996*, Macaulay Foundry, Berkeley, CA, 1996.

Laux, James, "Diesel Trucks and Buses: Their Gradual Spread in the United States," in *The Economic and Social Effects of the Spread of Motor Vehicles*, Theo Barker, ed., Macmillan, Basingstoke, Hampshire, UK, 1987.

Lenzke, James, ed., *Standard Catalog of Cadillac, 1903–2000*, Krause Publications, Iola, WI, 2000.

Luke, William, *Buses of ACF*, Iconografix, Hudson, WI, 2003.

Madderon, Chuck, *Crown Firecoach, 1951 through 1985; Photo Archive*, Iconografix, Hudson, WI, 2001.

Maurer, Maurer, ed., *The U.S. Air Service in World War I, Vol. II*, U.S. Government Printing Office, Washington, DC, 1978.

Montville, John, *Mack*, AXTEX, Tucson, AZ, 1979.

National Cyclopaedia of American Biography, Vol. XLIII, University Microfilms, Ann Arbor, MI, 1967.

Pattillo, Donald, *Pushing the Envelope; The American Aircraft Industry*, The University of Michigan Press, Ann Arbor, MI, 1998.

Pripps, Robert, *The Big Book of Caterpillar*, Voyageur Press, Stillwater, MN, 2000.

Reynolds, John, *Andre Citröen; The Henry Ford of France*, St. Martin's Press, New York, NY, 1996.

Sable, Charles F., Jonathan Zeitlan, and Maurice Aymard, *World of Possibilities; Flexibility and Mass Production in Western Industrialism*, Cambridge University Press, New York, NY, 1997.

Schafer, Mike, *Vintage Diesel Locomotives*, Motorbooks International, Osceola, WI, 1998.

Scott, Edward B., *The Saga of Lake Tahoe, Vol. I*, Sierra-Tahoe Publishing, Crystal Bay, NV, 1957.

Scott, Edward B., *The Saga of Lake Tahoe, Vol. II*, Sierra-Tahoe Publishing, Crystal Bay, NV, 1973.

Scranton, Philip, *Endless Novelty; Specialty Production and American Industrialization, 1865–1925*, Princeton University Press, Princeton, NJ, 1997.

Smith, Herschel, *Aircraft Piston Engines: From the Manly Balzer to the Continental Tiara*, Sunflower University Press, Manhattan, KS, 1986.

Sorensen, Wayne and Donald Wood, *Motorized Fire Apparatus of the West 1900–1960*, Transportation Trails, Polo, IL, 1991.

Strickland, F., *Motor Boats*, Sir Isaac Pitman & Sons, London, UK, 1933.

Vanderveen, Bart, *Historic Military Vehicles Directory*, Battle of Britain Prints, London, UK, 1989.

Wagner, William, *Continental!: Its Motors and Its People*, Aero Publishers, Fallbrook, CA, 1983.

Wik, Reynold, *Benjamin Holt and Caterpillar*, American Society of Agricultural Engineers, St. Joseph, MI, 1984.

Winkler, Allan, *Home Front U.S.A.: America During World War II*, Harlan Davidson, Arlington Heights, IL, 1986.

Articles and Pamphlets

Ayer, Robert L., "Kenworth," *Motor Coach Age*, Vol. XXXIII, Nos. 8 and 9, August–September 1981, pp. 4–33.

Bail, Eli, "Fageol," *Motor Coach Age*, November–December 1991, pp. 4–5.

Dunning, Lorry, "Simple Compact Crawler, Large Complicated History: The Story of Holt's 2 Ton," *Antique Caterpillar Machinery Owners Club*, Issue 54, March/April 2004, pp. 8–13.

Hall, E.J., "Reducing Transportation Cost by Means of Engine Design," Northern California Section Paper, SAE International, Paper No. 290010, Society of Automotive Engineers, Warrendale, PA, 1929, pp. 64–79.

Hall-Scott Motor Car Company, "Pertinent Facts About the Liberty Motor," pamphlet, circa 1919.

Herb, Charles, "Hall-Scott Marine Engines Aid Invasion and Defense," *Machinery*, Vol. 49, No. 1, September 1942, pp. 121–134.

Jones, Keith, "If Only in Another Time...The Story of the De Vaux–Hall Motors Corporation," *Automotive History Review*, No. 40, Summer 2003, pp. 42–45.

McCall, J.B., "Dieselization of American Railroads: A Case Study," *Essays in Economic and Business History*, Edwin Perkins, ed., Vol. III, 1984, pp. 152–159.

Meier, Albert, "ACF Buses," *Motor Coach Age*, Vol. XXIX, Nos. 11–12, October–November 1977, pp. 4–42.

Miller, Warren, "Hall's Comet," *Antique Automobile*, March–April 1975, pp. 22–24.

Packard Motor Car Company, "The Real Story of the Liberty Motor," circa 1919.

Tikker, Kevin, "Gustav Heine and His Cars," *Automotive History Review*, No. 15, Fall 1982, pp. 10–15.

Unpublished Reports and Manuscripts

American Car and Foundry, "Report on Hall-Scott Motor Car Company, Berkeley, California," unpublished report, 1931. Courtesy of Taylor Scott.

Bradford, Francis, "A History of the Hall-Scott Motor Car Company," unpublished manuscript, 1989. Bancroft Library, University of California, Berkeley, BANC MSS 93/104C.

Brittingham, Don, "The Hall-Scott Engine in the L.A. Fire Department," unpublished manuscript, circa 1980. Courtesy of Bill West.

Glidewell, John E. "Speed," "A Brief History of Hall-Scott Motor Company," unpublished address, 1956.

Guernsey, Charles, "Report of Investigation of European High Speed Diesel Engines," unpublished report, 1930.

Hercules Motors Corporation, "History, Growth & Expansion of the Hercules Motors Corporation," unpublished manuscript, circa 1963. Courtesy of Charles Balough Family Collection.

Nelson, William, autobiography, unpublished manuscript, 1963. Courtesy of William Nelson.

Pickering Advertising Agency, "Hall-Scott, Incorporated, Power Division, Total Marketing Analysis and Plan," unpublished report, 1957.

Periodicals

Aeronautics

Antique Automobile

Antique Caterpillar Machinery Owners Club

The Automobile

Automobile Magazine

Automobile Quarterly

Automobile Trade Journal

Automotive History Review

*Automotive Industries (*and *Automotive and Aviation Industries)*

Aviation

Aviation Age

*Commercial Car Journal (*and *Commercial Carrier Journal)*

Cycle and Automobile Trade Journal

Fleet Owner

Investor's Reader

Machinery (New York)

Metal Trades

Motor Age

Motor Boating

Motor Coach Age

The Motor Truck

Motor Truck and Coach

Motor West

Pacific Motor Boat

Port of Oakland Compass

Power Parade

Railway Age Gazette

Western Machinery World

Yachting

Newspapers

Berkeley Daily Gazette

Hall-Scott Invader Exhaust

The New York Times

The Oakland Tribune

*San Francisco Bulletin (*and *San Francisco Call-Bulletin)*

San Francisco Chronicle

The San Francisco Examiner

*San Jose Mercury Herald (*and *San Jose Herald)*

San Jose Mercury News

The Wall Street Journal

Archives and Collections

Bancroft Library, University of California, Berkeley, California

Benson Ford Research Center, The Henry Ford, Dearborn, Michigan

Berkeley Historical Society, Berkeley, California

California State Railroad Museum Library, Sacramento, California

Department of Special Collections, University of California, Davis, California

Department of Special Collections, Wichita State University Libraries, Wichita, Kansas

The Haggin Museum Library/Archive, Stockton, California

San Diego Aerospace Museum, Library, and Archives, San Diego, California

Transportation Library, University of California, Berkeley, California

Wm. McKinley Presidential Library & Museum, Canton, Ohio

Interviews

John Bodden, March 14, 2005

Dick Brown, November 13, 2002

Jack Fidler, March 6, 2004

Jody Kirsan, July 26, 2004

Al Outsen, October 25, 2005

Jim Ryan, April 19, 2004

Joseph Scheetz, November 8, 2003

Craig Smith, January 10, 2004

INDEX

ABOUT THE AUTHORS

Francis H. (Brad) Bradford graduated from Stanford University in 1934 with a B.S. in engineering and worked as a staff engineer at Hall-Scott from 1940 until 1958. Among the last Hall-Scott employees in Berkeley, California, Bradford oversaw the plant shutdown. In 1989, he wrote the first history of Hall-Scott, which was an unpublished manuscript. Francis Bradford passed away in 2005 at the age of 97.

Ric Dias graduated from the University of California, Riverside, in 1995 with a Ph.D. in history. He is a professor of history at Northern State University in Aberdeen, South Dakota. Dias has written on Kaiser Steel Corporation and the Cold War. In addition to this Hall-Scott book, Dias and Bradford collaborated on a number of articles concerning Hall-Scott.